FLORIDA STATE
UNIVERSITY LIBRARIES

JUN 23 1997

TALLAHASSEE, FLORIDA

Illusory Consensus

University of Delaware Press
Manuscript Competition Winners

Shakespearean Literature
John W. Blanpied, *Time and the Artist in Shakespeare's English Histories*
Robert Ornstein, *Shakespeare's Comedies: From Roman Farce to Romantic Mystery*
Donald W. Foster, *Elegy by W. S.: A Study in Attribution*
David Hoeniger, *Medicine and Shakespeare in the English Renaissance*
Peggy Muñoz Simonds, *Myth, Emblem, and Music in Shakespeare's Cymbeline*
Marvin Rosenberg, *The Masks of* Hamlet
Frederick Kiefer, *Writing on the Renaissance Stage: Written Words, Printed Pages, Metaphoric Books*

Early American Culture to 1840
Daniel D. Reiff, *Small Georgian Houses in England and Virginia: Origins and Development through the 1750s*

Military, Naval, and Diplomatic History
Richard J. Hargrove, *General John Burgoyne*

Eighteenth-Century Studies
Donald T. Siebert, *The Moral Animus of David Hume*
Ruben Quintero, *Literate Culture: Pope's Rhetorical Art*
Lois Bueler, *Clarissa's Plots*
Alexander Pettit, *Illusory Consensus: Bolingbroke and the Polemical Response to Walpole, 1730–1737*

American Art
Rowland Elzea, *John Sloan's Oil Paintings: A Catalogue Raisonné*
Thomas P. Somma, *The Apotheosis of Democracy, 1908–1916: The Pediment for the House Wing of the United States Capitol*

Illusory Consensus

Bolingbroke and the
Polemical Response to Walpole,
1730–1737

Alexander Pettit

Newark: University of Delaware Press
London: Associated University Presses

© 1997 by Alexander Pettit

All rights reserved. Authorization to photocopy items for internal or personal use, or the internal or personal use of specific clients, is granted by the copyright owner, provided that a base fee of $10.00, plus eight cents per page, per copy is paid directly to the Copyright Clearance Center, 222 Rosewood Drive, Danvers, Massachusetts 01923. [0-87413-592-3/97 $10.00+8¢ pp, pc.]

Associated University Presses
440 Forsgate Drive
Cranbury, NJ 08512

Associated University Presses
16 Barter Street
London WC1A 2AH, England

Associated University Presses
P.O. Box 338, Port Credit
Mississauga, Ontario
Canada L5G 4L8

The paper used in this publication meets the requirements of the American National Standard for Permanence of Paper for Printed Library Materials Z39.48–1984.

Library of Congress Cataloging-in-Publication Data

Pettit, Alexander, 1958–
   Illusory consensus : Bolingbroke and the polemical response to Walpole, 1730–1737 / Alexander Pettit.
     p. cm.
   Includes bibliographical references and index.
   ISBN 0-87413-592-3 (alk. paper)
   1. Bolingbroke, Henry St. John, Viscount, 1678–1751. 2. Great Britain—Politics and government—1727–1760. 3. Walpole, Sir Robert, 1676–1745. 4. Consensus (Social sciences) 5. Polemics. I. Title.
DA501.B6P44 1997
941.07'2'092—dc20
                                                                                       96-11942
                                                                                            CIP

PRINTED IN THE UNITED STATES OF AMERICA

*To Bernice Pettit
and to the memory of Henry MacMillan*

Contents

Acknowledgments	9
A Note on the Text	11
Introduction	15

Part 1. The Rhetoric of Consensus

1. Bolingbroke's *Remarks on the History of England* in the *Craftsman* and Elsewhere	35
2. Bolingbroke's Analogic Historiography	58

Part 2. The Illusion of Consensus

3. Squaring Off—or Not—over the Revolution of 1688	87
4. The Carolinist Challenge	115
5. Carolinism and the Church: The *Grub-street Journal* and the Curious Case of Dr. Francis Hare	139
6. Acting Out the Unstable Opposition	165
Conclusion	189
Notes	193
Bibliography	224
Index	237

Acknowledgments

I am particularly grateful to Thomas Lockwood and Marshall Brown, who have supported my work in countless ways, and to Jacqueline Vanhoutte, whose good sense and good nature recalled me to my better self repeatedly while I was writing this book, and whose critical and editorial skills assisted me inestimably in the final stages of my work.

Marilyn Morris and Hans Turley proved themselves excellent critics and faithful friends. Bertrand Goldgar and Simon Varey, whose influence is evident throughout these pages, helped when I most needed help, as did Kevin Cope and John Whalen-Bridge.

I have received liberal support from the staff, faculty, and administration of the University of North Texas, both financially and in less quantifiable ways. Thomas Preston has been a source of guidance and inspiration since my arrival in Texas. I am grateful as well to Nora Kizer Bell, James Duban, Melanie Hawkins, David Holdeman, Laura Kennelly, David Kesterson, Kenneth Lavender, James Ward Lee, Alice Mathews, Giles Mitchell, Jane Newcomer-Fuller, Monica Rais, Martin Sarvis, Rollie Schafer, L. Robert Stevens, James T. F. Tanner, J. Don Vann, Charlotte Wixom, and the many fine students with whom I discuss eighteenth-century literature and culture.

The following libraries and organizations funded my research: the Henry E. Huntington Library, the Harry Ransom Humanities Research Center at the University of Texas at Austin, the William Ready Division of Archives and Research Collections at McMaster University, the American Society for Eighteenth-Century Studies, the South Central Modern Language Association, the Rocky Mountain Modern Language Association, the University of Washington graduate school, and the University of North Texas office of sponsored projects. The Huntington deserves special mention for its repeated demonstrations of faith in my work. The library staffs were models of patience and professionalism.

For miscellaneous good deeds, I thank Edward Alexander, Jim Springer Borck, Eveline Cruickshanks, John Dussinger, Jay Halio, Brean Hammond, Geoffrey Hastings, Robert Hay, Robert Hume, J.

Paul Hunter, Don Kalbach, Katheryn King, Paul Korshin, Michael Koy, William Kupersmith, Melinda Luck, Thomas Marshall, Barry Menikoff, Dave Oliphant, Joel Reed, Otto Reinert, Cedric Reverand II, Elizabeth Reynolds, Jeffrey Seckendorf, Philip Winsor, Larry Wolff, and Julien Yoseloff. To those friends and colleagues whose efforts on my behalf are not recorded here, I offer apologies and tacit thanks.

※ ※ ※

Portions of this book appeared, in different form, in *The Age of Johnson* 7 (1994): 365–95; *British Journal for Eighteenth-Century Studies* 17 (1994): 41–53; *Philological Quarterly* 69 (1990): 437-53; and *1650–1850: Ideas, Aesthetics, and Inquiries in the Early Modern Era* 1 (1994): 109–36.

I regret that my production schedule prevented me from considering Christine Gerrard's *The Patriot Opposition to Walpole: Politics, Poetry, and National Myth, 1725–1742* (Oxford: Clarendon, 1994 [for 1995]) in this study. Readers may want to refer to my review of the book in *The Scriblerian* 27 (Spring 1996).

A Note on the Text

I have converted all dates to the New Style, which in any case was often favored in the 1730s. The slight to ultramonarchists and others who clung to the Old Style is justified, I hope, by a gain in consistency and thus clarity. Except in cases where emendation proved necessary to clarify meaning, I have not modernized or otherwise altered passages from eighteenth-century sources. Emendations are identified by square brackets.

When it has been possible to do so gracefully, I have used parenthetical documentation for references to eighteenth-century newspapers and pamphlets. When the information has seemed pertinent, I have noted the publication dates of pamphlets by day and month as well as by year. I have preferred short to long forms of titles for eighteenth-century works, except where the longer form enhances a portion of my argument.

Because part of my argument concerns the textual history of Bolingbroke's *Remarks on the History of England*, I have used the original folios of the *Craftsman* for my discussion of that work. Otherwise, I have preferred the 1844 edition of Bolingbroke's *Works* (rpt. New York: Augustus M. Kelley, 1967). This ensures that more readers will have access to the works that I discuss, for which reason I have also noted instances in which works by others authors are available in modern editions. Bolingbroke's essays from the *Craftsman*, excepting those that constitute the *Remarks on the History of England* and *A Dissertation upon Parties*, are available in Simon Varey, ed., *Lord Bolingbroke: Contributions to the* Craftsman (Oxford: Clarendon, 1982).

Illusory Consensus

Introduction

ONE of the defining characteristics of early eighteenth-century English culture is its insistence on the centrality of literature to the political debate. Whatever differences separated the revered poet Alexander Pope (1688–1744) from the obscure hack-writer Matthias Earbery (1690–1740), both assumed that the battle over the moral and political custodianship of society was preeminently a literary enterprise. Nowhere is this more evident than in the print wars of the 1730s, when George II's de facto prime minister Sir Robert Walpole (1676–1745) was continually attacked for his hostility to the belles lettres, his alleged disregard of the royal prerogative, and his concentration of power in an oligarchy of parliamentary "placemen."

Literary scholars have tended to regard this debate either as background to Scriblerian satire or as the occasion for the major political treatises of Pope's friend Henry St. John, Viscount Bolingbroke (1687–1751), cofounder, with William Pulteney, an M.P., and Nicholas Amhurst, a journalist, of the popular opposition weekly the *Country Journal: Or, the Craftsman* (1726–52). But this emphasis on a small and interconnected group of writers has caused scholars to lose sight of the diversity and the instability of the opposition to Walpole. The history of the opposition is recorded not only in the durable productions of authors like Pope and Bolingbroke, but also in many short-lived and less finely crafted plays, sermons, pamphlets, and newspapers that in their own time were regarded as significant contributions to political discussion. Scholars of the opposition have used ephemeral sources selectively or subordinated them to more recognizable landmarks of literature. This has prompted my reevaluation, from street-level as it were, of polemical literature during the print wars between Walpole and his detractors.

This study concerns ideological conflict among writers hostile to Walpole or skeptical about his methods of governance. More particularly, it analyzes the formation of and the reaction against the Bolingbrokean notion of a unified opposition, neither "Whig" nor "Tory," as the mythopoetic Bolingbroke would have it, but rather a "Revival of the true old *English Spirit*, which prevailed in the Days of our Fathers" (*Craftsman* 206; 13 June 1731). The idea of an opposition organized around Bolingbrokean thought has its modern apologists, as, more pervasively, does the idea of an opposition defined by beliefs (Jacobitism) or values (Scriblerian humanism) that were at one time or another espoused by Bolingbroke. But much of the polemical literature of the 1730s responds anxiously to Bolingbroke's prescriptive theorizing and questions or criticizes the terms of his appeals to consensus. Challenging the conclusions of scholars whose choice of source material allows them to find ideological cohesiveness in the opposition, I argue that the opposition was fundamentally in disagreement about how best to formulate its objection to modern government. Unlike Bertrand Goldgar, who—as Pope and Swift did—concerns himself with a like-minded group of "the most talented writers of a generation" and so finds an "apparent unanimity of political attitudes among a whole generation of writers"; unlike Isaac Kramnick, who focuses on the "circle" of the genteel Bolingbroke and so—as Bolingbroke did—declares the opposition homogeneous; and unlike Eveline Cruickshanks, whose work with the Stuart papers has led her to believe—as Walpole did—that even after the failed Jacobite rebellion of 1715 "*the leaders of the [Tory] party were Jacobites and answered for the party,*" I hold that the opposition is characterized by its resistance to ideological consensus, particularly on the terms offered by Bolingbroke.[1]

If scholars have tended to endorse versions of the opposition rooted in the early eighteenth century's own habits of self-representation, the dominating figures of the great poet Pope, the great politician Walpole, and the great polemicist Bolingbroke have in a sense asked them to. To borrow a term from Matthew Arnold, they seemed then, and seem now, the "representative men" of the literary and political debate. The contours of Pope's and Walpole's careers are well known and in any case not germane to the present study, but a few words about Bolingbroke's life are in order. His tortuous political career; his dazzling roster of acquaintances; his various, profuse, and occasionally brilliant literary output—all have helped ensure Bolingbroke a lasting reputation and have thus made him a rarity among polemicists, generally a fugitive breed. His name winds in and out of English and French history for the first half of the eighteenth century, typically attended by a testimonial to his excellent "parts" or his "mercurial" personality, and perhaps by a potshot at his moral laxity as well. He numbered among his friends Swift, Pope, Gay, Voltaire, and Chesterfield. Secretary of state to Queen Anne during the Tory revival of the early 1710s, by 1715 he occupied the same post under James Edward Stuart, the exiled pretender to the English throne encamped at St. Germain. Bolingbroke was convicted of high treason following his flight to France but was permitted to return to England unmolested eight years later, although, as his modern biographer notes, without being allowed to reclaim "his political rights, his title and his seat in the Lords."[2]

The repatriated Bolingbroke returned to politics trumpeting his devotion to the Hanoverian monarchy. This largesse did not extend to Walpole, the enemy, as Bolingbroke saw it, of the strong parliaments guaranteed by the Revolution Settlement of 1689. Barred from politics "indoors," Bolingbroke became an outspoken participant in the incipient print campaign against Walpole. He attacked Walpole with wit and something like genius in the *Occasional Writer* (1727), and with verve and determination in the *Craftsman*. Bolingbroke's best-known contributions to the *Craftsman*, the *Remarks on the History of England* (1730–31) and *A Dissertation upon Parties* (1733–34), delimit the period of his greatest influence as a polemicist and of the *Craftsman*'s greatest importance as an organ of opposition propaganda. Bolingbroke's work after the *Remarks* is generally unconcerned with practical politics; and, particularly after the fall of Walpole in 1742, theories that had shown themselves more interesting than useful were out of fashion. Unable to realize his dream of a united front and increasingly out of favor with others in the opposition, Bolingbroke retreated to France in 1735. He lived there for nine years before returning to his family estate at Battersea, where he died in 1751, his political philosophy generally in disrepute among his countrymen. His posthumous and deistical *Philosophical Works* (1754–77) were widely reviled and prompted Henry Fielding to remark, cynically, that "as the temporal happiness, the civil liberties and properties of Europe, were the game of [Bolingbroke's] earliest youth, there could be no sport so adequate to the entertainment of his advanced age, as the eternal and final happiness of all mankind."[3] In his *Dictionary* (1755), Dr. Johnson defined "irony" as "a mode of speech in which the meaning is contrary to the words: as, *Bolingbroke was a holy man.*"

※ ※ ※

As this study will demonstrate, many writers who shared Bolingbroke's dislike of Walpole also shared (or anticipated) Fielding's and Johnson's mistrust of Bolingbroke. By arguing against coherency in the opposition, I am contributing to a larger reaction, evident in both historical and literary studies, against once-orthodox notions of neoclassical "stability." Linda Colley and Paul Kléber Monod have recently questioned J. H. Plumb's influential thesis about the "political stability"—"almost monolithic," Plumb calls it—nascent in the last quarter of the seventeenth century and mature under Walpole's Whig oligarchy. Political stability, Plumb wrote in 1967, is "the acceptance by society of its political institutions, and of those classes of men or officials who control them." Norma Landau summarizes the rebellion against Plumb:

> As Plumb had associated a single-party regime with political stability, Colley and Monod had to explain how the presence of organized opposition to that single party affected political stability. Their strategy is to deny that 'political stability' is a concept that distinguishes the Walpolean era from its predecessors.... By stretching Plumb's definition of 'political stability' to its limit, Colley and Monod show that Plumb's definition is inadequate. For example, as Stuart historians have been arguing with some persistence, England before the civil war qualifies, according to Plumb's definition, as politically stable.

Nicholas Rogers moves farther still from Plumb than Colley and Monod do when he criticizes Colley and others for mistaking Parliament for the country at large and so retaining Plumb's focus on "high politics," the source of stability in Plumb's formulation.[4]

Colley, Monod, and Rogers, however, are not concerned with the tendency among many of Walpole's assailants to eschew institutional politics, to shun telic (and arguably anachronistic) ideologies like Jacobitism, and to question or even reject the totalizing strategies of the opposition's self-appointed leaders. And these scholars, reasonably for their purposes, finally find stability enough in the period anyway—note Landau's use of the term "organized opposition" in reference to Colley's and Monod's work. Colley argues for internal coherency in the "proscribed tory party" after the installation of the Hanoverian monarchy in 1714. Monod, although concerned that Plumb's "notion" of "political stability" has "imposed a new kind of rigidity" on the study of English politics after 1688, argues that "Jacobite political culture should be interpreted as a language, with its own internal logic or grammar, operating as a coherent system." Rogers believes that "urban political culture" and the "extraparliamentary public" describe a stronger and more cohesive force than previous scholars had realized.[5]

But the more distance we admit between the political debate and the formal institutions of political power, the less neat the debate appears. With respect to current historiography, my argument is an exercise in something like "onedownmanship": as an alternative to Plumb's and Colley's focus on national politics, Monod's on a precise if complex ideology, and Rogers's on the urban electorate, I intend to examine the anxieties of a literature that operated outside of these more-or-less institutional schemata but that shared with their representatives a dissatisfaction with Walpole's governance.

In literary studies, poststructuralist critics in general and new historicists in particular have followed Michael McKeon in finding an ideologically resonant "instability of generic categories" in seventeenth- and early eighteenth-century fiction. According to McKeon, this literature is an amalgam that ultimately gains a sort of uniformity in the "modern, 'institutional' stability" of the novel after 1740. McKeon invites scholars to be attentive to various genres when considering matters of ideology, or to consider ideological conflict as central to, but not as limited to, fiction. So it is odd that polemical literature, certainly what McKeon would call an "unstable" genre and one in any case plainly concerned with the diffusion of ideology, attracts little interest either in McKeon or in new historicists obsessed as McKeon is with suggestive collisions of genre and ideology.[6]

One reason for this omission is methodological and suggests my own departure from current trends in literary studies. Like McKeon, new historicists have tended to practice a highly selective approach to archival sources and thus to reassert the primacy of well-known works of literature even as they attempt to "contextualize" them. More specifically, they have shown little interest in ephemeral political productions often unapologetically distant from sturdier works of literature. Among John Bender's "broad, definitional traits of new historicism" are "a fairly pervasive use of original sources both literary and nonliterary" and "a redefinition through rereading of some canonical work, or previously uncanonized work, as a culturally operative text rather than as a strictly aesthetic object." Leaving aside the fact that Bender is begging the question (insofar as it is possible to determine what "culturally operative text[s]" are, it is difficult to imagine that Fielding—Bender's example here—didn't write them), I would note Bender's dedication to canonicity, however organized, and his tentativeness about the proper purview of research ("fairly pervasive," "literary" versus "nonliterary" sources, "some canonical work"). When Bender, elsewhere, takes up specific authors, his interest is in tracing points of correspondence among more and less familiar works by the very familiar authors Defoe and Fielding. The authors whom McKeon considers in detail are similarly "canonical," if more numerous. The new-historical attempt to revise the "orderly, well-reasoned, fundamentally hierarchical vision of Augustan England" that Bender finds championed by Maynard Mack finally sounds like a new way of talking about an old hierarchy.[7]

Chipping away at the notion of stability in the period requires more than juxtaposing big and little works, a widely read novel here and a little-known pamphlet there. Rather, we need to acknowledge the ways in which the period defended its own myths of stability against superevident threat. As I have already implied, one obstacle is the period itself. Any good undergraduate knows that many of the period's ablest representatives—satirists for the most part—were driven by their fear of cultural disintegration to insist upon the stabilizing value of wit, sense, taste, tradition, or other attractive but imprecise designations by which the period attempted to identify what the satirist possessed and what his opponents lacked. And for much of the twentieth century we have been content to regard the most eloquent accounts of the period as the most accurate, and therefore to legitimate the appeals to stability on which they are based.

This familiar problem in the study of satire also complicates any analysis of polemical literature, although literary critics have not shown much interest in the formal tendencies of eighteenth-century polemics or in the relation of polemics to other sorts of literature. A glance at Scriblerian satire and its correspondences to Bolingbrokean polemics should make Bolingbroke's program clearer to the modern reader. Plainly enough Pope saw himself as the remnant of a grand tradition of wit, virtue, and sanity, drawn by all that was dull into a lunatic debate, forced here to assail polemicists less lucid than he and there to excoriate professional politicians unimpressed by the old symbiosis of poetry and statescraft. The predictable antitheses of then and now, learned and ignorant, and genteel and professional describe stability—or stasis—as surely as they express a sense of culture in crisis. (The antitheses are honored in the title of Goldgar's *Walpole and the Wits*, the most important study of literature and politics in the period.) Pope's belief in his own historical connectedness usually keeps "universal darkness" at bay somewhere just beyond the *sanctum sanctorum* of his estate at Twickenham. But the posture is unconvincing; and it is not controversial to suggest that the swarms of hacks and halfwits that invade the sacred spaces of, say, *An Epistle to Dr. Arbuthnot* indicate the immense anxiety behind Pope's defense of a stable belletristic culture.

Scriblerian satire also advertises the tenuousness of its belief in stability by asserting its own importance at the expense of inferior works and so reminding its readers of the abundance as well as the menace of such works. Pope and Swift repeatedly invite their readers to acknowledge the heft of the literature that they dislike but to regard this literature as ridiculous or worse. This is not news, but it is an important reminder of the manner in which certain writers in the period struggled against attempts to represent the period in ways other than the ones that they themselves favored. C. S. Lewis commented long ago that "the number of things [Pope and Swift] do not want to hear about is enormous,"[8] and his observation reminds us that many of the most famous writers of the period shaped their careers in opposition to the diverse literary milieu to which they actually belonged.

Most notably, Swift, Pope, and "Scriblerus Secundus" Fielding positioned themselves against a crowded field of allegedly bad writers. Pope, in *Peri Bathos*, *The Dunciad*, and *An Epistle to Dr. Arbuthnot*, like Swift in his verses on Grub-street and like Fielding in *The Tragedy of Tragedies* and in his parodies of Richardson (*Shamela*) and of criminal biographies (*Jonathan Wild*), attests to as well as criticizes the verbal profuseness of his culture. When he declares himself the wielder of "the last Pen for Freedom,"[9] Pope asks us not to suppose that there was a shortage of pens but to recognize that there were, suddenly, more of them being used for less acceptable purposes. But he does not mean us to regard the literature that he loathes as anything but incentive for learned satire, a reductive and extraordinarily self-important enterprise. The world of Scriblerian satire was a small one by design; and Lewis is right to argue that "the terror expressed at the end of the *Dunciad* is not wholly terror at the approach of ignorance: it is also terror lest the compact little fortress of Humanism should be destroyed, and new knowledge is one of the enemies."[10] As many feminist scholars have observed, the best-remembered satirists of the period invite us to believe in a fraternity of wit that is exclusionary by design and anxious by nature.

The same is true of polemicists, Bolingbroke most pertinently. Like his friend Pope, Bolingbroke insisted on order in the teeth of chaos. He too was a resident of "the compact little fortress of Humanism"; and he peddled a master plan for the opposition no less totalizing than Pope's vision of ideal culture. Unlike "dunces" such as Daniel Defoe and Eliza Haywood, Bolingbroke's opponents in the print wars have not been rehabilitated by modern scholars. We have not, therefore, had the opportunity to consider the opposition in terms other than Bolingbroke's. For instance, most accounts of Bolingbroke have little or nothing to say about Earbery and William Arnall, prolific polemicists who attacked Bolingbroke with considerable energy throughout the early 1730s and who agreed on nothing but the perniciousness of Bolingbrokean rhetoric.[11] A result of omissions of this sort is the continuance of various monolithic models of the opposition, parallels to the Dunciadic view of literary history that has been under attack for some years. What was for Bolingbroke a rhetorical gambit has hardened into orthodoxy.

Again like Pope, Bolingbroke wrote in a genre that promotes its own superiority to common discourse as well as its ability to effect ideological consensus. I shall consider both these pretenses (or goals, or tendencies) briefly here, remarking first that the collocation is itself unstable, as comprising both disinterestedness and a readiness to fight tooth and nail for political influence. Like satire, polemical literature draws much of its meaning from the works to which it responds and, a bit more abstractly, from responses to it in other works. Jerome McGann has been arguing since 1983 that "literary works are fundamentally social rather than personal or psychological products."[12] The observation seems especially pertinent to polemics and satire, in which the idea of discreet meaning is self-evidently absurd. For example, Bolingbroke's *Remarks on the History of England*, the object of a good deal of attention in this study, is both a professedly disinterested survey of English history and an assault on progovernment historiography and indeed on the government itself. Like satire, polemical literature feeds on the flesh it mocks.[13]

And Bolingbroke was as intent as Pope on denying that he was engaged in any sort of polemical enterprise. Pope's disingenuous claim that "I sought no homage from the Race that write; / I kept, like *Asian* Monarchs, from their sight" has plenty of analogues in Bolingbroke.[14] Proscribed politically, Bolingbroke wrote tendentious pamphlets and newspaper-leaders that he masked as detached reflections on old history and new politics—factious arguments against "faction" that ultimately promoted nothing more than their author's headship of a coherent opposition of his own invention. To Joel Weinsheimer, the "sublimated despair" characteristic of Bolingbroke's writing is the result of Bolingbroke's frustrated desire "to be not a philosopher of history or even a student of it but rather the subject of history."[15] I would add that the philosophical trimmings of Bolingbrokean historiography often seem like attempts to obscure precisely the desire that Weinsheimer identifies, given that by the 1730s at least, Bolingbroke's attempt to participate in English history is really the attempt to dictate the terms, linguistic and practical, of the revolt against Walpole. His courtship of history was coy, marked by denial as surely as it was driven by despair. Bolingbroke sought to invent a "history" in which he could participate more directly than he could in the real England of the real 1730s. But presenting himself as distant from the contemporary hue and cry allowed Bolingbroke to foster the illusion of potency, decorum, and austerity that inheres in Pope's image of the "*Asian* Monarch."

Bolingbroke dramatizes his professed remove from the furor over his *Remarks on the History of England* in an incendiary pamphlet entitled *A Final Answer to the Remarks on the Craftsman's Vindication* (1731)—published, no doubt to its author's eventual irritation, three months before the end of the conflict that it attempted to conclude. Here Bolingbroke, writing anonymously, poses on the one hand as the power that has intervened between the (pseudonymous) author of the *Remarks on the History of England* and the necessity of direct polemical engagement, and, on the other hand, as the scourge of that author's enemies:

> After what has been here said, the *Gentleman*, in whose Defense I have appeared, can have no Reason of Honour to enter by *Himself*, or his *Friends*, into these Altercations; and if my Opinion can prevail, should these *Libellers* continue to scold and to call Names, They should be left to do it, without Reproof, or Notice. The Answer now given should stand as a *final Answer to all They have said, and to all They may think fit to say hereafter.* (31–32)

The myth of the magisterial "last word" is abundantly evident in the period, in polemical literature as in satires like *The Dunciad*, with its terminal invocation of verbally deadening darkness.

Bolingbroke's contemporaries saw this sort of thing as pretense and were justified in doing so. Indeed, we may reasonably regard polemical literature as the packaging of pretense as truth. The Walpolite journalist Arnall, writing about Pulteney's defense of Bolingbroke's final entry in the *Remarks on the History of England*, strikes an unexpectedly frank note when he dismisses Bolingbroke's and Pulteney's claims of disinterestedness by observing "[that] the Authors of both Sides in these *Political* Altercations and Disputes, are actuated by much the same motives with one another, and that the Reason that either Party gives for engaging in these kind of Contests, is very far from being the true one." Arnall is less egalitarian but perhaps no less accurate when he describes Bolingbroke, Pulteney, and an unseemly crew of "distinguish'd patriots" from times past as "all furious and hot-headed alike."[16] The rhythm of the exchange is simple: Bolingbroke and his allies assert their distance from interested political discussion; Arnall and his cohorts remind them of their immersion in it.

Appeals to consensus are as important in polemical literature as they are in Scriblerian satire. Pope's Horatian imitations posture populism even as they assert the unique moral qualifications of the poet. And Pope liked to bolster his satires by introducing paragonal characters—the Man of Ross in the *Epistle to Bathurst*, the poet's father in *An Epistle to Dr. Arbuthnot*—whose goodness is beyond question and who are thus invitations to a consensus structured in opposition to a chaotic world of duncehood and immorality. Bolingbroke's case for a unified "Country" opposition works in an analogous way. In *A Dissertation upon Parties*, as in the earlier *Remarks on the History of England*, Bolingbroke dismisses the conventional labels "Whig" and "Tory." He argues that "the bulk of both parties are really united; united on principles of liberty, in opposition to an obscure remnant of one party [Jacobites], who disown those principles, and a mercenary detachment from the other [Walpole's Whigs] who betray them."[17] As he characteristically does, Bolingbroke presents threats to consensus as aberrant—the products of greed, malice, or stupidity. In this way he expresses one of the animating dichotomies of polemical literature: to process data (typically historical) correctly is to concur with the polemicist about the state of contemporary politics; to process these data incorrectly is to promote faction. Pulteney's leader in *Craftsman* 127 (7 Dec. 1728) introduces a discussion of bribes and pensions by noting that

> Though the Methods, by which a State may lose its Liberties, appear to be various; yet upon a close Examination, we shall find all national Misfortunes generally owing to one, great original Source; and that is, when every Individual comes to consider Himself distinctly and apart from the Community, of which He is a Member, and is continually employing all his Parts and Talents on Means of obtaining to Himself Wealth, Power, Preferment or Titles; instead of advancing the Welfare and Happiness of his country.[18]

Bolingbrokean polemics pretends to construct a large monovocal community in opposition to a minority of self-interested individuals. The strategy is as familiar now as it was then, and the fallacy that underlies it hardly needs explaining. Like their claims of objectivity, the Bolingbrokeans' appeals to consensus are transparent affective devices, pulse-quickeners without much substance. Such appeals say plenty about how Bolingbroke and his fellow travelers imagined the opposition but very little about what the opposition really was. To endorse Bolingbroke's or Pulteney's self-serving rhetoric (as Kramnick does) is to tumble into what we once called "the intentional fallacy," or to resign ourselves to deducing meaning from an author's statements about meaning. Whether or not this is sensible practice in literary criticism is not an issue likely to generate much warmth at this late date, but certainly it is bad business when we are dealing with partisan political literature.

This book, then, is largely a study in pretense. The opening section is concerned with Bolingbroke's immensely popular *Remarks on the History of England*, published serially in the *Craftsman* in 1730 and 1731, and immediately the focus for the debate about print and politics that had been gaining momentum since the mid-1720s. I present the *Remarks* as the central document in Bolingbroke's attempt to establish himself as the spokesman for a populist opposition united by common values and a common vocabulary. I attempt to rehabilitate the *Remarks* not by offering inflated claims for their intrinsic merit, but by suggesting that their value is extrinsic or synthetic, the product of a noisy collaboration between the work and its readers rather than of Bolingbroke's often predictable utterances.

Chapter 1 considers the textual history of the *Remarks*, with particular attention to the tendency of reprint editions to vitiate the series by disregarding its topicality and its appeals to the conventions of middlebrow fiction and journalism. Editions in effect endorse Bolingbroke's own pretense of superiority to the polemical debate and reify his myth of an opposition united by its adherence to his own theories of government. Applying the ideas of McGann and other textual theorists, I argue that the intertextual nature of polemical literature poses a special problem for a tradition of textual editing accustomed to regarding authorial intention as an individual rather than a collective enterprise. Removed from the original *Craftsman* folios, the *Remarks* become the manifesto of a confident and learned opposition rather than Bolingbroke's attempt to graft coherency onto a diverse field of literature. The edited Bolingbroke is a philosopher first and a polemicist incidentally if at all, his *Remarks* a candidate for that singularly inert category "great literature," but barely recognizable as the interested intertextual exercise that they were. Oddly, perhaps, by calling attention to the ephemeral element in the *Remarks*, I hope to make the series accessible now, as it evidently was in the 1730s.

The *Remarks* perfected a rhetoric of historical analogy that had been the *Craftsman*'s modus operandi since its inception. Didactic comparisons of past and present, staples of historiography at least since Plutarch, were particularly useful to Bolingbrokean polemicists, adherents to a cyclical theory of history who believed that the Revolution of 1688–89 had reinstated the ancient Saxon "liberty" once manifest in (for instance) Elizabethan England, once undermined by (for instance) the Stuarts, and now again threatened by Walpole's government of placemanship. The second chapter demonstrates that the government's failed attempts to respond effectively to the *Remarks* in print and in court established analogic historiography as a safe and efficient mode of opposition rhetoric. But pro-government polemicists were not precisely the losers here. Confronted in the early 1730s by a swelling and multivocal opposition, they were willing enough to conflate ideological affiliation and rhetorical habit and so to dismiss their opponents as a unit that was as coherent ideologically as it was predictable methodologically. The convenience to the government's apologists was considerable. The *Remarks* promoted Bolingbroke's vision of a coherent opposition; the controversy that they inspired facilitated an analogous movement in pro-government polemics.

Anti-Bolingbrokeans within the opposition, then, had to contend with compatible homogenizing versions of the opposition, promoted on the one hand by the *Craftsman* and on the other by the pro-government press. A question introduced in the first section and addressed throughout the second asks what ideological and rhetorical options were available to opposition sympathizers unconvinced by the terms of Bolingbroke's bullish attempts to forge consensus. J. A. W. Gunn, sounding like Kramnick and quite a few less thoughtful commentators, claims that "'The Opposition' as a body was recognized by the early 1730s," and that Bolingbroke was this group's "effective leader."[19] But the assertion fails to account either for the often blurry boundaries between Bolingbrokean and Walpolite polemics or for a good deal of material written against both Walpole and Bolingbroke. Chapter 3 illustrates the shrinkage of the debate between the *Craftsman* and the pro-government press that resulted from the contestants' shared enthusiasm for the Revolution and their mutual willingness to reduce the print wars to a series of squabbles about who better understood the Revolution Settlement's prescription for limited monarchy. This way of defining the debate was repellent to the likes of the journalists Earbery and Richard Russel, who found Bolingbrokeans and Walpolites equally committed to the worst sort of historical revisionism, and equally tainted by their adherence to political philosophies hostile to the union of strong church and strong monarchy that had characterized pre-Revolution government.

This is not to say that Jacobitism had the vigor outside of Parliament that Cruickshanks believes it had "indoors." In order to facilitate my discussion of monarchist polemics in the 1730s, I introduce in the third chapter a term of my own coinage—"Carolinism"—as an alternative to Jacobitism, a frustratingly vague designation during the lull in pro-Stuart activity between the uprisings of 1715 and 1745. Jacobitism claims as its object the reinstallation of the Stuart monarchy. Carolinism does not. As practiced by Earbery, Russel, and others, Carolinism was a rhetorical stance rather than a political movement, a reductive language that opposed both linear pro-government historiography and circular Bolingbrokean historiography by juxtaposing single-mindedly the England of Charles I (1600–49) and his archbishop William Laud, and that of George II (1683–1760) and his secular first minister Walpole. In contrast to Bolingbroke, the Carolinists did not care whether or not Walpole was subverting the ends of the Revolution. Rather, they criticized him for severing the monarchic and ecclesiastical estates and thus reviving the republicanism of England under Oliver Cromwell. By discounting the analogic—hence, didactic—utility of the Revolution, Carolinist rhetoric contradicts the historical foundation of Bolingbrokean ideology even as it attacks Walpole. Carolinism refutes Bolingbroke's program of ideological amalgamation.

This militantly conservative rhetoric was the language of a motley group of nonjurors and divine-right theorists, ideological descendants of mid-seventeenth-century apologists for Charles I. Chapter 4 examines in more detail the eighteenth-century adaptation of what J. P. Kenyon, speaking of the seventeenth century, calls "the cult of Charles I."[20] Here I investigate the manner in which Carolinist polemicists—particularly Earbery, Russel, the Tory clergyman Joseph Trapp, and the Oxonian Thomas Hearne—incorporated the Caroline ethos into their critique of modern government and the modern political debate. Charles's reign and execution had been treated mythopoetically since the 1640s. Stuart apologists in the 1730s thus had ample material to use in their struggle against what they regarded as the rampant Erastianism and antimonarchism of their own day. Modernity provided no better materials, since the "old pretender," James Edward Stuart, could neither inspire confidence in propagandists nor offer hope to would-be insurrectionists. Spurned by modernity (to risk abstraction), the Carolinists preferred myth to practical politics. This gave them an excellent position from which to criticize the present, but one that alienated them from the practical interests of the Bolingbrokean opposition as surely as it distanced them from the historiographical habits of that group.

High-church apologists were largely responsible for the diffusion of Carolinist rhetoric into the public sphere. Chapter 5 first takes up the role of Russel's weekly *Grub-street Journal* (1730–37) in interrogating both the administration and its Bolingbrokean opponents. Readers in our own century have been puzzled by the political stance of the *Journal*, presumably because the *Journal* never bothered to formulate its criticisms of the government in what we have been content to regard as the language of the opposition: Bolingbrokean polemics. Unmistakably critical of Walpole, often resistant to the Bolingbrokean party line, and staunchly devoted to the memory of the "martyred monarch" Charles I, the *Journal* attests to Carolinism's position as a third stream of political discourse.

Chapter 5 concludes with an analysis of the controversy surrounding a King Charles Day sermon preached in 1732 by Francis Hare, bishop of Chichester (1671–1740). I present the sermon as an illustration of the government's anxiety about even the most derivative use of Carolinist rhetoric. Hare, a friend of Walpole and a pro-government servant of long standing, had typically asserted his own political opinion only when the Walpolite program was undefined. The renewed agitation in the 1730s for the repeal of the Test and Corporation Acts—seventeenth-century measures hostile to Catholics and dissenters—was such a moment; and in his sermon Hare argued against repeal by invoking the Carolinist analogy of murderous puritans then and menacing dissenters now. Walpole had wavered on repeal, but a strong court faction favored the claims of dissent and pounced on Hare's rhetoric in an effort to discredit him with Walpole. Hare's adversaries strove, illogically but with some success, to cast him as a Jacobite. His later career is marked by resolute but not wholly effective attempts to regain the status that his presumably innocent miscalculation had cost him.

The final chapter is a coalescence, an investigation of the role of the drama in expressing the ideological instability that I discuss in the earlier chapters. Analyzing generic differences between the historical drama of the half-dozen years before Walpole's Licensing Act of 1737 and the more focused polemical literature with which critics have often confused it, I suggest that many of the plays regarded as "opposition" by (among others) John Loftis and Robert Hume are in fact deeply anxious about the Bolingbrokean program. I concur with Hume that the drama of the period typically trades in "political commonplace" rather than in heartfelt ideologies.[21] But, unlike Hume, I find "political commonplace" in the drama frequently a skeptical or parodic commentary on opposition sentiment rather than a blandly supportive recitation of it. The drama often appropriated Bolingbrokean rhetoric in ways that replicated concerns about Bolingbroke reiterated less imaginatively by polemicists for and against Walpole.

Throughout this study, I show that the opposition looks very different—and a good deal less tidy—when we view it as the product of competing systems of genre, rhetoric, and historiography rather than as the expression of institutionalized consensus. Mine is a version of the political debate, I think, that would have been familiar to a coffee-house politician in the 1730s, but that several centuries of emphasis on "high politics" and "high literature" have taught us to disregard.

※ ※ ※

I have concentrated on the period 1730 to 1737 in order best to illustrate my claim that during the height of Walpole's power the opposition was a disparate bunch that resisted, as it continues to resist, easy definitions. The period is delimited on the one side by the publication of the *Remarks on the History of England* and on the other by the passage of the Licensing Act, which authorized pre-performance censorship and so virtually abolished politically suggestive drama. The Bolingbrokean strain asserted itself most forcefully in 1730 and 1731, was attacked and defended widely during the next half-dozen years or so, and finally dwindled into a vague point of reference in the works of the later "patriot opposition." By 1737, Bolingbroke had returned to France, the *Craftsman* was foundering, and *Fog's Weekly Journal*, the other major opposition newspaper, had been rendered toothless by the government.[22] If there was something that we could call a "Bolingbrokean moment," it was over by 1737.

The years 1730 to 1737 are different attitudinally from those that precede and succeed them. Consensus had seemed attainable in the heady mid-'20s. Goldgar observes that a "literary opposition" solidified in 1726 around the coalition of Bolingbroke and Pulteney. Most importantly, December 1726 saw the founding of the *Craftsman*, which quickly attracted a considerable audience. As Goldgar notes, these years were characterized by a gradual intensification of hostility between writers for and against the government.[23] But I do not find much evidence from this period of significant ideological diversity within the opposition other than that which is implicit in the distance (often slight) between the Jacobitical *Mist's Weekly Journal* or its successor *Fog's* and the professedly (and unconvincingly) pro-Hanoverian *Craftsman*.

On the other end of the spectrum, the years between the Licensing Act and Walpole's resignation in 1742 are marked by a generational shift in the opposition away from the *Craftsman* and its representatives. With Bolingbroke once more an expatriate and Pulteney fast losing credibility, the opposition became the property of a younger group of "boy patriots" rallying around Frederick, Prince of Wales, and represented in print by an increasingly angry and vocal Pope and by relative newcomers James Thomson and George Lyttleton. Goldgar calls this "a more vigorous and determined opposition."[24] Unquestionably it was a more coherent opposition as well and one that was eager to distance itself from its immediate forebears.

The intervening years are a good deal harder to characterize. I think that Goldgar understates the case when he claims that in the period 1734–37 "the increase in volume and intensity of antigovernment literature . . . [is] still not quite the result of an organized, directed program."[25] Rather, these years and those immediately preceding saw the invention—and the interrogation—of the myth of organization and direction. This is something quite different from a steady, whiggish march toward consensus.

Part 1
The Rhetoric of Consensus

1
Bolingbroke's *Remarks on the History of England* in the *Craftsman* and Elsewhere

THIS chapter is concerned with the textual history of Bolingbroke's *Remarks on the History of England*, specifically with the role of textual editing in legitimating the specious appeals to consensus on which Bolingbroke based the series. The transmission of the *Remarks* from the original folios to Nicholas Amhurst's and Isaac Kramnick's editions of 1731 and 1972, respectively, is accompanied by a loss of immediacy or "context."[1] This sort of slippage is unfortunate in the editing of, say, a novel, but is crippling in editions of an intrinsically intertextual genre like polemical literature. Editions of the *Remarks* sever the series from the numerous contemporary works (pamphlets and other newspapers) and genres (popular fiction and middlebrow journalism) with which it interacted. In this way, editions promote the myth of a monovocal, Bolingbroke-centered opposition that the present study opposes.

Conventional editing circumscribes polemical works in ways that belie their status *as* polemical works, or works that generate meaning by responding to other works. Polemical pieces like the *Remarks* are part of a synthetic textual environment inaccessible to editorial practices predicated on a belief in what Jerome McGann calls "the autonomy of the isolated author," a fallacy that McGann finds "grounded in a Romantic conception of literary production."[2] By distancing Bolingbroke from his contemporaries, bibliographically speaking, we have given him the last word in the print wars. This is legerdemain, a wishing-into-existence of an authority that no polemicist ever actually has.

During the decade of Bolingbroke's involvement (1726–36), the *Craftsman* was England's most widely read political paper. The apex of its popularity corresponds to its publication of the twenty-four installments of Bolingbroke's famous series, professedly a disinterested survey of English history but in fact a vehicle for historical analogies unflattering to the government. The series ran from 13 June 1730 (No. 206) to 22 May 1731 (No. 255); the best estimate of weekly sales during 1731 is twelve to thirteen thousand.[3] Numerous newspaper-leaders and at least thirty-three pamphlets were published in response to the series. Even in a period obsessed with print and politics, the numbers are extraordinary. By way of comparison, the *Grub-street Journal* (1730–37), a very popular paper in its early years, printed more than two thousand copies only twice in the period 8 January 1730 to 28 January 1731.[4]

Bolingbroke wrote the *Remarks* for the *Craftsman* during his busiest twelve months as a contributor, when he was most committed to effecting political change through the medium of popular literature.[5] The series was the summa of the partisan historiography that he and his fellows practiced in the *Craftsman*. Borrowing from classical and early modern traditions of polemics and historiography, the *Craftsman* had since its inception sniped at Walpole analogically by enumerating the alleged crimes of historical figures like Sejanus; Thomas Wolsey; and George Villiers, first duke of Buckingham—"wicked ministers," respectively, to Tiberius, Henry VIII, and James I and Charles I. But the *Remarks*—popular, plainly written, and bolder in their analogies than the *Craftsman*'s earlier efforts had been—intensified the analogic attack by targeting not only Walpole but, to the irritation of pro-government writers, George II himself. In 1730 and 1731, Bolingbroke was at his boldest and his most ambitious.

The structure of the *Remarks* is simple. Three introductory numbers outline the series and establish the fictional personae that Bolingbroke will employ. The survey of some seven centuries of English history will be cast as the lucubrations of an unnamed "Gentleman," recorded by one Humphrey Oldcastle and submitted as letters to the *Craftsman*'s fictive editor Caleb D'Anvers. Twenty numbers then appraise monarchs, ministers, and the status of popular "liberty" from the days of Saxon rule through the reign of Charles I (1625–49). The concluding number is Oldcastle's spirited response to the pro-government polemicists who had attacked Bolingbroke and his fellow *Craftsman*-writer William Pulteney during the course of the *Remarks*.

There has never been any doubt that the "general Remarks on the *English History*," as the *Craftsman*'s editor Amhurst winkingly called the *Remarks* (No. 213; 1 Aug. 1730), were in fact highly particular reflections on contemporary England. Bolingbroke was being characteristically disingenuous when he described the *Remarks* as "general and inoffensive Reflections on the Nature of *Liberty* and of *Faction*" (No. 255; 22 May 1731); and Kramnick sensibly observes that "the intent of the *Remarks* is overtly partisan, as its entrance into the world in the form of weekly essays in *The Craftsman* attests."[6] Bolingbroke's focus on his own time is implicit in his cyclical theory of history. Like Machiavelli, whom he admired and emulated, Bolingbroke believed in the *corso* and *ricorso* (ebb and flow) of history. The belief manifests itself in the pointedly "exemplary" readings of history at which Bolingbroke excelled.[7] In the series as elsewhere, Bolingbroke presents English history as the continual competition of the "spirit of liberty" and the "spirit of faction." Among others, Queen Elizabeth is characteristic of the former quality; and, among others, the Stuart monarchs embody the latter.

George II's relationship to various unsavory monarchs of the past is evident throughout the *Remarks*, as in Bolingbroke's attack on the minister-ridden and antiparliamentarian Richard II (No. 217; 29 Aug. 1730), which, along with the previous entry in the series (No. 215; 15 Aug. 1730), prompted the arrest of the *Craftsman*'s printer Richard Francklin. The *Remarks* attempt to counteract what Bolingbroke regarded as the tendency of Walpole and George II to subordinate to the "spirit of faction" the libertarian principles institutionalized in the Revolution Settlement of 1689.

In his first letter, Bolingbroke's Gentleman observes that limited monarchies are generally regarded as occupying a *"middle Point"* between *"absolute Monarchies"* and *"perfect Democracies,"* and are therefore thought susceptible to any "Deviation [that] leads on one Hand to *Tyranny*; and, on the other, to *Anarchy."* Without precisely contradicting this truism, the Gentleman recasts the dichotomy of tyranny and democracy in terms of "faction" and "liberty," thereby making proper government less dependent upon the inclinations of the monarch and more so upon the coherent participation of a right-minded populace.

After proposing this subtle but significant shift in emphasis, the Gentleman suggests that *"Liberty* would be safer, perhaps, if we inclined a little more than we do to the *popular Side."* Here as throughout the series, Bolingbroke bases his argument on his interpretation of British history:

> I may safely appeal to every impartial Reader of our *History*, whether any Truth he collected from it ever struck him more strongly than This; that when the Disputes between the *King* and the *People* have been carried to such extremes, as to draw national Calamities after them, it has not been owing primarily to the Obstinacy and weak Management of the *Court*, and is therefore unjustly charged on the just *Spirit of Liberty.* In Truth a *Spirit of Liberty* will never destroy a free Constitution; a *Spirit of Faction* may. But I appeal again, whether Those of our Princes, who have had Sense and Virtue enough to encourage the *one*, have had any Thing to fear from the *other*.
>
> Now if Experience shews, as I am persuaded it does, that the Prerogative and Power of a *Prince* will never be in any real Danger, when he invades, neither openly nor insidiously, the *Liberties of his People*; the same Experience will shew that the *Liberties of a People* may be in very real Danger, when, far from invading the *Prerogative and Power of the Prince*, they submit to one, and are even so good as to encrease the *other*. The Reason of this Difference is plain. A *Spirit of Faction* alone will be always too weak to cope with the legal Power and Authority of the *Crown*; and the *Spirit of Liberty*, in the whole Body of the People, which contradistinguishes this Case from the other, may be rais'd by the Fear of *losing*; but cannot be so raised by the Hopes of *acquiring*. The *Fear* is common to *all*; the *Hope* can only be particular to a *few.* The *Fear* therefore may become a general Principle of Union; the *Hope* cannot.

The *Remarks*, then, will attempt to inspire "the whole body of the people" to protect ancient liberties once again under assault by factious monarchs and ministers. Not surprisingly, the series proves to be equally a recitation of English history and an attack on modern English government, equally an appeal to consensus and an expression of hostility toward those who would resist the terms of consensus that Bolingbroke was offering.

The *Remarks* were Bolingbroke's first sustained attempt to present his vision of the opposition to a popular audience and so to promote the unified front with which he was becoming increasingly preoccupied. The journal's impressive sales-figures may or may not suggest that Bolingbroke's readers found his series persuasive, but they certainly imply that readers at least liked it. An interest in currying a broad readership, not evident in Bolingbroke's Scriblerian *Occasional Writer* (1727), is implicit in the medium that Bolingbroke chose for the *Remarks*. The appearance of such a series in a popular political newspaper guaranteed a lively intertextual controversy of a sort that had considerable popular appeal, or so we may infer from the abundance of such controversies and from the tendency of publishers to prolong controversies by printing pamphlets "on both sides of" a given issue, to borrow a common phrase of the day. Significantly, the *Monthly Chronicle*'s register of books for the period 1728–32 coded new pamphlets according to the controversy in which they participated.[8] Bolingbroke and his colleagues knew that controversy was a good market.

In the folios, the *Remarks* are contextualized by their participation in popular culture, as they cannot be in the reprint edition. Bolingbroke's original leaders go elbow to elbow with stock prices; London, national, and international news; notices of lost wives and servants; and the advertisements for pamphlets and quack medicines that call attention to the inglorious breeding grounds of much "neoclassical" literature. In news briefs written by Amhurst or taken from other papers, the folios present reports of the ongoing legal battles between the *Craftsman* and the ministry. In leaders by Bolingbroke and others, the journal comments on these battles.

For instance, the "London News" section of number 218 (5 Sept. 1730) reports that Francklin has been arrested for printing number 215 (15 Aug. 1730), an encomium on Edward III, and number 217 (29 Aug. 1730), the diatribe against Edward's successor Richard II. An item in number 219 (12 Sept. 1730) notes that Francklin has been released from custody. In the same number, Bolingbroke's confident seventh letter of the *Remarks* suggests that the *Craftsman* is relishing its legal victory. Bolingbroke uses a cursory account of the civil strife during and after the reign of Henry IV as an excuse for a stab at the pro-government *London Journal*, an analysis of the proper balance of power in a constitutional monarchy, and a barely disguised attack on the subordination of Parliament by George II and Walpole, here typed as the antiparliamentarian Charles I and a bevy of menacing minions. Amhurst presses the journal's advantage harder still in number 220 (19 Sept. 1730), a defense of Bolingbroke against the pro-government writers who had found ample specificity in the "general Remarks." In number 222 (3 Oct. 1730), Bolingbroke swaggers into a new round of analogic fisticuffs, this time criticizing the "Cruelty," "Rashness," and "Incontienence" [sic] of the usurping Edward IV—his most offensive analogy to date, according to the pro-government press.[9]

This pugnaciousness continues into the new year. The attitude is evident in the *Remarks* themselves and in the journal's publication on 2 January 1731 (No. 235) of the seditious "Hague letter"—a report from Walpole's supposedly secret negotiations toward the second Treaty of Vienna (1731). It is softened by Francklin's arrest for printing that document—reported in number 237 (16 Jan. 1731)—and is converted into a strident sort of anxiety in leaders responding to the arrest (Nos. 239, 241; 31 Jan., 13 Feb. 1731), and in leaders concerned more generally with the government's harassment of the journal (Nos. 243, 244; 27 Feb., 6 Mar. 1731). 1731 is marked by constant bickering between the *Craftsman* and the pro-government press. The contest takes a parodic turn when William Arnall ("Francis Walsingham") publishes in the *Free Briton* a parallel series against Bolingbroke and Pulteney entitled *The History of Patriotism*. This squabbling continues into and beyond *Craftsman* 255, the strident "vindication" of himself and Pulteney with which Bolingbroke concluded the *Remarks:* the number inspired thirteen pamphlets and a handful of leaders and prolonged the controversy by four months.[10] This is the larger cultural "text" of the *Remarks*—brash, busy, and relentlessly intertextual.

Bolingbroke's decision to publish the *Remarks* in the *Craftsman* illustrates his interest in reaching a broad audience. Bolingbroke makes his intentions more explicit still by allying his series to popular literature, notably fiction and journalism. These modes of appeal, as I shall demonstrate shortly, are muted in the 1731 edition and virtually obliterated in Kramnick's 1972 edition. But the generic allegiances declare themselves immediately in the pretense on which Bolingbroke based the *Remarks*. The series begins with the introduction of a fictive group of conversationalists, headed by Oldcastle, whose "Minutes," the journal proclaims at the start of each letter, are the source of the information that the series replicates. Bolingbroke's "Company, which often meets, rather to live than to drink together" (No. 206; 13 June 1730), is descended from Joseph Addison and Richard Steele's "Spectator club" and Eliza Haywood's "tea table."[11] By presenting the *Remarks* as the record of a conversation among peers, Bolingbroke courts a generation of readers raised on the journalistic fictions of the likes of Addison, Steele, and Haywood, all of whom promoted the illusion that their own didactic commentary was transcribed from the discussions of a lively and inquisitive coterie.

We learn in the first letter that Oldcastle and his companions have been spurred to a discussion of politics by their reading of the *Craftsman* and "several of Those [papers], which have been written against [it]." The men quickly—and preposterously—

dismiss the notion that the *Craftsman* "could be suspected to be written in Opposition to the *present M[iniste]rs.*" The first letter identifies "an *antient venerable Gentleman*" from Oldcastle's set as Bolingbroke's mouthpiece; it is he who defends the *Craftsman* against the charge of partisanship. The *Craftsman*, the Gentleman argues, has arisen to reassert an ancient and vital strain of English "liberty" now in eclipse, not to traffic in sedition like the Jacobitical *Fog's Weekly Journal*. The Gentleman wastes no time in addressing the stock pro-government claim that the *Craftsman* had at its inception introduced discontent into a tranquil world, a claim that would soon be reiterated in Arnall's charge that the paper had been "instrumental in raising that Spirit of Complaint, at a Time when the Nation enjoyed the most perfect and undisturbed Calm" (*Free Briton* 64; 18 Feb. 1731).[12] Note the yearning toward a homogenized rhetoric of opposition, evident in the Gentleman's characteristically Bolingbrokean attempt to collapse incompatible ideologies:

> I agree that, since that Time, Things are very much altered. A *Ferment,* or *Spirit,* call it which you please, is raised; but, I bless God, it is not the blind and furious *Spirit of Party.* It is a *Spirit* which springs from Information and Conviction, that has diffused itself not only to all Orders of Men . . . but to Men of all Denominations. Even They, who act against it, encourage it. You cannot call it *Tor[y]ism,* when such Numbers of *independent Whigs* avow it. To call it *Whigism* would be improper likewise, when so many *Tories* concur in it. He, who should call it *Jacobitism,* would be too absurd to deserve an Answer. What is it then? It is, I think, a Revival of the true old *English Spirit,* which prevailed in the Days of our Fathers, and which must always be national, since it has not Direction but to the national Interest.

The *Remarks,* as their readers would shortly see, will illustrate the Gentleman's position by tracing the "true old *English Spirit*" throughout history, or by presenting "liberty" as a repeatable historical phenomenon that modern England can decide to nourish or to subordinate to the "furious *Spirit of Party.*" "Liberty cannot be long secure, in any country, unless a *perpetual Jealousy* watches over it, and a *constant determined Resolution* protects it in the whole body of the nation," the Gentleman declares, simultaneously reciting for his listeners (fictive and actual) the platitudes of Bolingbrokean thought and introducing the didactic purpose of the *Remarks.*

Bolingbroke dramatizes the Gentleman's rhetorical potency by writing into the first two letters a young pro-government apologist over whom the older man gains ascendancy. (Pope does something analogous in the *Epilogue to the Satires* [1738], in the character of the poet's skeptical but stupid pro-government "friend.") The first expression of the straw man's mistrust of the *Craftsman* prompts the speech from which I have quoted. One week later, the youngster "owns [him]self a good deal reconcil'd to the *Craftsman* by the Discourse you held, when We were last together," and asks the "*old Sage*" to speak further so that "the few Doubts I have still may be removed" (No. 208; 27 June 1730). The Gentleman of course obliges; and we may take the silence of his one-time adversary as assent to his further comments on "liberty" and "faction" and the *Craftsman*'s role in safeguarding one and exposing the other. The unnamed listener, so easily convinced of the error of his thought, is a useful emblem of the *Craftsman*'s intentions: within and without the series, the journal will convert such skeptics to the truths retailed weekly in its pages.

Oldcastle closes his second letter by promising to report back to D'Anvers if the Gentleman should "resume the Discourse." The Gentleman will do so in his fourth letter (No. 213; 1 Aug. 1730), but only after Bolingbroke's third letter (No. 210; 11 July 1730) develops the fiction of the series's corporate authorship and stresses the topicality of the *Remarks*. Oldcastle begins the third letter by noting that he has been called into the country on personal business and has passed the "Minutes" of the Gentleman's "Conversations" to D'Anvers "in Hopes that the Subject will not be left imperfect for as long a Time as my Affairs may oblige me to be absent." Oldcastle quits the series shortly after he delivers his manuscript to D'Anvers; he lingers only to answer the responses to the series that were already starting to appear in the pro-government *Daily Courant* and *London Journal*. The next two folios (Nos. 211, 212; 18, 25 July 1730), written by Amhurst, are further interruptions of the series. But both continue the volley against the pro-government press initiated by Oldcastle, and both thereby stress the similarity of Bolingbroke's historiography to the less high-minded business of unmediated polemical attack.

In number 212, Amhurst, as D'Anvers, notes that he has received from Oldcastle "the Minutes of the succeeding Conversations, mention'd in his last Letter":

> I have great Reason to wish that his Affairs had allowed Him to digest these Materials into Form; being very sensible of my own Inability,

even with the Advantage of his Assistance, to follow such an excellent Master of History and political Reasoning; but since He hath done me the Honour to commit this Trust into my Hands, I will exert my best Endeavours to execute it as it deserves, and in the Manner, which He hath directed; by dividing his Remarks into select Dissertations and publishing them, from Time to Time, as Occasion requires.

Amhurst and Bolingbroke are acting as mock editors in the tradition of Aphra Behn (Oroonoko [ca. 1688]); Jonathan Swift (A Tale of a Tub [1704]); Daniel Defoe (Moll Flanders [1722], among others); and, later, Samuel Richardson (Pamela [1740–41] and Clarissa [1747–49]). The pretense of corporate authorship is an appeal to an audience acquainted with the conventions of popular literature.

The prevalence of this pretense should not blind us to its potency. Richardson is a useful analogue. In Clarissa, the characters convert seriatim to the Christian ethos endorsed by Richardson and expressed by his heroine. Clarissa's message—her purity, less abstractly—is first tested by her family and then, more dramatically, by Lovelace. But this suffusive quality is dominant by the end of the novel, chastening—instructing, to press the analogy—the Harlowes, Belford, and even Lovelace. Pamela's moral triumph over Squire B. is of precisely the same order. And with Amhurst's help, Bolingbroke is up to something analogous. By assigning his political program to the Gentleman by way of Oldcastle and his fellows, and by disseminating it with the compliance of the popular D'Anvers, Bolingbroke packages an idiosyncratic ideology as common intellectual property. In Bolingbroke as in Richardson, didacticism insists on its own persuasive or hegemonizing power. In the Remarks, the appeal to consensus is advanced narratively by the fiction of corporate authorship much as the straw man's conversion acts it out dramatically. The interaction among different but compatible voices illustrates various ways of getting to a single truth. This is perhaps most evident in Bolingbroke's notorious twenty-fourth letter, in which Bolingbroke, as Oldcastle, simultaneously defends the Gentleman's libertarian political philosophy and his own and Pulteney's careers as the apostles of "liberty." By alternating personae throughout the series, Bolingbroke enforces an artificial but expedient distinction between polemical writing and historiography, assigning the first to Oldcastle and the second to the Gentleman. Both modes operate as appeals to consensus.

Contemporary readers would presumably have recognized as designedly specious the attempt to distinguish between "low" polemics and "high" historiography. The categories merge too frequently and too obviously in the period for it to have been otherwise. Scholars of Bolingbroke, however, have had no interest in Bolingbroke's use of the middlebrow conventions of his own day. Although no one seems to have noticed it, the *Remarks* do not pretend to be the utterances of Bolingbroke or, for that matter, Humphry Oldcastle.[13] Bolingbroke presents his series as the transcriptions by Oldcastle of the meditations of the "*antient venerable Gentleman*" who moderates the discussion at the outset of the series. The only exceptions are letter 1 (which introduces the Gentleman and is largely given over to him); letter 2 (which includes introductory and concluding paragraphs by Oldcastle and is otherwise spoken by the Gentleman); letter 3 (Oldcastle's comments on the pro-government press and his introduction of the survey portion of the series); and letter 24 (Oldcastle's defense of Bolingbroke and Pulteney). This is not to say that the *Remarks* are anything other than Bolingbrokean historiography. But what is more important here is that Bolingbroke dresses his historiography in very current costume, the more evidently so for the series's epistolary format.

Although both Oldcastle and the Gentleman are manifestations of Bolingbroke, the personae are complementary, not identical. Oldcastle is a polemicist, rooted in the here and now and unapologetically gunning for his opponents. His third and twenty-fourth letters are largely indistinguishable from many miscellaneous leaders in the *Craftsman* and from scores of pro-*Craftsman* pamphlets. On the other hand, the Gentleman is a coolly detached theorist who favors the indirection of historical analogy to Oldcastle's less elaborate rhetorical strategies. The Gentleman's few direct appeals to contemporaneity create a sense of moderation that plays off of the evident bias of his analogies, as when, in the second letter, he presents the *Craftsman* as equally distant from the ideologies of *Fog's Weekly Journal* and the *Daily Courant*.

Interestingly, the Gentleman mentions Oldcastle only once, and then to invoke him in his own uncharacteristic attempt "to speak . . . without any *Metaphor*"—without recurring to historical analogy, that is. In the seventh letter, the Gentleman quickly abandons his discussion of the houses of York and Lancaster. He turns first to a theoretical discussion of constitutional monarchy and then to a thinly disguised criticism of taxation under George

II, pausing to glance derisively at the pro-government press's excuses for France's rebuilding of fortifications at Dunkirk—a violation of the Treaty of Utrecht (1713). But until the direct hit on the government's apologists, the Gentleman makes politics a corollary from morality. When the pitch of his argument rises, he bows out to Oldcastle. Here the Gentleman is lamenting what he sees as his opponents' disregard for the proper balance of power among monarch, ministers, and Parliament:

> One would be ashamed to insist thus much on a Point so very clear, if *some Men* were not so harden'd to all Sense of Shame, as to maintain the contrary; and that there are Men capable of doing This, is one of those melancholy Symptoms which characterise the *present Age*. I could almost appeal to the cool Thoughts, and the private Reflections of some of *these Writers*, whether any Thing can be more scandalous than the Task they have undertaken. To skreen their *Patrons*, They endeavor to distinguish us out of our greatest *national Advantages*; as was observed in the Case of *Dunkirk*. To reconcile the Minds of Men to *such Measures*, as their *Patrons* may want, and as no *honest* Man will take, They endeavor to demolish the very *Corner-stones*, on which the whole Fabrick of *Liberty* rests. Their Iniquity, it must be confess'd, is very systematical. When They write for the *Corruption*, they write for the *Means*. When They write for the *Dependency of the Parliament on the Court*, They write for the *End*. Well might *Oldcastle* say of *these Writers*, their *Patrons* and *Abettors, that the* Mask *was pull'd off on one Side*.

As it happens, the Gentleman misremembers. The phrase "the mask is pulled off" is his own construction from the second letter, presented not as part of an attack on the pro-government press but rather as a general, if obviously barbed, illustration of the tendency of Bolingbroke's beloved "spirit of liberty" to ferret out factious enemies of constitutional monarchy. Both the Gentleman's invocation of Oldcastle and the slip of his memory—intended or not—illustrate the tension in Bolingbrokean polemics between direct and mediated discourse.

Oldcastle's pugilistic ranting is thematically compatible with the Gentleman's loftier rhetoric, which suggests the fallacy behind the Gentleman's pretenses to objectivity. As I have demonstrated, Bolingbroke, like his friend Pope, liked to imagine himself as far from the madding crowd of polemicists. But this sort of posturing is one of the defining characteristics of polemical literature and is, as such, another of Bolingbroke's attempts to rely upon familiar contemporary conventions. Consider the pose that Pulteney strikes in his rebuttal of John, Lord Hervey's attack on the *Remarks*:

> Many Persons now alive remember *Bass Brown*, Verger of *Westminster-Abbey*. He had but one Secret for keeping Himself unrival'd in his Sovereign, the *Dean*'s Favour, and often partaking of his Bounty; which was driving the *Dog*'s out of the Church; but that He might, at the same Time, make his *Ministry* the more necessary, *Bass* took Care to whistle them into it. This may be call'd *Plot-making*; and when the Terror of his *Whip* had made all the stragling Curs forsake even the Cloisters, I am told that *Bass* kept a *Boy* hid in a Corner, who could *bark*. This I call *Pamphleteering*.[14]

The problem here is that the pamphleteer Pulteney is whistling and barking as loudly as anyone, including Hervey. Bolingbroke shuffles in a similar way in the terminal number of the *Remarks*, in which he describes himself and Pulteney as "*Gentlemen*" and the assailants of the *Remarks* as "all the Powers of Scurrility and Calumny," and, more simply still, "*Insects*." However much some contemporary readers of the *Craftsman* might have enjoyed Bolingbroke's and Pulteney's assertions of distance from their enemies, it is unlikely that readers of any stripe actually believed them. This sort of angry diminution is clubbish rather than properly didactic, and panders to the prejudices of old readers rather than seeking the sympathy of new ones. It is not an attempt at truth, the more obviously for having been the property of no particular party. Such hyperbolic self-aggrandizement would have been broadly recognized for what it was: an affective posture, of a piece with the other familiar pretenses and modes of appeal that Bolingbroke wrote into the *Remarks*.

I have been suggesting that Bolingbroke designed the *Remarks* as an exercise in popular literature, accessible to an audience lacking the erudition and the attentiveness to tonal nuance required to master, say, Bolingbroke's later *The Idea of a Patriot King* (written 1738[?]; published 1749) or the *Letters on the Study and Use of History* (1752). If I have been justified in doing so, then it follows that to lose sight of the contemporary contexts of the series is in a very real sense to lose sight of the series itself. By falling into this error, we render the series inert, a predictable sequence of swipes at a silent adversary—Walpole— who is all the more easily dismissed by readers today as having been a favorite butt of the great Augustan satirists. Unquestionably, the *Remarks* have lost vitality. In 1976 Bertrand Goldgar referred easily enough to "the tedious series of historical parallels" that constitutes the Remarks. Eight years later Simon Varey acknowledged that the contemporary popularity of the Remarks "may now be difficult to understand."[15] It is not hard to appreciate the lack of enthusiasm. Bolingbroke's immense sense of self-importance, the unrelieved astringency of much of his rhetoric, and his tendency to rehearse a very few very simple and not very original ideas endlessly and as though they were somehow revolutionary—these are not endearing tonal characteristics in any case and are less so when we encounter them in isolation, untempered by mitigating response. How is it, one might ask, that readers in the 1730s found so engaging a work that now seems alternately carping and lifeless?

Even to pose the question is to advertise our own tendency to read polemical literature anticontextually. This tendency manifests itself as a willingness to ignore the contemporaneous element in a literature that masquerades as superior to contemporary discourse as part of its pretense of objectivity—a literature that stoops to conquer while asking its readers not to notice that it is stooping in the first place. Specifically, the 1731 and 1972 editions of the Remarks recast Bolingbroke's leaders as a disinterested treatise, protected from rather than participating in the print wars. The editions present the Remarks as Bolingbroke justified them, not as he designed them.

Reprinting polemical journalism as stable and durable works is probably a doomed enterprise. Before taking up the 1731 and 1972 editions individually, I shall state the problem in more general terms. Surely it is uncontroversial to posit as the goal of textual editing the recuperation of an author's meaning, whether we consider the author as an autonomous entity (as editors often have) or as part of a social network of production (as McGann and other theorists suggest that we should). Because polemical literature has little or no intrinsic meaning, to reprint polemical pieces separately from the works with which they interact is to ignore their most basic source of meaning. And if one supposes that polemicists knew that they were writing polemically, then one must acknowledge that reprinting necessarily obscures, rather than clarifies, authorial intention, however broadly construed. Although a great many people are saying a great many curious things about textual editing these days, I do not believe that anyone has suggested that obscuring authorial intention is a laudable result of the process.

Additionally, polemical literature tends to be ephemeral literature. Polemical works are often *Dunciads* without rhyme or wit, repositories of period-specific data that on the face of it would seem to discourage the wide-ranging thematizing practiced by Kramnick in his analyses of Bolingbroke's thought.[16] Writing in 1770, Oliver Goldsmith acknowledged the contemporary appeal as well as the ephemerality of Bolingbroke's polemical writing:

> His letters in a paper called the Craftsman, were particularly distinguished in this political contest [i.e., the print wars of the late 1720s and the early '30s]; and though several of the most expert politicians of the times joined in this paper, his essays were peculiarly relished by the public. However, it is the fate of things written to an occasion seldom to survive that occasion: the Craftsman, though written with great spirit and sharpness, is now almost forgotten, although when it was published as a weekly paper, it sold much more rapidly than even the Spectator.[17]

The challenge that Bolingbroke poses to editors is clear from Goldsmith's observation: how does one present as meaningful a work "written to an occasion" that itself lies beyond the reconstructive powers of conventional editing?

Like much else in textual theory, the problem is easier to illustrate than it is to answer. Bolingbroke's terminal letter of the *Remarks* exemplifies the restrictive commitment to "occasion" that Goldsmith finds in Bolingbroke's polemics. The number was not the first time that Bolingbroke used the series to answer his detractors. He had on several occasions peppered his letters with attacks on pro-government journalists, and Amhurst repeatedly interrupted the series to publish essays by himself and others against the Walpolite press.[18] But in *Craftsman* 255, Bolingbroke no longer bothers to couch his argument in the expansive language of English history. He takes aim at "the whole Posse of *ministerial Scribblers*" who had cast Pulteney as a turncoat motivated by "*the Stings of disappointed Ambition*" and had presented Bolingbroke himself as a Jacobite ungrateful to his old supporters the duke of Marlborough, the earl of Godolphin, and George I himself. The essay is the product of earlier pieces by pro-government polemicists like Hervey and Arnall, whose barbs had perhaps stung Bolingbroke more than he acknowledged when he portrayed himself and Pulteney, loftily, as in "Contempt" of the "strain of Malice" directed against them. Meaning in this essay is synthetic or extrinsic, the more so considering the controversy that the number itself generated. We may understand *Craftsman* 255 as one entry among many in a certain controversy, but without this context the number only exemplifies the transiency that Goldsmith ascribed to Bolingbroke's entries in the *Craftsman*.

Reprint editions have not restored breadth to the series. The 1731 edition, for instance, presents *Craftsman* 255 as the triumphant climax of a controversy recorded only in the *Craftsman*'s words and contained within the covers of the edition's seventh and final volume. Necessarily, given the constraints of conventional editing, the 1754, 1841, and 1844 diplomatic editions of Bolingbroke's *Works* present the number transhistorically, as one entry in a sequence of works, polemical and otherwise, by Bolingbroke.[19] Kramnick deletes the number, presenting the *Remarks* as timeless rather than time-bound and so artificially protecting the series from the fate recorded by Goldsmith. Editions variously obscure what I have been arguing is the series's most vital characteristic: its intertextuality, or, again, its commitment to contemporaneity.

Current textual theory helps us understand this shortcoming of editorial practice. In 1991 McGann introduced the idea of a work's "bibliographical code," which he distinguishes from the "linguistic code," or the verbal signifiers of meaning that he believes "we tend to privilege when we study language-based arts like novels and poetry." The bibliographical code is the record of "the symbolic and signifying dimensions of the physical medium through which (or rather *as* which) the linguistic text is embodied."[20] McGann's own examples are Blake's elaborate (and elaborately signifying) page designs and the different tables of contents in editions of Arnold that suggest different relations among Arnold's poems. McGann argues that it is "the business of critical editing" to clarify "differences" resulting from alterations in a work's bibliographical code.[21] Working from McGann's schema, George Bornstein coined the term "contextual code" to address the sequencing of material within an edition. "On the one hand," Bornstein writes, "[the] contextual code is bibliographic in that it pertains to the physical constitution of the volume; on the other, the contextual code is linguistic in that it is made up of words."[22]

The problems that I find in the 1731 and 1972 editions result from alterations in the bibliographical and contextual codes of the original work. Prepared by Amhurst and printed by Francklin, the seven-volume collected edition of the *Craftsman* begins the detemporalizing of the *Remarks*. Amhurst and Francklin regarded the *Remarks* as the cornerstone of the edition. By packaging and promoting the edition as they did, they in effect endorsed the fictional Gentleman's sense that the series was something more than mere polemic.

An advertisement in *Craftsman* 253 (8 May 1731) promised that the edition would appear "*at the latter End of next Week*" and would include reprints of leaders "to the Conclusion of Mr. *Oldcastle*'s Remarks." Clearly Amhurst was considering Bolingbroke's twenty-third letter (No. 254; 15 May 1731) the terminal entry in the series. But someone (presumably Amhurst) decided to put off publication until 1 June, more than two weeks after the appearance of number 254. Advertisements in numbers 254 (15 May 1731), 255 (22 May 1731), and 256 (29 May 1731), all of which present different publication dates, allow us to speculate that Amhurst was uncertain about what sequence of entries would constitute the "final" version of the *Remarks*. Given the evidence of the first advertisement, we may tentatively conclude that Amhurst had decided to delay publication of his edition until it could accommodate Bolingbroke's vitriolic coda to the series in his twenty-fourth letter. By including that number, Amhurst (unlike Bolingbroke's later editors) replicates Bolingbroke's intratextual sequence. But by plucking it from the controversy that even then surrounded it, and by printing it with the entries designed, however disingenuously, as "general Remarks" on English history, Amhurst attempts to add dignity and authority—erudition, even—to a particularly nasty and small-minded polemical tract. Repackaged, the widely discussed number maintains a distinguished distance from its detractors: it becomes a smug and dismissive conclusion to a series that itself comes to stand as a validation of the claims of disinterestedness that Bolingbroke advances in the twenty-fourth letter.

The decision to postpone publication says something about the prestige that Amhurst and Francklin believed the popular series would bring to what otherwise would have been simply a collection of discreet newspaper-leaders. The edition was a publishing event of an altogether different order from the production of a weekly political paper, as readers would see when the edition finally appeared in June 1731. The unbound folios become handsomely bound octavos with copperplate frontispieces; and the series is purged of advertisements, stock prices, and other "low" reminders of commerce and contemporaneity. Authors are now identified by initials appended to the essays: Bolingbroke's "O" marks off the *Remarks* as a distinct single-author work, nudging the series away from the cloak-and-dagger anonymity of newspaper polemics and toward the respectable forthrightness of mainstream literature.²³ The work's bibliographical code has been rewritten; and the cultural meaning of the work has changed considerably, even if its linguistic text has not.

With very few interruptions, the *Remarks* make up the seventh and final volume of the 1731 edition. Amhurst thus presents the series as the conclusion of the *Craftsman*'s first three and a half years, or as the last word on didactic historiography, to be somewhat fanciful about it. In order to fit the *Remarks* neatly into one volume, Amhurst or Francklin assigned new numbers and dates to the folios published from 13 June 1730 (No. 206) to 10 April 1731 (No. 248).²⁴ Although this shuffling does not alter the work's linguistic code, it scrambles the contextual code. Again, the meaning of the work is altered. Not only does one lose the running commentary of the news items (deleted from the edition), but one is unlikely to recognize the many points of correspondence among the *Remarks* and the contemporaneous publications that "answer" the series. In the most striking example, the original number 243 (27 Feb. 1731), Amhurst's denunciation of Francklin's arrest for printing the "Hague letter," becomes number 216 in the reprint edition (22 Aug. 1730), moved from six weeks after to four and a half months before the legal incident that inspired it, or transformed from an angry topical response into an oddly unfocused tantrum. The intertextual debate becomes a recitation of utterances that often seem (literally) uninspired and unchallenged, more oblique the more they trade in topical detail. Bornstein argues that editorial resequencing helped convert Yeats's "Song of the Happy Shepherd" from a politically rich moment in "Irish renaissance" literature to a bland example of "international modernism."²⁵ The 1731 edition of the *Craftsman* neutralizes the tenor of Bolingbroke's politics no less efficiently.

What the edition gains is narrative coherency, somewhat like what a Victorian novel gains when it is promoted from the pages of a magazine to a first edition. The edition "reads" as briskly as such material can read, but it does so because it has largely disowned its relationship to the environment in which its component texts were produced.

Surprisingly, Kramnick ignores the folios in his research.²⁶ This is emblematic of what I take to be Kramnick's tendency to minimize the contemporaneous element in Bolingbroke. Bound with Bolingbroke's high-toned *Letters on the Study and Use of*

History,[27] printed with modernized spelling and punctuation, and introduced by an essay that does not mention either Oldcastle or the Gentleman, Kramnick's 1972 edition presents a version of the *Remarks* that is substantially different from the one presented in the folios or the 1731 edition. In Kramnick's introduction and the text itself, the *Remarks* become a self-contained and self-indulgent exercise in political theory, representative of important trends in the history of ideas but lacking the immediacy that Bolingbroke built into them. Kramnick's erudite introduction sharpens its readers' appreciation of Bolingbroke's place in intellectual history. But the effect of the introduction, like the effect of the emendations that I shall discuss, is to promote Bolingbroke the philosopher at the expense of Bolingbroke the polemicist, or, more dramatically, to make of Bolingbroke the autonomous author pronounced mythic by McGann.

The packaging of the book poses an initial problem. It is easy enough in these days of resolute multiculturalism to cry foul at the proud Anglo-centrism of a series title like "Classics of British Historical Literature," perhaps easier still when the words are embossed in gold letters on the cover of a handsome edition published by an august university press. But it is more useful to note that the packaging and the series title, although not attributable to Kramnick, nonetheless prefigure the detemporalizing tendency of his edition. The idea of a "classic" of "historical literature" is sensible enough. I am not convinced, however, that the designation fits the *Remarks*, or, rather, that to apply the designation to the *Remarks* is not to misrepresent Bolingbroke's series at the outset. And the idea of a "classic" of polemical literature is unsettling: the categories pull in opposite directions. Presenting the *Remarks* as a "classic" recalls the unfortunate tendency of some anthologists and authors of introductory studies to make satire accessible to a general readership by liberating it from the grip of topicality.[28]

Kramnick consistently ignores the topical content of the *Remarks*. For example, following the lead of the 1754, 1841, and 1844 editions of Bolingbroke's *Works*, he does away with an addendum to the seventh letter that refers to Francklin's arrest for publishing Bolingbroke's two previous entries. In the folios and the 1731 edition, the seventh letter is introduced by Amhurst's dig at the government for its "uncommon Proceedings upon Mr. *Francklin*" and by his promise to exercise his "Privilege" of publishing the "*Abstract of the English History.*" "As for Mr. *Oldcastle* and *my self*," the notice continues, "we shall always take particular Care not to assert any Thing, in the Course of these *Remarks*, but what we can justify by undoubted Authority from the *best Historians*." The deadpan and cheeky passage, and Bolingbroke's direct assault on the government that follows it, records the *Craftsman*'s mockery of the government for its inability to prosecute Francklin for the sort of sedition that Amhurst's introduction denies but that Bolingbroke's leader delivers. In the folios and the 1731 edition, Amhurst and Bolingbroke collectively test the government's patience, virtually daring Walpole to take further action against the journal. In Kramnick's edition, Bolingbroke just writes about history.

Kramnick chose not to include Bolingbroke's third and twenty-fourth letters, in which Oldcastle stands in for the Gentleman and steers the *Remarks* from the past to the present. As I have noted, in the third letter Bolingbroke solidifies his fiction of corporate authorship. It would be impossible for the reader of Kramnick's edition to determine whether or not the Gentleman had kept his promise, made in the second letter, to "resume the Discourse" that had captivated his listeners. Kramnick's reader, therefore, would not know precisely who was "speaking" the series. If the series were meant only to promote broad truths of history and politics, the deletion is insignificant. But if, as I have been arguing, the series is additionally a self-conscious exercise in contemporary polemics—or an exploration of the means by which the truths of history and politics might most successfully be disseminated—then the deletion matters quite a bit.

Omitting the terminal letter deprives the reader of the logical culmination of the series in more ways than one. In the folios as in the 1731 edition and the various editions of Bolingbroke's *Works*, the effect of the conclusion of the *Remarks* is tremendous: it is as though Oldcastle (the author of the letter to D'Anvers) and Bolingbroke (with Pulteney the letter's subject) have dismissed the mild Gentleman and are marching in lockstep against an enemy at whose presence the Gentleman had hinted, but not acknowledged, for most of his series. Oldcastle continues to defend the "general and inoffensive Reflections on the Nature of *Liberty* and *Faction*" offered, or so he claims, by the *Remarks*. But his real interest is in Bolingbroke's and D'Anvers's detractors, "*Those*, who not content with the Merit of being your *Adversaries*, have declared Themselves such at last to the very Being of the *British Constitution* and to the Principles, on which the *present Establishment* is built, and on which alone it can stand."

Narratologically speaking, this is both climax and closure.

Back in July 1730, Amhurst, as D'Anvers, had acknowledged receipt of the text of the *Remarks*, "in which the *general Positions*" enumerated in Bolingbroke's first and second letters "are apply'd to the *English History*, from the Conquest to this Time" (No. 212; 25 July 1730). This description of the chronological scope of the series is repeated without significant alteration in the heading of number 213 (1 Aug. 1730), the beginning of the historical survey section of the series. Yet the twenty-third letter takes the reader only through the reign of Charles I—nearly a century from "this Time." *Craftsman* 255 brings the series up to the minute, presenting Walpole's apologists as the embodiments of the "spirit of faction" that the Gentleman had been describing in more distant terms. History becomes modernity, and historiography becomes polemics. The transition could not surprise any reader of the *Remarks* in earlier editions, but it is invisible to the reader of Kramnick's edition. Kramnick is right to note that in the *Remarks* "English history is one long endorsement of the Opposition."[29] But by leaving off Bolingbroke's final installment he does not let his reader see that this "endorsement" was equally the product of Bolingbrokean political theory and Bolingbrokean polemical practice. Amhurst's inclusion of the number produces one set of problems; Kramnick's deletion of it another.

By ignoring Bolingbroke's careful layering of authorial personae, Kramnick recasts as monovocal (and "classic") a work built around popular pretenses of corporate authorship and demonstrably mindful of the need to address a large contemporary audience. A final example suggests the extent to which the most innocent emendations can distort meaning in a polemical work. Following is a transcription of the heading of the twenty-second essay of the *Remarks*:

The COUNTRY JOURNAL: N°. 253

OR, THE

CRAFTSMAN

By CALEB D'ANVERS, *of* GRAY'S-INN, *Esq*;

SATURDAY, MAY 8, 1731

Remarks on the History of England *continued.*
From the Minutes of Mr. Oldcastle.

In the folio as in the 1731 edition, the essay begins, "IN our Paper, of *March* the 13th, We have spoken of the State of *Parties* at the Accession of K. *James.*" Kramnick omits the journal's heading, number, and date. His entry begins, "In letter 18, we have spoken of the state of parties at the accession of king James."[30]

Mindful of Kramnick's others deletions, we may appreciate the manner in which this simple emendation further subverts any sense of Bolingbroke's role in the contemporary political debate. Most obviously, D'Anvers is absent, as he is from Kramnick's introduction. Varey discusses the significance of D'Anvers's name. He observes that the Biblical resonance of "Caleb" suggests "a loyal leader, faithful to a cause"; and he notes the *Craftsman's* own affiliation of "D'Anvers" with Antwerp, hence with the Holy Roman Empire, and hence with the Hanoverian succession, to which the journal habitually pretended devotion. Varey notes that D'Anvers "was obviously a screen to conceal the identities of the paper's contributors, but he could also usefully break down the barrier between the author and the reader."[31] The connection with law, established by the Gray's-Inn address, identifies D'Anvers's social position as impressive but not awesome.[32] The convenience of the eidolon is obvious: D'Anvers allowed the aristocratic Bolingbroke and the well-bred Pulteney to interact imaginatively with a populace whose support they sought but with whom they were disallowed less mediated contact.[33]

Kramnick's emendation removes not only D'Anvers, but the country gentleman Oldcastle as well—a comfortably mythic type to an urban audience, I would guess, in the years between the appearances of Addison's Sir Roger de Coverley and Fielding's Squire Allworthy. And Oldcastle in turn takes with him the narrating Gentleman alluded to in the original heading's reference to Oldcastle's "minutes." This leaves only Henry St. John, Viscount Bolingbroke, presumably in his own voice a more suitable vessel for the transmission of serious historiography than a fictional character could be. Oldcastle's "minutes," the bequest of a group of gentlemen-collaborators to the populace, become Bolingbroke's personal "remarks."

Having done away with the personae invented to relate the *Remarks,* Kramnick threatens the notion of the series *as* a series by removing the reference to its continuity ("REMARKS *on the History of* England *continued*"). And Bolingbroke's allusion to his own series ("IN our Paper, of *March* the 13th") is stripped both of its reference to corporate authorship and of its defining temporality: the possessive pronoun "our" is deleted, and

"*March* the 13th" becomes "In letter 18." Particularly in a publication environment in which controversial pamphlets appeared frequently and usually disappeared quickly, "*March* the 13th" does not mean "letter 18" in any comprehensive sense, but encourages us to acknowledge the presence of those pamphlets and newspapers that were published approximately at the time that Bolingbroke identifies and that contribute to the larger meaning of the *Remarks*. In March 1731 were published, among other historical and political tracts, two installments of Nicholas Tindal's new translation of Paul de Rapin-Thoyras' *History of England* (a work to which Bolingbroke often refers in the *Remarks*); a poem entitled *The Compromise: Or, a Dialogue between W[alpole] and P[ulteney]*; and a derivative pamphlet entitled *An Appeal to the Nation: Or, the Case of the Present Minister of Great Britain Truly Stated in an Impartial View of the Fortunes and Fate of All Those Ministers Who Have Born the Office of Lord High Treasurer, from Henry IV. to This Time*. These works, too, are part of the textual history of the *Remarks*.

Since 1983, McGann has been arguing for "a socialized concept of authorship and textual authority" that would account for "the dynamic social relations which always exist in literary production—the dialectic between the historically located individual author and the historically developing institutions of literary production."[34] That McGann initiated a revolution in textual theory rather than textual editing is often remarked and is not, I think, contrary to his design; his interest has been in new ways of conceptualizing "textual authority" primarily and new ways of editing texts incidentally. So, for example, noting that "practical editorial matter is not my principal concern at this moment," he proposes as the most satisfying method of editing Dante Gabriel Rossetti's *The House of Life* either the compilation of diplomatic texts that "would yield at least four distinct 'Houses of Life'" or the assembling of a "genetic" edition (after Hans Gabler's edition of Joyce's *Ulysses* [1984]) designed "to display the work's evolution from its earliest to its latest productive phases in the author's lifetime."[35]

By rejecting the principles of eclecticism, McGann seems to propose an exhaustive sort of diplomatic editing (as opposed to "critical editing," in the old nomenclature) as the proper method for editions that would recreate, or at least meaningfully allude to, the social bases of literary production. Curiously, with this apparent abdication of editorial responsibility, McGann has made—or allowed—what is arguably his most important contribution. Through the efforts of McGann, Bornstein, and quite a few others, editors and theorists have come to question the primacy of eclecticism and to consider the possibility that a "text" may usefully be defined as the sum of its linguistic, bibliographical, and contextual "codes," as well as by extratextual considerations such as its reception-history. The apparatus of the eclectic critical edition, in a sense, is proposed as the substance of the "postmodern" edition, for lack of a better term. In eighteenth-century studies, the utility of this expansive notion of textuality is evident in AMS Press's *Clarissa* Project (1990–), a compendium of the third edition of Richardson's novel (1751), the author's commentary on the novel, his own volume of material deleted from earlier editions, the "moral and instructive sentiments" that Richardson distilled from his fiction, and a liberal cross-section of the criticism that has contributed to the history of the work from Richardson's day to our own.[36] In this edition, as in McGannian theory, eclecticism gives way to inclusiveness.

The lead is a good one. A useful edition of Bolingbroke's *Remarks* would reprint in facsimile the original folios along with a sampling of the pamphlets and leaders written in response to the series. Of course, world and time will not allow such a venture. Frustratingly, then, the most useful source for the *Remarks* is likely to remain either the 1731 edition or one of the diplomatic editions of Bolingbroke's *Works*, as all these editions have the advantage of presenting the *Remarks* in their entirety. Furthermore, the 1754, 1841, and 1844 editions, by reprinting polemical pieces such as Bolingbroke's *Final Answer to the Remarks on the Craftsman's Vindication* (1731), at least remind their readers that Bolingbroke was a polemicist. But neither these editions nor Kramnick's acknowledges the controversy initiated by the *Remarks* or represents the other sources that, with Bolingbroke's, recorded the debate. Whether or not this sort of thing is, as McGann has averred, "the business of critical editing" is an open question. But it seems reasonable to conclude that our critical work will benefit from a "socialized" approach to polemical literature. Indeed, without such an approach our criticism will be likely to follow reprint editions in regarding Bolingbroke as separate from the print wars, dictating, rather than negotiating, the terms of the debate.

2
Bolingbroke's Analogic Historiography

"It is impossible," wrote John, Lord Hervey in 1734, "to judge of any human Institution, any more than of any human virtue, but by Comparison."[1] Hervey's plain speaking here only briefly conceals his anxiety about what he, like other pro-government polemicists, regarded as the attempt by writers hostile to George II and Walpole to control the recasting of history as analogy and thus its conversion into partisan political rhetoric. Many readers have noted the tendency in Pope's later poetry to suggest that modern English culture is degenerate because, to simplify just a bit, it isn't ancient Roman culture. This habit of thought is evident in the poetry of Dryden and others. It is anticipated more nearly in numerous ephemeral publications that attack Walpole by implying, to simplify not at all, that he is entirely unlike such and such a good minister or very much like such and such a bad one. When Hervey defines his target as those "modern Authors [who] . . . have often insisted on the Faults of the present Government, by extolling the Felicity of Times past" (4), he is acknowledging what everybody knew anyhow: that analogic argumentation had become the preferred language of the opposition.

Had Hervey written his comments before the publication of Bolingbroke's *Remarks on the History of England*, they might have seemed like a focused personal attack on Bolingbroke, the more so because Hervey had been harassing Bolingbroke since 1727.[2] But by 1734, Hervey could count on them being read as a condemnation of a strain of rhetoric practiced widely by a variety of opposition polemicists, some supportive of Bolingbroke, others not. The controversy initiated by the *Remarks* attests to Bolingbroke's success in authoring a more-or-less uniform rhetorical method for the opposition. Pro-government polemicists were willing to regard the prevalence of this method as prima facie evidence that the opposition had the ideological coherency that Bolingbroke wanted it to have.³ The controversy illustrates the confluence of Bolingbroke's myth of unity and the government's need to simplify its response to an increasingly vocal and diverse opposition. By examining the controversy surrounding the *Remarks*, we are able to appreciate the process by which Bolingbroke and the *Craftsman* came to occupy the center of the polemical debate, in appearance if not in fact.

As we have seen, Bolingbroke structured the *Remarks* as a series of appeals to consensus. The idea of an opposition organized around his own political philosophy would occupy Bolingbroke throughout the 1730s, most notably in the *Remarks* and in *A Dissertation upon Parties*, published in the *Craftsman* from October 1733 through December 1734. Representations of the opposition in the pro-government press of the period indicate that Walpolite writers were often more willing to endorse Bolingbroke's vision than many of Walpole's other opponents were. The pro-government literature of the early 1730s, unlike that of the late 1720s, is full of references to the *Craftsman*-centered opposition. Writing in his *London Journal* shortly after the conclusion of the *Remarks*, James Pitt ("Francis Osborne") complained that "We know of no Ills *at home*; and had it not been for *one infamous Journal, or weekly Libel* against the Court and Ministry, the People would not have a Word to say against the Government" (No. 625; 17 July 1731). The following year, a contributor to *Applebee's Original Weekly Journal* dubbed the 1730s a "Craftsmanick" age and claimed that "the Authors of the *Craftsman* have Vanity and Ostentation enough to imagine they can lead all the World by the Nose" (2 Sept. 1732). "All the World" did not in fact offer its collective nose to Nicholas Amhurst and company. But Hervey nonetheless came close to justifying the *Craftsman*'s "Ostentation" two years later when, writing about the journal's role in organizing resistance to Walpole's failed Excise Bill of 1733, he referred to "the *Craftsman*'s Sect" and to "that Speaking-Trumpet of the whole [opposition] Party the *Craftsman*."⁴ Like the *Craftsman* itself, apologists for the government had stopped trying to distinguish between Amhurst's journal and "the opposition."

Hervey's remark about "Comparison" is not the only indication that the pro-government press regarded analogic historiography as a trait of the opposition. Pitt answered Bolingbroke's twentieth letter of the *Remarks* (*Craftsman* 248; 10 Apr. 1731) by agreeing that James I "[built] up *his Prerogative* upon the Ruin and Destruction of the *People's Rights*" (*London Journal*

613; 24 Apr. 1731). But he argued that any analogy between James I and George II was specious, an attempt to build from old materials "the [new] *Opposition*, which Mr. OLDCASTLE so *unreasonably and whimsically* contends for now."[5] Three years later, a like-minded polemicist could again criticize the presumptuousness of Bolingbroke's enterprise, but not its incipiency. One "R. Freeman," in *The Merits of the Crafts-Men Consider'd: Or, a Display of the Injuries Offer'd by That Party, Not Only to the Ministry but to Their Majesties and the Constitution* (1734), claimed to have identified "what the *Chiefs* in the *Opposition* plead as the *Source* of their extraordinary Behavior":

> It is in few words this: That all *Kings*, having a propensity to *Tyranny*, and all *Ministries* being alike ready to promote the *Views* of their *Masters*, in order to promote their own *private Interests*; it is therefore a Happiness to a *free People*, that they have a Party always among them zealously inclined to oppose the *Court* in whatever Measures it takes; their whole Conduct resting on a *Scripture Rule* inverted, viz. *Do no Good, lest of it there come Evil.* (10)

By 1734 the historical and methodological bias codified in the *Remarks* was being cited as the defining characteristic of an opposition clustered around Bolingbroke and Bolingbrokean historiography. A weekly newspaper had become "That Party"; a trope, in effect, had been converted into an ideology.

Walpole's ministry harassed the *Craftsman* throughout the late 1720s and the early '30s, typically without a great deal of success. Although the *Craftsman*'s printer, Richard Francklin, was brought to trial for libel only in November 1729 and July 1731 and was found guilty only on the latter occasion, secretary of state Thomas Pelham-Holles, duke of Newcastle, authorized eight warrants for his arrest from January 1727 to January 1731.[6] One warrant was issued on 1 September 1730. The *Craftsman* (No. 218; 5 Sept. 1730) soon reported that Francklin had been arrested and examined by Newcastle on 3 September for printing numbers 215 and 217 (15, 29 Aug. 1730), the anti-Hanoverian fifth and sixth letters of Bolingbroke's *Remarks*. A notice in number 219 (12 Sept. 1730) informed readers that Francklin had been detained for one week, then released on bail. We may take the absence of information about the case in the Public Record Office as proof that Francklin did not stand trial on this occasion;[7] and textual evidence that I shall discuss suggests that the case was dropped toward the end of October. In any event, the author of the pro-government pamphlet *Liberty and the Craftsman: A Project for Improving the Country Journal* (17 Dec. 1730) claimed that Francklin was "bound over to attend the first and last Day of a Term for three Terms" (4), a simple form of probation and, as the pamphleteer notes, a sentence more likely to publicize the journal than punish its printer.[8] Details of the fall arrest and its aftermath are sketchy, but there is no doubt that the affair did nothing to strengthen the government's position in the print wars.[9]

The author of *Liberty and the Craftsman* had reason to complain about "the Method the Secretary's Office takes in combating Francklin" (4), which obviously was in need of reexamination. Understandably not content with the outcome of its autumn campaign, the government soon struck again, and with considerably more force than it had previously used. On 9 January 1731, the king's messengers arrested Francklin for printing the "Hague letter" in *Craftsman* 235 (2 Jan. 1731). Simon Varey notes that after the publication of Bolingbroke's feverish tenth letter of the *Remarks* (No. 226; 31 Oct. 1730), "Walpole was casting about for any reason at all to arrest [Francklin], or in some other way to stop the *Craftsman*."[10] Whatever its immediate cause, Francklin's second arrest was a response to the *Remarks* as surely as the first one was. Mindful of the unsuccessful prosecution of 1729, the government carefully limited the power of the jury, this time taking full advantage of the new Juries Act (1730), which, as Laurence Hanson notes, "enabled the judges to empanel 'special juries' with much larger property qualification in cases tried at the courts in Westminster."[11] Francklin's counsel succeeded in having the trial postponed on the basis of a legal technicality; but the government pushed on, arresting Francklin later in July for printing William Pulteney's *An Answer to One Part of a Late Infamous Libel* (1731), a reply to William Arnall's *Remarks on the Craftsman's Vindication of His Two Hon[our-a]ble Patrons, in His Paper of May 22, 1731* (1731).[12] The trial resumed in December 1731. On 12 February 1732, Francklin was sentenced to one year in jail, fined £100, and required to produce "security for his good behavior" amounting to £2,000.[13] Bolingbroke and Pulteney paid the fine and provided the "security," and Francklin continued to work for the journal from jail,[14] but the government had nonetheless notched an impressive victory.

On the face of it, then, Walpole, Newcastle, and attorney general Philip Yorke, first earl of Hardwicke, had plenty of leverage against the opposition press. The case of the journalist John Tutchin in 1704 had formalized a definition of seditious libel that allowed prosecution not only for writing against the monarch and his or her ministers, but for writing against measures approved by the government.[15] This conveniently elastic definition was tested and reaffirmed in Francklin's trial and sentencing of 1731 and 1732. So it is surprising to learn from Michael Harris that after Francklin's prosecution, "the application of consistent legal pressure was abandoned and it seems possible that a deliberate decision was taken to step up the distribution of ministerial papers as a viable alternative."[16] One might wonder why the government had adopted such a toothless strategy in the aftermath of its only significant victory against its most popular and persistent adversary.

Certainly the government had good reason to be wary of the repercussions of even a successful prosecution. The *Craftsman* was popular and, thus, powerful; and Walpole of course recognized this. He could not have been cheered by Abel Boyer's report that during Francklin's abortive trial of July 1731, Pulteney had been "loudly huzza'd" by "a vast Crowd of Spectators" as he exited Westminster Hall, an event that Boyer chose to regard as evidence of "the Fondness of the People of *England* for the Liberty of the Press."[17] Commenting on Francklin's eventual conviction, Varey observes that "the effect of [Francklin's] sentence was to make him a martyr and thereby raise the circulation of the *Craftsman*." Harris notes more generally that "the considerable boost to the notoriety, and hence the sales, of a paper that results from legal action was generally accepted."[18] But this hardly explains the oddity of the government calling an end to five or six years of systematic harassment only after the first hint of success. To round out the picture, we need to examine more carefully the manner in which the rhetoric of analogy and evasion practiced in the *Remarks* redefined the limits of political expression by allowing a more comprehensive means of attack on the government while reducing the likelihood of effective retaliation.

Bolingbroke signaled the commencement of the historiographical portion of the *Remarks* by introducing his fourth letter with the slotted headline, "Some general Remarks on the *English History*, from the *Conquest* to this Time" (No. 213; 1 Aug. 1730). Letter four surveys England under the Saxon and Norman kings innocuously enough; but the next entry (No. 215; 15 Aug. 1730) is considerably less cautious. One of the numbers for which Francklin would be arrested in September, the fifth letter initiated a comparison, continued two weeks later (No. 217; 29 Aug. 1730), of the reigns of the libertarian Edward III and his successor Richard II, "a violent, haughty, obstinate and weak prince" undone by "*favourite Ministers*" and "flatter[ers] . . . who, to fasten Him to *themselves*, made the *Nation* odious to Him, as They made Him odious to the *Nation*, by their Rapine, their Insolence, and by a weak Administration" (No. 217). Bolingbroke praises the earlier monarch for, among other things, "the great Care he took of extending and improving *Trade*" and therefore restoring to the citizenry monies that he had taken from it in taxes.

In the summer of 1730, it would have been impossible to regard the claim as innocent. The parliamentary opposition, newly bolstered by support from the mercantile community, had been attacking Walpole's handling of finances more vehemently than ever in 1729 and 1730. Sentiment was particularly strong against Walpole's request for increased allotments to the Civil List and his attempts to continue funding costly Hessian troops.[19] The *Craftsman* had been outspoken against both measures; Bolingbroke himself had contributed leaders to numbers 186 (24 Jan. 1730) and 199 (25 Apr. 1730) lambasting the government for bankrolling foreign mercenaries.

Craftsman 215, therefore, had the force of a well-established polemical battle behind it, if one previously constrained by the *Craftsman*'s reluctance to acknowledge George II's support for Walpole's policies. The antiministerial rhetoric was old hat by now; but the swipes at the monarchy were fresh and daring, presumably indicators of the opposition's frustration with its failure to make significant headway against Walpole.[20] By applying the *Craftsman*'s old habit of analogic argument to an account of the English monarchy, Bolingbroke could discuss issues of polity, like the Civil List and the Hessian troops affair, that advertised a cooperation between Walpole and George II unaccounted for in the *Craftsman*'s posture as the defender of the monarchy against subversive ministers.[21] "A *Prince* who lives a rent-charge on the Nation he governs," Bolingbroke wrote in *Craftsman* 215, ". . . ought to blush at every Grant he receives from a *People*, who have never received any Benefit from *Him*." The pitch rises higher still when Bolingbroke introduces a direct address into his closing sentence: "When you have increased the *Riches* and advanced the *Prosperity* of the Nation, you will have some Right to make *these demands* upon us; but till then we shall think that you have none." "You," "us," and "we" are not pronouns likely to promote the cool sense of distance upon which the *Remarks* are predicated. Still more to the point, Bolingbroke seemed to be saying that he was no longer content simply to spin out analogies against Walpole, but would now move against George II himself.

The shift in focus was not lost on the pro-government press. Pro-government writers began treating the *Remarks* as evidence that Bolingbroke had begun practicing the plainest and most easily actionable form of libel: writing against the monarch. Pitt pressed the point in the *London Journal* by claiming that the *Craftsman's "false Arts, Corruption of History* [and] *Insinuation of parallel Instances and opposite Characters"* were evidence of a plainly anti-Hanoverian program (No. 577; 22 Aug. 1730).[22] As apologists for the government would throughout the period, Pitt finds in Bolingbroke's method proof of his fundamental hypocrisy. The essay includes a section that parodies Bolingbroke's first letter of the *Remarks*:

> But had Mr. OLDCASTLE kept to his own Definition of a Spirit of Liberty, *That it exerts itself in Favour of good Princes, and is slow to act even against the worst,* he would have preserv'd himself from the Infamy of some of his late Papers. For, *if a Spirit of Liberty* is slow to act even against the *worst Princes*, what is that Spirit, *which is forward to act against the best?* What Name shall we find for *that Spirit, Faction* is too good for it, which shall misrepresent former and present Transactions; and abuse, by *parallel Stories*, all Persons and all Things, with a manife[s]t Intention to distress a Government, under which *Laws and Liberty* were never better preserv'd, nor more strongly secur'd?[23]

The purpose of the *Craftsman*'s analogies, Pitt argues, is to "strive to beget in the Minds of the People an *ill Opinion* of the King, his Councils and Actions, and to make his Government hated at Home and despised Abroad." If Pitt was justified in reading the *Remarks* in this way (and he was), then the *Craftsman* had burst into a dangerous legal territory that it had previously skirted, coyly but carefully.

Bolingbroke's rather sudden change of direction offered a new convenience to Walpole's polemicists. The author of the 1729 anti-Bolingbroke pamphlet *Observations on the Occasional Writer, the Craftsman, and Other Papers* had only been able to complain about the "great Error" of the *Craftsman's* analogic redactions of Walpole, and to ask "what Character is given to that Prince, who employs and maintains in his Service, a person so notoriously resembling *Sejanus, Wolsey, Leicester* and *Buckingham,* in their Crimes, but not in their Virtues?" (37–38). The 1729 pamphlet posits a flaw in the *Craftsman*'s method by remarking that the king to whom Bolingbroke claims fidelity appears, as a corollary from Bolingbroke's own anti-Walpole analogies, culpable or even obtuse. But the pamphlet tacitly acknowledges Bolingbroke's deftness in sidestepping the awkward question of the monarch's cordial relations with his minister. The author of a contemporaneous pamphlet can only insist that the *Craftsman* is an "Enemy . . . both to his King and Country, however . . . much a *Palavre* [sic] (as the *Portuguese* call it) he would seem to be otherwise."[24] Lacking evidence, the first pamphleteer relies on deduction; the second merely splutters. In neither case does the charge have any legal correlative.

One year later, however, Pitt could accuse Bolingbroke of libel more convincingly. By charging that Bolingbroke had raised the stakes in a campaign that ministerial writers had long accused him of waging, Pitt's leader in *London Journal* 577 makes a point of equal rhetorical and legal substance—or so it must have seemed in the early days of the controversy. One imagines a note of satisfaction behind Pitt's pronouncement that "things seem coming to a Crisis: 'Tis not *the Ministry now,* but the *King and Government* are attack'd. Let any Man of common Sense read the last CRAFTSMAN, and he will acknowledge, *That greater Infamy could not be designed to be thrown upon* both."

Part of Pitt's smugness here is the conventional posturing of the polemicist, but we may assume that the case looked awfully clear to him and his allies in the wake of Bolingbroke's fifth and sixth letters. However much discussion the legal sanctity of ministers occasioned in the political press, no one would have argued that attacks of the sort noted by Pitt were protected by law. Proving Bolingbroke's analogies libelous stood to give the government the legal leverage that it had been seeking at least since January 1727, the date of Newcastle's first warrant for Francklin's arrest.

As I have noted, Francklin was arrested on 3 September 1730, about two weeks after the publication of *London Journal* 577, and incarcerated until 10 September, at which time he was released on bail. The charges against the journal apparently did not have the force that the government had imagined they would. Because the press reported on cases in court but did not generally have access to the closeted deliberations of the ministry, it would be difficult to say precisely when the government decided not to pursue a case against Francklin. Certainly the decision antedated Francklin's next arrest in January 1731. Textual evidence favors the possibility that the charges were dropped more promptly still. Some additional consideration of the matter is worthwhile, because it is difficult to account for the progress of the controversy in the absence of reasonable speculation about the status of the case against Francklin. Around October 1730, the government apparently decided against a full-scale prosecution based on the methodology of Bolingbroke's series and so initiated a brief period of frustration among pro-government writers and confidence among the *Craftsman* and its apologists.

The *Craftsman's* first comments on the arrest demonstrate the bellicosity of Bolingbroke and the less-assured defiance of the *Craftsman's* editor, Amhurst. Amhurst's short preface to Bolingbroke's seventh letter (No. 219; 12 Sept. 1730), noted in the previous chapter, remarked on the "*uncommon Proceedings upon Mr. Francklin*" and promised that the *Craftsman* would continue to assert its "*Privilege . . . to give the Publick an Abstract of the English History.*" The notice concluded with a reiteration of the journal's basic defense, its appeal to disinterested authority: "*As for Mr. Oldcastle and my self, we shall always take particular Care not to assert any Thing, in the Course of these Remarks, but what we can justify by undoubted Authority from the best Historians.*" The *Craftsman* would continue doing what it had been doing because there was nothing wrong with doing it. That Francklin's arrest was hardly "uncommon," that the "privilege" of the press was dangerous grounds for assumption in the period, and that pro-government responses to the *Remarks* generally questioned Bolingbroke's application of history rather than his rehearsal of the details that constitute it—these are matters that Amhurst chooses to overlook here and would continue to overlook in his future defenses of the *Remarks*.

In the furious essay that follows Amhurst's remarks, Bolingbroke, combative where Amhurst had been defensive, takes the arrest as an opportunity to introduce a profusion of examples of "faction" from the fourteenth and fifteenth centuries. Bolingbroke takes aim at "the *wicked* and *hated Ministers*" of Richard II; the "*illegal* and *tyrannical Actions*" of his successor, Henry IV; the "horrid Scene of *Iniquity, Folly,* [and] *Madness*" and "the scandalous Management of *publick Affairs*" under Henry VI; and the factionalism and the antimonarchism of parliaments during the Wars of the Roses. He brings the essay to modernity by shifting his attack to "the *London Journalist*" (Pitt) and "his *Patron*" (Walpole), claiming that he fears neither the "*Arguments*" of one nor the "*Power*" of the other. Then he lurches back to the seventeenth century in order to pair analogically Walpolite writers and apologists for Charles I. Having zigged and zagged through two and a half centuries of bad monarchs and a century's worth of bad political writers, Bolingbroke concludes by declaring the *Craftsman* and its sympathizers "the truest Friends to his Majesty King George and the *Protestant Succession.*"

Bolingbroke challenges the ministry boldly enough in this letter, but he retreats to his previous habit of indirection in his treatment of the monarchy. And at this early date, he gives no indication that the *Craftsman* had beaten the recent charge of libel. His essay and Amhurst's introduction to it are quick responses to a threat that evidently seemed very real. Both "answer" passionately, and thus admit the gravity of, the government's accusations of antimonarchism.

Amhurst interrupted the *Remarks* for two weeks by inserting essays of his own (*Craftsman* 220, 221; 19, 26 Sept. 1730) between Bolingbroke's seventh and eighth letters. The delay of the series may indicate that Amhurst was reluctant to move ahead while the case against Francklin was pending, and the urgency of Amhurst's essays would be difficult to account for had the legal attack been called off. Amhurst, quoting from but not naming Pitt's leader in *London Journal* 580 (12 Sept. 1730), notes that the *Craftsman* had been warned

> that if we continue these Papers, the Government cannot subsist without Power and Terror; that this licentious Way of Writing ... naturally brings a Nation from Freedom to Slavery; and from a Government by Wisdom and Goodness to a Government by dreadful Power and lawless Authority. (No. 221)

Confronted with this monolithic presentation of reactionary government, Amhurst's task becomes again the familiar one that Bolingbroke seemed increasingly to disregard: to defend the *Craftsman's* method in such a way as to present the paper as the champion of a libertarianism that it shares with George II but that is threatened by the ministry and its apologists. At the conclusion of number 219, Bolingbroke had declared allegiance to Hanover in a manner that was arguably ironic, indisputably tendentious, and in any case tacked on to an argument that had found a good measure of unpleasantness in the history of the

English monarchy. But Amhurst, a workaday journalist who stood to lose more than Bolingbroke did by a successful prosecution of the *Craftsman*, takes as his theme the sincerity of the journal's support for the monarchy. He restricts his quarrel to those agents of the ministry who would interfere with "the *Liberty of the Press*" and so, to his way of thinking, would "Attempt to destroy his Majesty's Title, and to absolve the People from their Allegiance" (No. 221). Faced with threats of suppression that presumably would not have found their way into the progovernment press without the sanction of Walpole or his treasury solicitor, Nicholas Paxton, Amhurst appealed to the highest authority in the land by questioning, as the *Craftsman* always had, the right of the press to speak for the king.[25]

An earlier acknowledgment by Amhurst of the antiministerial intent of his journal's "parallels" highlights the significance of his leader in *Craftsman* 220. In 1727 Amhurst had freely admitted the convenience of using "*parallel Instances*" in arguments against scheming ministers—but only ministers. Further, he had averred that only "a *Lunatick*" would favor a more direct approach (*Craftsman* 31; 24 Mar. 1727). But Amhurst could not afford to be so forthcoming in response to the new accusations of antimonarchism. In *Craftsman* 220, he dodges, rather than addresses, the charges circulating against the *Remarks*:

> We were no sooner enter'd upon this Undertaking than the *pensionary Writers* of the Times began to exclaim against a factious, seditious, and at last a treasonable Design of drawing *Parallels*. Instead of applying our *Principles*, according to our profess'd Intention, to the Purposes of *Liberty*, They apply them to the Purposes of *Faction*; and endeavour to prove that our Design is to asperse the *present Reign* by an historical Representation of Those, which are past; whereas it is manifest that our only Design . . . is to shew that the present Enjoyment of our *Liberties* is owing to that *Spirit*, which hath exerted itself through all Ages in its Defense; that our *best* and *most glorious Princes* have given it the greatest Encouragement; and that *Those*, who have endeavour'd to suppress it, have always proved the most *unfortunate*. It appears likewise, from this Abstract of the *English History*, that most of our *unhappy Princes* owed their Misfortunes to *wicked Ministers* and *Favourites*.

Amhurst is attempting to reassert the old emphasis on ministers, rather than kings, that had been the *Craftsman's* professed modus operandi before the *Remarks*. When Amhurst observes that "most of our *unhappy Princes* owed their Misfortunes to *wicked*

Ministers and *Favorites,*" the regular reader of the *Craftsman* immediately realizes that George II is being shunted aside so that Walpole may be attacked more forcefully. But George II was not being shunted aside any longer, at least not by Bolingbroke. Amhurst, defensively, pretends that the *Remarks* are a continuation of the antiministerial program that had been exonerated legally in 1729, when Francklin had been cleared of the charge of writing libels against the ministry.

Bolingbroke did not help Amhurst sustain this pretense. His eighth letter (No. 222; 3 Oct. 1730), published just two weeks after Amhurst's defense of the *Craftsman's* method, finds him doing what looks very much like "drawing parallels" and, furthermore, doing so with the royal family in mind. Of Edward IV, Bolingbroke remarks that "his good and his bad Qualities work'd the different Effects of supporting, exasperating and increasing *Factions.*" Bolingbroke had been denouncing Walpole in virtually identical language for nearly four years. But now he stresses his new focus by invoking the earl of Warwick, initially Edward's supporter but ultimately his archrival and as such the perfect illustration of Bolingbroke's stock claim that the minister Walpole was an enemy to the monarch George II—Bolingbroke's thesis in the seventh letter of the series and, more generally, the shaky foundation on which his "Gentleman" built the *Remarks.* In the eighth letter, however, Bolingbroke was not content merely to remind his readers of the flexibility of his analogies. Additionally, he tempted fate by positing the complicity of Edward's queen Elizabeth Woodville in creating "a Reign of *Faction.*" Although there is little about the analogy to suggest that Bolingbroke intended any pointed commentary on Queen Caroline, he must have known that his detractors would find precisely this motivation behind the number, as of course they did. Given the fact that for three weeks Amhurst had been attempting to guide the debate away from precisely the sorts of charges that such a number was sure to inspire, one may well ask for what effect Bolingbroke was aiming.

Was Bolingbroke rashly provoking the government by resuming the *Remarks* with the sort of rhetoric that Amhurst claimed the journal did not practice, or did he know by then that the government had decided not to proceed against Francklin? Certainly Bolingbroke could be hotheaded, and the difference between his tone and Amhurst's in *Craftsman* 219 indicates that the editor and his most famous writer were capable of contradictory behavior on the same occasion. So impetuosity might account for the bluster of *Craftsman* 222. But it seems more likely that sometime in the first three weeks of October, the *Craftsman* knew or at least began to suspect that Francklin would not be prosecuted in any significant way. During September, Amhurst bided his time with the *Remarks*. In the four weeks between the arrest and *Craftsman* 222, only Bolingbroke's seventh letter represented the series (No. 219; 12 Sept. 1730). But in the fourteen weeks from 3 October 1730 until 9 January 1731 (No. 236), when Francklin was arrested again, Amhurst printed seven letters from the *Remarks*; in the final eighteen weeks of the series, he printed ten. And the material placed between entries in the *Remarks* in September and early in October, although politically barbed, is of a piece with the sort of material that the government had let pass without notice since the *Craftsman*'s early days. In addition to Amhurst's essays in numbers 220 and 221, the journal ran during this period a stock accounting of the *Craftsman*'s superiority to the pro-government press in matters of "*Truth*" and "*Argument*" (No. 218; 5 Sept. 1730), and an unimaginative and entirely safe "Analogy between *Politicks* and *Foxhunting*" (No. 223; 10 Oct. 1730). Neither essay was written by a significant contributor and neither mentions the *Remarks* or offers any topical clues to suggest that it was not filler pulled from an old file.[26] The next interruption of the series (No. 225; 24 Oct. 1730), however, would come in the form of a rebuttal by Bolingbroke himself of an attack on the *Remarks* in the pro-government *Daily Courant*. Sometime around 17 October, Amhurst reaffirmed his commitment to the *Remarks*. It seems reasonable to suppose that he did so because he had some assurance that he could proceed with relative safety.

Additional evidence, inconclusive in itself, supports the hypothesis. An editorial insertion in the "London News" section of *Craftsman* 224 (17 Oct. 1730) demonstrates that the characteristically stiff-lipped *Craftsman* was treating the arrest with a levity that poses a contrast to its earlier pronouncements on the matter; the new tone would have been incautious (and strange) had Francklin's case still been under consideration. In his windy defense of the *Remarks* in *Craftsman* 220, Amhurst had claimed that "This Argument [against 'parallels'] might be still press'd a great deal farther; and the whole *English History* might be prov'd a Libel upon the *present Government*, by the same Rule of Interpretation." Therefore, he continued, "every *Bookseller*, who publishes *Kennet*'s, *Echard*'s, or *Rapin*'s History, is as liable to a Prosecution as Mr. *Francklin*." In number 224, the acerb argument resurfaces as a poke at the government for its zeal in persecuting purveyors of what the *Craftsman* is content to consider disinterested historiography. Amhurst reports that the printer George Knapton had been arrested for publishing the *History of England* by the recently deceased Paul de Rapin-Thoyras, "in which it is said the Author hath drawn a *treasonable Parallel* between some *former Reigns* and a *certain Reign*, that should happen after his Death." The sense of threat has abated, and the *Craftsman* is enjoying a good laugh. By 24 October, the government seems to have decided that it would have a hard time assembling a case against the *Craftsman*'s "Abstract."

The pro-government press's irritation with what it saw as the *Craftsman*'s disingenuousness about its position on George II had been evident in the summer and early fall of 1730; but Hervey's *Observations on the Writings of the Craftsman* (Oct. 1730) was the first sustained attempt to call the *Craftsman*'s bluff. Although dating the pamphlet precisely is not possible, Hervey's interest in it on material from *Craftsman* 222 suggests that it was written, if not necessarily published, shortly after 3 October, the date of that number of the *Craftsman*. The emphases on legalism and Bolingbroke's method suggest that the pamphlet was written prior to the government's cessation of action against Francklin.[27] The pamphlet is also the first in a series of publications that demonstrate the government's inability to stand up to the *Craftsman* in the fall of 1730.

Hervey presents a jaundiced rhetorical history of the *Craftsman*. He argues that the journal, having exhausted substantive means of criticizing Walpole in the here and now, has turned, desperately, to more arcane rhetorical strategies: "When the Sources of their Invention grew dry, Libraries were ransack'd, the Annals of all Ages were turned over, and Extracts made, out of the worst Characters, that the Historians, or *Calebs*, of other Times ever transmitted to Posterity, to be applied to these" (11–12). But Hervey charges that the *Craftsman*'s analogic attack on Walpole had quickly shown itself ineffective. The *Craftsman* had therefore reformulated its approach once again, this time deciding "to temporize no longer, but openly to attack even that sacred Person, which hitherto they had only dared obliquely to touch, and collaterally to glance at" (17)—George II, of course. Sounding much like Pitt in *London Journal* 577, Hervey claims that

> The Transition was easy from Ministers to Princes and the same Methods that had served to defame the one, were now imployed to

depreciate the other. The whole Artillery of Pamphleteers, Balladmongers, and Libellers was drawn out; they recurr'd again to History for Parallels, they quoted Tyrants in Italicks, show'd by what Steps Revolutions might be form'd; and resolved, since they could not prevail on the King to change his Ministry, to try if they could not perswade the People to change their King. (17–18)

The common charge that the *Craftsman* was promoting the overthrow of the Hanoverian monarchy was silly, as Hervey himself presumably realized.[28] More important is that the reversion to old ad hominem charges indicates the paucity of rhetorical options available to Hervey. Although similar to it in tone, the pamphlet lacks the freshness and optimism of Pitt's earlier offering. By October, Hervey could do little more than insist that the *Craftsman* was doing what it claimed not to be doing—or perhaps what the government had been unable to prove that it was doing.

Pulteney's *Answer to a Late Pamphlet, Intituled, Observations on the Writings of the Craftsman* (Nov. 1730) could not, therefore, have been a simpler affair. Amid renewed assertions of devotion to George II and Caroline and a good deal of quibbling about grammar, Pulteney brushes aside Hervey's charge about antimonarchic "parallels": "I affirm that this Method of attacking an *Author* is mean and ungenerous," he sniffs, "It is not the language of the *Law*; which, in all Censures for Male-Administration, excludes the *present Possessor of the Throne*" (17). Pulteney declines to discuss the method of the *Remarks*, treating it as a matter now governed by legal precedent. His arch reminder of the illegality of writing against the monarch must have been particularly galling to the *Craftsman*'s detractors, who had of course been pushing this very argument, although to no satisfactory end. The controversy had reached a standstill, with the *Craftsman*'s writers in the enviable position of having garnered legal support for their rote denials of libelous intent. The author of *Liberty and the Craftsman* was left to regret that "Scandal and Abuse of the King and Ministry are too valuable to mercenary Scriblers and Printers, and too pleasing a Gratification of the Malice and Envy of discontented Gentlemen to vent their Passion[,] to be easily laid down" (4). The tone of dejection is understandable.

Hervey, too, was increasingly frustrated, or so we may infer from the two pamphlets that he published against the *Remarks* between 1 and 16 December. Different in their approaches, the pamphlets variously attest to the difficult position of pro-government writers between October 1730 and January 1731. The *Sequel of a Pamphlet Intitled Observations on the Writings of the Craftsman*, a further response to Bolingbroke's comments on Edward IV in *Craftsman* 222 rather than a follow-up to Hervey's own pamphlet, is a tour de force that, like Bolingbroke's first number of his short-lived *Occasional Writer* (1727) and like some of Swift's contemporaneous prose, illustrates the imaginative grasp of the best polemical literature of the period. Hervey still insists that Bolingbroke had intended offense to the royal family in *Craftsman* 222. But he now lays hold of the analogy that had animated that number and writes into it Pulteney and Bolingbroke as the dukes of Buckingham and Gloucester, presenting them as restive powermongers under Edward IV and as the orchestrators, upon Edward's death, of the murder of the youthful heir Edward V that had cleared the way for Gloucester's coronation as Richard III. Hervey cannot resist noting Buckingham's break with Richard and his eventual execution at the King's command. He closes the pamphlet with a resounding dismissal of the rhetorical method that he has borrowed from the *Craftsman* only in order "to shew those who deal in it, that if one did approve, or would give one's self the Liberty they take of Fighting in Disguise, and Stabbing in the Dark, how easy such Historical Masks and Daggers are to be found" (29).

Its cleverness notwithstanding, the *Sequel* is more effective as parody than polemic. And even its status as parody is compromised: the pamphlet is animated by its author's frustration over the inacessibility of his target, rather than by the giddy belief of the parodist that his response can expose previously unseen weaknesses that render the parodied work laughable. Henry Fielding's *Shamela* (1741) irritated Samuel Richardson, author of *Pamela* (1740–41), in part because Fielding posited moral improprieties in Richardson's novel that Richardson (and many of his readers) would never have imagined existed there but that immediately became part of the ongoing debate about the morality of that novel. But Hervey's *Sequel* fails as contributive parody because its argument was by late 1731 an old one and, more particularly, because the debate to which it attempted to contribute had been abandoned by the government. The *Remarks* were beyond the slings and arrows of even the best rhetoric; Hervey's finest rhetorical moment elicited no response from the *Craftsman*'s writers because they had no reason to respond to it.

That the government was unwilling to continue operating at a disadvantage soon became clear. Hervey's *Farther Observations on the Writings of the Craftsman* was published a week or so after the *Sequel*. Like the contemporaneous *Liberty and the Craftsman*, the pamphlet hints that the government might fashion less wordy weapons to combat the proliferation of what Hervey had in October, with a telling lack of precision, called "guarded Treasons."[29] In large part a reaction against Pulteney's legalistic analysis of the alleged limits of monarchic power in his *Answer* to Hervey's *Observations*, the *Farther Observations* are the most reactionary entry in the controversy and the strongest evidence that the government was rethinking its strategy against the *Craftsman*. Given that in the first half of 1730 Hervey had established himself as one of Walpole's most trusted servants both in and out of print, and given Walpole's involvement in the newspaper- and pamphlet-campaign against the opposition,[30] it is reasonable to assume that Walpole, and perhaps others in the ministry, shared Hervey's frustration over the government's ineffective persecution of Francklin.

Like Pitt, quoted by Amhurst in *Craftsman* 221, Hervey is concerned with the *Craftsman's* alleged manipulation of laws that are intrinsically benign but that have been rendered inadequate by the increasing rhetorical subtlety of the opposition. Hervey continues the old harangue against the "open and flagrant" attacks on George II and Caroline in Bolingbroke's eighth letter (6), and, unsurprisingly, asks whether the *Craftsman's* writers "can ... be so vain, as to imagine they can impose upon any one Man to believe, that all their Examples are not intended by them for Parallels?" (25). But Hervey is criticizing the laws that allow the *Craftsman* to publish against the monarchy as forcefully as he is criticizing the *Craftsman* itself. He quotes Pulteney's taunting pun that the alleged "guarded Treason" of the *Craftsman*—"guarded" in Hervey's original signification as demonstrating covertness—can only be "guarded" insofar as it is protected by a legal system that "hath not declared [it] to be Treason." Hervey accuses Pulteney of "an idle playing with ... Words" (11), but can only attempt to rebut him by acknowledging the validity of his argument even as he criticizes the conditions that allow it: "There is no Difficulty in understanding what is meant, or any Absurdity in affirming, that there is a Treason, which may very properly be term'd Guarded Treason, Treason guarded by Law, that is, Treason which the Law hath not declar'd to be Treason" (12–13). Beneath this sophistry lies an admission: Hervey has virtually accepted Pulteney's revision of his original use of "guarded" and now agrees with Pulteney, angrily, about the legality of the *Craftsman*'s method.

Hervey's real complaint concerns what he sees as an ineffective means of judging "treason." Commenting almost hysterically on Pulteney's vindication of the *Craftsman*'s commitment to the Revolution Settlement of 1689 and the system of constitutional monarchy that it ensured,[31] Hervey asserts that Pulteney and the *Craftsman* have come out against George II's very right to rule. He claims that

> though this manner of asserting that His Majesty has forfeited His Right [to the crown], shall do infinitely more Mischief, than if the same had been declared in so many words; yet such is the Happiness of our Law and Constitution, that though the Authors of this Guarded Treason shall be esteemed no better than the vilest and most detestable Traytors to their King and Country; yet these Men ought not to be adjudged Guilty of Treason in a Court of Justice. (12)

Hervey's irony in his final clause is of a particularly crabbed and bitter sort. The tone of the pro-government attack on the *Remarks* has changed notably since Pitt's leader in *London Journal* 577. Pitt had explicated the apparent illegality of the *Remarks;* Hervey's *Observations* largely restated the position. But the *Farther Observations* both admit that the *Remarks* are protected by law and strongly suggest that they ought not to be. Such a pamphlet, written by someone as knowledgeable as Hervey was of court affairs, might have given the *Craftsman* reason to suspect that it was being watched and warned.

The *Remarks* themselves imply that the *Craftsman* was aware of the government's restlessness. Bolingbroke's twelfth letter (*Craftsman* 232; 12 Dec. 1730) seems to have been written in response to Hervey's *Farther Observations*. Bolingbroke strikes a familiar pose in his introductory diatribe against the "*shameless crew*" of pro-government writers who have claimed "scandalous Licence" by "draw[ing] *odious Parallels*" and "imput[ing] these *Parallels* to us." He predicts that as the *Remarks* move closer to the present time, "they will become the Occasions of louder Complaints"; and he promises that such responses will only encourage the *Craftsman* "to pursue the honest Design, to which We have devoted ourselves with Constancy and Vigour."

The twelfth letter intensifies the discussion of the limits of law that had been introduced in numbers 230 and 231 (28 Nov., 5 Dec. 1730) and continued in Pulteney's *Answer* to Hervey's *Observation* and in Hervey's own *Farther Observations*.[32] After tossing off the conventional (and accurate) charge that the pro-government press was in the pay of Walpole, Bolingbroke offers an "address" directly to Walpole, "Him, who guides [the] pens" of the pro-government press.[33] He accuses Walpole of using the press to "threaten" the *Craftsman;* and he claims that the *Craftsman*'s own writers "have not offended the *Law*" and that "they are safe, as long as the *Laws* and *Liberties* of their Country are so." Bolingbroke closes his introduction with what looks like an acknowledgment of the government's readiness to discontinue its unproductive sallies into textual exegesis in favor of less imaginative and presumably more effective strategies of harassment: "When next you meditate Revenge on your *Adversaries*, remember this Truth. *The Laws must be destroy'd, before* They *can suffer, or* You *escape.*" That George II might not be guiltless is suggested by the essay's subsequent survey of parliaments corrupted by pressures from the monarchy—a reformulation of the *Craftsman*'s habitual claim that bad ministers make good monarchs bad, too. The *Craftsman* had evidently registered the threat expressed in the *Farther Observations* and *Liberty and the Craftsman* and was building its case against the legality of any move to suppress the *Remarks*. Bolingbroke's twelfth letter is the *Craftsman*'s last statement before Francklin's arrest in January. He could hardly have presented a more direct challenge.

Newcastle would not issue the warrant for Francklin's arrest until 9 January 1731, the day of the arrest.[34] But the courtier William Yonge's *Sedition and Defamation Display'd* (Jan. 1731), like Hervey's *Farther Observations*, indicates that the action had been discussed in court circles and that word of it was being leaked through polemicists connected to the upper echelons of government. A full week elapsed between the publication of the "Hague letter" and the arrest; *Sedition and Defamation Display'd* appeared during this week. The pamphlet and Hervey's introductory dedication "To the Patrons of the *Craftsman*" (that is, Bolingbroke and Pulteney) were the government's last statements before the arrest.[35]

In his dedication to Yonge's pamphlet, Hervey initiates the sequence of personal attacks on Bolingbroke and Pulteney that would culminate in the responses to Bolingbroke's vindication of himself and Pulteney in *Craftsman* 255 (22 May 1731). Hervey again steers clear of the discussions of Bolingbroke's method that had animated his *Observations* and the *Sequel* to them. Instead, he nicks Bolingbroke for his Jacobitism and his alleged ingratitude to the government that had allowed him to return from exile, and he hits hard at Pulteney for his opportunistic abandonment of his old cohorts among the Walpolite camp. The urgency of the *Observations*, the taut inventiveness of the *Sequel*, and the rage and frustration of the *Farther Observations* are gone. The energy that Hervey had invested in the *Observations* to proving the *Remarks* libelous is expended in a quasilegalistic recitation of evidence against the characters of Bolingbroke and Pulteney. Hervey now finds it less useful to analyze the rhetoric of his opponents and more so to focus on those moments in their pasts that might bolster a case against the *Craftsman* as the product of avowed enemies of the government.

Yonge does mention the *Craftsman*'s "odious *Parallels*" (6), and does make a point of finding them covert attacks on George and Caroline. In contrast to Hervey's *Observations on the Writings of the Craftsman*, however, the tone is dismissive, admonitory, or simply contemptuous, rather than alarmist. Sounding a note that would echo in writings against the *Craftsman* throughout the 1730s, Yonge begins his argument by presenting the freedom of the *Craftsman* and the Jacobitical *Fog's Weekly Journal* to act as "Retailers of Lies, Scandal, Sedition, and Treason" as evidence of the benevolence of a government not bound to protect such forms of expression (2–3). Yonge, that is, now assumes the *Craftsman* guilty of "treason," whereas Hervey had previously argued that it was. As Hervey had been, Yonge is concerned with the gray area between the letter and the spirit of the law. Again like Hervey, he tries to reconcile legal and propagandistic "definitions" of libel. But, as Hervey had not done, Yonge treats the *Craftsman*'s guilt as a matter of fact, if not yet one of record.

According to Yonge, the *Craftsman* lacks the "Shame to forbid them insulting and calumniating the best of Queens" and, more ominously, the "Prudence" to keep them from "vilifying their lawful Sovereign" (36). Yonge imagines the government and the populace acting in concert against the aberrant *Craftsman*, scoffing at a rhetorical method that had once seemed safe and powerful. No longer duped by the *Craftsman*'s pledges of loyalty to the Hanoverian succession, "Men begin to be astonish'd how they could thus long have been deceived with idle Pretences to *Patriotism*, and the *Love of Liberty*; when they see the Reigns of the worst of Tyrants, produced as *Parallels* to the best of Kings" (33). While Bolingbroke, in his twelfth letter, was building a populist case for the *Craftsman* by calling attention to what he took to be the letter of the law, Yonge, in *Sedition and Defamation*

Display'd, was currying popular favor by presenting the *Craftsman* as a transgressor against the spirit of the law.[36]

Whether or not that useful but amorphous group "the people" was in fact "astonished" by the *Craftsman*'s new direction would be impossible to determine, although the popularity of the series suggests that a good many of them either were not astonished at all or were unwilling to let their astonishment interfere with their weekly reading. But the implication of Yonge's argument is clear enough: the government would no longer bother to combat the *Remarks* rhetorically, but would move against the *Craftsman* as the conscience of the state, if not quite its laws, demanded that it should.

Francklin's arrest in January was a carefully orchestrated affair. On the sixteenth of the month, the *Craftsman* reported that

> on Saturday last, Mr. R. Francklin, the reputed Printer of this Paper, was taken into Custody by four of his Majesty's messengers, for printing and publishing the *Country Journal* or *Craftsman* of last Saturday and the Saturday before, who broke open several Locks and Doors, tore down his Books, and seized many of his Papers.
> (No. 237; 16 Jan. 1731)

The *London Journal* said nothing of the violence that the *Craftsman* alleged but did add that on the same day that Francklin was arrested, Elizabeth Nutt, Anne (or Ann) Dodd, and one Mrs. Pearce were arrested "for publishing the said Craftsman" (No. 598; 16 Jan. 1731). Later in the month, Felix Farley and John White, printers at Bristol and Newcastle respectively, were arrested for reprinting the "Hague letter."[37]

All this adds up to a stronger and more effective assault than the government had made in September 1730, or indeed at any time in the past. The period between the arrest and the trial was a particularly busy one for polemicists of either stripe. The opposition's response to the arrest illustrates the difficulty of continuing a literary controversy that, abruptly, had been declared not a literary controversy at all. The facile and effective denials of libelous intent give way to anger about the government's change in strategy. Meanwhile, pro-government polemicists battled the opposition willingly enough over issues like the "Hague letter," the Hessian troops, and Walpole's impending second Treaty of Vienna (1731). But they were no longer easily tempted into discussions of rhetorical method.[38]

The *Craftsman* responded to Francklin's arrest by charging Walpole with precisely the violation of law—or "liberty"—that it had in effect challenged him to attempt. In the first number published after 9 January, Amhurst asserted the *Craftsman*'s legal "Right" to discuss the "Hague letter" and blasted the "extraordinary Liberties" taken against the paper by "a *certain Gentleman*"—Walpole—and his "*Advocates*" (No. 237; 16 Jan. 1731). According to Bolingbroke in December, the government would have to violate the law in order to be able to prosecute the *Craftsman*; according to Amhurst one month later, the government had done just that.[39]

Pulteney's *Proper Reply to a Late Scurrilous Libel; Intitled, Sedition and Defamation Display'd* (21 Jan. 1731) demonstrates the ferocity with which the opposition press could respond when its claims of innocence were answered out of print by force and in print by character assassination and smug reminders of its dependence upon the indulgence of the government. As his rabid response to William Arnall's *Remarks on the Craftsman's Vindication of His Two Hon[oura]ble Patrons* (June 1731) would remind readers, Pulteney was quick to assign authors to anonymous pamphlets, although his instincts were hardly those of a bibliographer. His questionable assumption that Walpole himself had written the June pamphlet animated his astringent *Answer to One Part of a Late Infamous Libel* (19 June 1731), for which his name was struck from the list of George II's privy counsellors.[40] In January, his erroneous assumption that Hervey had written *Sedition and Defamation Display'd* inspired the *Proper Reply*, one of the ugliest personal attacks of a period not leery of verbal savagery.

In the *Proper Reply*, Pulteney gives short shrift to the *Craftsman* itself and to the rhetoric of *Sedition and Defamation Display'd*; his interest is in Hervey's effeminacy and bisexuality and thus, by extension, his unfitness for participation in public affairs. Hervey is, among much else, "a *delicate hermaphrodite*" (6), "a pretty, little, *Master-Miss*" (6), a "pert, little creature" (22), and "our *pretty, little Scribbler*" (26). The pamphlet builds not toward a rebuttal of the charges against the *Craftsman*, but rather toward the linkage of Hervey's sexual inclinations and Walpole's habits of governance. Pulteney's potshots culminate in an extended pun on the political "*Corruption*" of Walpole and the sexual "*Corruption*" of Hervey; Pulteney presents Walpole as the "*Agent*" and Hervey as the "*Pathick*" of a homosexual union that Hervey finds particularly delightful (27–28). Pulteney is accusing Hervey of more than subservience to Walpole or lack of qualification for public service: he is charging him with a widely prosecuted capital offense and publicizing something about a servant of the government that George II's court was evidently willing to ignore, but could hardly have wanted advertised throughout the bookstalls of London.[41]

Pulteney's pamphlet prompted a duel between its author and Hervey.[42] This conclusive rejection of verbal combat is oddly appropriate, given that in six months the controversy had first proclaimed, then exhausted, and finally all but discarded an interest in rhetorical method. Contrary to Bolingbroke's prediction in the twelfth letter of the *Remarks*, the series did not draw "louder Complaints" as it moved closer to the present (*Craftsman* 232; 12 Dec. 1730). Rather, Walpole's press was increasingly deaf to Bolingbroke's shrill rhetoric. Of the seventeen leaders that the *London Journal* printed against the *Craftsman* from 9 January 1731 (No. 597) to 29 May 1731 (No. 618), for instance, only six concern the *Remarks*. Except for the denunciation of Bolingbroke's use of analogy that Pitt published during the last week of Bolingbroke's series (*London Journal* 617; 22 May 1731), these leaders are content to mention Bolingbroke's method in passing, or merely to allege its shortcomings, rather than to argue against its legality. The *London Journal*'s emphasis during the period is on the *Craftsman*'s carping against the peace negotiations in Vienna and, after the signing of the treaty in March, against the Peace itself. Pitt still claims that the opposition's propaganda is or at least ought to be illegal. But he now frames the charge, as Walpole and Newcastle had done extratextually in January, around the publication of the "Hague letter." "Must [the government] tamely sit still," asks Pitt,

> ... and hear it said of them, printed, and sent over all *Europe, That they are going to make Treaties, or have made Treaties, which break in upon all their other Treaties, and render 'em perfidious Wretches, and Violators of their Faith*; and yet not lift up their Heads in their own Defence? No; the Authors of such *infamous Libels* ought to be punished, in Justice to the Community. (No. 605; 6 Mar. 1731)

The government itself was silent on the matter of rhetorical method; and its press had apparently decided—or been informed—that analogic historiography was one offense among many and one that no longer merited the attention that it had received in the second half of 1730. The *Craftsman* was more vulnerable elsewhere.

A few itinerant hack writers, not subject to the same controls (or rewards) that Walpole's journalists were, attempted to keep the controversy alive, but opportunistically and only half-heartedly. Their efforts were doomed because they did not have access to the fund of information necessary to sustain the controversy on any but a superficial level. In the four months after the arrest, a number of broadsides and pamphlets were published that commented on the controversy in one way or another. Some, mainly sensationalistic, concerned the duel; some, for the most part baldly encomiastic, concerned the character of Pulteney; at least one, Eustace Budgell's(?) characteristically weird *An Essay upon Something, or Something of an Essay* (23 Feb. 1731), is beyond categorization.[43] But all advertise the passing of the controversy from principals to seconds, and all punctuate the controversy's abandonment of once-pressing matters of rhetoric.

Budgell's pamphlet is a send-up of the ad hominem attacks on the *Craftsman*'s writers (here addressed collectively as the *Craftsman*'s editorial persona, Caleb D'Anvers) that had only recently served as alternatives to substantive argument among polemicists angered by the inability of the government to suppress the *Remarks*. The pamphlet's subtitle accurately expresses its logorrheic brand of parody: "a full and compleat Answer to all *that has been, or can be published,* by that Infamous, Knitty, Lousy, Shabby, Scabby, Paultry, Insignificant, Venomous, Billingsgate, Pickpocket Son-of-a-Whore Caleb D'Anvers Esq." Mindful of Pulteney's recent go-around against Hervey, Budgell makes D'Anvers "Sodomitical" and "a Catamite" (9). The pamphlet parodies the tenor and the terms of the controversy, but the extravagance with which it does so calls attention to Budgell's lack of interest in the controversy as anything but fodder. Budgell sends up the question of rhetorical method much as he sends up everything else: he incorporates a rote "pro-government" attack on the *Craftsman*'s analogic arguments into a designedly absurd defense of what he pretends to regard as Walpole's useful bribery of Parliament (11–12).

If Budgell was willing to subordinate the controversy to his own (incomprehensible) ends, a later pamphleteer was willing to pronounce it dead and buried. *A Full and True Account of the Sad and Deplorable Death of Caleb D'Anvers Esq* (5 May 1731), published two and a half weeks before the conclusion of the *Remarks*, claimed that D'Anvers (here, both Bolingbroke and Pulteney) had survived the duel with Hervey, only to be rendered fatally ill by news of Walpole's success in concluding the Treaty of Vienna. In a "*woful* Soliloquy" over the body of D'Anvers, the author asks, "Where are now thy harmless *unmeaning Parallels,* thy *innocent well-grounded Innuendo's?* . . . Are they not gone down with thee to the *Dust* from whence they came, are they not gone to the Land where all things are *forgotten?*" (19–20). On one level, the pamphlet is a simple revenge-fantasy, a common subgenre of polemical literature. More pertinently, its eulogy for a trope that Bolingbroke was still busily promoting in the *Remarks* suggests the difficulty that Bolingbroke faced when he attempted to continue the debate about government past and government present in a language that the government now chose to ignore.

The controversy flared up for the last time after the publication of Bolingbroke's final letter of the *Remarks* (No. 255; 22 May 1731). The essay was followed by a round of pamphlets largely given over to rehearsals of familiar observations on the characters and politics of Bolingbroke and Pulteney. Like their immediate predecessors, these pamphlets have little to say on the method of the *Remarks;* they look much like the pamphlets written against the *Craftsman* before the publication of the *Remarks.* By late September 1731, this final phase of the controversy had flickered out, and the *Remarks* had ceased to be a regular topic of discussion. Significantly, the sturdiest attack on the *Craftsman* published in 1732, *The Danverian History of the Affairs of Europe, for the Memorable Year 1731,* reviews every number of the *Craftsman* from 28 November 1730 (No. 230) to 11 December 1731 (No. 284), but mentions the *Remarks* just once, and then only to note that Bolingbroke had revealed himself as their author in *Craftsman* 255 (37). By restricting its comments to the *Craftsman's* handling of domestic and foreign news, *The Danverian History* presents a *Craftsman* that is one-dimensional and therefore gratifyingly easy to answer. As the government itself had done, ministerial writers endeavored to forget their unsuccessful and embarrassing attempts to pin down the rhetoric of the *Remarks.*

In his 1727 essay on "parallels," Amhurst had argued plausibly that the *Craftsman* had been forced into analogic argument by the possibility of legal action. The debate about the *Remarks* attests to the success of this originally defensive strategy. The great convenience of the rhetoric popularized by the *Remarks* is that it offered its sympathetic reader precisely the suggestive resonance that it withheld from its hostile reader. To grant that any rhetorician wants "to have it both ways," but usually cannot, is to grant that this was an effective if not a terribly sophisticated strain of rhetoric.

So resistant to attack was the *Craftsman's* analogic rhetoric, in fact, that apologists for it could afford to be perfunctory or even absurd. The author of *The Doctrine of Innuendo's Discuss'd* (Jan. 1731) is stirred to a runty sort of righteousness by the government's assault on the alleged antimonarchism of Bolingbroke's "plain and ingenuous" *Remarks* (6).[44] The pamphleteer attempts to defend the *Craftsman* against "the Advocates for the Validity of *Parallels* and *Innuendo's*, that is to say, the Advocates for the putting what Construction they please upon another Man's meaning" (12). He assails pro-government lawyers who claim, as he believes, that the *Craftsman's* defense does not allow a court "to understand a Paragraph in the same Sense wherein it is understood by all the People in *England*" (9). The response to this fancied charge is even more extraordinary than the pamphleteer's appraisal of the prosecution:

> Let me ask these angry Gentlemen one Question: Did they ever consult all the People in *England*, to know in what Sense they understood these Papers? . . . Nay, were they ever inform'd that that *upright* and *incorrupt* Gentleman, their Patron, was imagin'd by the Nation to be alluded to, whenever a *Sejanus*, a *Wolsey*, a *Menzikoff*, or a *Coscia* was mention'd by the *Craftsman*? (9)

Argument this shabby makes few converts. But the subtext is noteworthy: what is being discussed is the question whether or not a polemicist is obliged to acknowledge any but the most superficial meaning in his writing.

The controversy initiated by the *Remarks* finally validates the underlying assumption of the *Doctrine of Innuendo's Discuss'd*: that indirection and denial were the opposition polemicist's best tools. Two related conclusions were clear by the end of January 1731, and would be borne out by the developments of the next six months. First, the government was a formidable opponent when the opposition sought to illuminate state secrets, or to engage in what we now call investigative journalism. Secondly, the opposition had earned the right to practice with impunity a strain of rhetoric that may or may not have been libelous but that could not be proven to be so. Although the opposition press was virtually under siege in January 1731, the government around that time conceded it a lasting victory by giving it carte blanche to practice a form of rhetoric the legality of which had been debated for six months. It is no wonder, then, that the opposition appeared to be united by its rhetorical habits: superficially, it was. And it is no wonder that the pro-government press was henceforth typically content to regard the opposition as so many images of the *Craftsman*, practitioners of a sort of rhetoric that had reached the public through the same libelous medium as the "Hague letter" had. If the glory of sounding what Hervey had called the opposition's "Speaking-Trumpet" went to Bolingbroke, the convenience of blanket dismissals went to the government.

That polemicists in the 1730s took advantage of the government's "gift" is evident from the profusion of analogic publications that appeared until Walpole's Stage Licensing Act of 1737, a reaction to the analogic habits of a genre against which it was never terribly difficult to direct public sentiment. Pamphlets like Hervey's *Ancient and Modern Liberty Stated and Compar'd*, noted at the beginning of this chapter, demonstrate that pro-government writers after the *Remarks* could still take the trouble to argue against analogic rhetoric. Until 1737, however, they did so without legal support from Walpole, Newcastle, or Paxton. Commenting in the *Observations on the Writings of the Craftsman* on Bolingbroke's suggestively antigovernment criticism of the Yorkist Edward IV, Hervey declared that "the Peace and Happiness of *England* are too deeply rooted in the *present House of York*, for the Nation ever to be mad enough at the Instigations of the *Craftsman*, to risque the transplanting them into *his House of Lancaster*" (31). This was probably true enough, as far as it reflected on the generality of the English. But Hervey might more honestly have said that the government, wearied by tracking the *Craftsman* through the dim corridors of medieval England, was unwilling to continue what had become a fruitless pursuit. In his witty literalizing of the *Craftsman*'s rhetoric, Hervey ignores the fact that the house of York (for instance) offered safe cover for polemicists harried by legal threats and intent on developing an effective way of sniping at their powerful adversaries.

Part 2
The Illusion of Consensus

3
Squaring Off—or Not—over the Revolution of 1688

TOWARD the end of the controversy provoked by the *Remarks on the History of England*, Bolingbroke observed that his detractors had endeavored "to make all the disputes about national affairs, and our most important interests . . . pass for nothing more than cavils, which have been raised by the pique and resentment of one man, and by the iniquity and dangerous designs of another."[1] He refers first to William Pulteney and secondly to himself. Bolingbroke was right to suggest that the debate had shrunk to a narrow compass, with two men absorbing the brunt of the government's counterattack. And certainly he could be expected to bridle at the pro-government press's attempts to portray his motivation and Pulteney's as personal rather than populist.

But Bolingbroke had little justification for complaining about what amounted to the metonymical substitution of "Bolingbroke and Pulteney" for "the opposition." We have seen that in the *Remarks*, Bolingbroke lobbied for a homogeneous opposition organized around his own vision of England past and present; he would develop the argument in *A Dissertation upon Parties* (1733–34). And we have seen that the argument was attractive to pro-government polemicists as well as to Bolingbroke and his fellow writers for the *Craftsman*. As a result of this confluence of interests, a diverse polemical contest came increasingly to be represented as a simple tilt between "*Caleb* [D'Anvers] and Company, and their Adversaries," in the words of the 1731 pro-*Craftsman* pamphlet *The Doctrine of Innuendo's Discuss'd* (5). In appearance though not in fact, the print wars were polarized rather than polyvocal.

I intend first to analyze this perception and second to examine its inadequacy as an indicator of how political argument was conducted in the period—an endeavor that will concern me in various ways for the remainder of the study. J. A. W. Gunn's claim that "there is no denying the fact that Bolingbroke's Opposition chose the terms of the debate and placed Government writers in a defensive posture" does not identify a "fact" at all, but rather reiterates a misconception that crops up in countless incidental mentions of the print wars and even in the weightier analyses of Isaac Kramnick.[2] In order to arrive at a more catholic sense of polemics under Walpole, we need to consider ways in which the period itself encouraged the class of error that Gunn's remark exemplifies. The false sense of polarity, it seems to me, is a result of an ideological and rhetorical habit common to Bolingbrokean and Walpolite polemicists: the tendency to cast the contemporary debate as an argument about the so-called "Glorious Revolution" of 1688–89. Polemicists of either stripe claimed to champion the values of the Revolution Settlement, and both groups were equally willing to conduct the print wars as an inquiry into the contemporary status of "Revolution principles," to use a common term from the seventeenth and eighteenth centuries. The problem is that this model excluded a significant number of polemicists who were contemptuous of Bolingbroke, Walpole, and their mutual insistence on the Revolution Settlement as the blueprint for eighteenth-century government.

Shelley Burtt glances at the importance of the Revolution to polemics in the 1730s, and at the attraction for contemporary polemicists of its reordering of the constitution. In order to portray "Court Whigs as the agents of corruption and their Country opponents as the epitome of public virtue," she argues,

> Bolingbroke must give the familiar categories of republican thought—liberty, virtue and corruption—new content. Without reworking, they will not yield the uncompromising condemnation of Walpole that Bolingbroke wants. Thus Bolingbroke reduces the notion of political liberty to the maintenance of formal constitutional structures: an independent parliament and balanced constitution. To deviate from this ideal, either through error or innovation is to enslave—whatever the actual political experiences of English citizens.[3]

Burtt's "formal constitutional structures" are the bequests of the Revolution. Burtt does not say so, but they are the bases of Walpolite theories of government as surely as they are of Bolingbrokean theories of opposition. Nor does Burtt consider the determination with which the government and its apologists would resist the appropriation of ideas and institutions that they regarded as their own legacies from 1688. Bolingbrokeans and

Walpolites were fighting for the same turf. At least until Bolingbroke's departure from the *Craftsman* in 1735, both groups attempted to portray the argument over Walpole's governance as a squabble between two rival camps, each claiming ideological descent from the Revolution and each protesting its devotion to the memory of William III, James II's son-in-law and successor.

In a more focused analysis of the Revolution in eighteenth-century polemics, Kathleen Wilson acknowledges the importance of 1688 to both camps and argues that "the political discourse of opposition under Walpole challenged establishment Whig arguments that security of the *form* of government—of Britain's mixed and balanced constitution—ensured the preservation of liberty under it."[4] The argument reasonably assumes that 1688 is a moment of more-or-less equivalent significance to Bolingbroke and to Walpole's apologists, whose disagreement did not concern the value of the constitution but rather its application or maintenance. Wilson is again on firm ground when she notes the centrality to opposition polemics of Bolingbroke's interpretation of the Revolution.[5] Still more pertinent to my interests is Wilson's acknowledgement of the conflict between Bolingbroke's "bipartisan view of 1688" and the position advanced in *Fog's Weekly Journal* that "the Revolution had been the act of the people at large."[6] Appropriately for her purposes, Wilson limits her consideration of discord within the opposition to this single point; she does not consider opposition polemicists who declined to quibble about 1688 as *Fog's* did, as the *Craftsman* did, and as a host of pro-government papers did as well.

Bolingbrokeans and Walpolites both benefited from their emphases on the Revolution. Bolingbroke knew that the Revolution was typically regarded as the barrier between modern England and a noxious aggregate of libertinage, divine-right monarchy, and crypto-Catholicism. And he knew from experience that these were behaviors or ideologies with which his enemies were willing to associate him. By casting his lot with the vanquishers of Stuart "tyranny," Bolingbroke advertised his renunciation of Jacobitism and aligned himself with a recent and tremendously important event that most people regarded favorably or even reverentially. In this way he could advance the populist campaign that he had mounted in the *Remarks,* presenting his coherent (and mythic) "country" opposition as the custodian of values authorized by the Revolution and therefore fundamental to the political structure of modern England.[7] The pro-government press, understandably leery of fighting the print wars on multiple fronts, was willing to dispense with the difficulty of battling a various opposition. Walpole's writers tended increasingly to present the opposition as Bolingbroke's property and to cast Bolingbroke as an insincere apologist for a revolution the goals of which were antithetical to the Jacobitism by which he had been tainted. Whatever their differences, "*Caleb* and *Company*, and their Adversaries" came increasingly to use a common historical vocabulary, the prevalence of which suggests an easy means of circumscribing the political debate.

Easy but unsatisfactory. The twin notions of a dichotomous debate and a coherent opposition are undermined by the refusal of opposition polemicists to concur about what moments from the seventeenth century "mattered" most and about the manner in which the people and events of that century should be converted into modern polemics. A third stream of polemicists, Stuart-sympathizers but not Jacobites in any useful sense of the term, abhorred the Revolution and its modern apologists and thus were opposed with equal vehemence to Walpole and "Caleb." Because of their mythopoetic attachment to the reign of King Charles I (1625–49) and their fascination with the regicide that ended it, I call these polemicists "Carolinists." My representatives are two nonjuring divines: Matthias Earbery (1690–1740), fierce opponent of the Hanoverian monarchy—and, eventually, of Bolingbroke—and Richard Russel (ca. 1685–?), editor of the popular *Grub-street Journal* (1730–37) and general skeptic about the Bolingbrokean program. Earbery, Russel, and a handful of vaguely like-minded polemicists illustrate the diversity and the lack of coherency in an opposition that Bolingbrokeans liked to imagine as unified and that the pro-government press tended to portray as monolithic. In subsequent chapters I shall analyze more particularly the presence of Caroline England in anti-Walpole and anti-Bolingbroke polemics. Here I mean to establish the Carolinists' hostility to the Revolution and thus to stress the threat that they posed to the stability of the political debate.

A substantial body of literature advertises the tendency to organize the political debate around competing interpretations of the Revolution. John "Orator" Henley, *The Dunciad*'s "Zany" and editor of the anti-*Craftsman Hyp-Doctor* (1730–42) and *Free-Mason* (1733–34), provides an introductory example. In *Hyp-Doctor* 65 (7 Mar. 1732), Henley presents Walpole as "a Friend to . . . the true Liberties and Interests of *England*, on the footing of the Revolution, [which were] the main Views and Sentiments of K[ing] WILLIAM." He then attempts to discount the *Craftsman's* claim to the "glorious steady Principle" of Williamite ideology. Two years later, Henley would criticize the first installments of Bolingbroke's *A Dissertation upon Parties*. He decried "the Craftsman's total Deduction of Parties in his last Papers and others in order to [form] a *Coalition*." The *Craftsman's* intention, Henley opined, was obvious: "That *all* may *joyn* against the Protestant Succession and Interest" (*Free-Mason* 8; 7 Jan. 1734).[8]

Henley recasts Bolingbroke's pro-Revolution and ostensibly pro-Hanoverian *Dissertation* as evidence of an amalgamated, Bolingbroke-centered opposition's hostility toward the Revolution and the Hanoverian succession. In his dismissal of the opposition as anti-Protestant and guided by the *Craftsman*, Henley hints at the advantage to pro-government polemicists of accepting Bolingbroke's claim to speak for a unified opposition. Although Henley questions Bolingbroke's motives for seeking to abolish English "parties," he does not question the homogenizing element in Bolingbroke's rhetoric. Bolingbroke's "coalition," fictitious or not, is as convenient for Henley as it is for Bolingbroke. The trick is to present one's opponent as an enemy to the Protestant libertarianism institutionalized by the Bill of Rights (1689), the legislative manifestation of the Revolution Settlement. If Bolingbroke would try to lay claim to the Revolution, Henley and like-minded writers would try to snatch it back. The terms of the rebuttal are easy, repeatable, and largely indistinguishable from the terms of the attack. The scope of the argument is small and would have seemed more so still in the aftermath of Bolingbroke's discursive *Remarks on the History of England*.

Evidence of this circumscription abounds in the period. *The Doctrine of Innuendo's Discuss'd* follows up the charge noted above by applauding the *Craftsman* for defending "the Principles of the *Revolution*" (8), and by presenting the journal's critics as retrogressive or pre-Revolutionary tyrants who would demand "an implicit Faith in the Ministry, which is a Step that leads as directly to Slavery as an implicit Faith in the Traditions of the Church of *Rome* does to Popery" (9). The same week, in *Sedition and Defamation Display'd* (1731), Sir William Yonge enlisted the memory of William III against Bolingbroke, whom he called

> a *Patriot* who desires *another Revolution* . . . [and] who attempts to raise Discontent, Sedition, and Rebellion, at a Time when we are blessed with the full Enjoyment of our Civil and Religious Liberties,

under a Prince who owes his Title to that glorious Event, and gives us daily Cause to shew our Gratitude, not only to himself, but to the Memory of our late IMMORTAL DELIVERER. (41)

Such exchanges are shoddy stuff. But the posturing is significant because it suggests the single-mindedness of many polemicists. Yonge and the author of The Doctrine of Innuendo's Discuss'd have found common ground. The lengths to which some polemicists were willing to go to defend this territory is evident in the anonymous pamphleteer's absurd tu quoque: the claim that pro-government apologists—and not, as such as Yonge and John, Lord Hervey liked to allege, "Caleb" and his crew— were descended from the Romish stock of the Stuarts. The reversal is telling. Like the florid pro-William prose profuse in both Bolingbrokean and pro-government sources, it reminds us that Bolingbroke and his most powerful opponents used essentially interchangeable vocabularies when they discussed the Revolution. This was not the case when Bolingbroke and Hervey did battle over the relative merit of the House of Lancaster—that is, when they argued about the past rather than the present.

The Craftsman needed the Revolution more than ever, rhetorically speaking, after 1731. The controversy about the Remarks on the History of England had established the political debate as hopelessly unstable—a contest in which no points could be scored because no terms could be agreed upon, given Bolingbroke's avid and idiosyncratic appropriation of seven centuries of English history, and given the pro-government press's reluctance to filter the debate through the distant past. The failure of the government's legal campaign against the Remarks left the Craftsman's writers free to spin out their analogies, but to what end, practically? Caleb was probably preaching to the choir.

And it may be that the emergence of certain important issues— notably Walpole's doomed Excise Bill, the central concern of Parliament and the press in 1732 and 1733—prompted the Bolingbrokean opposition to adopt more focused rhetorical strategies as it confronted, briefly, the possibility of winning its old game against Walpole. The Craftsman could hardly have claimed that the Remarks had had any real impact on affairs of state. But in April 1733, Nicholas Amhurst was publicly pronouncing Walpole's withdrawal of the Excise Bill a validation of Bolingbrokean theories about "the Spirit of Liberty," "the original Power of the People," and "the silly Denominations of Whig and Tory" (Craftsman 355; 21 Apr. 1731).[9] Amhurst's interpretation is self-serving, but it illustrates the fact that the *Craftsman* had a means of applying its theories about history and "party" in 1733, as it had not when Bolingbroke was writing the *Remarks*. The times had changed. J. H. Plumb, uncontroversially, identifies the years 1733 and 1734 as the start of Walpole's "slope towards defeat and retirement."[10] For the opposition, the stakes were higher than they had been previously. A new sense of urgency seems to have inspired a willingness to conduct the debate in terms the importance of which—if not the application of which—was largely unquestioned.

There are good reasons why the Revolution offered this broad utility. In the early eighteenth century, both Whig and Tory theories of history made the Revolution a crucible from which had emerged competing versions of old history and new politics. In an argument that has passed into orthodoxy, Kramnick demonstrates that an about-face of pre- and post-Revolution Whig and Tory ideologies occurred in the early part of the eighteenth century. A result of this swap was that Bolingbroke and his fellow outsiders—"Tories," in eighteenth-century nomenclature, however much Bolingbroke disliked the term—came to identify themselves with the old Whig argument that posited an ancient constitution as the source of English "liberty" and English institutions. And the Walpolites were forced by the logic of their favored status under the Hanoverian monarchy to adopt the old Tory belief that "liberty" was the product of modern political institutions—particularly of the strong Commons authorized by the Bill of Rights.[11] So in 1729, the *Craftsman* could praise "the *antient Spirit* and *Principles* of that [Whig] Party, which our Fore-Fathers exerted in Defence of their Liberties against the encroachments of *arbitrary Princes*, and the Depredations of *rapacious Ministers*," while lamenting that "the *Whiggism*, at present in Fashion, is quite a different Thing, and not worth preserving" (*Craftsman* 166; 6 Sept. 1729).[12] Five years later, Hervey, commenting on the Bolingbrokean opposition's infatuation with ideal Whiggery, could dismiss "[such] chimerical Whig-principles as are imbibed from *Eutopian Speculation*," and could cry up "the only honest and good Whig-principles, those of preserving a limited Monarchy in the Shape and Fashion we now enjoy it."[13] The Revolution was the emblem of both Bolingbroke's attachment to earlier Whiggery and the pro-government theorists' "old Tory" emphasis on modernity.

To consider the matter from a related perspective, the Revolution was the one point at which Bolingbroke's cyclical theory of history intersected the linear theory advanced by Walpole's apologists. In Bolingbrokean historiography, the Revolution was the most recent occurrence of an ancient "spirit of liberty" that was slipping away under Walpole. In linear pro-government historiography, 1688 was the source of a novel "liberty": England had shaken off the age-old yoke of tyranny at the Revolution, the "gloriousness" of which had been formalized by the Bill of Rights in 1689, safeguarded by the Act of Settlement in 1701, reified by the succession of George I in 1714, and defended by the suppression of the Jacobite rebellion in 1715. Both interpretations posit the Revolution as the definitional moment of modern government, and both of course value the Revolution positively.

By claiming the Revolution as an inheritance rather than promoting it as an invention, Bolingbroke and the *Craftsman* squared off against Walpole's apologists, for whom 1688 divided a fuzzy and uncomfortable past from the practically miraculous present praised (or imagined) in tedious encomia like Colley Cibber's annual birthday odes to George II. When Bolingbroke says that "by the coming in of King *William* our *Religion* and *Liberties* were preserved from the Designs and Projects then on Foot to destroy *both*" (*Craftsman* 375; 8 Sept. 1733), his choice of verb is contentious: William III "preserves" an ancient "liberty" that Bolingbroke knew full well his adversaries needed to regard as newly minted.[14]

Hervey's *Ancient and Modern Liberty Stated and Compar'd* (1734) demonstrates that the pro-government position could be equally combative. Hervey attacks "Anti-ministerial Writers"—specifically Bolingbroke and Pulteney—who "have as often prostituted the *Name* of Liberty, as they have abused the *Enjoyment* of it" (2). He brushes aside the notoriously oblique debate about the legality of William's ascension, and he dismisses everything that antedated the Revolution. "From King *James* the Second's Banishment, Abdication, Deposition, or whatever People please to call it," Hervey asserts, "I date the Birth of real Liberty in this Kingdom, or at least the Establishment, if not the Commencement, of every valuable Privilege we now enjoy" (40). An overly legalistic analysis of the succession would have been of no service to a pro-Hanoverian writer; and Hervey's dismissal of the terms of James II's departure from the throne—an issue that had vexed William III's Convention Parliament in 1689 and that troubled Jacobites and nonjurors throughout the first half of the eighteenth century—is consistent with the pro-government emphasis on the here and now.¹⁵ *Avant nous le déluge.* To Hervey, William's reign inaugurates, rather than revives, libertarian government.

Bolingbroke and the pro-government press had found a historical moment on which each could take a stand. This had not been the case in 1731, when the government had finally opted to arrest Francklin rather than to prolong its futile attempt to "answer" Bolingbroke's volley of recondite historical examples.

Bolingbroke had sought to provoke partisan discussion of the Revolution as far back as his first *Occasional Writer* (1727), in which, as Simon Varey notes, he had argued for "preserv[ing] the rights won in 1688: liberty of conscience, liberty of trade, and political rights consequent on the ownership of property."¹⁶ Bolingbroke has little to say about William during the next few years. But in the vindicatory essay with which he concluded the *Remarks on the History of England* (*Craftsman* 255; 22 May 1731), he engages in one of the favorite rhetorical tricks of the period: the presentation of oneself as the defender of the Revolution against pretenders to its legacy. Bolingbroke portrays his and Pulteney's detractors as enemies to "The *Revolution* and the *Acts of Settlement*," and charges them with "promot[ing] some Interest, which is repugnant to the Ends, for which the People of this Nation established the *Protestant Succession.*" As is characteristically the case in Bolingbroke's polemical writing, the charge here is that Walpole has usurped power from George II and subverted the Revolution Settlement's mandate for a balance of parliamentary and monarchic power. Walpole becomes a bastard offspring of the antilibertarian monarchs exposed in the *Remarks*.

William and the Revolution turn up more frequently in Bolingbroke's writing during the following years. In *Craftsman* 375 (8 Sept. 1733), for instance, William is the "*glorious Deliverer of our Country*" and the guarantor of "*free Parliaments*, and consequently [of] our *Constitution* and *Liberties.*" In his *Letters on the Study and Use of History* (1752), Bolingbroke claimed that "King James's mal-administration rendered a revolution necessary and practicable." He described his treatise as an attempt "to develope all the wise, honest, and salutary precepts, with which [the Revolution] is pregnant, both to king and subject."¹⁷

To Bolingbroke, these "precepts" were being violated by Walpole and ignored by the Hanoverians. The most sustained recitation of the charge occurs in *A Dissertation upon Parties* and its dedication to Walpole, reprinted separately in 1735, for the first of many times, as *The Famous Dedication to the Pamphlet, Entitled, A Dissertation upon Parties*. Here Bolingbroke presses his point without depending on the coy analogies of the *Remarks on the History of England*. On the title page of the Dedication, Bolingbroke identifies his dedicatee—his target, that is—as "the Rt. Hon. Sir ROBERT WALPOLE." He is bolder still when he tells Walpole that "the style of my dedication will be different from that which is commonly employed to persons in your station."[18] By 1733, Bolingbroke apparently considered the agile satire of the *Occasional Writer* and the studied evasiveness of the *Remarks* inadequate vehicles for his attempt to overhaul modern politics. Indirection was no longer the order of the day. Bolingbroke would now address Walpole directly and would condemn him as the enemy of the Revolution.

In the Dedication and the *Dissertation*, Bolingbroke presents his homogeneous "country" opposition as the force that would restore to English government the libertarian principles codified in the Bill of Rights. In the Dedication, he outlines his fantastic vision of an England that has transcended the need for party distinctions. The appeal to unity, he claims, is authorized by the Revolution:

> [The essays] are designed ... to expose the artifice, and to point out the series of misfortunes, by which we were divided formerly into parties, whose contests brought even the fundamental principles of our constitution into question, and whose excesses brought liberty to the very brink of ruin.
>
> They are designed to give true ideas of this constitution, and to revive in the minds of men the true spirit of it.
>
> They are designed to assert and vindicate the justice and honour of the revolution; of the principles established, of the means employed, and of the ends obtained by it.
>
> They are designed to explode our former distinctions, and to unite men of all denominations in support of these principles, in the defence of these means, and in the pursuit of these ends.[19]

For Bolingbroke, adherence to Revolution principles—by the 1730s, a somewhat vague melding of personal and commercial liberties—is the litmus test of political cooperation.[20] The logic is disarmingly simple: Revolution principles are clear and incontrovertible statements against "parties" (or for "liberty"); a true believer in the Hanoverian monarchy is perforce a believer in these principles; therefore, anyone professing support for the Hanoverian monarchy must endorse a political model founded on the absence of factious parties. So Walpole, by dint of his hostility to Bolingbroke's opposition, becomes the enemy of the Revolution and, even, of the Hanoverians. The only thing wrong with the syllogism is that its major premise assumes consensus about the meaning of "liberty"—an undefinable term that political writers of all sorts quarreled about endlessly in the period. Undaunted by the speciousness of his logic, Bolingbroke pretends astonishment that his program could have left anyone unconverted:

> Who could have expected that attempts to revive the doctrines of old whiggism, and the principles and spirit of the revolution . . . would give any umbrage, or cause any alarm, among men, who still affect to call themselves whigs, and pretend zeal for a government, that is founded on the revolution, and could not have been established without it?[21]

The question how to account for those who fail to appreciate the salutary effects of Bolingbrokean hegemony does not concern Bolingbroke. First proclaiming himself heir apparent to the Revolution, Bolingbroke subsequently reduces to a position of insignificance anyone not willing to endorse his political philosophy. In the first installment of the *Dissertation*, for instance, Bolingbroke reiterates both his claim to the title "whig" and his contention that the Walpolites' similar claim is spurious. He then dumps Walpole and his apologists into the same hold in which he stows his (and their) Jacobite opponents. Having dismissed the possibility of an opposition characterized by diversity, he finds one defined by consensus:

> The bulk of both parties are really united; united on principles of liberty, in opposition to an obscure remnant of one party [i.e., the Jacobite faction], who disown the principles, and a mercenary detachment from the other [i.e., Walpole's administration], who betray them.[22]

This purposively reductive vision allows Bolingbroke to bolster his proprietary claim to the Revolution and thus, given the terms of his argument, to promote his own headship of the opposition.

Walpole's writers were as eager as Bolingbroke was to square off around the Revolution: William III was "King *William* of Glorious Memory" to the author of the generally pro-government *Whitehall Evening-Post* (No. 2283; 16 Dec. 1732) as surely as he was to Bolingbroke.[23] H. T. Dickinson observes that "in order to combat Bolingbroke's campaign Walpole believed that it was essential to challenge his interpretation of the Revolution since this threatened to establish the Tories as more loyal to the Revolution than the Whigs."[24] In polemical literature, this "challenge" manifests itself in part as a fondness for totalizing representations of the opposition.

James Pitt ("Francis Osborne") exemplifies the pro-government press's tendency to defend its territory by dismissing its opponents as enemies of the Revolution. During the agitation surrounding the attempt to repeal the Test and Corporation Acts in 1733, Pitt tried to appease restive Protestant dissenters by arguing for "a FIRM UNION among all the *real* and *original* Friends to the *Revolution* and *Hanoverian Succession*" (*London Journal* 741; 8 Sept. 1733). Mindful of the *Craftsman*'s attempt to woo the dissenting interest, Pitt frames his offer of ideological camaraderie as an attempt to discredit the *Craftsman*. He dismisses Amhurst's paper along with *Fog's Weekly Journal* as a "*jacobite* Journal ... wrote by *artful* Men, full of *deep* Resentment and *Malice*." The *Craftsman* becomes the product of protean "*Jacobites*" who "appear under all Shapes and Forms, of Whigs, Free-Thinkers, and Republicans." By making the *Craftsman* the enemy of true Whiggery, the established church, and constitutional monarchy, Pitt presents that journal as a standing attempt to refute the Revolution Settlement, the libertarian spirit of which might cautiously be shared among parties who resist the amalgamated threat that he finds in Bolingbroke's opposition. Pitt's "firm union" is a defensive posture, a bulwark against a monolithic opposition intent on destroying the benefits of the Revolution. One senses that Pitt is only incidentally concerned with dissenters, who were left to plead for "liberty" of a distinctly nonabstract sort throughout the period.[25]

Pitt was not alone in attempting to discount Bolingbroke's enthusiasm for the Revolution. In one of his many harangues on the matter, William Arnall ("Francis Walsingham") presented Bolingbroke's *Famous Dedication* as evidence that the Pretender's one-time secretary of state would "CONDEMN the *Principles of the Revolution*, when they were essentially necessary to *introduce* the *House of Hanover*, and ... ASSERT the *Principles of the Revolution*, when *Resistance* and *Charge* may *remove* the *House of Hanover*" (*Free Briton* 278; 6 Mar. 1735). Writing a year earlier, Hervey had been more succinct: "What can be more absurd than to suppose, that either a Revolution Government could be supported by Men of Anti-revolution Principles, or that any Regal Authority at all could be supported by Men of Republican Principles?"[26] And the notion of an opposition organized around Bolingbroke and united by its misapprehension of the Revolution Settlement is central to a 1735 pamphlet entitled, breathily, *A Coalition of Patriots Delineated. Or, a Just Display of the Union of Jacobites, Malecontents, Republicans, and False Friends, with an Attainted Old Traitor, to Revile the Ministry; Impose upon the People; Set Aside the Succession; and Bring in the Pretender.* The author finds Bolingbroke's "*coagulated Crew*" advocates "for *no King at all*, but for setting up an IDOL, they don't know well what, in the *room* of a *King*; they are for that *many-Headed Monster* a COMMONWEALTH, which has ever appear'd so *inconsistent* with the *Humour* of the *British Nation*" (6). Bolingbroke becomes "the *Chief* of the *Clan*, the HEAD of the FACTION" (26). As the alleged point man for the Pretender, he is, again, the antithesis of the values that animated the Revolution Settlement. Predictably, political threat is located in the dark days before 1688.

But were the print wars really contests between "clans" of "Calebs" and "Robins"—code, like "Great Man," for Walpole—peddling different versions of the Revolution? Kramnick thinks so. Stating his disagreement with disciples of Sir Lewis Namier who dismiss "Bolingbroke's opposition" as "an alliance of groups in a similar strategic position, outside the government," Kramnick argues that

> the opposition was . . . based upon political ideas and principles and not merely the common interest of the outsider. . . . The opposition was held together by a particular set of ideas. It had an image of an ideal political order and of the threat to this order which it felt had arisen in England since the Glorious Revolution. The Walpole government and the Bolingbroke opposition represent, then, two different sets of ideas about society, government, and economics.[27]

For Kramnick, a certain attitude toward the Revolution and its aftermath gives the opposition its coherency and distinguishes it ideologically from Walpole and, presumably, from the Hanoverians. If there were "oppositions" other than Bolingbroke's, Kramnick does not consider them. Indeed, in his monograph on Bolingbroke and his "circle," Kramnick qualifies his homogenizing comments about "the opposition" only to the extent of noting that "an extraparliamentary opposition with Bolingbroke at its center [was] the focus of the opposition to [Walpole's] rule."[28]

Kramnick's response to Namierite historiography is accurate insofar as it represents the Revolution as a normative point of reference for both Bolingbrokeans and Walpolites. But the implication that the exchange between these groups comprised the political debate ignores the fact that opposition polemicists like Russel and Earbery cared little for William III and the Revolution, and generally declined to distinguish between apologists for the Revolution like Bolingbroke and Walpole.[29] The presence of such polemicists casts doubt upon Kramnick's model (and Gunn's) and upon Dickinson's broader observation that "throughout the eighteenth century no major debate involving any discussion of fundamental political principles took place without the events of 1688–89 being used as a source of inspiration or guidance."[30]

One might be tempted to call the likes of Russel and Earbery Jacobites, insofar as the term signifies, blandly, a fondness for the Stuart monarchy. But one might reasonably expect the term to mean something more than this, to denote a settled preference for the current Stuarts over the current Hanoverians, or an interest in returning the one line to the throne and removing the other from it. The term comes up short when we attempt to tack it onto "Carolinist" polemicists who, in the 1730s at least, did not trouble themselves with the dubious proposition of bringing the pretender "James III" to the throne of England and so violating the spirit of the Revolution Settlement and the letter of the Act of Settlement.

As the endless and almost random bandying-about of the term in the 1730s suggests, Jacobitism had become an imprecise category, perhaps not surprisingly, given that the early '30s fell right between the uprisings of 1715 and 1745, the only coherent manifestations of collective Jacobitism in the eighteenth century. James Edward Stuart was never an easy person to support; and after the military losses at Preston and Sheriffmuir in 1715, his status was irretrievably low. Unlike the earlier Stuarts, he was a professed and unregenerate Catholic, which posed a problem for the nonjuring Anglicans like Russel and Earbery who accounted for the bulk of the Carolinist opposition. Moreover, James never developed a productive relationship with the opposition press. *Fog's Weekly Journal*, the only paper loosely connected with James, declines to mention him and indeed offers up only sparing, if complimentary, remarks about his family. Of course the desire to avoid prosecution figures here, but the fact remains that the bungling and bullheaded Pretender did little to inspire propagandists.³¹ James is virtually absent from the annals of the opposition press in the busy years 1727–35.

Time was not James's ally. Nicholas Rogers argues that

> in the summer of 1715 some of the ultras may well have contemplated insurrection. But outside of the inner circle they were already bickering among themselves and, unnerved by the Whigs' iron will and the dilatory response at St. Germain [the temporary court of the Pretender], retired to their cups and kennels.³²

The likes of Fielding's Squire Western were already in evidence some thirty-four years before the publication of *Tom Jones*. The glory days of 1715 quickly faded to a memory that would lie dormant until the final flowering of Jacobitism in the 1740s under James's "bonnie" and charismatic son Charles.

Even the succession was not a heated or a particularly relevant topic in the 1730s. When on the occasion of George I's coronation in 1714 an anonymous pamphleteer had written that "I can find no more *Glory* in 1714, than in 1701, or in 1688, the Year of that Great Revolution, upon the Bottom of which the Succession of 1714 is entirely grounded," these were—and were meant to be—fighting words.³³ But fifteen or twenty years later, with the Hanoverian monarchy settling into a comfortable middle age, such utterances had become the stuff of habit, still heard here and there and still met with derision and even with a certain studied alarm, but on balance more of an invitation to rote rebuttal than a source of genuine anxiety to the government's apologists. Although Jacobitism survived in City government and in pockets of Parliament, the "movement" had little coherency or popular appeal. Bruce Lenman is being safe enough when he observes that "there is little doubt that at the high noon of his greatness Sir Robert Walpole presided over a political system which left very little opportunity for the mounting of a serious Jacobite rebellion."³⁴

It is not odd that writers like Earbery and Russel, opportunistically scorned by some of their contemporaries as "Jacobites," do not gain much definition when we who have no reason to scorn them nonetheless regard them in this same light. Carolinist polemicists passed over the Revolution in favor of the England of Charles I, roseate reconstructions of which they juxtaposed single-mindedly against the new age ushered in by the Revolution and fought over by its modern apologists. Earbery, whom I shall consider in more detail momentarily, always considered the

Revolution "a Rape upon common Sense," as he framed the point in 1717.³⁵ And the *Grub-street Journal* characteristically refused to couch its criticism of Walpole in the terms advanced by Bolingbroke and the *Craftsman;* the Bolingbrokean cycle of repression, struggle, and liberation contradicts Russel's dour cynicism. In an article abusing the *Craftsman* and the pro-government *London Journal,* the *Grub-street Journal* finds in the post-Revolution about-face of Whig and Tory not the means of separating true from false claimants to Revolution principles, but rather, evidence that "when the two Parties had changed their ground . . . wit and folly were blended together by each Party." In such a hybrid system, "every person of either [party] must be partly a Wit, and partly a Fool" (No. 76; 17 June 1731). While Bolingbroke was acknowledging the role of resistance to the monarchy in the events of 1688 and thereby attempting to distance himself from his old Jacobite cohorts,³⁶ the *Grub-street Journal* was caustically observing that the rhetoric of politicians "on both sides of the question" had brought the people "to that maturity, as to be able to discern exactly, when they are to obey, and when to resist their governors, which is the very highest pitch of all political knowledge" (No. 166; 1 Mar. 1733). The distance between the two "opposition" papers is immense.

The *Grub-street Journal's* skepticism about both the Revolution and the *Craftsman's* appropriation of Williamite "liberty" came to the fore late in the fall of 1731, in response to the Jacobitical London Common Council's decision not to hear a petition for the erection of an equestrian statue of William III in Cheapside. The pro-government press was furious and, like the *Craftsman,* interpreted the incident as a slur against the memory of William. Arnall wrote two long leaders against the City governors in which he supposed that they would be more inclined to authorize a statue of the Pretender (*Free Briton* 101; 4 Nov. 1731); he condemned the Council as "*Advocates of Slavery*" and "Advocates of *absolute* Power [who] have ever objected against Liberty" (*Free Briton* 103; 18 Nov. 1731).³⁷ Presumably reluctant to alienate its City readers, the *Craftsman* shied away from the controversy during its height. But after the fact, Bolingbroke suggested that the inscription on such a statue should have praised William for his "*Hazardous and glorious Enterprize* [which] *preserved the British Nation from the imminent Danger of Popery and Slavery*" and for having "*confirmed and strengthened* [England's] *Liberties by such excellent Laws as the* TRIENNIAL ACT" (*Craftsman* 375; 8 Sept. 1733). Predictably, Bolingbroke faults the present ministry for failing to follow the path paved by William. He uses the Council's decision as an opportunity to bring up the controversial question of parliamentary elections. His attitude toward William, the statue, and the Council, however, is indistinguishable from Arnall's.[38]

The *Grub-street Journal* would have none of this, and established its anti-Williamite position in a series of articles on the proposed statue.[39] Having expressed considerable irritation about the pro-government press's Williamite rhetoric and its lack of regard for the integrity of the Common Council, the paper concluded its series on 16 December 1731 (No. 102) by lampooning a recent *Daily Courant* (No. 9390; 13 Dec. 1731) that had criticized the *Grub-street Journal's* hostility toward the proposed statue by allegorically praising William for saving England from James II. The *Daily Courant* had presented William as "a Dutchman" who had saved England ("an *East India* Man," or "an *East India* Ship," in the *Grub-street Journal's* rendering) from the piratical Catholic James II ("the Captain . . . a *Moor* in principle"). In its response, the *Grub-street Journal* reopened the old dispute about the manner of James's departure from the throne: "Did the *Captain steal into his long-boat* [as the *Courant* had claimed], or was he *obliged* by the *Dutchman* to get into it and sheer off?" Continuing this rather dangerous strain of argument, the anonymous author questions the *Courant*'s claim that "the ungrateful majority of the Crew" had been seduced by James's Catholicism ("his base principles"). He notes, reasonably enough, that "if the *Majority* was thus *tainted*, it was very strange that the first *Captain*, who *did all he could to betray them* to the Moors, did not succeed in his treachery."[40]

The *Grub-street Journal's* version of the pirate allegory stops short of vindicating James II. The essayist settles for a send-up of William's pecuniary interest in the throne and a swipe at William's modern-day apologists:

> The fathers of the persons on board the ship had formerly been saved from shipwreck by a *Dutch* Pilot, who came to them in distress; and whom they afterwards, out of gratitude, chose to be their Captain, a post of great honour and profit. After his death, the sons retained a grateful memory of the deliverance of their fathers, which they expressed by pictures and statues of the Deliverer, and even in this very ship they had a fine picture of [him] in the cabbin, and a statue upon deck.

Modern liberty, that is, is the product of an impecunious prince meeting a foolish people and inspiring a debased idolatry in their progeny. So much for the "Glorious Revolution."

There is no room for this sort of discord in Kramnick's or Dickinson's schema. Nor is there any room for those who would question the liberty of the press, in Bolingbrokean polemics a marker between pre- and post-Revolutionary England, and, in the wake of Francklin's arrest, that "liberty" against which Walpole seemed to be moving with the most determination. No doubt due to the government's harassment of Francklin, quite a few pamphlets and newspaper-leaders were published in 1731 and 1732 about the possibility of regulating the press, particularly the *Craftsman*. No one argued the case against the *Craftsman* more belligerently than Earbery.[41] Earbery sneers unmistakably when he observes that "Liberty of Conscience, and Liberty of the Press, are the *Craftsman's* dear and everlasting Topicks."[42] And when the *Craftsman* defended itself for having published the "Hague letter" by insisting that "the *only Liberty of writing*, which We enjoy above slavish Nations, is That of examining all Matters of *Religion* and *Government*" (No. 241; 13 Feb. 1731), Earbery, the inveterate enemy of the *Craftsman's* persecutors, responded with the vitriolic third number of his *Occasional Historian* (1731–32), in which he argued that "an absolute Liberty of the Press would be a Madness in any Government to allow" (1731; 33).

Russel was of a like mind. In his preface to the *Memoirs of the Society of Grub-street* (1737), a two-volume collection of essays from the *Grub-street Journal*, Russel discusses the conditions that had prompted his decision to found the weekly. He runs on at great length about the potential evils of the free press, noting the profusion of irreligious writing since the relaxation of licensing laws in 1695, satirically lamenting that the "genius" of the Grub-street writers had once been cramped by licensing (1:ii), and lashing out at the "late epidemic Bibliomany" that he finds characteristic of English culture (1:viii). In the preface as throughout the *Journal's* seven-year run, Russel is skeptical about Bolingbrokean arguments for a free press. In his epigram "On the liberty of the press," Russel accuses the Whigs under Anne of having pined "O Liberty, O virtue, O my country" but of having forgotten their libertarian principles once in power. But Russel does not rest after what at first looks like a knee-jerk opposition taunt. He concludes, "What means this charge! The sum of all the story's: / Tories oprest are Whigs, and Whigs in pow'r are Tories" (No. 147; 26 Oct. 1732). Russel's lack of enthusiasm for the period's reevaluation of ideal whiggism is again evident, as is his use of the charge—a staple of Walpolite polemics—that Bolingbroke's pleas for a free press were preposterous coming from a man who, as secretary of state to Queen Anne, had routinely suppressed Whig journalism.[43]

The rhetorical alliances here are interesting. By questioning the utility of an unlicensed press, Earbery and Russel are participating in a reaction against "free" expression characteristic of Walpolite polemics—and Walpole's policies—in the late 1720s and the early '30s.[44] Yonge, in his response to Francklin's arrest, had argued that the *Craftsman* and *Fog's Weekly Journal* were "at once, the Demonstration and the Reproach of that unlimited Freedom we enjoy, and of the Lenity and Goodness of the King, and that Government which the Authors are hired to Defame" (*Sedition and Defamation Display'd* [1731], 2–3). To the author of *The Danverian History of the Affairs of Europe* (1732), the publication of the "Hague letter" was a "dangerous Attack" upon England's "inestimable Liberty of the Press"; the culprits are the *Craftsman's* writers, "who make a Noise with the Word *Liberty* while they are tricking and betraying us out of that valuable Branch of it, which conduces so much to the Security and Defense of the Rest" (75). Several years later, Henley would respond to the *Craftsman's* jubilation over the defeat of the Excise Bill with an ill-natured dig at the *Craftsman's* infatuation with "liberty" and a none-too-subtle reminder that the administration could silence the opposition press if it chose to (*Hyp-Doctor* 127; 24 Apr. 1733).[45] In this matter at least, these supporters of Walpole sound like Earbery and Russel.

Earbery illustrates the drift from the committed Jacobitism of the teens to the far less precise and optimistic Carolinism of the 1730s—a phenomenon somewhat less conclusively evident in the careers of Russel and the Oxonian antiquary Thomas Hearne, and in the transformation of the Jacobitical *Mist's Weekly Journal* into the less militantly pro-Stuart *Fog's Weekly Journal*.[46] Because Earbery challenges our received sense of what the opposition was, ideologically speaking, the contours of his career deserve closer examination.

Earbery began publishing polemical and controversial treatises in 1716, a year after Bolingbroke's abandonment of the Pretender's cause. In 1717 Earbery, already a professed nonjuror, printed at his own expense an energetic condemnation of the hangings at Preston that had followed the Jacobite uprising of 1715. The full title of the pamphlet suggests the author's drift: *The History of the Clemency of Our English Monarchs. The Usage Prisoners, Who Surrender'd at Discretion, Have Met With from Their Hands. Compar'd with Several Matters of Fact Which Have Lately Occurr'd in This Kingdom. With an Account of the Manner of Issuing Forth Acts of Grace and Pardon in Former Reigns. Written for the Information of the Present Age, and of Posterity.* Toward the foot of the title page is a motto from Ecclesiasticus 10.3: "An unwise King destroyeth his People."

Earbery's comparisons did not tend toward the greater glory of George I or toward the exoneration of the maneuvering that had landed him on the throne. His thesis is that the Preston Jacobites had been treated with an unwarranted and unprecedented severity.[47] Earbery's apparent juridical liberalism might surprise anyone familiar with his later defense of the penal methods used in Charles I's Star Chamber;[48] but it is clear, and may be inferred from Parliament's eventual pardon of the rioters, that his sympathy for the rioters was not idiosyncratic. W. A. Speck notes that Lord Nottingham and other Tory M.P.'s had pressured George on the matter; and the Tories, out of power after Anne's death in 1714 and discredited in the aftermath of the Jacobite rebellion of 1715, would presumably have needed public support to carry the point.[49]

The analogic treatment promised in Earbery's title is made explicit in his preface, in which Earbery castigates the English General Charles Wills for his treatment of the surrendered Jacobites:

> General *Wills* confesses, that they [the rebels] at last Surrendred at Discretion, and he defines Surrendring at Discretion thus. That it was in our Power to cut them all to Pieces, but I would give them their Lives till farther Order.
> But this Definition as he is pleas'd to call it, is opposite to the universal Opinion of Mankind, both of the present and past Ages, nor is there any General in *Europe* will agree to this Definition.
> (N.p.)

Earbery attempts to prove his point by developing a series of contrasts between the official response to Preston and the responses of other governments threatened by revolt. Among the examples that Earbery plucks from English history are William the Conqueror's allegedly indulgent response to his son Robert's uprising of 1078–80 (1), and Henry II's supposed patience with various (and proverbial) "high Provocations from his own Flesh and blood" (3–4).[50] Not surprisingly, Earbery dwells on what he regards as Charles I's magnanimity toward his rebellious subjects and Charles II's grace upon his restoration. Having dispensed with English history—and having ignored the ugly business of James II's suppression of Monmouth's rebellion in 1685[51]—Earbery moves into classical and European history, ending the pamphlet with a wildly unorthodox account of what he sees as the exemplary treatment by the Hapsburg emperors Leopold I and Joseph I of the participants in Ferenc Rákóczi's Hungarian rebellion of 1703–4.[52] Various appendices include the texts of pardons and acts of attainder extended to rebels by Edward II, Richard III, Henry IV, and Henry VI. The hostility toward the Hanoverian monarchy, for which Wills is a metonymy, is constant and undisguised.

Earbery was not born under a forgiving star, and his timing in publishing the pamphlet was typically unfortunate. As he notes in a nervous and hastily assembled preface, the publication of *The History of the Clemency* coincided with the parliamentary pardon of the surviving insurrectionists. Earbery's assertion that his pamphlet "was in the Press before I had the least Knowledge or Sight of the said Act" (n.p.) is plaintive and perhaps truthful; but he could hardly have expected it to win him any credit with the monarch whom he had so bluntly offended. *The History of the Clemency* earned Earbery a Bill of Indictment at the Hicks Hall Sessions, 9 September 1717. Almost exactly one year later at the Hicks Hall Sessions, Earbery, according to Philip Yorke, the first earl of Hardwicke, was "returned & outlaw'd upon the said Indictment."[53]

Between his indictment and his sentencing, Earbery may have been in Paris: his understandably frantic *Vindication of the History of the Clemency, with Reflections upon the Late Proceedings against the Author* is dated from that city 30 May 1718, and is said on the title page to have been written in Paris and addressed by its author "to his Friend in London." Because title pages and colophons on political pamphlets are notoriously unreliable (and because the author's claim to be resident at "*L'Ho'tell de Salamander*" [167] sounds a tad creative), these statements may or may not provide accurate information about Earbery's whereabouts. But at the very least they tell us that Earbery was willing to say that he was in France and so to affiliate himself with a country that was far more tolerant of Jacobitism than England was, even after the Pretender's move to Italy in 1717.

Even as he was writing the *Vindication*, under indictment and in need of leniency, Earbery could not contain his loathing of the Hanoverian monarchy. He feigns surprise at the charge that his motto from Ecclesiasticus about the "unwise King," tacked on as it had been to a book about the Preston hangings, had been designed as commentary on George I. Rather than plainly pretending innocence—as Bolingbroke would do when he was accused of arguing analogically in the *Remarks on the History of England*—Earbery mixes into his defense a further condemnation of George I:

> Wou'd King *Charles* II. have been stung with such a Motto; wou'd it have entred into his Heart, that he was the foolish King who destroyed his People? no he was as free from Guilt as from Suspicion; and such a reflection wou'd have rather sweeten'd into a jest than sowr'd into Resentment. (v–vi)

If only George had been a *funnier* fellow, Earbery seems to suggest.... Not content even with this dangerous contrast, Earbery continues to convert opportunities for apology into occasions for offense. His assertion that his commentary on Preston was the work of "an Historian ... oblig'd by the Eternal Laws of Justice, to confine himself to Truth" (iii) is both conventional and ridiculous, as Earbery himself surely knew. In staking his claim to objectivity, Earbery digs himself in still deeper:

> Neither their [the prosecution's] justice or Clemency is directly thro' my fault Concern'd in the Book; I only Acted the part of an Historian, and if that is reflecting upon the Government, Let all history, all Memorial of past Ages be burnt or destroy'd; and may the World Commence only from the first Year of this present Reign; then indeed General *Wills* Definition of surrendering at discretion may stand good. (ii–iii)

Earbery failed to convince attorney general Robert, Lord Raymond, who, Hardwicke notes, had him jailed in 1722 for writing *The History of the Clemency* and "another seditious Libel"—presumably the *Vindication*. In 1722 Hardwicke reports that the hapless journalist is "[lying] in Custody of the Marshall of Kings Bench."[54] Earbery's later accounts of this period suggest that his library was seized and that he was tortured in custody. The legal battle would drag on at least until April or May 1723, when Earbery, arguing his own case, overcame the initial objections of Raymond and several other justices and won a writ of error by claiming that the government had unjustly "outlawed" him for contempt after he had declined to appear in court to respond to the initial charge against him.[55] I have found no evidence to suggest that the government continued the case against Earbery, although it could have done so legally, since the writ of error released Earbery only from the "outlawry," not from the charge of having written against the government. Earbery may or may not have had a specific trial in mind when, in 1730, he complained that he had been "successively persecuted and betray'd for sixteen Years past."[56]

Earbery's later legal history is rockier still. He was arrested again in 1732, this time for writing Universal Spy 12 (22 Sept. 1732), a snide commentary on Queen Caroline's hermitage, home to busts of such exempla of irreligion as John Locke and the deists Samuel Clarke and Thomas Woolston. In The Whole System of English Liberty (1738), his blatantly seditious account of the debacle, Earbery asserts that he was jailed from December 1732 until June 1733; and it is a matter of record that in November 1733, the court denied his motion to have the case dismissed due to (acknowledged) procedural errors in the arrest.[57] His trial, and apparent acquittal, took place only in April or May 1738.[58] Unlike the genteel Bolingbroke and the M.P. Pulteney, Earbery dealt with the most pressing sort of legal difficulty throughout his life.

The brouhaha over The History of the Clemency and the Vindication first reminds us that Jacobite polemics were a dangerous business in the early decades of the eighteenth century and, secondly, demonstrates that the young Earbery was an ardent, and even a foolhardy, Jacobite polemicist. It may be that Earbery's later abandonment of the Jacobite party line was dictated by legal expediency or even by maturity, but it is every bit as likely that he became disillusioned with an old cause that no longer had much urgency about it. As early as the Vindication (i–ii), Earbery had expressed irritation about what he saw as the lack of support offered to him by the Jacobites whom he had defended in The History of the Clemency. And by 1733, at least, Earbery's relations with his fellow nonjurors were seriously strained, apparently the result of his having sided with the nonjuring bishop Thomas Brett (and against Richard Russel) in Brett's attempt to settle the Usages Controversy that had riven the ranks of the nonjurors since 1717.[59] There is no doubt that Earbery became progressively uncertain of Jacobitism and nonjurism, the once-stable ideologies that had informed his early polemical writing.

To invoke Matthew Arnold, "the man" and "the moment," having converged in the teens, diverged in the '20s and '30s. Earbery maintained his devotion to the Stuart monarchy, but not his belief in doctrinaire means of supporting that monarchy. When he finally swore allegiance to Hanover, probably after June 1738, Earbery wrote,

> It is some comfort to me, that I have endeavoured to perform my allegiance [to the exiled monarchy] that I swore, as sincerely as the iniquity of the times would permit, & that I have yielded up no part of it, but what is extorted by the conquering power; which how it do[e]s excuse, I must leave it to God alone to judge.[60]

The intense dedication to the Stuart monarchy is evident here, but so is the belief, or the realization, that such sentiment was by the '30s a moral posture with no correlation to practical politics or, even, to contemporaneity. If Earbery is any measure, Jacobitism had become an anachronism.

For nine years after his sentencing in 1722, Earbery kept a low profile, publishing infrequently and cautiously. In his 1724 reply to Gilbert Burnet's posthumous *History of His Own Time*, he again vindicates the Stuart monarchs and several times advertises his belief in the doctrine of nonresistance; but Earbery here is not interested in commenting on the present day, directly or by analogy. No doubt leery of further scrapes with authority, however, Earbery published the book under the safe and shopworn pseudonym "Philalethes."[61] His 1727 translation of Thomas Burnet's *De Statu Mortuorum* (2 vols.), published by the "dunce" Edmund Curll, was presumably undertaken to earn Earbery some quick money during what must have been a difficult time for him. Otherwise we hear nothing from Earbery during this period.

He reemerges with the *Occasional Historian*, four long pamphlets designed as rebuttals of the *Remarks on the History of England* and other entries in the *Craftsman*.[62] By this time, Earbery's loathing of the Revolution Settlement had become fodder for a campaign against Bolingbroke and his journal rather than an argument for the resuscitation of a monarchy that had by and large lost its appeal, romantic or practical.[63] The devotion to pre-Revolutionary England becomes a mythopoetic point of reference—a standard, or a trope—rather than a call to arms, as it had been in the teens. In the *Occasional Historian* and its short-lived sequel *The Universal Spy: Or, the Royal Oak Journal*

Reviv'd (1732), Earbery is as dedicated as ever to the older Stuarts and as hostile as ever to the Revolution Settlement. But the tenor of the argument has changed. George II does not receive anything like the attention that George I had received in Earbery's earlier work; and, at least in the copies of the journal that have survived, there are no hints of support for James Edward Stuart.[64] The target now is a political debate that Earbery believed was being conducted along exclusionary lines, a clubbish dialogue between participants united by their loathing for England before the Revolution and their enthusiasm for England after it. Writing in the *Universal Spy* as "Sir John Perspective," Earbery promises that he will monitor the *Craftsman* as well the pro-government press and that he will eavesdrop even on the private conferences of George II and Walpole:

> I shall be a Spy upon the *Craftsman*, when he abuses the *Stuarts*, and adulterates *English* History, and borrows Parallels as aukward as his own, with the antient *Roman* Patriots.... I shall be a Spy upon the *London Journal*, when he blasphemes, varnishes, gilds and colours; when he sends for Stuff to Court every Week, when the Devil is not at Leisure to supply him with Impiety from Hell to gloss over: Perhaps I may spy likewise the Closet, see two sit like a Cock and a Hen; one to write, and the other to brood alternately, some very monstrous Position to startle human Nature; as, for instance, *That the Principles of the Revolution, constitute the Being of a God.* In short, all Lying, from whatsoever Quarter it comes, I shall detect; so that the Statesman shall no longer deceive with Success.
> (*Universal Spy* 1; 29 Apr. 1732)

"Lying" here is endorsing the Revolution Settlement, and the lying "statesman" here seems equally to be the present minister Walpole and Queen Anne's old secretary of state Bolingbroke. By attacking the *Craftsman* and its enemies in power in the same terms and with equal zeal, Earbery was trying to undermine the very basis of Bolingbrokean consensus.

Earbery's attack on Bolingbroke takes the form of an attempt to discredit the soundness of Bolingbroke's sense of the English past, or, rhetorically speaking, to question the bases of the "aukward" analogies on which Bolingbroke built his series. In the preface to the first *Occasional Historian*, Earbery states his intention to "rescue as much of *English* History as [he] can from Pyrates of all sorts" (n.p.). Advertisements for the series, like the title pages of the pamphlets, name the *Craftsman*; so there may be no doubt about precisely what "Pyrate" Earbery had most in mind. He observes, accurately, that Bolingbroke, the great enemy of the Stuarts generally and Charles I in particular, had excused the rebellion against Charles I precisely as he had justified the Revolution of 1688. According to Earbery, by January 1731 the *Remarks* were promoting Bolingbroke's belief that "the War against King *Charles* was just, and absolutely necessary to prevent Subversion; nay, as necessary as he tells us the Revolution was." Bolingbroke's design, Earbery insisted, was to "transmit the individual Quarrel of the last rebellious Age to the present."[65]

In Earbery's reading of Bolingbrokean historiography, the Revolution is the moment that had sanctified rebellion, and the Bill of Rights is the document that had institutionalized the possibility of rebellion by making the monarch accountable to his or her subjects. Earbery thus daubed both "new Whigs" and "old Whigs" with the same brush. Like the pro-government polemicists Pitt, Arnall, and Hervey, Earbery was disturbed by Bolingbroke's application of England's past to its present. But while Walpole's apologists took offense at Bolingbroke's efforts to claim for himself the ideological inheritance of the Revolution and other great instances of "liberty," Earbery's complaint concerned Bolingbroke's eagerness to focus the political debate on the Revolution and so, as Earbery saw it, to advertise consensus between himself and the court-Whigs even as he sought to promote consensus within the opposition. To Earbery, Bolingbroke offered no "opposition" to Walpole at all.

The second *Occasional Historian* illustrates Earbery's habit of conflating Bolingbroke and those in power. Earbery's target is Bolingbroke's seventeenth letter of the *Remarks on the History of England* (*Craftsman* 242; 20 Feb. 1730). In that number, Bolingbroke had praised the allegedly libertarian era of Elizabeth I at the expense of the factious reigns of James I and Charles I and, implicitly, the "reign" of Walpole and the Hanoverians. Earbery is enraged by the notion of an ancient "liberty" squelched by the Stuarts and reaffirmed by their ouster at the Revolution:

> Mr. *Craftsman* has manifestly shewn that he can blend with History any Fictions to support an Hypothesis, or he would never have recommended Queen *Elizabeth's* Reign, contrary to the concurrent Testimony of Parliaments themselves, as a Reign of Liberty, which secur'd to us the Ballance of Property.
> He would never represent the *Stuarts* as arbitrary, who transmitted to us the greatest Share of Liberty we now enjoy. He would never

strain the Revolution to a greater height than its most eminent Patriots ever fix'd it at, and make it a Restoration to what we never had.
(N.p.)

Earbery's pitch rises as he makes Bolingbroke's devotion to the Revolution emblematic of a modern disease common to Bolingbroke and his enemies in power. If Bolingbroke—"Mr. *Craftsman*"—continues to insult the Stuarts and praise the Revolution, Earbery threatens,

I shall proceed . . . to lay open great Weaknesses in his Writings, his ministerial Enemies have not Sense enough to come at: Who are in like manner affected, and are sick together with him as Brethren, tho' they know it not; with this only Difference, His is the Expectation of Reward, and theirs the actual Enjoyment thereof; and we can easily know to whom they belong, as well can the Master of a Servant with his Lord's Livery upon his Back. (N.p.)

To Earbery as to the authors of the *Grub-street Journal*, speakers "on both sides of the question" look much the same: the *Craftsman* and its "brethren" in the pro-government press both argue from a faulty premise and both act on mercenary motives. In the same number, Earbery notes that Walpole's apologists and the *Craftsman* are equally given to carping about "Liberty of Conscience" (27); the language is meant to bring the Revolution Settlement to mind. Earbery eventually dismisses Bolingbroke as a historiographer of the same sort as the *London Journal's* Pitt: "yet how the *Craftsman* flourishes like Mr. *Osborn[e]* without supporting one Flight, one Insinuation with Fact: If he knew not *English* history, why does he pretend to give us his Magisterial Memoirs?" (58).

Earbery's enmity toward the Revolution's various apologists ensured that Earbery would balk at Bolingbroke's attempt to claim headship of the "opposition." In the first *Occasional Historian*, he criticizes the *Craftsman*'s "Schemes to get into Power himself" (3) and glances caustically at Bolingbroke's "Qualifications to be a prime Minister" (4). In the second number, Earbery employs two of his favorite analogies—the regicide of 1649 and the Revolution of 1688, and the regicides of the 1640s and the Revolution-worshippers of the 1730s—in order to ridicule Bolingbroke's attempts to speak for a coalition defined by its belief in constitutional monarchy. Earbery claims that in Bolingbroke's seventeenth letter of the *Remarks*,

> the King is said . . . to be trusted with a Power, and like a true trustee is intitled to no Benefit of popular Legacies: Liberty and Property the People bequeath to themselves, and make the King a Guardian, and themselves Guardians over him, *Trincolo's* all, and Mr. *Craftsman* the greatest *Trincolo* in the whole Play. (77)

To Earbery, Bolingbroke was the "greatest" participant in a drama that was intrinsically absurd. Bolingbroke's grand accomplishment was to position himself atop a heap of scoundrels—Revolution-worshippers and de facto regicides. Taking the cue from Earbery, we too may want to recall Shakespeare, whose Troilus—in a play far less lovely than *The Tempest*—sounds much like Earbery and Russel when he dismisses the great ruckus over Helen of Troy by snarling, "Fools on both sides!" As adamantly (and perhaps as naively) as the young Troilus, the Carolinists believed that their idol "must needs be fair" and that his detractors were condemned by their own stupidity.[66] This attitude is at quite a distance from the notion of a debate conducted by rival apologists for the Revolution, and from the myth of an opposition defined by its enthusiasm for Revolution principles.

4
The Carolinist Challenge

In the nearly imperceptible process by which a moment becomes first a memory and finally a myth, the original moment—or event—becomes increasingly susceptible to didactic reinterpretation. Through the agency of literature—poetry, sermons, oral and written history, or what-have-you—the actors and actions of a specific time become abstractions, the bases of opportunistic representation. Much historiography untouched by the postmodern fondness for relativism tends to present itself as the attempt to arrest this process, or to isolate points along a continuum, claiming for each a more-or-less precise and perhaps even discreet meaning. There is nothing to be gained by being cynical about this endeavor, but it is useful to note that history imagined in this way is potentially inert. Any polemicist knows this. In particular, writers in the eighteenth century often subverted their professed interest in replicating history verbally, by attempting to apply the lessons of history, polemically, to the present. Bolingbroke, the century's greatest proponent of "exemplary historiography," was not primarily interested in the Revolution; he was interested in how the Revolution called attention to the failure of Walpole's government. The point may be made with reference to rhetoric. If analogy, the trope that frees the past for use in the present, inspires historiography, it also destabilizes it by replacing the historiographer's pretense of objectivity with the polemicist's desire to criticize, to reform, or otherwise to operate in the here and now.

The present chapter examines the means by which early eighteenth-century polemicists converted the Caroline past, an amalgam of event and myth, into modern political argument. I shall concentrate on the conflict between the beliefs of the Carolinist polemicists whom I introduced in the previous chapter, and the tenets that I have established as characteristic of the Bolingbrokean opposition. On the face of it, Carolinist rhetoric could not have been simpler: post-Revolutionary England was measured against the Caroline standard and found wanting. Common during the interregnum and the Restoration, this rhetoric was sustained in the eighteenth century by polemicists—self-proclaimed "historians," in some cases—like Matthias Earbery, Richard Russel, Thomas Hearne, and Joseph Trapp, all of whom tended to regard both Bolingbrokeans and Walpolites as manifestations of the spirit of regicide introduced into England by Charles I's execution, and legitimated (or so the reasoning went) by the Revolution Settlement's authorization of constitutional monarchy.

Carolinism was a static and pessimistic rhetoric that operated outside the main stream of opposition discourse, challenging the debate to abandon the stability that it had come to assume by relying on increasingly programmatic disagreements about the Revolution. By attempting to localize the debate in the 1630s and '40s, Carolinism mounted a rearguard action against the historiographical, and thus polemical and ideological, basis of the mainstream political culture of the early eighteenth century. As I have demonstrated, arguing about the Revolution gave Bolingbrokeans and Walpolites the opportunity to plead for their particular interpretations of the event that both groups regarded as the cornerstone of enlightened government. But to argue about Caroline England was to enter into a violent and anxious past that both groups conventionally used as the emblem of the "tyranny" that the Revolution Settlement had vanquished. In the quarrels about the 1630s and '40s as in the sparring over the Revolution, Bolingbrokeans generally lined up with their Walpolite "adversaries," while the Carolinists sniped at the lot from the sidelines. Carolinism rejected the dominant language of the political debate and in this way attacked Bolingbroke's proprietary notion of the Revolution-centered opposition even as it opposed Walpole's system of governance.

The terms of the debate about Caroline England were different from those used to discuss the Revolution. They were less familiar, because the 1640s had witnessed the rejection of an old dispensation (divine-right monarchy) that seemed broadly anachronistic by the 1730s, whereas the 1680s, *pace* Bolingbroke, saw the institutionalizing of a new one (constitutional monarchy) that was of course still current in the 1730s. They were less legalistic, because virtually no one after the Stuart Restoration in 1660 attempted to justify the manner in which

Oliver Cromwell and his kind had pulled Charles from the throne, while the manner in which William had replaced James II had been validated by a series of laws that seem to have been broadly acceptable to the English. They were less "practical" as well: Carolinists had little interest in the "national affairs" and the "most important interests" that concern Bolingbroke in a characteristic passage that I reproduced at the beginning of the previous chapter.[1] And, no doubt as a result of this compelling lack of precision, the terms of this debate were more mythopoetic. The figure of the ethereal Charles I ensured as much: the monarch lent himself perfectly to interpretive literary representation, as the stolid William III did not.[2]

All this made Caroline England appealing to conservative monarchists alienated by the eighteenth-century's habits of worship and governance—by modernity, more simply. Under Charles, church and monarchy were strong and, for a time at least, growing stronger; and party affiliation was defined by support for the king or seditious resistance to him. Unlike the late seventeenth century, the Caroline era was untroubled by what later polemicists like Earbery would regard as Bolingbroke's or Walpole's (or Parliament's) bewildering attempts to praise the king while usurping his power. And unlike the Revolution, the Civil War was everywhere acknowledged to have been a conflict between monarchic and antimonarchic factions, in or out of Parliament. The relative clarity of questions of political affiliation in the 1640s aided eighteenth-century apologists for divine-right monarchy who had often attempted—without much success—to group the participants in the Revolution into these same categories.

And the Caroline period had the combined appeal of immediacy and distance. Like the periods preferred by historical novelists from Daniel Defoe to (and beyond) George Eliot, the England of the 1640s was in the early 1730s located just at the fringes of memory. Discussions of Charles and his death—framed mythically even in the decade after the regicide, as Lois Potter has demonstrated[3]—had by the 1730s been shaped by eighty-some years of amalgamated fact and fancy, remembrance and invention, historiography and polemic. The passage of time shot through with mythopoeia events that even in their own day had seemed fantastic, not to say portentous. The later period clung to its Caroline past with exaggerated intensity, sometimes expressed as abhorrence, sometimes as reverence, sometimes simply as awe.

First-hand accounts of the regicide still surface in the early 1730s. As in the seventeenth century, the accounts are rarely perfunctory or unadorned. Even routine descriptions tend to accent the imagistic potency of Charles's execution and thus to portray the event as supraverbal, something that can be described in words but not quite comprehended by them. Consider, for example, an entry in the *Daily Post* from 23 December 1730 (No. 3514), nearly eighty-two years after the king's execution:

> One Margaret Coe ... Died a few Days since, in the 104th Year of her Age. She was 21 years old when King Charles the First was beheaded, and was a Servant at Whitehall; she saw the Executioner hold up the Head after he had cut it off, and remember'd the dismal Groan that was made by the vast Multitude of Spectators when the fatal Blow was given.

Margaret Coe's memory, or the press's account of it, suggests the mythic potential of the regicide and thus the attractiveness of the "martyr" who made the myth. The tableau that the passage creates, with its somber aural accompaniment, is conventional. But it is so in part because of its timelessness, its spinning-backwards to include, as it were, familiar images from mythology: the simple posture of executioner and executed, frozen in time and space, suggests Perseus and Medusa, Judith and Holofernes, and other familiar groupings. Furthermore, the passage emphasizes what was literally sensed (seen and heard) rather than what happened. Charles's death is rewritten as Margaret Coe's experience; transcribed from memory, the experience is imagistic rather than primarily verbal and is therefore endlessly suggestive. Although no doubt unintentional, the newspaper's error in arithmetic (had she been 104 in 1730, Coe would have been twenty-four or twenty-five when Charles died) points up the blurring of what happened and what was experienced in a way that is characteristic of Carolinist polemics. A journalist's reworking of an old woman's experience—perhaps passed along by her friends or family—takes on the language of myth. In a genre governed by convention as journalism is, it could not do so this easily if the period were not accustomed to mythologizing the regicide.

The Carolinist takes subjective "moments" like Margaret Coe's and makes them over as more expansive units of meaning. Given the eighteenth century's anxiety about the Caroline period, the enterprise was unavoidably controversial. The *Craftsman*'s editor, Nicholas Amhurst, spoke from experience when he complained in 1732 that "it [is] almost impossible for a Writer to speak of [Charles's reign], without giving Offence to *one of those* Parties which continue to espouse the different Principles and Conduct of their Forefathers" (*Craftsman* 298; 1 Apr. 1732). His target is the Carolinist opposition, which had been accusing his journal of "giving offense" at least since the publication of the *Remarks on the History of England*. Amhurst's griping earned no points with Earbery, who one month later noted "how exactly the *Craftsman* and Mr. *Walsingham* [i.e., William Arnall of the pro-government *Free Briton*] agree together in insulting the Memory of King *Charles* I" (*Universal Spy* 2; 6 May 1732).

Earbery's observation, if petulant, is accurate. Because of their mutual enthusiasm for the principles of constitutional monarchy, Bolingbrokean and pro-government pamphleteers tended to present the reign of the antiparliamentary Charles as leading inexorably to rebellion, war, and regicide. The regicide was the regrettable consequence of an inevitable rebellion. It is easy to see that Charles invited the charge: a monarch who had prorogued Parliament as readily as he had was the antithesis of the values formalized in the Bill of Rights. James Pitt ("Francis Osborne") framed the point succinctly when he claimed that Charles "ruin'd himself by reigning *twelve years without a Parliament, and against the Laws*" (*London Journal* 661; 26 Feb. 1732).[4] John "Orator" Henley, unfettered by tact or sanity, pushed the point harder when he opined that "all who are Enemies to the Memory of K. *Charles* I. for unparliamentary and illegal Proceedings, are oblig'd by that Principle to be zealous Friends to K. *GEORGE* II. and his Ministers for contrary Measures and Temper" (*Hyp-Doctor* 94; 26 Sept. 1732). The logic is Henleyan, to be sure; but Henley is merely rendering explicit the connection between praising Hanover and damning Charles that Pitt had been content to imply. So when Earbery notes that the *Craftsman* "lays it down as a Maxim, that King *Charles* the First, by transgressing the Bounds of the Constitution, brought on a Revolution" (*Occasional Historian* 3 [1731], 11), he could just as easily be talking about any one of a number of Walpole's apologists.

No one in the 1730s would have been foolish enough to argue that the regicide had been justified—not *quite*, at least. But friends of Hanover, real or professed, had no trouble arguing *post hoc, ergo propter hoc* when the discussion turned to Charles's reign and its dramatic culmination. The mealy-mouthed bishop White Kennett did so when he declared Charles emblematic of a social malaise that had made England susceptible to civil war. In his 1720 King Charles Day sermon before the House of Lords, Kennett, referring to the Civil War, decried "the Corruption and general Depravation of Manners, that usher'd in that Stupidity, and those Calamities upon us." He added that under Charles "the Liberties of the Stage, and indecent Representations, and vitious Interviews . . . had tended to soften and taint the Minds of the People."[5] To Kennett, the Caroline era was an invitation to rebellion tendered by a grasping monarch to an addled populace. John, Lord Hervey said the same thing more explicitly in 1734, when he excused "the Struggle made for Liberty when the People could bear no longer the lawless oppressive Conduct of King Charles the First."[6] Like Pitt and Kennett, Hervey is expressing a commonplace of the period.

Always eager to appear weary of the whine of faction, the *Craftsman* frames its antipathy to "the disastrous Reign of King Charles the *first*" in terms of the consensus it habitually pretended to observe and to represent: it finds agreement "on all Sides" for its tendentious (if common) assertion that "the Foundation of those Distractions and Calamities, which broke out in the Year 1641, was laid many Years before, in the weak, ridiculous and scandalous Conduct of King *James* the *first*" (No. 298; 1 Apr. 1732). Bolingbroke himself is unreservedly negative about Charles I and Caroline England. In the twenty-third letter of the *Remarks on the History of England* (*Craftsman* 254; 15 May 1731), he wrote that Charles I

> had, in a Manner, renounced the *Constitution*; and instead of governing with the Assistance and Concurrence of a *Parliament*, He govern'd by *illegal Acts of Power*, which the *Council*, the *Star-Chamber* and the *High Commission* exercised. . . . Not only the *Government* was carried on *without Law*, or *against Law*, but the *Judges* were become the Instruments of *arbitrary Power*, and that *Law*, which should have been the Protection of *Property*, was rendered, by their corrupt Interpretations of it, so great a Grievance that *the Foundations of Right* were, to the Apprehension and Understanding of wise Men, says my Lord *Clarendon*, never more in *Danger* to be destroyed.

(Clarendon, of course, is Edward Hyde, first earl of Clarendon, author of the magisterial *True Historical Narrative of the Rebellion* [1702–4].) Bolingbroke goes on to posit Charles's final dismissal of Parliament in 1640 as irresistible provocation to rise against the king. It is not difficult to understand Earbery's tendency to conflate the "opposition" and that which it claimed to oppose.

Carolinism comes down squarely against this alliance and the assumptions that define it. To Carolinist polemicists, the regicide was a corollary from, not a mutation of, the spirit of rebellion against Charles. With its origins in the tenacious doctrine of "passive obedience," made much of by nonjurors and other anti-Williamites in 1688–89, the argument against "resistance" to the monarch accommodates the essential movement in Carolinist rhetoric: the analogy of Cromwell's roundheads and the Revolution's apologists—or the Stuart-bashers—of the late seventeenth century, and, somewhat less convincingly, the eighteenth century. The analogy takes advantage of a significant weakness in the rhetoric of libertarianism and Revolution-worship. Apologists for the Revolution Settlement could represent William III as a savior who had healed the rupture caused to national polity by the tyrannical Roman Catholic James II. The roles of villain and hero are easily assigned and in a sense had been codified by the laws governing the succession. But, due to the universal loathing for Cromwell after the Restoration, these same polemicists, when they attempted to justify the rebellion against Charles, were in the uncomfortable position of arguing for the inevitability of an uprising against tyranny without being able to produce a satisfactory personification of the libertarian impulse—rather like Trafalgar without a Nelson. Eighteenth-century proponents of divine-right monarchy found in the 1640s something like the antithesis of right and wrong that Bolingbrokean and Walpolite writers found in the 1680s. But their position, based only on the abhorrence of regicide, was more resistant to attack than that of those whom Earbery, dismissively, called the "*Whig Revolutioners*" and the "*Tory Revolutioners.*"[7]

Carolinist rhetoric prospered during times of stress in church and state such as the Jacobite uprisings of the late seventeenth and early eighteenth century, the trial of Henry Sacheverell (1710), and the Bangorian Controversy (1717). Its premises are easy to identify. Published in the wake of the Sacheverell trial, the miscellany *Whig and Tory: Or, Wit on Both Sides* (1713), offers a clear, if inelegant, introduction. The book's central motif is the resurgence of a "commonwealth" mentality among enemies of the church and, thus, according to a certain turn of thought, to the state. Verses entitled (for no evident reason) "Said to Be Found upon a Great Lady's Toylet" present the Caroline analogy in its basic form:

> OA—a! see, the prelude is begun,
> Again they play the Game of Forty One,
> And he's the Traytor that defends the Throne.
> Thus *Laud*, and thus the *Royal martyr* dy'd,
> Impeach'd by *Clamour*, and by Traytors try'd.
>
> (3)

"Laud" is Charles's archbishop William Laud, a central figure in Carolinist rhetoric in the seventeenth and eighteenth centuries, and, by the 1730s, often a counterpoint to George II's unblushingly secular first minister Walpole. The condemnatory and cautionary strains are animated by the least imaginative sort of analogy: as then, so now, without qualification. Richard Russel's contemporaneous poem *The Impeachment: Or, the Church Triumphant* (1711) strikes the same chord at much greater length.

With more reach and grasp, the 1714 pamphlet *Advocates for Murther and Rebellion, the Pest of Government* identifies issues that had been part of political discourse since 1649, that were central to the struggles over the ouster of the Stuarts and the installation of the Hanoverians, and that would survive in the Carolinist vocabulary during the Walpole era:

> The execrable and unprecedented Murther of King *Charles* I. has laid such deep and broad Foundations for Rebellion, that our mild and wholesome Laws have hitherto been hardly able to keep under, much less to extirpate wholly this growing Evil. Ever since that fatal Epoch of Anarchy, it has been the Business of a certain busy Sett of Men to transmit the poisonous Principles from Father to Son, and to settle them by (what they are, in other Cases, no great Friends to) Hereditary Right; who, by black'ning the Conduct of that innocent Prince, and the Management of his Ministry[,] endeavour to extenuate the Parricide of the Butchers. (3)

The passage, characteristic of the pamphlet, is noteworthy in two respects. First, it stresses the analogic and conflational nature of Carolinist rhetoric by presenting the regicide as emblematic of the modern spirit. What the author presents as a pure and simple genealogy of regicide is actually a complex history of rebellion, regicide, revolution, and adjustments in the succession; but Carolinism defies precisely this set of practical distinctions. More specifically, by noting with irony the secular appropriation of divine right, the passage identifies the threat to the royal prerogative initiated in the Civil War and allegedly sustained by its latter-day apologists.

Recent scholarship posits an organic connection between the Carolinist rhetoric of the seventeenth century and that of the first two decades of the eighteenth century. Although it would be difficult to say why, this work has not considered the Carolinist strain in the 1730s; but it may still help us appreciate with what sources later Carolinists were working and what uses they made of them. Tim Harris notes that the propagandistic comparison of roundheads and Whigs was common among royalists from the 1660s through the 1720s:

> Typically the whigs were represented as trying to revive the "good old cause." This argument was so common that the whigs even satirized it in their propaganda. The charge could be made in a variety of ways, the most blatant being through explicit parallels with the 1640s.[8]

Harris errs in supposing the 1720s the terminal decade of Carolinist rhetoric, but he is right to note the prevalence of interest in Caroline England well after the king's death.[9]

There is reason for this allure and this longevity. As a good number of scholars are now arguing, Charles's reign had substantially more merit than several centuries of historiography (including Bolingbroke's) have allowed it. Recent revisionist scholarship comes down against the durable Whiggish presentation of Charles's reign as repressive and antipopulist. Kevin Sharpe, for instance, argues at length against the tenacious belief in Charles's so-called "eleven years' tyranny."[10] Raymond Anselment analyzes "loyalist" poetry during the interregnum and finds devotion to Charles prevalent—and justified—during that period. Stressing England's economic prosperity in the 1630s and its detachment from the Thirty Years' War in Europe, Anselment argues that "when the period is considered without the hindsight of the civil war and without the assumption that the conflict was inevitable, the real benefits of the king's peace cannot be easily dismissed."[11] Anselment applauds and advances recent scholarship that endorses the beatific vision of the 1630s presented in the *Eikon Basilike* (1649) and in the writings of poets and historians who praised the 1630s overtly before the Civil War and covertly during and after it.[12]

Modern scholarship on Charles himself is compatible with Sharpe's and Anselment's findings on the Caroline period, and tends again to stress the monarch's mythic status.[13] Some time ago, Helen Randall analyzed the "foundations of a political myth of the Royal Martyr" in terms of the "serious tactical errors on the part of the regicides." Immediately after Charles's execution, she argued, "both the real character of Charles and most of the tangible circumstances of his life [gave] way to a stylized representation of an already legendary figure who owes his lineaments more to sacred than to contemporary history."[14] Charles and Laud were made mythic by their assassins—a transformation rich in analogic potential and attractive to eighteenth-century nonjurors and other defenders of the role of episcopacy in government. In 1730, the Tory divine Joseph Trapp balked— slightly—at the analogic pairing of Christ and Charles I. But the analogy is nonetheless a commonplace of Carolinist rhetoric and one that hints at the mythic resonance with which Randall is concerned.[15]

Although she does not mention Randall, Lois Potter develops Randall's interest in an archetypally resonant Charles. She attributes Charles's literary or mythic refashioning to the confluence of his character and the needs of his apologists, and she finds evidence of mythopoetic transformation even before the execution. Central to Potter's study is the idea that Charles presented himself and was represented by others in a manner that facilitated mythopoetic interpretation—a larger version of the sort of thing we have seen in the telegraphic narrative about the death of Margaret Coe. Potter's Charles is an imagistic rather than a verbal king, much given to dancing and little to speaking.[16] Calling Charles "the royal actor," Potter notes that he was "perceived" by portraitists "to be acting a series of emblematic roles."[17] Poets, too, conventionally emphasized the king's "external aspect"; and Potter believes it possible that "Charles's own reserved manner made it necessary for [his] secretive temperament to be elevated into a virtue."[18] Charles's barely audible speech on the scaffold and his silent funeral become symbolic moments to Potter.[19] His death, like his life, makes the monarch a tabula rasa for the use of his disciples and their descendants.

Potter maintains that after Charles I's arrest in 1641, royalist writers had to choose between what amounted to literal and figurative versions of Charles. "By 1645," she writes,

> the events of the civil war had reached a point where Charles needed either to be condemned as a devious schemer or condoned on the

dubious grounds that he had not really known what was going on. To refuse to accept either proposition—to attribute to the king a degree of wisdom which was totally independent of his observed actions—required such an effort of double-think that it is worth trying to unpick its tangled motives.[20]

Part of the yield of Potter's "unpicking" is her observation that "a cult of personality is capable of surviving even the most damning discoveries: the believer abstracts the 'real' hero from the confused mass of words and actions which are his historical being."[21]

Charles's eighteenth-century apologists sustained this "cult of personality" by negotiating among the options that Potter outlines, specifically by proposing a passive, Christ-like monarch undone by evil ministers and vicious republicans.[22] In this way, they transformed an arguably incompetent Charles to one guilty only of the "failing" of trusting overmuch—a positive trait, it is worth remembering, in the satire and sentimental fiction of (among others) Alexander Pope, Samuel Richardson, and Henry and Sarah Fielding. This Charles provided the basis of a forceful "opposition" analogy that identified strong-willed ministers as the enemies of benevolent monarchy.

The anonymous prologue to William Havard's pseudo-Shakespearean *King Charles the First: An Historical Tragedy* (1737) develops the notion of the trusting, victimized Charles, "By Nature Virtuous, tho' mis-led by Slaves, / By Tools of Power, by Sycophants and Knaves" (n.p.). Charles's chaplain, William Juxon, is the normative figure of tragedy who eulogizes the dead hero at the end of the play. In Juxon's oration, the qualities that have facilitated Charles's victimage—"Patience" and "Charity" (61)—are also the markers of his special dignity. Havard recommends the king simultaneously to heroism and analogic utility:

> ... his Pray'r
> Was for his Foes more earnest than himself,
> Because their Wants were greater—Thus fell *Charles!*
> A Monument of Shame to the present Age—
> A Warning to the future. . . .
>
> (60–61)

Charles's "foes" are equally the cabinet ministers who would control him and the puritans in Parliament who would dethrone him. The temporal scope introduced in the last line assures us that Juxon means both to warn modern meddlers with the monarchy and to criticize their forebears.

The passive Charles is also the subject of Robert Dodsley's absurdly affected *Chronicale of the Kings of England from The Norman Conquest unto the Present Time* (1742). Dodsley's Charles is the victim of the Romish Laud and the scheming George Villiers, first duke of Buckingham, counselor to both James I and Charles I.[23] Dodsley, here writing as "Nathan Ben Saddi, a priest of the Jews," had been a contributor to the *Grubstreet Journal;* and, although he apparently did not share the editor Russel's enthusiasm for Caroline religion, he did endorse the Carolinist view that Charles was not accountable for the policies that had marred his reign or for the civil war that had ended it.[24] Dodsley presents Charles's crypto-Catholicism as the fruit of his dealings with Laud, who "was suspected of debauching the King into this lewd Amour" with the "inveigling Harlot" of Rome (48). Furthermore, Dodsley—in opposition to Kennett, for one—claims currency in the seventeenth century for the idea that Charles was the victim of Villiers: "Then the Anger of the People waxed great, and they said amongst themselves, The King is ill advised, his Counsellors are naught; let us remove the Wicked from before the King, and his Throne shall be established in Righteousness" (46). The paraphrase of Proverbs 25.5 aligns Dodsley with the opposition to Walpole: a 1730 sermon by Samuel Croxall on the same text had created a ruckus among the pro-government camp.[25] In 1742, when Walpole's enemies were finally prying the minister from the king, it would have been impossible to read the pamphlet nonanalogically.

Dodsley was not sufficiently solicitous of Charles's reputation to have satisfied a resolute Carolinist, but he nonetheless absolves the king of responsibility for his own actions and so leaves him open to the sort of mythic interpretation that interests Potter. An anecdote—often retailed in the eighteenth century—about the head of Charles's cane falling off during his trial recalls the supernaturalism of much seventeenth- and eighteenth-century commentary on Charles (50).[26] And Dodsley, conventionally, presents Charles's procession to the scaffold as a reenactment of the procession to Calvary: "And they treated him with great Insolence, spitting upon him, and puffing Tobacco in his Face, which they knew was hateful to him. Howbeit he bore with Patience their Insults, neither opened he his Lips against them" (50). The monarch-as-text with whom Potter is concerned has retained his air of silence and mystery; he has not done but has rather been done to. Again, Margaret Coe's tableau comes to mind.

In their reconstructions of Charles, eighteenth-century writers like Havard and Dodsley sustained the "royalist style," of which Potter says "context was everything and literal meaning nothing."[27] No doubt due in large part to Charles's peculiarly abstract status, eighteenth-century Carolinist argumentation is typically beyond the clamor over the facts of constitutional history that had marked the seventeenth- and eighteenth-century debate about the Revolution and the accession of William and Mary. Earbery—an oddity in any company—was always ready to argue fine points about the succession. But other nonjurors like Russel and the antiquary Thomas Hearne tended to treat issues and events incidentally—as obscured by myth, so to speak. For them as for the cavalier poets noted by Potter and investigated by Anselment, the emphasis is often on the emblematic function of Charles. The *Grub-street Journal,* for instance, caps off a debate about church behavior by presenting Charles as the paragon of respect for the divine service.[28] Another entry dwells on Charles's ethereal, quasi-divine state: the author of the weird metaphysical poem "The Apotheosis of that ever blessed Martyr KING CHARLES I" imagines a decapitated monarch who ascends far over the "horrid gloom" of earth and (improbably) "smil[es] at the sportive malice of his Foes" (*Grub-street Journal* 56; 28 Jan. 1731).

Hearne, known more for his dry-as-dust pedantry than for his mythic imagination,[29] provides a useful example of the diffusion of the Caroline "moment" into the eighteenth century. An Oxonian Jacobite and a nonjuror of the old school, Hearne peppers his diaries with references to George I as "ye Duke of Brunswick" and to James Stuart as "K. James III." His objection to the Hanoverians is inseparable from his commitment to the Stuart succession; but his devotion to the Stuarts is focused on "that excellent Prince" Charles I, rather than on the exiled Pretender.[30]

Hearne is interested in some of the substantive issues of Charles I's reign. He is quick, for example, to absolve the king of responsibility for his role in the Irish Rebellion of 1641, and for his maneuvers in Scotland in 1646.[31] But Hearne spends more time exploring the umbrous region that lies beyond conventional historiography: throughout the teens and '20s, his diaries and letters attest to an interest in Charles that is inseparably historical and mythical. Hearne is fascinated, for instance, by the uncertainty surrounding Charles's burial. In a 1715 diary entry, he claims to have "receiv'd it from very good Hands that K. Charles I^{ts} body was never put into y^t Coffin that was buried at Windsor, but that this Coffin was filled with Stones and other Trumpery, and y^t the body was really buried under a Dunghill in Scotland Yard" (11 Aug. 1715).

This much perhaps falls within the province of scholarship or at least antiquarianism, but the entry ultimately indicates the extent to which Hearne could indulge himself in mythical renderings of the Caroline past. Hearne's informant (one Mr. Tyrell) has told him that

> Dr. Walter Charleton, the famous Physitian, was one of those Physitians that were present at y^e opening of K. Ch. I$^{st's}$ Body, & that the D^r affirmed that all his vitals were so very intire y^t he might have lived in all probability to an extreme old age (perhaps an 100 years) but that his Features & hair were much decayed & altered by reason of his great Afflictions. The D^r also told him [Tyrell] y^t he was credibly informed that the Room where the said operation was performed was much haunted for some considerable time after, in so much that no body would venture to lye in it.[32]

In the next decade, Hearne reports a rumor that the king's body had been accidentally disinterred in St. James's Park, and records an account of an old woman who "had a Kinswoman . . . that dipp'd a Handkerchief all over in the King's (K. Charles Ist) Bloud, when he was beheaded, wch she kept as a sacred Thing to her dying day, above 30 years since."[33]

In their emphasis on myth and oral history, Hearne's remarks remind us that the Caroline presence in the eighteenth century had evolved from earlier representations of Charles. Three quarters of a century after the king's death, Hearne gives evidence of Potter's "cult of personality," or of what Anselment calls "the uncertain blend of fact and fiction surrounding Charles's monarchy."[34]

This is not to say that the meaning, or perhaps the function, of Carolinism remained constant from the seventeenth century to the 1710s and into the 1730s. With Jacobitism's decline in vitality in the years after Hearne's obsessive lucubrations, Carolinism tended more and more to manifest itself as rage against writers "on either side of the question" who were attempting to cast the modern political debate in the language of "liberty," Revolution, and "resistance" to the monarch. "Resistance" is pitched a bit differently than it had been in earlier years. In the 1730s, conservative polemicists used the term to signify the (alleged) resistance of a powerful Commons rather than to identify the more overt—or discernible, a skeptic might say—strategies of antimonarchism practiced in the 1630s and '40s. The Caroline analogy has a certain force and, arguably, a certain accuracy when it is deployed against the prosecution of a highchurchman like Sacheverell in a year as fraught with political tension as 1713 was, when Jacobitism was in the air and the old cry of "Church in danger" retained an urgency that it would shortly lose. The twin blows of the (surprisingly smooth) accession of George I in 1714 and the (unsurprising) failure of the Jacobite revolt of 1715 ensured that Carolinism would surrender the slight means it had of addressing practical politics and would drift toward anachronism. Carolinist rhetoric survived not because of its persuasive power or its ability to focus complex political issues, but because it provided a mythopoetic retreat from just this sort of complexity. What had been a contributive strain of opposition discourse became the conduit for anger against those who maligned the memory of Charles I and were now attempting to gather the opposition under the aegis of the Revolution. The "new" Carolinism targeted the derivative and suffusive spirit of republicanism and Revolution-worship, regardless of by whom it was embodied.

Russel and Earbery are the most visible representatives of Carolinism in the 1730s. When Russel criticizes those who would condone Charles's deposition but condemn his decollation, he is simultaneously commenting on Caroline history in a familiar way and admonishing apologists for the Revolution like Pitt, Henley, and "Caleb D'Anvers." The nicety of distinction "*betwixt rebellion and regicide*" concerns Russel in entries in *Grubstreet Journal* numbers 214 (31 Jan. 1734) and 266 (30 Jan. 1735), both of which are concerned with accommodationist interpretations of the Civil War. In number 266, the *Journal* laments, "This hair, betwixt king-fighting and king-killing, / Vainly to split how many still are willing!" How many, indeed. This is precisely the "hair" that Bolingbroke had split in the *Remarks on the History of England,* that other writers for the *Craftsman* were still splitting, and that apologists for the Revolution Settlement and the Hanoverian monarchy had been splitting since the late 1680s.[35] The *Journal's* complaint taps into a familiar fund of rhetoric, but gains its immediacy from the fact that "hair splitting" seemed to have been institutionalized in contemporary politics and polemics.

An anonymous epigram in *Grub-street Journal* 271 (6 Mar. 1735) intensifies this attack by employing the familiar analogy of modern Whig and puritan rebel:

> At last 'tis plain, some Whigs are as of yore;
> The same in forty-eight and thirty-four:
> Kings and all kingly government they hate;
> And Whig and Round-head differ but in date.

It is perhaps useful to imagine Carolinist historiography as the gradual accretion of "roundheads," a thickening of analogues to a single, fixed referent that was itself increasingly beyond the reach of memory. The enemies are more numerous in the 1730s than they had been, say, in the 1680s. Later Carolinist polemics, therefore, are more astringent and more broadly dismissive. But they are less convincing as having to rely on the juxtaposing of an old argument and a new context—the newness of which the Carolinists refused to acknowledge.

Earbery illustrates the point even more neatly than Russel does. In his "advertisement" for the first number of the anti-Bolingbroke *Occasional Historian*, Earbery attacked Bolingbroke's use of Caroline history in the strongest language:

> Whereas the CRAFTSMAN has for some Time past openly declared himself to be a Root and Branch Man, and has made several injust and scandalous Reflections upon the Family of the STUARTS, not sparing even King CHARLES the First: This is to give Notice, That if he reflects further upon any ONE of that Line, I shall shake his rotten Common-Wealth Principles into Atoms.[36]

A "root and branch man" is here a proponent of the overhaul of venerable institutions, specifically the monarchy. With more conviction than logic, Earbery asserts that Bolingbroke cannot be an advocate of monarchy of any sort, because he has criticized the Stuarts in the *Remarks on the History of England*. Earbery finds Bolingbroke's ideological heritage not in any tradition of monarchist polemics, but in the Commonwealth, the dread locus of extravagant antimonarchism.

In another attack on Bolingbroke published about six months after the first *Occasional Historian*, Earbery asks, "In God's Name, is *English* Liberty confin'd only to Republicans, Fanaticks and Rebels?" (*Occasional Historian* 3 [1731], 32). To Earbery, Bolingbroke's "principles" are again the stuff of Cromwellian republicanism, and his "liberty" is that quality that had ousted two Stuart monarchs and that was finding sponsorship once more in the impious 1730s. The debt to the Carolinist sources from 1713 and 1714 is obvious enough; and like his predecessors and like his contemporary Russel, Earbery regards the menace to (and of) modernity as a recrudescence of the spirit that had reduced England nearly to ruin in the previous century. But it is difficult to imagine that this sort of rhetoric had quite the force in 1731 that it did twenty years earlier. Indeed, in a decade addicted to intertextual bickering, Earbery's attacks on the *Craftsman* seem to have generated only one passing response from anyone connected with that journal.[37]

Earbery's third *Occasional Historian* (1731) exemplifies the anger of Carolinist apologetics and its tendency to lash out at its enemies while scorning the issues with which they were most concerned. The incentive for writing the number was an essay hostile to the Walpolite Pitt in *Craftsman* 241 (13 Feb. 1731)—hardly someone whom one would expect Earbery to defend. *Craftsman* 241 had included an attack on the previous week's *London Journal* (No. 601; 6 Feb. 1731), in which Pitt had criticized the *Craftsman* for publishing the "Hague letter" and, implicitly, had marveled at the mildness of the government's response. After having noted Plutarch's account of "*an Athenian, who was cruelly tortur'd for telling a Piece of News, pernicious and dishonourable to the Commonwealth, though it was* true," Pitt had declared "our *English Patriots*" worse than such as Plutarch's Athenian for their readiness to "invent Falshoods [sic], and send 'em all over the Kingdom, and all over *Europe*, on purpose to disgrace the Government abroad, and render it contemptible at home!" The arrest of a printer was a slight price to pay for such perfidy, in Pitt's reckoning. The *Craftsman*'s anonymous contributor, no doubt wary of direct combat in the aftermath of Richard Francklin's January arrest, had answered Pitt indirectly, by comparing Plutarch's Athens and Cromwell's England:

> I could tell *this Author* of several *Englishmen*, in former Reigns, who have been as *cruelly tortur'd* for speaking the *Truth*; and these arbitrary Proceedings were recommended, not long ago, as proper Precedents to be put in Practice at present; though They had contributed to several Revolutions of Government, and the *Court*, which had been guilty of them, is abolish'd by Act of Parliament.

The *Craftsman*'s reference was to the 1637 Star Chamber trial of the puritan pamphleteers John Bastwick, William Prynne, and

Henry Burton, "the graphic stories" about which, Sharpe observes, have long "besmirched the court of Star Chamber and the episcopate and government of Caroline England."[38] The *Craftsman*'s habitual linkage of Stuart and Walpolite "tyranny" completes the essayist's meaning: suppression now was beginning to look very much like suppression then.

The *Craftsman*'s accusations infuriated Earbery. But he refused to cast his response in the terms favored by the *Craftsman* and the *London Journal:* current events like the fiasco over the "Hague letter" do not interest him even obliquely, nor does the quibbling "verbal criticism" tossed back and forth between polemicists of the period, evident in *Craftsman* 241 and many contemporaneous pieces. Earbery is concerned only with the *Craftsman*'s particular use of Caroline history—the vehicle of that journal's metaphor, not its tenor, so to speak. In his characteristically immoderate response to the *Craftsman*, Earbery shows some interest in mythic Hearnean Carolinism: Charles I is "a Saint in his private Life," "a Martyr at the Block for both Church and State," and so on (18). Again familiarly, Earbery makes ample use of the old Caroline analogy, for instance attacking "that glorious *Craftsmanical* Establishment of [16]48, when a Veil was drawn over Monarchy, Episcopacy, and Laws at once, and even Juries were banish'd from their pretended Courts of Justice" (36–37). Although he has virtually nothing to say about contemporary politics, Earbery goes to great lengths to vindicate Charles I and to eviscerate Elizabeth I, the former of whom was despised by Bolingbroke and the latter of whom was revered by Bolingbroke and hated by Earbery.

By now, Earbery is practicing something different from the political "activism" of his predecessors in the 1710s, and from the unfocused residual Jacobitism of Hearne. Departing even from his own earlier work, he no longer concerns himself with the Stuart succession, but rather concentrates on rehabilitating the reputation of Charles I and undermining those of Bolingbroke and Walpole. The "opposition" theme in the pamphlet is stated quickly, then dispensed with. Sounding for the moment like Bolingbroke, Earbery strikes out against "Ministers, too often the common Plagues of Society . . . [who] make the Liberty of the Press so essential a benefit to Society, whenever the Rights of a Nation are notoriously invaded" (36). The hit at Walpole is not subtle and is not intended to be. But neither is it Earbery's primary interest. Earbery announces his larger purpose when he argues that Bastwick, Prynne, and Burton—the *Craftsman*'s tellers of "truth"—were subversives whose freedom of expression ought not to have been protected by law and, indeed, had not been protected by the wary and judicious Charles. When Earbery calls the puritan trio "unear'd Patriots, convicted by Law" (37), he looks squarely at the once-proscribed "patriot" Bolingbroke (and anticipates Dr. Johnson's durable line about scoundrels and patriotism). An attack on "evil Ministers" (36) becomes a slam on Walpole, but the "opposition" impulse is immediately subsumed by Earbery's apology for the selective repressiveness of Charles I. Earbery is longing for the ethos of another time rather than attempting to prescribe policy to the present one, as Bolingbroke and Pulteney did, if vainly for the most part.

Earbery's apparently limitless interest in the minutiae of Caroline politics suggests the importance that he attached to his self-appointed role as custodian of Charles I's reputation. It is almost as though he had lost interest in what we may imagine as the tenor of the analogy, and was content endlessly to forage around in the vehicle, or the referent. Most of Earbery's energy in *Occasional Historian* 3 goes into a burdened analysis of the origins and the legal status of the Star Chamber. Arguing, as Bolingbroke liked to, from a constitutionalist position, Earbery claims that the Star Chamber was not, as Bolingbroke had contended, the invention of Charles I, but was rather "as ancient as any known Part of our temporal Constitution" and ipso facto a commendable institution. Earbery admits that the Caroline Star Chamber "inflicted Punishments by Pillory, Papers, Whipping, Loss of Ears, Tacking of Ears, [and] Stigmata in the Face." Unmoved by the weight of this concession, however, he submits that chambermen under Charles "neither distorted the Limbs, nor cut off Genitals, nor embowl'd Persons alive; therefore their Tortures are reduced to a very narrow Compass." Earbery, evidently still smarting from his own imprisonment in the King's Bench, concludes that the Hanoverians' fondness for torture, like Elizabeth's, leaves apologists for that monarchy little room for criticizing Charles: "'Tis very hard to load the *Star-Chamber* with Reproach, for using Punishments that are common to all Societies, and are now in Use at this Day" (12).

The shabbiness of Earbery's argument only contributes to my point: Earbery, the practitioner of an anachronistic discourse allied to but distant from mainstream opposition rhetoric, marked off for himself a corner of history that he defended with tooth-baring ferocity, savaging all trespassers equally. The "political" agenda is nothing more specific than a preference for the imagined moral simplicity of a crepuscular past to what Earbery regarded as the moral laxity of Hanoverian England.

By the 1730s, this rhetoric was no longer the exclusive property of crusty nonjurors and disenfranchised Jacobites, or so we may infer from a 1730 King Charles Day sermon preached by the Tory divine and pamphleteer Joseph Trapp before a congregation headed by Richard Brocas, Lord Mayor of London, and the sheriffs John Barber and John Williams. As Earbery does, Trapp melds his attacks on Walpole and Bolingbroke. His sermon illustrates the proximity of the Carolinist and pro-government positions on Bolingbrokean polemics and so calls attention to the fissure in the opposition created by disagreements about the proper application of seventeenth-century history.

Trapp was not a nonjuror; and there is no reason to think that he was a Jacobite, or even that he had been one in the 1710s, when the term had a more precise meaning. Hearne, always friendly to nonjurors and Jacobites and generally unfriendly to everyone else, abhorred Trapp's dual position as a juring clergyman and an opponent of Walpole's administration; he regarded Trapp as a lackey jockeying for preferment within the church that he (Hearne) had left.[39] But Trapp's opposition credentials were in order and had been at least since the days of Queen Anne, when he published the first of his many anti-Whig or (later) anti-Walpole pamphlets. In 1711 he wrote a lively tract ridiculing the emergence of the newly wrought Whiggery, which he regarded as symbolic of the errors of the Revolution Settlement and, more specifically, as "weakening the just and legal Powers both of the Ecclesiastical and Civil Constitution" (*The Character and Principles of the Present Set of Whigs* [1711], 394). Trapp would later write a number of sophisticated anti-Walpole essays for the *Grub-street Journal*; as late as 1738, he would chide the administration for having failed to carry the Excise Bill in 1733, and would ridicule Walpole's positions on dissent, the Stage Licensing Act of 1737, and military involvement with Spain.[40] Some of Trapp's positions—the opposition to the Excise Bill and the mistrust of Walpole's pacifism—indicate a sympathy with the Bolingbrokean platform. Some—the cynicism about Whiggery and the Revolution Settlement and the hostility toward dissent—do not.

Trapp's distance from any clear party line is evident throughout the 1730 sermon.[41] The City functionaries provided a good audience for Trapp. Given what was at least a tincture of Jacobitism in City government at the time, Trapp could express his fondness for divine-right monarchy without fear of giving offense.[42] Given the nature of the day itself, he could praise Charles I without having to feign devotion to the exiled Pretender or even to the Stuarts after Charles I.[43] And of course he was under no obligation to placate the national government with which the City was perenially at odds.

The sermon was in part a transparent attack on policy under George II and Walpole. In a sarcastic aside on the Commonwealth, Trapp snarls, "What glorious *Liberty* was it to be ruled by the *lawless arbitrary Will* and *Pleasure* of a *base usurping Tyrant*, or *Tyrants*, back'd and supported by a *standing Army!*" (14). The analogy of Cromwell's army and George II's peacetime band of Hessian mercenaries would have been plain as day to any reader of the *Craftsman* or *Fog's Weekly Journal* in the late 1720s or early in 1730, or to any follower of Parliament in the same period.[44] (And although a polemicist like Bolingbroke might try to deny that his essays were intended as analogies, to make such a claim about a sermon, an analogic genre by nature, would be absurd.) In the dedication to Brocas, Barber, and Williams that he appended to the sermon, Trapp seemed anxious to fly his "opposition" colors. He laments Cromwell's destruction of "the *Rights, Liberty,* and *Property* of the *Subject*" and his practice of "*Tyranny* and *arbitrary Power*" (n.p.). Were Trapp not also suggestively criticizing the erosion of monarchic privilege during the Commonwealth (and were he not speaking in a church), one might be forgiven for mistaking him for such as Bolingbroke.

Or such as Pitt, Arnall, or Hervey—and this is the key to the sermon itself, tonally speaking. As in the dedication, where Trapp drifts in and out of the local concerns of the Bolingbrokean opposition, in the sermon proper he again shows little regard for the conventional markers of political "sides." Trapp's treatment of the twin themes of "liberty" and the Civil War strengthens this sense of nonaffiliation by suggesting that Trapp was as unconvinced by Bolingbroke's platitudes as he was by Walpole's. "It will ever be found, as it ever has been," he observes, "that Those who make the greatest Noise about *Liberty,* when it is [in] no Danger, intend to *destroy* That *Liberty,* and make *Themselves Tyrants:* And when they are so, are of *all* Tyrants the *worst* and most *insupportable*" (13). Of course Trapp is talking about the regicides here, and at least one contemporary reader believed that he intended a nod as well at the Revolution and its beneficiaries.[45] But we have seen that many people were making a good bit of "noise about liberty" in the 1730s. The phrase "when it is [in] no danger" is reduced to nonsense if we suppose that Trapp intended it to designate Walpole's own noisemakers—themselves, of course, funded to reiterate precisely the sort of appeal to the status quo that Trapp offers here. The *Craftsman*, not the *London Journal* or the *Free Briton*, seems to be on Trapp's mind. "Liberty" is an unstable quantity in his sermon, a vague gesture of affiliation with the Bolingbrokean opposition, but finally a red herring. The word is the cant of the Revolution-worshippers, and as such is subordinate in Trapp's schema to his paeans to divine-right monarchy and his criticism of the modern nation still obligated, Trapp maintains, "to make God forget This most horrid Murder and Parricide" by "for ever . . . remember[ing] it Ourselves" (22).

The somber call for penance with which Trapp concludes his sermon is a motif in eighteenth-century Carolinist polemics. The question whether or not England was bound continually to seek absolution for the sins of the regicides was a frequent point of contention among high- and low-churchmen who preached on King Charles Day. The author of *Anti-Papismus: Or, a Letter to Dr. Trapp* (1731), a hostile response to Trapp's sermon, found in Trapp's use of the motif an echo of the nonjuror Thomas Brett, who, the pamphleteer claims, "rendered the Priesthood superior to God himself; pronouncing *ex Cathedra*, That our *Repentance and Conversion cannot blot out our Sins*" (20). The linkage of Trapp and a professed anti-Hanoverian is convenient for the anonymous polemicist, although it would have irritated both Trapp and Brett. But what matters most here is the evasive mythopoeia of the "perpetual atonement" claim. The argument, a hardy holdover from the King Charles Day sermons of the seventeenth century, is expressed most famously in Jonathan Swift's 1726 King Charles Day sermon.[46] Like Swift's sermon but with greater topicality, Trapp's sermon sidesteps the discussion of libertarianism and social change that by 1731 was characteristic of the Bolingbrokean opposition. For Trapp, as for earlier Carolinist polemicists, the endless carping about "liberty" is beside the point, a ridiculous plea for privilege by a nation polluted by a rank antimonarchism that had been declared in the 1640s and reinforced repeatedly since.

Carolinism's bleak and focused dismissiveness is not an aberration in literary history. One may find an analogous frame of mind in the Scriblerians' tendency to use Rome under Caesar Augustus as a yardstick against which to measure England under Walpole.[47] In Pope's *Epilogue to the Satires* (1738), for instance, the poet mixes ideality and hopelessness in a manner reminiscent of Carolinist rhetoric. Perhaps Swift's Augustinianism comes to mind as well—his belief that by "projecting" schemes of perfection, postlapsarian humankind only advertises its innate foolishness. Or one may find in the Carolinist position an anticipation of the reactionary fulminations of Thomas Carlyle, who, in *Past and Present* (1843) posited a stern but ideal past in opposition to the Benthamite "Greatest-Happiness Principle," a privileging of commercial and personal expression that looks something like Bolingbrokean theories of "liberty" filtered through the Industrial Revolution. It is no coincidence that the very pious and very angry Swift and Carlyle both operated uncomfortably outside the more doctrinaire and telic political schemata of friends like Bolingbroke or Charles Dickens and (late in his life) John Stuart Mill. Both Swift and Carlyle, like the Carolinist polemicists, rejected the secular premises on which the debates of their own times were predicated. And both, like the Carolinists, believed in their darker moods that a culture in collapse was a culture beyond the reach of the easy nostrums of practical politics—hence Swift's suffusive despair and hence the militant intolerance of Carlyle's later polemical essays.

An oppressive sense of irreversible decay is fundamental to Carolinism, as it cannot be to a polemics based, like Bolingbroke's, on a cyclical model of history. Several poems in *Phoenix Britannicus* (1732), Joseph Morgan's miscellany of seventeenth- and eighteenth-century nonce pieces, emphasize what their authors take to be the fundamental inversion of cultural priorities effected by the puritan assumption of power and prolonged by the modern tendency to restrict the royal prerogative. As it will later be for the *Grub-street Journal*, Cromwell's corruption of the Stuart maxim "No Bishop, No King" is at the root of the problem.[48] Representative verses from 1661 rather ingeniously pair Cromwell and Laud as the king's nemeses and as the progenitors of the modern vogue of populism:

> A *Scot* and *Jesuit* join'd in Hand,
>   First taught the World to say,
> That Subjects ought to have Command,
>   And Princes to Obey.

> They both agreed to have no King;
> The *Scotchman* he cries further,
> No Bishop: 'tis a Godly Thing
> States to reform by Murther.[49]

Leaving aside the fact that Bolingbroke's antiepiscopalianism was a refrain in Carolinist polemics, one may still note that in Bolingbrokean polemics, negative examples from history—analogous to this early bit of doggerel—have cautionary or exemplary value: they are markers of what ought not to have happened before and what might happen again to a culture unmindful of its history. But in Carolinist polemics, the negative example—*the* negative example, that is—is a moment that replays itself endlessly, always condemning the present but never offering, as Bolingbroke does, the possibility of regeneration or rectification. The pitch of the undistinguished verses from *Phoenix Britannicus* rises as the poet deduces from the regicide a vision of ultimate, omnidirectional threat unlike Bolingbroke's (at least implicit) optimism, but very much of a piece with the fear of anarchy expressed in eighteenth-century works like *The Dunciad* or Swift's playful but strongly Augustinian "excremental verses":

> The King dethron'd! the Subjects bleed!
> The Church hath no Abode:
> Let us conclude they're all agreed,
> That sure there is no GOD.
>
> (175)

Like Pope in *The Dunciad*, the poet fears the Godless society. Unlike Pope, however, the scribbler-at-hand finds a precise causal relationship between a specific political phenomenon—the erosion of the royal prerogative—and a general social and moral collapse. The poem, in this typically Carolinist and utterly un-Bolingbrokean, is not interested in how to undo the damage done to England in the middle of the previous century, or, even, in how to avoid a reenactment of it.

5
Carolinism and the Church: The *Grub-street Journal* and the Curious Case of Dr. Francis Hare

ACCORDING to his modern biographer, by the 1730s Bolingbroke had decided that "religious issues, in particular the privileged position of the Church of England, did not excite such passionate debates as twenty years earlier."[1] As Bolingbroke certainly realized, this was a safe stance in a period wary of reviving the divisiveness that had characterized relations among church, state, and populace in England for much of the seventeenth and early eighteenth centuries. The 1720s and '30s were generally more attracted to the ease of low churchmen like White Kennett than to the stridency of "high fliers" like Bolingbroke's one-time crony Francis Atterbury, the Jacobite bishop who had been banished to France in 1723. But Bolingbroke's unwillingness to debate "religious issues" placed him at odds with the Carolinist opposition, defenders of the muscular union of monarchy and church epitomized in the relationship of Charles I and William Laud, and localized in an England not yet vitiated by the Civil War and the Revolution.

This chapter comprises two analyses of the role of Carolinism in Anglican apologetics, both of which illustrate the diversity and the complexity of political rhetoric in the 1730s and so illuminate the fallacy behind Bolingbroke's uniformitarian program for the opposition. I shall first examine the religious, political, and historiographical program of Richard Russel's Carolinist weekly, the *Grub-street Journal* (1730–37). The *Journal*'s opposition to Walpole was tempered by its dedication to high-church apologetics; consequently the weekly was often at odds with the secular Bolingbrokean opposition. By faulting modern government for its failure to replicate the Caroline symbiosis of monarchy and episcopacy, Russel consigned the *Journal* to the fringes of the opposition, or at least Bolingbroke's construction of it. The *Craftsman*'s lack of interest in the *Journal*—a contrast to its harassment of the pro-government papers and its generally laudatory notices of *Fog's Weekly Journal*—suggests either that the *Craftsman* did not know what to make of the *Journal* or that it found no reason to make anything of it at all. But this probably says more about the *Craftsman*'s habit of ignoring fissures in the opposition than it does about the *Journal*. The *Journal* could not have been easy to overlook: a surviving ledger proves that the paper was printed in significant quantities during its first fourteen months, the only period covered by the document. These data and numerous references to the *Journal* in other papers suggest that a good number of people were talking about the *Journal*, even if the *Craftsman* chose not to.[2]

The Carolinist strain may or may not have contributed substantially to the *Journal*'s success. At the very least, however, the data indicate that Carolinism was "in the air" in the early 1730s. There is more, and more precise, evidence. In the second part of this chapter, I illustrate the pro-government press's anxiety about Carolinist rhetoric by investigating the controversy surrounding a 1732 King Charles Day sermon by Francis Hare, the Walpolite bishop of Chichester and dean of St. Paul's. Hare's encomiastic sermon on Charles was condemned as antigovernment in spite of strong evidence that Hare did not intend it to be so. The controversy found Walpole's hireling Thomas Gordon denouncing Hare, Earbery quite nearly endorsing him, and the *Grub-street Journal* evidently confused by the whole business. The heat of the controversy, like the data on Russel's weekly, suggests that Carolinism was a familiar mode of political thought in the 1730s, and one capable of arousing considerable debate. More broadly, both the paper and the sermon remind us that there was little agreement in the period about precisely what qualified as opposition rhetoric.

Although no one denies that the *Grub-street Journal* was primarily interested in literary matters (typically controversial ones), there is general agreement that the paper was in some measure sympathetic to the opposition. Even James Hillhouse, the author of the only book on the *Journal* and a scholar generally disinclined to question the *Journal*'s satiric claim of political neutrality, grudgingly concedes that "what political leanings [the *Journal*] betrays are Tory, and Jacobite." Bertrand Goldgar, who calls Hillhouse's appraisal "an understatement," believes that "the *Journal* showed a constant bias against the administration." More recently, Brean Hammond has acknowledged, although not examined, the *Journal*'s interest in opposition politics.³

But the *Journal*'s politics need to be clarified if we are to understand its status both as an organ against Walpole and as a challenge to Bolingbrokean hegemony. The easy labeling of the *Journal* as a "Jacobite" paper, for instance, is difficult to reconcile with the paper's absence from the abundant literature that chronicles the Jacobite movement.⁴ The *Journal* was not in sympathy with the reformulated Jacobitism of the period 1715 to 1745, when City coalitions and party politics replaced treasonous intercourse with the Pretender and his transient foreign allies. The *Journal*'s correspondent "Timothy Zeal" was justified in mocking Walpole's preoccupation with sniffing out international Jacobite intrigue in the '30s (No. 258; 5 Dec. 1734). Lucy Sutherland argues that by the end of the Walpole era, Jacobitism was absorbed into the City nexus of "united parliamentary Oppositions, composed of combinations of discontented whigs and broken tories."⁵ However much scholars might debate the currency or potency of English Jacobitism between the two rebellions, it is clear enough that a relatively high concentration of this uncertain quantity was localized in the City and in Parliament. "Caleb D'Anvers" and his cabinet of refurbished Whigs catered to the amalgam that Sutherland identifies, but Russel did not.

The *Journal* deduced its political opinions from the anachronistic religious tenets of the nonjuring clergyman Russel, the paper's principal writer and shareholder as well as its editor.⁶ Unlike his fellow nonjuror Earbery, Russel did not engage in a systematic program of harassment against Bolingbroke. Rather, his opinions conformed to or contradicted those of the mainstream opposition depending on whether or not the opposition was discussing matters pertinent to the church or approachable by way of church history—or, of course, by way of Caroline England. While Earbery's hostility to Bolingbroke and the *Craftsman* was virtually a matter of policy, Russel's interests alternately intersect, ignore, and deviate from the interests of the Bolingbrokean opposition.

This was inconvenient for pro-government writers, who, as I have shown, were always eager to homogenize the opposition in order to dismiss it more easily. In an essay that begins as an attack on the *Craftsman*, James Pitt ("Francis Osborne") turns to Russel in order to portray the opposition as a collection of "Nonjuring *Jacobite* Priests, shabby wandring, vicious, ignorant

Parsons *without a Cure*, Night-House-Wits, and beggarly Poet-tasters" (*London Journal* 565; 30 May 1730).⁷ Pitt is trying far too hard to hang the anticlerical (and nonmendicant, and nonpoetical) Bolingbroke and Russel by the same rope. His attempt to conflate journals as distinct as the *Craftsman* and the *Grub-street Journal* is self-evidently absurd and finally points up the diversity that he wishes to deny.

Later commentators have been no more inclined than Pitt to see substantive differences between the *Journal* and the bulk of the opposition press. Only one reader, in a short essay published over a century ago, has noted the nonfraternal relationship between the *Grub-street Journal* and both the *Craftsman* and *Fog's Weekly Journal*. Writing in 1888, W. Roberts called the *Grub-street Journal* the "persistent rival" of the *Craftsman* and claimed that "the conductors of [the *Grub-street Journal*] apparently had an inveterate hatred for *Mist's Journal*, *Fog's Journal*, *The Craftsman*, and the *Daily Journal*."⁸ The *Grub-street Journal*'s dislike of the pro-government *Daily Journal* is no surprise; and one wonders why Roberts, who notes that *Mist's Weekly Journal* had become *Fog's Weekly Journal* in 1728, supposes that the *Grub-street Journal* had any interest in the defunct *Mist's* at all. But the comment about the *Journal*'s "hatred" of *Fog's* and the *Craftsman*, if overstated, is not inaccurate. Goldgar notes that *Fog's Weekly Journal* had accused the *Grub-street Journal* of being in league with the ministry; and in *Grub-street Journal* 84 (12 Aug. 1731), Russel remarks that the *Craftsman* had also charged the *Journal* with writing for Walpole.⁹ Such claims are useless on their own terms, but they do suggest the ambiguity of the *Journal*'s political posture. Indeed, the sparring with *Fog's* becomes comprehensible only when one realizes that the *Journal* had twitted that weekly for religious heterodoxy.¹⁰

The *Journal*'s conservative political and religious stance is part and parcel of its basic satiric pretense. In his preface to the *Memoirs of the Society of Grub-street* (2 vols., 1737), Russel allies the current generation of pro-government scribblers to the "Grubeans" from "the seditious times of King CHARLES I . . . [who] from their garrets and cellars dispersed those false reports and reasonings, which were very instrumental in stirring up the people at last to a rebellion" (1:i).¹¹ The ethos of this earlier England provides the raw materials of Russel's own conservatism:

> There is a fashion in Learning, Politics, and Religion, as well as in Cloaths; and the alteration of the fashion in those is as unaccount-

able, tho' not so frequent, as in these. As it is not always the effect of reason and conviction, but proceeds from accidental and external motives, this change in reading, principle, and practice, is sometimes for the worse; as persons lay aside rich, convenient, and decent habits, as old-fashioned, to put on those of a newer mode, tho' meaner, inconvenient, and indecent. (1:vi)

Russel perhaps intends a sideswipe at the *Craftsman*, defenders of the press and critics of Charles's suppression of free expression; here he sounds like Earbery, who in *Occasional Historian* 3 (1731) had approved Charles's actions against antigovernment journalists.[12] In any case, Russel's longing for the functional garb of divine-right monarchy repeatedly leads him back to Caroline England. Pat Rogers finds in Russel's preface a "significant correlation of Grub Street with puritan publicism at the time of the Civil War."[13] The "correlation" is in fact the basis of the *Journal*'s political rhetoric throughout its run.

Carolinism was Russel's alternative to a Jacobitism now distant from the tenets of the nonjurors that had once given it its spiritual ballast—tenets in which Russel, like Earbery, passionately believed. This somewhat stale orthodoxy accounts for the aura of anachronism that hovers around much of the religious writing in the *Grub-street Journal* and helps distinguish it from the more overtly "political" opposition press. Many of the entries on religion address interests common only to the few who shared Russel's extreme orthodoxy. A piece on the Usages Controversy (No. 17; 30 Apr. 1730) takes up an internecine quarrel among the nonjurors; the *Journal* acknowledges the public's lack of interest in prolonged religious controversy even as it persists in satirizing those nonjurors who would resolve the controversy. A defense of eastward adoration—a high-church tenet the merits of which had been debated earlier in the century[14]—would have had still less contemporary appeal (No. 121; 27 Apr. 1732).

Such concerns were hardly modish in the 1730s, and Bolingbroke was not alone in regarding "religious matters" as unworthy of discussion. Writing in 1742, the Walpolite *Dunciad*-dweller John Oldmixon claimed that as early as the 1720s "the stale Cry of the Church's danger became indeed ridiculous"; he taxed the "Jacobite and inveterate Tory faction" with artificially maintaining the musty argument for divine-right monarchy in order to undermine the new succession.[15] Oldmixon conveniently (and conventionally) inflated the threat of Jacobitism; but it is hard to discount his claim about the decline of the "church in danger" faction. Like Jacobites, nonjurors were a vanishing breed. The seven bishops who had refused to swear loyalty to William III were all dead by 1730, and the repressive legislation of the first quarter of the century induced many of their successors to conform. Abjuration Oaths of 1701–2 and 1714 deprived the rank and file of souls less stalwart than Russel, who paid for his refusal to swear the latter oath with the loss of two livings. A 1722 legislative attack on both nonjurors and Catholics, brought about by the Atterbury plot of that year and retrospectively ridiculed in *Grub-street Journal* numbers 142 (21 Sept. 1732) and 341 (8 July 1736), authorized domestic confinement, seizure of property, further taxation, and further demands for formal abjuration. Predictably, the ranks again diminished.[16] Although one should not dismiss lightly the substance of a body of men that included theologians and controversialists like Thomas Hearne, Thomas Brett, and Richard Rawlinson, nonjurors were by Russel's time probably best known to the public through caricatures such as Colley Cibber's Tartuffean Dr. Wolf in *The Nonjuror* (1717), a play that was revived briefly in 1734.[17]

By 1730, then, a devout nonjuror like Russel would have seemed a transplant from a time remote from Erastianism and loyalty oaths, a time that had perhaps ended with the flight of Atterbury. A sneer at this disjunctive status underlies Pitt's reference to the *Journal*'s "nonjuring, *Jacobite* Priests." The epithet demonstrates the tendency to rely upon a monolithic presentation of a stance equally religious and political, the specifics of which had been blurred by time.[18] The merger was expedient for the ministerial press and had long been a staple of its offensive strategy. Pro-government writers had rarely troubled themselves with distinctions between Jacobites and nonjurors; and by the late teens, as Henry Offley Wakeman noted some years back, "the Whigs determined to make their position secure by treating all Tories as if they were Jacobites, and all High Churchmen as if they were both."[19]

This facile conflation might have been justly condemned by anyone sympathetic to the opposition. Indeed, we have already seen the acrobatics that Bolingbroke performed to distinguish his "country" opposition from Toryism, Jacobitism, or indeed any formal ideology whatsoever. But the *Journal* is not offended by the pro-government attempt to gather the opposition under the old aegis of the high church. Its response to Pitt's reductive attack opens with an ostensibly reluctant abandonment of the mask of disinterestedness originally donned in number 3 (22 Jan. 1730):

> Tho' this Society passed a Resolution, Jan. 21. not to publish any Political Dissertations in their *Journal*, yet since several of our Members do it weekly in other Papers, those Dissertations come properly under our cognizance, and we ought to commend or censure those, whose labours in that kind deserve either our approbation or our animadversion. (No. 22; 4 June 1730)

Russel here ironically presents the *Journal* as descending to political discussion only as an exercise in literary criticism. What follows, however, is more notable for its refusal to distinguish between opposition politics and Caroline religion than for any appraisal of the literary endeavors of Russel's staff. Russel aligns Pitt with Charles's murderers and charges him with having "taken upon him intirely to alter the old Martyrology, striking out at once all the Martyrs of Antiquity, and placing in their room a new set of Saints, even the Rebels of Forty one [i.e., 1641]." The accusations tendered against the *Journal* are puffed into the moral prerogatives of a righteous opposition:

> I think it much more reputable to be a *Parson without a Cure*, or a *beggarly Poetaster*, speaking or writing his own real sentiments, as occasion offers, than to be a *Parson* highly preferred, or a well-fed *Poetaster*, vilely prostituting his pen for pay to the dictates of others.

Russel equates the Whig anti-Carolinists, the latitudinarian clergy, and the Grubean lackeys of Walpole; but he does not bother to question the connection between his politics and his status as a nonjuror.

As a committed nonjuror, Russel could assure himself that the corruption that he saw in the government was the consequence of a ruptured succession. He could thus locate his objections to the government on the level of efficient causes. His political stance is a series of corollaries from a single proposition: the government was damned at the outset by its refutation of divine right. Local abuses—patronage, excise bills, and so forth—were merely the wages of sin. To Russel no less than Earbery, William III and the Hanoverians were guilty of allowing the erosion of monarchic privilege and the compensatory elevation of secular government. In verses by Russel (No. 96; 4 Nov. 1731) and in a vigorous essay probably written by Joseph Trapp (No. 62; 11

Mar. 1731),[20] pro-government "grubs" are accused of sanctioning Parliament's appropriation of privileges traditionally reserved for the monarch. Goldgar is correct in regarding Trapp's essay as a denunciation of the ministry,[21] but what counts is the causal sequence behind the corruption that it attacks: Erastianism, not Walpole, is Trapp's complaint. Russel later argues that the glorification of secular government forces kings, now de facto electees, to become "beasts of burthen" to the mob (No. 167; 8 Mar. 1733). Predictably, he traces the inversion to Oliver Cromwell.[22]

The discord that must follow the untuning of the sacred string of divine right is the subject of several leaders in which the *Journal* portrays the Hanoverians' repeated demands for loyalty oaths as doctrinal proof of unstable government. The *Journal* states the essence of its grievance against the oaths in number 341 (8 July 1736): "All state Oaths are the product of human invention . . . they are, indeed, of a very modern date, and have all been prostituted to servile ends and purposes. They are the natural offspring of divisions in principles of Religion and Government." This essay and an earlier piece (No. 281; 15 May 1735) present multiple oaths as invitations to opportunism and insincerity, as novelties unknown elsewhere in the Christian world, and as irreligious attempts to understand matters properly beyond the scope of human comprehension.[23]

State oaths are emblems of the new dispensation ushered in by the Revolution. To one such as Russel, the recent Abjuration Oaths both accented the distance of Hanoverian from Stuart England and suggested the modern era's dedication to the new and vicious values installed with the Revolution Settlement. The *Journal* sets its sights on the errors of 1688 in a mock vindication of "the ingenious and learned pieces published in defence of the [Abjuration] oaths, which fully explain the nature of our constitution, as placed upon a new basis at the Revolution" (No. 142; 21 Sept. 1732). The essay, probably by Trapp, begins as satire but quickly becomes invective.[24] The author taxes "those who injoined" the oaths—the "declared enemies to all implicit blind obedience"—with creating an unmanageable activism among a citizenry previously content to regard divine-right monarchy as a condition of reasonable government:

> It has been frequently matter of wonder to me, that some persons, who pretend to be the greatest friends to our excellent constitution, should blame this inquisitive temper of our people, and censure them for meddling with matters relating to government; since they

were formerly, and many of them are still, obliged either to swear with their eyes shut . . . or else to inquire into the rights of princes; and consequently, either to become formally perjured, or to become politicians.

Oaths demanded in support of the spurious monarchy, that is, make one a hypocrite or a revisionist—or an affiliate of the opposition. This portrayal of the post-Revolution political system suits Russel perfectly and exemplifies an opposition politics based on historical imperative rather than immediate practical interest.

The *Grub-street Journal* did at times share an interest in City politics with its supposed fellows in the opposition. But Russel's hatred of the religious dissent prevalent among anti-Walpole City merchants (and defended in the *Craftsman*) tempered any enthusiasm he might have felt for the Jacobites' move into political amalgamation.[25] Although, as Goldgar points out, the *Journal* "sometimes spoke directly on political issues, especially when they involved the City of London," it sometimes did not do so, or did so in ways that accent its lack of sympathy with the *Craftsman*'s pro-City program.[26]

The *Journal* plays the party line when it harangues William Arnall's pro-government *Free Briton* for its criticism of the high-church and Jacobitical Common Council (Nos. 97, 98, 99; 11, 18, 25 Nov. 1731), and when it notes the increasing disregard of George II's court for the City (No. 330; 22 Apr. 1736). But the tenuousness of the *Journal*'s relationship with the City opposition is evident in its response to the Excise Crisis of 1732–33, one of the rare occasions on which, as George Rudé notes, "City Radicalism . . . harnessed the political energies of the capital as a whole."[27] There is no doubt that the *Journal* disapproved of Walpole's scheme for broader and more invasive forms of taxation. Its interest in the Excise Bill, however, hardly kept pace with the prevailing frenzy: from November 1732 to March 1733, while every *Craftsman* concerned either the Excise Bill or Walpole's pleas for a fortified standing army, the *Journal* presented only one leader on the excise (No. 164; 15 Feb. 1733). If one is to agree with Goldgar that "in 1733 the *Journal* consistently attacked Walpole's excise scheme," one must also acknowledge that its attacks were not nearly as "consistent" as the *Craftsman*'s.[28]

Nor were they similar in tone to the *Craftsman*'s strident essays. The *Journal* registers surprisingly few direct hits against the bill. During the height of the crisis, the *Journal* offered only the following pronouncements: a punning bit of bawdry called "The CONSTITUTION Clap'd," in which the bill is likened to "a pox . . . [that] Must ruin the constitution" (No. 160; 18 Jan. 1733); a letter from the stupid, opportunistic, and upwardly mobile "Will Traffick," in support of the bill (No. 164; 15 Feb. 1733); and an essay by Russel chiding Arnall for his hostility toward the anti-excise Common Council (No. 173; 19 Apr. 1733). The *Journal*'s opposition to the bill is oddly out of focus. A potentially strong blast from one "Oliver Grub" appears some thirteen months after Walpole had withdrawn the bill (No. 230; 23 May 1734). Other anti-excise pieces are unabashedly silly. A "*humble REMONSTRANCE of the ladies in and about the cities of London and Westminster*" against "*any further extension of the laws of excise*" (No. 164; 15 Feb. 1733) is more concerned with winking genital references and the supposed frivolity of women than with the bill proper.[29] A promising satirical attack on the role of the *Craftsman* in the anti-excise movement, published two days after Walpole withdrew the bill, degenerates into a derivative proposal that the excise be extended to "a staple commodity, called *Dullness*" (No. 172; 12 Apr. 1733).[30] The nod to Pope is more important here than the articulation of any clear political stance. Hero worship, not opposition to the excise, carries the day.

The *Journal*'s assault on the bill is often retrogressive and indirect, and again attests to Russel's identification with the politics and religion of Caroline England. "The CONSTITUTION Clap'd," for instance, introduces its criticism of the bill by positing a connection between supporters of the excise and the puritan rebels of the previous century. This conceit also informs the letter from "Will Traffick." The conflict that this poses to the *Craftsman* is clear: the very terms of the *Journal*'s opposition to the bill stress Russel's disagreement with the *Craftsman*'s stance on Caroline history. Russel and his writers criticize the bill by comparing its supporters to the puritan rebels routinely exonerated in the *Craftsman*—the locus of anti-excise sentiment.

That this conflict registered in Russel as ambivalence toward the *Craftsman*'s campaign against the bill is suggested by the relative paucity of material against the bill in the *Journal* and by the unsettled or evasive tone of much of what the *Journal* did print on the subject. In an epigram published during what proved to be the final week of the battle against the bill (No. 171;

5 Apr. 1733), Russel leaves no doubt that his skepticism about (in particular) Bolingbroke had tempered his enthusiasm for the campaign against the bill. With the anti-excise forces on the verge of victory, Russel was qualifying his support by sniping at Bolingbroke. He opens the verses by again pairing Cromwellians and their latter-day equivalents. But he now uses the comparison to comment caustically on the "country party," the seventeenth-century denomination that Bolingbroke had borrowed for his own allegedly non-partisan assemblage of libertarians:

> In forty one, on godly ends intent,
> Poor men in crowds petition'd parliament.
> The country party thought them all profound heads:
> The Court abusively nick-nam'd 'em round heads.
> But modern courtiers give their approbation,
> To all those steps that led to reformation.

The Carolinist distaste for populism is evident here, as it is whenever the *Journal* discusses the antimonarchic faction of the 1640s. More fundamentally, Russel accuses the populist "country party"—the puritan insurrectionists—of political maneuvering in Parliament. As readers familiar with his position on Charles I and the Civil War would have realized, this was virtual sedition to Russel. The parallel to Bolingbroke and the *Craftsman* is unmistakable; and what is finally most striking about the epigram is the nexus of "country party" and "modern courtiers" and, barely beyond the verses, Bolingbrokeans. The conflation of Bolingbrokeans and Walpolites, that staple of Carolinist polemics, is irresistible to Russel even as he was lending some measure of support to a cause that Bolingbroke championed.

The epigram's concluding couplet, then, can hardly have come as a surprise: "In every age all courtiers are the same; / And, as the Great direct, applaud, or blame." The tone is one of weariness and generalized disgust, and the charge that lingers is the one levelled against the "godly ends" of the Cromwellians and those whom Russel takes to be their modern apologists. The verses are more or less equally hostile to the bill, its promoters, and its most famous opponents. Russel was not to be "harnessed" alongside of such as Bolingbroke in Rudé's sturdy team of "City Radical[s]."

Shortly after the Excise Crisis, the *Grub-street Journal* and the *Craftsman* again lined up on the same side of an issue, this time without any evident reservation on Russel's part. But the *Jour-*

nal's position on the unsuccessful motion for the repeal of the Test and Corporation Acts in 1736 reminds us, no less than its role in the anti-excise campaign does, that Russel operated from very different premises than the *Craftsman* did, even after Bolingbroke's departure from England in 1735.

Archibald Foord notes that in 1736 the parliamentary opposition was "sadly riven" by proceedings on such measures as the Quakers' Tythes Bill and the proposed repeal of the Test and Corporation Acts.[31] The *Craftsman* had suddenly embraced the cause of dissent in August 1733, but it had offered no convincing reason for doing so and had therefore left itself open to the charge of opportunism.[32] *Fog's Weekly Journal*, on the other hand, seems to have been consistently skeptical about repeal.[33] One might expect the *Grub-street Journal*, with its attachment to clerical privilege and its antipathy to dissent, to have sided with the vocal-if-vestigial "church in danger" faction in the matter of repeal, as it did in the debate about the Quaker Bill.[34] But the *Journal* reached beyond simple reaction and opted for a vindication of repeal on the grounds of Christian doctrine. The *Journal* again subordinated political to religious considerations and developed its position through a thoughtful and extended analogy between the nonjurors—those who had refused to swear—and the contemporary dissenters—those of whom swearing was continually demanded.

The doctrinal nature of the *Journal's* opposition to "state Oaths" is laid out in a quotation reprinted from a speech before Parliament by George Savile, marquis of Halifax, in which Halifax had objected to the Test Act of 1673. Halifax had wondered

> whether assertory Oaths, which were properly appointed to give testimony of a matter of fact . . . can lawfully be made use of to confirm or invalidate *doctrinal* propositions; and whether that legislative power, which imposes such an Oath, doth not necessarily assume to itself an infallibility.

Halifax had consulted church history and concluded that Grotius "seems to make it clear, that such [multiple] Oaths are forbidden by our Saviour in the Gospel" (No. 341; 8 July 1736).

The nonjuror Russel agreed. He and Halifax are strange bedfellows. It was the Williamite Halifax whose parliamentary maneuvering had ensured that James II would not be invited back to England after his "abdication," and it was he who had engaged James in a battle of rhetorical one-upmanship for the affection of the dissenting interest.[35] The *Journal* could have sought historical sanction for its position on repeal from James himself, but it turned instead to his rival. Is the *Journal* passing judgment on the sincerity of James's on-again, off-again courtship of dissent—or, more to the point, on his intermittent demands for loyalty oaths? Quite possibly so; and if so, we are reminded, as we were by Earbery's journalism and Trapp's King Charles Day sermon, that Carolinism is not Jacobitism and does not imply any obligation to the later Stuarts. In any case, the *Journal* endorses and extends Halifax's argument. The author concludes the discussion of oaths by wondering whether "from such shameful and unchristian practices, we can expect, nothing but political Swearing and Tests, which is a strange method of propagating the Protestant religion."

A similar objection is voiced by an anonymous dissenter who argues that repeal is part and parcel of "our duty as Christians, as Protestants, and as Dissenters" (No. 325; 18 Mar. 1736). Hillhouse identifies this as a "devout and pious utterance,"[36] but he fails to comment on the significance of the *Journal*'s sympathy with a body that it had long treated with contempt. The *Journal*'s position on repeal is clearly anti-Walpole; the method by which it reaches it, however, is neither Jacobitical nor Bolingbrokean. By following it, the *Journal* again indicates its irregular status in the opposition.

Although nonjurors like Russel were prohibited from preaching publicly, the pulpit played a vital role in the eighteenth-century debate about Charles I. King Charles Day sermons were mandated by law until 1858, and were required equally of those churchmen who cherished the memory of Charles I and those who despised it.[37] Not surprisingly, there was considerable disagreement about the proper method of observing the day. Two mutually hostile treatments of Charles recur in the sermons preached from the Revolution until the fall of Walpole in 1742. Pro-government bishops typically used the occasion to condemn the factious 1640s and to recite the blessings of the Hanoverian succession. Their version of recent history was Whig meliorism at its most familiar, praising the Revolution as the antidote to civil and religious discord, and promoting the Hanoverian succession as the fulfillment of the Revolution. Charles is dredged up from an unhappy past once a year in order to call attention to the blessings of the "present happy establishment," to use one of the period's favorite clichés. White Kennett's sermon of 1720, noted in the previous chapter, is a case in point. Clerics sympathetic to the conservative high-church opposition, on the other hand, tended to present the regicide as a populist usurpation of benign monarchic power, an aberration that they found resurgent in Walpole and his network of placemen. Theirs is the "official" version of the Carolinist rhetoric practiced elsewhere by nonjurors like Hearne, Earbery, and Russel. Their sermons are animated by the analogic pairing of puritans and modern dissenters, puritans and Erastians, puritans and apologists for strong parliaments, and so forth. Trapp's 1730 sermon exemplifies the type.[38]

But if certain sermons tended to position clerics politically, they did not do so infallibly. As the split between William III and the original nonjuring bishops faded further into memory, there was less reason for the rhetoric of religion to replicate the battles of 1689, when to praise the old monarchy was unequivocally to blame the new. In their responses to Francis Hare's King Charles Day sermon of 1732, however, some pro-government polemicists were willing to ignore this simple truth and so to condemn the loyal but idiosyncratic Hare in virtually the same terms that they had previously reserved for declared enemies of Walpole. The Carolinist opposition proper, meanwhile, had a tough time figuring out what to make of Hare.

The controversy demonstrates that political argumentation in the 1730s authorized a strict correspondence between attitudes toward Charles I and attitudes toward the present government. But this "correspondence," closer analysis suggests, was spurious. Hare's debacle calls attention to a Carolinist rhetoric that operated across party lines and that became particularly volatile during the renewed agitation for the repeal of the Test and Corporation Acts in the early 1730s, prior to the concerted pro-repeal effort of 1736. Hare sought to protect the church from the encroachments of dissent that some of his pro-government colleagues regarded instead as reasonable pleas for rights or privileges. His militant position on dissent, although not anomalous within Whiggery, nonetheless tempted him into a rhetorical territory that his detractors could easily, if inaccurately, describe as antigovernment. Like the government's legal assault on Earbery, the hostile reaction to Hare suggests that when it suited them to do so, Walpole's apologists could regard Carolinist rhetoric as a threat on the order of, but distinct from, the Bolingbrokeanism that they were at other times content to regard as the "opposition."

Politically speaking, Hare had a good deal more in common

with Kennett than Trapp, as we may deduce from the fact that Hare, like Kennet twelve years earlier, had been selected to preach his sermon before the House of Lords. As one would expect of a cleric chosen to address the upper house on a potentially sensitive occasion, Hare had an impressive record of pro-government connections and activities. He had been tutor to the duke of Marlborough's son and to the young Robert Walpole, and in 1700 had written chummy letters to his "Dearest Bob," congratulating Walpole on his forthcoming marriage and, a few months later, consoling him on the death of his father. Hare had been Marlborough's chaplain during the Flanders campaign and his biographer after Blenheim; and he had written extensively in support of Marlborough's role in the war and against Swift, Mary de la Riviere Manley, and their fellow Harleyite Tories. Throughout his career, Hare was a favorite of both Walpole and Queen Caroline. He was offered the lucrative ushership of the Exchequer by Walpole in 1722. In the 1720s and 1730s, his other friends or correspondents in the government included Henry Pelham; Pelham's brother Thomas Pelham-Holles, the duke of Newcastle; and Edmund Gibson, bishop of London.[39] Hare seems just the sort of person to have treated the occasion as it had been treated by his immediate predecessors to the honor, the dully predictable William Bradshaw and Robert Clavering.[40] And to a certain extent he did this, offering ample praise to the establishment to which he owed his advancement. The Lords were satisfied with Hare's performance: they voted their thanks for the sermon and requested its publication.[41]

But within six weeks, Hare and his sermon were under fire from pro-government pamphleteers, who were in turn attacked by, among others, Earbery and an anonymous contributor to *Fog's Weekly Journal*.[42] One "P. C." invoked the habitual charge against the Jacobite opposition when he accused Hare of "engag[ing] on the Side of despotick Power" (*A Letter to [. . .] the Lord Bishop of Chichester*, 16). Walpole's hired hand Thomas Gordon recalled the old claims against Henry Sacheverell when he reviled Hare as "an Apologist who hides or adulterates the Truth" and "an Inflamer, who would create Rage and Strife" (4). In consecutive leaders, *Fog's* defended Hare against Gordon, accusing Gordon of "raking up all the Dirt and Stones you can meet with, to pelt the Clergy of the Church of *England*" (No. 187; 3 June 1732). Earbery, in his ultramonarchist *Universal Spy*, lashed Gordon for his anticlerical and anti-Caroline assault on Hare. Fourteen pamphlets or newspaper-leaders were published on the sermon;

some of the pamphlets went through several editions. Five editions of Gordon's pamphlet were published. Earbery acknowledged the "great sale" of this "pestiferous Libel," and *Fog's* lamented "the stupid Attention of the People to [Gordon's] incoherent Ravings" (No. 186; 27 May 1732).

Two related explanations address these curious alignments: one concerns what Hare said; the other, how he said it.

First, Hare's sermon is an argument against relief for dissenters. Hare to a certain extent invited the controversy by positioning himself against dissent at a time when the government was responding indecisively to agitation for the repeal of the Test and Corporation Acts. Hare's stance could have surprised no one. Although Hare had not entered the fray over the Occasional Conformity Act (1711) and the Schism Act (1714)—he would have been busy with the Marlborough pamphlets during the earlier and harder-fought campaign—he had often defended George I's antidissent position during the period 1709 to 1721. Hare had justly spoken of himself as an old hand against relief for dissenters in the preface to *Church-Authority Vindicated* (1719; 5), one of his three publications against the concessive low-churchmanship of bishop Benjamin Hoadly during the Bangorian Controversy, initiated by Hoadly's Erastian sermon before George I in March 1717. But the Bangorian Controversy, however astringent, was conducted as an examination of doctrinal difference rather than as an inquiry into political loyalty. Of the four responses to Hare's anti-Hoadly writing, for instance, none questions Hare's commitment to his government. As he would later in his career, Hare in his early work attempted both to support government policy on dissent and to discourage further concessions to dissent. And in the early part of the century, when Jacobitism was the more tangible threat, Hare's position apparently did not put him at odds with the Whig establishment.[43]

It need not have done so in 1732. N. C. Hunt has analyzed the increase in political activity among dissenters in the period 1731 to 1733. He observes that dissent cohered in response to Walpole's inability to relieve Irish dissenters, Parliament's failure to pass an Indemnity Act, the exclusion of dissenters from government posts in Liverpool, and the abuses of the Mansion House building fund, which extorted monies from dissenters both disqualified from serving public office and penalized for not doing so.[44] Hare was an early respondent to this resurgent "threat," but this does not make him unique among the Whiggish bishops of the period. Gibson, still powerful and very much in favor in 1732, was as outspoken against relief as Hare was. And Walpole was perenially oscillating between his need for the support of the dissenting interest and his reluctance to grant dissenters any but the token relief of the intermittent Indemnity Acts.[45] Several weeks after Hare preached his sermon, the Walpolite *London Journal*, supposedly under the thumb of Hare's opponent Gordon, would argue against repeal. The terms of its argument are less passionate than Hare's, but its ultimate position is identical.[46]

In its strictures against repeal, Hare's sermon also recalls a 1726 King Charles Day sermon by his old adversary Swift—not a great admirer of Walpole's government, I need hardly add. Hare irritated his future assailants by arguing, as Swift had, that observance of the day remained an act of national penance, or even a measure of national security.[47] And Hare's sermon is part of a more nearly contemporaneous body of nonce literature that includes "church-in-danger" pamphlets by Gibson and Swift, as well as the arch-Anglican periodicals the *Grub-street Journal* and the *Weekly Miscellany* (1732–41), the latter founded as an outlet for antirepeal writing. This motley group again testifies to the fact that hostility to dissent did not imply a specific party affiliation and, more locally, suggests the inappropriateness of the charges against Hare.

But even more important than Hare's position on dissent is the manner in which Hare represented Charles I. If the political theme of the sermon gave Hare's detractors a motive, its treatment of Charles gave them a vocabulary. The sound of Hare's sermon seems to have overwhelmed its sense, or at the very least to have allowed his assailants to pretend that it had done so.

Hare's text is Proverbs 24.21: "My son, fear thou the Lord and the King, and meddle not with them that are given to Change." The passage is a familiar one in the King Charles Day sermons of the century, but it was not the property of any one party or faction. On 30 January 1700, the Williamite John Sharp, archbishop of York, had used the text to argue against clerical "meddling" in matters of state. Twenty-six years later, Swift struck an altogether different note when he alluded to it in his politically charged sermon against dissent and church reform.[48] Hare's use of the text is more inclusive than Sharp's or Swift's: his sermon is equally a condemnation of the rebellion of the 1640s, a warning against Jacobitism, an argument against tinkering with the legal status of dissenters, and a statement of support for the Hanoverian monarchy. Hare, that is, refuses to observe the praise-

and-blame conventions of the occasion, ignoring or obscuring the distance between sermons hostile or indifferent toward Charles and supportive of the Revolution Settlement (like Sharp's), and those reverential toward Charles and disdainful of the Settlement or its beneficiary Walpole (like Swift's).

Hare begins innocuously enough, observing that "the Use of History in general is to direct us in the conduct of our lives, and point out to us the Things we should follow or avoid, to promote either our own Happiness or the publick Welfare" (5). The sermon seems to promise a conventional slap on the wrist to the regicides, to be warming up to the suggestion—central to milk-and-water King Charles Day sermons by Kennett, and, more recently, Bradshaw and Clavering—that one had best stay away from power-grubbing on the one hand and king-killing on the other if one is to enjoy fully the abundant blessings of constitutional monarchy.[49]

Hare's tone, however, changes abruptly:

> But of all the Facts recorded in the *English* History, as no one is more execrable and impious than that we are this Day assembled in the House of God to express our humble and sincere Abhorrence of, so is none fuller of good and useful Lessons for our future Conduct, if duly and seriously attended to. (5)

Hare's "lessons" concern the dangers of legitimating dissent now and then and thus undermining the beneficent cooperation of church and state. Hare builds the early portion of his argument outside of any temporal context, railing against undifferentiated "Enthusiasts" before noting that "the Men of this Turn are the Pests of all Governments, and the Misfortune is, that they swarm most in the best, in those that in the Constitution of them are the mildest, and the most indulgent to the Subject" (10). At this moment, Hare makes explicit his unorthodox pairing of Caroline and Hanoverian monarchies as equally sympathetic to and equally harassed by dissenters "given to change": one need only accept the proposition that Hare means both the Caroline and Georgian monarchies when he speaks of "the best" and "the mildest." That Hare praises both governments throughout the sermon makes the conclusion inescapable. When Hare presents Cromwell's roundheads as having "resolved on a Change of Government at any Rate, and, in order to [accomplish] it, to destroy the King" (14), his "lesson" is clear.

To Hare's detractor Gordon, Charles was seized by "[a] Thirst of unbounded Power" (5). To another participant in the controversy, Charles "fatally trod in the same Steps with his Father" by subordinating himself to the same counsellors who had corrupted James I (*Principles and Facts*, 25). The claims, as we have seen, are commonplace manifestations of anti-Carolinism in pro-government writing as well as in the *Craftsman* and other opposition sources. But Hare's Charles, like the Charles now being promoted by Kevin Sharpe and other revisionist scholars whom I noted in the previous chapter, is a populist monarch. In Hare's reckoning, Charles was a victim who "gave up entirely those Branches of the Prerogative, which were most liable to be made an arbitrary use of," and who strove unsuccessfully "to remove all jealousies, and restore a good Harmony between him[self] and his people" (12). The regicide becomes a symbol of the belligerence of an impious mob to a benevolent (and protoparliamentarian) king. The event adapts nicely to the analogic requirements of Hare's attack on dissent.

Hare's presentation of Charles's fall and the meaning that he extrapolates from it are in some ways congruent with the views of the Carolinists Earbery and Russel. For these writers as for Hare, dissent was a by-product of, or a malady coeval with, the "republicanism" revived in Walpolite England. The targets common to Earbery, Russel, and Hare are deviants from national religion first and monsters of political error consequently; they are, as Hare would have it, "men, who have in them a Tincture of Enthusiasm, [and] are very apt to be seduced with Pretences to a more perfect Way of Worship; and when once seduced, are always restless and impatient" (8).[50] Such "hypocrites" are to Hare canting anarchists who hide behind the ready mask of "liberty": "When such Men can't ruin the Established Religion this Way, then they set up for zealous Asserters of the Rights of Subjects in Religious Matters, and declare loudly for an absolute Exemption from all Authority whatever, as an Invasion of Liberty" (8).

The deference to "established religion" and the sneer at "liberty" again recall the rhetoric of the Carolinist opposition. And again like the Carolinists, Hare presses his use of analogy, finding in the 1730s a residue or even a recrudescence of the 1640s: "Tho' the Men are gone who perpetrated this horrid Fact," he observes, "the Spirit still remains" (16). This sentiment, endlessly reiterated in pulpit and pamphlet attacks on Walpole and his apologists, seems the stuff of the *Occasional Historian* and the *Grub-street Journal*.

But the similarity to the Carolinist opposition is apparent only. Unlike the Carolinists, Hare is not arguing against the primacy of parliament in Hanoverian England, and he certainly implies no disrespect toward the current monarch. He is arguing two points, both timely, as Carolinist rhetoric tends not to be, and both cautionary rather than critical of extant circumstances or policies. Hare is interested in, first, the importance of continuing to observe the day and, secondly, the necessity of defending the Test and Corporation Acts. He stresses his distance from the conservative high-church opposition by including Jacobites under the heading of "them that are given to change." Those who would look for assistance to the Pretender's court in Italy are as noxious to Hare as those who would seek reform from Parliament at Westminster. The conflation of dissenters and Jacobites came easily to Hare, who had practiced this dubious strain of argument as far back as 1722, in a sermon at Worcester published the following year as the second of his *Two Sermons on Rom. 13.1,2*. In the 1732 sermon, the anti-Catholic strain addresses a notoriously awkward problem for Jacobite and nonjuring polemicists:

> For we can't but observe, that under a Republican Spirit there lurks one very different. The Men who are so loud for Liberty upon the Republican Scheme are joined by a Party of Men who mean nothing less than what in Appearance they are so zealous for. They act by Direction from another Quarter, and to serve another Cause; 'tis for that they endeavour to weaken the King at Home, and to expose him Abroad; 'tis to bring in a Power destructive of the Religion and Liberty of their Country, that they espouse so warmly the Cause of Liberty, and join with Men of quite different Principles: Which makes it more than ordinarily necessary in these Times for the Friends of the Government to be vigilant, and take Care that they be not deluded into a Security that may prove fatal to them. (18)

Far from being a manifesto of "despotick power," Hare's argument is entirely compatible with its author's pro-government sympathies. In its position on dissent, the sermon is strongly opinionated where strong opinions were the order of the day; in its denunciation of Jacobitism, it is of a piece with Walpolite orthodoxy. The sermon is familiarly conservative insofar as it damns "meddling" and "change." But the conservatism is of recent vintage, assuming support for the Revolution Settlement rather than for the Stuart line that the Settlement had, in effect, terminated. Unlike any Jacobite or high-flying Tory, Hare attempted to define for himself a position that accommodated obedience to the Hanoverian succession, respect for the church, and adherence to a new philosophy of government—constitutional monarchy—that reduced the importance of both king and church. This triune interest ultimately forced Hare to abandon analogic argumentation and so to desert the method of the Carolinists even as he had spurned their ideology. Arguing against the strength of modern "meddlers," Hare is careful not to extend his analogy in such a manner as to suggest an irreparable rent in the fabric of government. Hare seems almost to retract his previous use of analogy:

> 'Tis not indeed so easy now for the disaffected to play over the same Game with the same Success. The Monarchy is now so limited and bounded by Laws, that it is not in the Power, no more than it is in the Will, of the Prince now upon the Throne, to give the same provocations that were given then; by which the Crown, however weakened in Appearance, is in Reality more firmly established. (17)

Hare's conclusion is strained, but it is not disingenuous. The terms of his argument are unorthodox, but there is nothing in the sermon to indicate that Hare intended to advance anything more seditious than equal measures of respect for Charles I and George II.

On 16 May 1732, however, an anonymous pamphleteer would comment that "the service of the Church was hardly over before a report was spread, that the Bishop of *Chichester* had preached a *Scandalous* and *Villainous* Sermon, at *St. James's*" (*Examiner Examined*, 2). The author exaggerates the speed of the response—the controversy really flared up after "P. C."'s pamphlet of 9 March—but not the tenor of the argument. "P. C."'s pamphlet presents the essence of the case against Hare, which was largely built on Hare's application of Caroline history. In keeping with the norms of pro-government rhetoric, "P. C." regards Caroline England didactically but not analogically and promotes a meliorism antithetical to the analogic strategies of the opposition. "P. C." finds England wiser and more jealous of its "liberties" than it had been in the days of Stuart priestcraft (12), and on this basis ridicules Hare's equation of past and present (23). The polemicist will grant the justice of Hare's censure of "Libellous Writings" against the government but is "far from thinking they amount to any thing like the Spirit of Forty-one, which arose and spread itself from a Sense of real, not imaginary Grievances" (25–26).[51]

"P. C." accuses Hare of apostasy, observing that the bishop's one-time "Admirers"—he counts himself as one such—found in the sermon surprising evidence of a "*High-church Spirit*" and "a compleat System of Slavery" (7). (John, Lord Hervey would later make a similar charge, remarking that Hare "set out in the world a zealous Whig in the state and a heretic in the Church; but ended in the character of a monarchial high-church persecutor."[52]) "P. C."'s claim drew fire from Hare's supporters, one of whom, entering the battle, unimaginatively, as "C. P.," praised Hare at the expense both of Alured Clarke, whose 1732 King Charles Day sermon before the Commons had included a dig at the factious Caroline bishops, and of Robert Warren, who had used the occasion to lecture the City government on the dangers of deism and dissent. "I can't but observe," writes "C. P.," "how contrary to the Bishop's Moderation is the *High-Church Spirit* you charge him with. Neither *Bishops* on the one hand, nor *Dissenters* on the other, are once named in the Sermon; all invidious Party-Words, with respect to them, are carefully avoided" (19).[53] "C. P." is being either obtuse or disingenuous in his reading of Hare's position on dissent. But the point is that he is refusing to endorse the notion, also present in Gordon's pamphlet against the sermon (4), that Hare's rhetoric identified him as an opponent of constitutional monarchy.

Several pamphleteers defended Hare by extrapolating from his sermon a greater breadth of analogy than Hare could possibly have intended. Their error, like that of Hare's detractors, is responding to the sermon as though it extended Hare's interest in Caroline history beyond the limits defined by Hare's loathing of dissent and into the realm of unchecked historical analogy. Typically subtle in its own use of analogy, *Fog's Weekly Journal* said, "Do you think the Bishop did not know that Kings had their Faults then, as well as at any Time since? But he thought it more becoming his Character and the Place where he stood, to draw the Curtain, than to expose the Royal Blemishes" (No. 186; 27 May 1732). The same month, a pro-Hare pamphlet called *The Examiner Examined* recited the charges against Hare in order to prove "that there are among us Men of the same principles, and of the same temper and disposition, with those who were the agents, or instruments, in the detestable wickedness of the day" (2). This same circular logic, a staple of defensive Carolinist rhetoric, turns up in a pamphlet by "Titus Britannicus," who claims that the accuracy of Hare's Caroline analogy is evident "from the very Writings of his Adversaries" (37). But reading Hare's argument as a conventional Carolinist equation of regicides and pro-government writers is as misleading as finding in it an attack on the government. Nowhere in Hare's career is there an instance of Hare battling the Walpolite (or pre-Walpolite Whig) journalists to whom some of his apologists placed him in opposition.

The *Grub-street Journal* was among the first sources to respond to Hare's sermon but was apparently unwilling to regard Hare as a kindred spirit. Russel's weekly, unlike the *Craftsman*, regularly observed the anniversary of Charles I's murder. Encomiastic verses, essays on the regicide, and reprints of King Charles Day sermons often appeared in the *Journal* in late January and early February.[54] The *Journal* might have been expected to praise Hare's warmth on the occasion, but its position in the controversy is tellingly ambiguous. In number 111 (17 Feb. 1732), the *Journal* reproduces portions of the three official King Charles Day sermons for the year. Joining Hare's are sermons by court chaplain Clarke and by the high-churchman Warren. Clarke's sermon is stock ministerial fare: melioristic and contrastive, it asks its listeners "to make a just application to Ourselves ... that We may *not be as* Our *Fathers*" (2). Clarke apportions blame for the Civil War more or less equally among "ignorant" ministers, the "*corrupt* part of the Clergy," and the "oppressed" citizenry (2–4). He argues that the guilt for the regicide expired with the deaths of the regicides and concludes with a panegyric upon the present glory days of "civil and religious Rights" (20). Clarke thus delicately supports the cause of dissent and exonerates the Erastianism of Walpole's government.[55]

Warren is cut from the same cloth as Russel. His sermon immediately proclaims a thoroughgoing hostility to deism, offers a thinly veiled pairing of Christ and Charles, and, in terms like those that Russel would later use, praises Charles's piety and his devotion to the national church.[56] Warren's conclusion is antithetical to Clarke's, reducing the importance of secular government where Clarke would elevate it:

> The *Sum* and *Substance* therefore of *this* Discourse is *wholly this*— That *no humane* Power is *secure* from *those Trials* in the State of *Probation* in which *Providence* has *placed us*. That the *divine Assistance, will never* be *wanting to those* who serve Him with Repen-

tance, Faith and Obedience, Charity, Devotion, and *constant Perseverance*. (22)

To Warren, England under Walpole is a "probationary" state to be endured and triumphed over only by those pious souls possessed of an adequate fund of the "Christian fortitude" archetypally embodied in the martyred Charles. This is far more dangerous territory than Hare would have attempted or approved.

By reproducing fragments from each sermon at the end of the text proper, the *Journal* reminds its readers that Hare had called Charles "the good King" only once during his sermon and that Clarke had called him "the unhappy King" only twice. But Warren had been more effusive, offering one "Blessed Martyr" and four "Royal Martyr[s]" in his sermon. A reader familiar with the *Journal*'s treatment of Charles would have recognized the endorsement of Warren's sermon: Warren's terminology echoes or anticipates the language of many of the *Journal*'s frequent entries on Charles.

The *Journal*'s subtle snub of Clarke and its sympathy for Warren are consistent with the church politics of that paper. But the *Journal* is less sure of itself in its presentation of Hare's sermon. One would not gather from the *Journal*'s distillation of the sermon into the bland phrase "the good King" that Hare had been profuse in his praise for Charles. It seems likely that the *Journal*, like later and more hostile commentators on the sermon, was confused by Hare's refusal to behave either like a spokesman for the government (as his post suggested that he should) or like an affiliate of the Caroline opposition (as his use of analogic argumentation suggested that he should).

Number 112 (24 Feb. 1732) illustrates the *Journal*'s uneasiness. A satiric letter to Clarke from the boobyish "Consciencious Doubtful" compares Clarke's and Hare's sermons on the questions of inherited guilt and continued repentance. The writer dismisses Hare's sentiments as "Tory notions" and finds his own habits of worship congruent with those enjoined by Clarke:

> I never go to Church on that day, till after the Prayers are over. And am glad to find my practice seemingly justified by your opinion; according to which, tho' I appear at Church only just as the Preacher mounts the pulpit, I have time sufficient to perform *the Whole of my duty on this occasion, in begging God to keep far away the evil of past days*.[57]

The letter presents Clarke as a time-server, a hypocrite, and an egotist and would seem at least to imply that the *Journal* endorsed the "Tory notions" that its straw man rejected. But Russel's epigram in the same number suggests otherwise by portraying Hare as insincere and as protected by his position from any responsibility for his rhetorical choices:

> When you preach on the thirtieth day of January,
> With your station and audience let your doctrine vary:
> If with Mitre you're grac'd, before the noble Peers,
> You may Parliament blame, praise King and Cavaliers:
> But if not—mind your hits—take a different tone;
> Lay the blame on both sides alike, or on none:
> Would you shine as a Dean, above Clerical Proctor,
> Tho' you think like a BISHOP, still preach like a DOCTOR.

According to Russel, Bishop Hare's Carolinism was lip-service only and would be excused (or so it seemed at the time) by virtue of his station: it was a simple matter of assuring nobles and kings that nobles and kings were, and are, guiltless. In comparison, Doctor Warren—safely absent from the letter but the beleaguered hero of the epigram—is required to hide his Carolinism beneath a cloak of disinterestedness. That this assessment in no way tallies with the specifics of Warren's sermon is immaterial. What matters is that the *Journal* is unwilling to defend with any clarity someone who would shortly be accused of a political orientation very much like its own. Similarly, Earbery would avoid a substantive discussion of Hare's sermon, concentrating instead on an attack on Gordon, Walpole, and those who would defile "the precious Memory of a Saint in Paradise" (*Universal Spy* 2; 6 May 1732). The Caroline opposition was attracted to Hare's sermon but was mistrustful of the speaker and uncertain how—or if—to translate the sermon into its own polemical vocabulary.

It may not be possible accurately to appraise Hare's own reaction to the controversy. Hare opted for silence after his initial statement, as he had not done in his disputes with the Harleyites and Hoadly. Formulating a response would have been difficult, as the possibility of repeal became, in the second half of 1732, the concern of pressure groups and politicians less interested in ecclesiastical squabbling than in political exigency.[58] Hare's letters to his son in the period 1737 to 1740 prove that Hare remained devoted to the ministry and the royal family and hostile to the opposition. Like his letters to Gibson during roughly the same period, they demonstrate that Hare—Hervey's accusations notwithstanding—was an active supporter of the government until the end of his life. But Hare seems to have said nothing publicly about the controversy during which his support for the government had been questioned so harshly.[59]

The best clue we have about Hare's political stance in the early '30s is a friendly but somewhat anxious letter from Hare to Newcastle dated 18 August 1733.[60] In it, Hare responds to Newcastle's request for assistance in promoting pro-government candidates for office, a call to arms necessitated by Walpole's recent humiliation in the Commons over the Excise Bill. What we know about Hare's behavior in the period immediately preceding the election of 1734 indicates that Hare was eager to reassert his commitment to Newcastle and to the Walpolite cause generally—an eagerness presumably focused by Newcastle's own tolerance of dissent.[61] The letter may contain a sidelong glance at the recent controversy, and its insistent tone suggests that Hare wanted to clarify his loyalties:

> The Gentlemen in the opposition want not to be informed what side I am of, not one of them having ever come near me since I had any concern in this Country. . . . & indeed they would be greatly mistaken if they thought otherwise; I am in all views and upon all acct[s] entirely in the interest of the present Governt. & the present ministry; and wish nothing so much as that they would steadily pursue those measures, that will tend most surely to support themselves.[62]

Hare concludes with a shot at the "stupid creatures" who had opposed Walpole on the excise. We are left with a sketch of a party-man protesting sincerely in the aftermath of an unexpected and probably bewildering attack.

Hare finally looks like a dependable Whig, like Gibson, vocal where church interests were concerned and where party platform was unformulated, and, like his foes Gordon and Hervey, loyal where party interest was at stake. The inappropriateness of the charges against Hare and the unsettled response to him by the Carolinists Russel and Earbery indicate the partisan violence that praise for Charles I was capable of inspiring in the early eighteenth century. The controversy illustrates the tendency of political rhetoric in the period to operate in defiance of the categories "opposition" and "pro-government" opportunistically promoted in Bolingbroke's day and naively endorsed in our own.

6
Acting Out the Unstable Opposition

Much of my argument thus far has concerned two related points: first, that notwithstanding the assertions of Bolingbroke and his latter-day apologists, Bolingbrokean polemics did not constitute a broadly accepted language of opposition to Walpole; and, second, that the period's anxiety about Bolingbroke and the *Craftsman* is superevident in sources that have not received much scholarly attention. Both claims benefit from being tested against the historical drama of the Walpole era, an underexplored body of work that is usually regarded, when it is regarded at all, as a subgenre committed to political discourse generally and Bolingbrokean ideology in particular. A motley and unfocused group of plays has been made over as a series of simple polemical exercises. This should give us pause, if only because drama does not characteristically "work" this way in the first place. To be Bakhtinian about it, the drama tends to resist ideological control, the more so when one allows for the infinite interpretive nuances of performance. The present chapter challenges the settled habit of regarding political drama under Walpole as a monolith of opposition sentiment, virtually a forum for acting out the simple praise-and-blame conventions of Bolingbrokean polemics. Like many of the pamphlets and sermons that I have been discussing, much of the historical drama of the period interrogates the rhetoric of the mainstream opposition rather than merely recording it.

There is no doubt that a substantial amount of the drama in the period is somehow "political," even in the less inclusive sense in which we used the word before modernity somehow slid (past itself, apparently) into postmodernity. Self-evidently, politics in general and opposition politics in particular are central concerns of dramaturgy in the late 1720s and the 1730s. Plays of the period delimited on one end by the production of John Gay's *The Beggar's Opera* (1728) and, on the other, by the invocation of the Licensing Act of 1737 to prevent the staging of James Thomson's *Edward and Eleonora* (1739) and Henry Brooke's *Gustavus Vasa* (1739), are profuse in the language of Bolingbrokean polemics. One encounters repeatedly in the drama the touchstones of Bolingbroke's cyclical theory of history and politics: praise for monarchs attentive to populace and Parliament, and blame for ministers who usurp the power of the constitutional monarch and so undermine the ancient English "liberty" cried up by Bolingbroke in works like the *Remarks on the History of England*, *A Dissertation upon Parties*, and, later, *The Idea of a Patriot King* (written 1738 [?]; published 1749).

But using Bolingbrokean rhetoric is not the same thing as promoting it. I am uneasy about even a cautious formulation like John Loftis's durable claim about "clear and recurrent patterns" in the political tragedies of the period: "In so far as this political theory is coherent," Loftis asserts, "it is that to which Bolingbroke gave systematic exposition in his *Idea of a Patriot King*."[1] I find very little coherent theorizing, Bolingbrokean or otherwise, in early eighteenth-century drama, although the illusion of coherency may perhaps be created by what Robert Hume identifies as the tendency of Restoration and eighteenth-century plays to reproduce "political commonplace" rather than to endorse precise ideologies.[2] We would do well to consider the "commonplace" element in the political drama as comprising both the rhetoric of Bolingbrokeanism and the contemporary reaction against that rhetoric. Certainly some plays attacked Walpole— the Licensing Act accurately suggests as much. And without a doubt most plays that did so relied for their ammunition on the platitudes of the Bolingbrokean opposition. But the drama often subverted Bolingbrokean rhetoric in ways that replicated broad concerns within English culture about Bolingbroke and his program—for instance the suspicion that Bolingbroke sought to weaken the monarchy and to promote anarchy, expressed repeatedly by Walpolite writers like John, Lord Hervey as well as by ultramonarchist opponents of Walpole like Matthias Earbery. The drama claimed the same latitude of opinion about Bolingbroke that the rest of the literate community claimed. The effect of Bolingbrokean rhetoric in the drama is sometimes to promote the ideology that it expresses, occasionally to reject it, and often to question or to complicate it.

In order to define a satisfactory position from which to discuss political meaning or ideological inquiry in these plays, we must acknowledge some generic differences between the plays and the polemical literature with which scholars have tended to confound them. The drama is poorly equipped to transmit meaning polemically. Most obviously, it trades in sustained patterns of verbal and narrative irony foreign to polemical literature. No one will need to be convinced that most early modern plays, operating without the convenience of disembodied authorial commentary, create meaning by developing contradictions—ironies—between what a character says and what he or she does. Our sense of Iago's honor comes not from Iago's language but from his actions and from the complications that they produce. We should judge Bolingbrokean rhetoric in the drama with the same steady awareness of potential irony that we bring to less overtly political plays, asking ourselves who uses this rhetoric and toward what result action based on it tends.

Addressing these points calls attention to considerable diversity in the drama. In the plays that I shall discuss, stirring Bolingbrokean rhetoric is often the language of frauds, demagogues, or incompetents who behave in unimpressive or unattractive ways. In polemical literature, however, right rhetoric produces right action historically and would inspire one to it in the here and now. And when polemical literature is ironic, we discover the irony not when the speaker's persona is clarified narratively—by the accumulation of evidence against the validity of what the speaker does—but because it is defined statically—by the speaker's habitual and immediately evident inability to say what he or she means. We recognize this simplest sort of irony when *Fog's Weekly Journal* builds a leader around mock praise for Walpole's "wise and steady Administration" (No. 125; 17 Apr. 1731), or when Bolingbroke, in the first number of the *Occasional Writer* (1727), presents himself to Walpole as "a man whose affection for your person and zeal for your service, must be above all suspicion."[3] When it is being ironic as when it is not, polemical literature asks its readers to identify what the speaker is, not, as in the drama, what the speaker becomes.

Furthermore, polemical literature insists that closure is negotiable, to be created by a readership—metonymically, a population—in an extratextual or "real-time" future from materials, typically historiographical, presented by the polemicist. The reader, in a manner of speaking, is asked to bring the polemicist's narrative to the conclusion desired by the polemicist. To read the work as it is designed to be read is to endorse and ideally to act upon the writer's ideology. The analogic intent and, thus, the exhortative purpose of Bolingbrokean historiography are clear enough: evil ministers are toppled, duped monarchs are rehabilitated, and libertarian government is installed and defended. The causality is absolute and, given the logic of the genre, repeatable. Closure validates ideology, however much Bolingbroke and the *Craftsman* tried to pretend otherwise in their defenses of the *Remarks on the History of England*.

Closure in the drama, however, supposes no such causality. The drama can act out less rigid and predictable possibilities, and closure allows options that are not necessarily congruent with ideologies themselves presented sympathetically. Tragedy, for instance, is often the study of sympathetic ideologies (or simply sound moral virtues) rendered useless by the inability of the community or its representatives to live up to them. In any political literature, meaning is determined in large part by the fate of ideology, and to complicate or to neutralize ideology as the drama often does is to raise questions about the ability of ideology to implement the changes upon which it insists.

The relationship of genre and ideology, then, distinguishes much political drama from most polemical literature. I intend nothing recondite in my terms. By genre I mean simply the formal or conventional structures toward the support of which plot tends. By ideology I mean the values, social and political in this case, generated or supported by plot and by language when plot suggests that we read it sympathetically.

I shall discuss a handful of representative plays among those that Hume calls "application plays," although I prefer the blander term "history-plays" as reducing an emphasis on analogy that I find clearer and more insistent in polemical literature than in the drama.[4] I propose three subcategories of the history-plays: Bolingbrokean comedies, anti-Bolingbrokean tragedies, and generically and ideologically imprecise plays that belong in neither group. The comedies demonstrate a conventional harmony of genre and ideology; they reify the exhortations of the polemicist, or enact the sorts of teleological possibilities for which polemical literature argues. These plays are repositories of opposition commonplace, valued positively. They are compatible both with the regenerative domestic and political conventions of comedy and with Bolingbroke's belief that strong ministers have no place in post-Revolution government. The action of William Bond's *The Tuscan Treaty* (1733), for instance, propels the misguided King Porsenna toward the reconstituted home and state characteristic of comic closure, the achievement of which validates and ensures the continuance of the libertarianism that Porsenna has come to embody.

Genre and ideology work together in the tragedies as well. In William Havard's anti-Bolingbrokean tragedy *King Charles the First* (1737), plot moves toward the destruction of the saintly Charles of the Carolinists. The regicide signals the demise of benevolent monarchy and the triumph of pseudolibertarianism, the language of which the character Oliver Cromwell has borrowed from the Bolingbrokean opposition. The king's state and his home collapse together. Tragedy here is the destruction of nondoctrinaire ideology and the triumph of cant.

Radically different in their politics but buoyed up to a similar level of confidence by their easy reconciliation of genre and ideology, the Bolingbrokean comedies and anti-Bolingbrokean tragedies represent the endpoints of a spectrum of responses to opposition rhetoric. The intermediate plays are animated by a tension between genre and ideology. In them, closure renders disjunctive the values of public and private life, rather than reconciling them positively as Bond's play does, or negatively as Havard's play does. Like Bond's play and its kind, these plays declare themselves tragedies on their title pages but close with structures of government recast along ideological lines that have been articulated sympathetically throughout the play. But as in Havard's play (and, less neatly, in the anonymous *Majesty Misled* [1734]), the force of tragedy disallows any sustained movement toward regeneration and contradicts the optimistic political values that promote such a movement. The political gains made in these plays are tenuous and unprotected.

Even a trite and professedly Bolingbrokean recipe like *Gustavus Vasa* may stand as an example of this problematic subcategory. The libertarian hero Vasa springs ready-made from the pages of *The Idea of a Patriot King* to the support of the oppressed Dalecarlians, whom he saves from the tyrant Cristiern. But Vasa fails to effect the terminal marriage that would have ensured comic closure by bringing him familial and political entrenchment. In the absence of marriage, Vasa can offer his people only rulership without succession. In *Vasa* and plays like it, genre qualifies opposition ideology by dramatizing the difficulties of achieving closure satisfactory both to the public (or political) and the private (or domestic) spheres. These plays present unstable versions of "liberty" that lack ballast and futurity, and that advertise the distance between political theory and practical government.

※ ※ ※

The Bolingbrokean comedies have been analyzed sensibly by the other critics whom I have mentioned, if in ways that suppose them broadly representative of political drama in the period. I shall comment on them only as they provide points of contrast to the other and less predictable plays in which I am interested. The comedies present the beleaguered but reclaimable monarch (or monarchy) of Bolingbrokean theory, the belief in which allowed Bolingbroke unapologetically to profess loyalty to George II even as he attacked measures and habits of governance of which the king approved. This is the model of monarchy that Bolingbroke derived from his belief in an ancient constitution and from his theory of cycles of liberty and faction. In these plays as in Bolingbroke's work, monarchs who lean toward absolutism always had been and always must be corrected by the ancient mechanisms reinstated by the Revolution Settlement of 1689: the action of Parliament and the action of the populace.

I include in this category William Hatchett's(?) controversial *The Fall of Mortimer* (1731), Bond's *The Tuscan Treaty*, George Lillo's *The Christian Hero* (1735), and Thomson's *Edward and Eleonora* (1739).[5] Robert Dodsley's farce *The King and the Miller of Mansfield* (1737) is ideologically identical, but unlike the comedies it poses no significant impediments to the institutionalizing of libertarian ideology, which is effected without either a change of monarchs or a fundamental change in the monarch himself.

Two of the plays quickly tip us off to the unstable relationship of genre and ideology in the drama of the period. *The Tuscan Treaty* and *Edward and Eleonora* bill themselves as tragedies although they are clearly comic in structure. The question becomes under what circumstances might we imagine the plays as tragedies, and the answer has to be when we admit the greatness of the discredited minister or king who falls from power. Joseph Addison's *Cato* (1713) suggests that neoclassical drama can authorize such a situation, but political dramatists could not have expected their plays to be read this way in the 1730s. We are left to conclude that the conventions of genre are less important to the Bolingbrokean writers than the promulgation of ideology. The substitution of "tragedy" for "comedy" merely suggests an irony by claiming anything more than incidental pathos for the destruction of designedly repellent characters.

The movement in all the plays in this category is conventionally comic: toward a better state and a better home. The events of Thomson's play propel young Edward I to a greater realization of the rectitude of popular monarchy and therefore qualify him for blessings both domestic (he recovers a wife who he thought had died), and political (he will ascend the throne wary of the "corrupt, corrupting Ministers and Favourites" who ruined his father [50]).[6] Only the focus differs in Dodsley's farce and its sequel, *Sir John Cockle at Court* (1738), in which Henry II is chastened by his encounter with the patriot-miller Cockle, whose homely philosophy shields the king from the influence of vicious courtiers and earns Cockle and his family considerable domestic advantages. Bond's Porsenna frees himself from the scheming minister Quintus and sheds his lust for the fair Valeria, embracing instead "Roman" principles of popular monarchy and gracefully accepting his role as senex when he gives Valeria— and thus the future of the state—to his worthy son, Aruns (65). Althea, beloved of Lillo's monarch, Scanderbeg, will be in her marriage to him "an equal blessing to [him]self and people" (76). The interests of ruler and ruled are inseparable, and the happy state and presumably its continuance are based on the happy home. On the busy final page of Hatchett's play, Edward III, freed of his reprobate mother, Isabella, and her lover, Mortimer, rewards the Bolingbrokean cut-out Mountacute by marrying him to Maria, the one-time object of the evil minister Mortimer's attention. Mountacute is given a new title, and the couple is given Mortimer's estate. Parliament will be convened; and of his "good Commoners," Edward says, "I'll lose my own, or fix their Liberty" (63). In these plays, purity supplants corruption in public and private spheres. The terms of the Revolution Settlement (or the Bolingbrokean opposition's sense of them) have ushered in and will now support the refurbished government.

The further we move from this small group of plays, the more difficult it is to find unqualified endorsements of the Bolingbrokean program. *King Charles the First*, an enactment of the commonplaces of Carolinist polemics, is the drama's most concerted assault on Bolingbrokean ideology. In this lugubrious tragedy, genre assists the dismantling of an ideology of monarchism far more attractive than the opportunistic pseudo-libertarianism to which it is contrasted.

More than any of the history-plays, *King Charles the First* has suffered at the hands of critics given to "opposition" readings. Loftis, Hume, and Vincent Liesenfeld all find the play a useful example of anti-Walpole drama. All note Lord Chesterfield's strictures on the play, although, curiously, none notes that neither Chesterfield nor his contemporaries ascribed any political meaning to it.[7] And none finds it odd that Havard, a workaday repertory actor with no apparent interest in the opposition or need to curry its favor, would abruptly take up its cause—or for that matter would abandon the cause, if he *had* adopted it, after the success of *King Charles the First*.[8]

Still more to the point, none of these critics accounts for the fact that the Bolingbrokean strain is voiced most frequently by Cromwell's lackey Bradshaw and by Cromwell himself, here as everywhere in the period a tyrant and a vulgarian. Liesenfeld even cites a comment by Dr. Johnson's early biographer, Sir John Hawkins, who believed that Havard's play contained "sentiments suited to the characters of republicans, sectaries and enthusiasts."[9] But Liesenfeld does not consider that republicanism, sectarianism, and enthusiasm received very little good press in the 1730s, or that Havard was using these "sentiments" to identify his villains rather than to counsel violent resistance to the monarch. Hawkins, like Chesterfield and like his own subject Johnson, simply believed that some subjects were less suitable for representation than others. Havard's intentions did not concern him.[10] Furthermore, the extravagant insincerity of the Cromwellians' encomia on "liberty" is emphasized in the printed version that Loftis, Hume, and Liesenfeld all produce as evidence of Havard's sympathy with the opposition. Far from being, in Hume's words, "a dangerously outspoken 'parallel' play,"[11] Havard's play suggests that a counterfeit rhetoric of libertarianism can be a weapon against legitimate monarchy. Perhaps opportunistically, Havard wrote a play based on the tenets and the rhetoric of Carolinism, which had become familiar to the public through the efforts of the polemicists whom I have discussed in the preceding chapters.

Much of the problem with the discussion of *King Charles the First* has been an insistence on pinpointing conventional Bolingbrokean "parallels," a method that works well enough with the *Remarks on the History of England* but not well at all with the drama. Hume, who reads the play as an attack on George II, follows the tradition of Loftis and Liesenfeld when he says that Havard's play "is particularly striking because its 'majesty misled' theme leads to such dire consequences."[12] The claim is an odd one: the loyalists Bishop Juxon and the duke of Richmond, like Charles himself, are sensitive and circumspect in staid sentimental fashion.[13] When Charles is pressed into service as the type of the misled monarch (as he often is by the *Craftsman*), the evil ministers required by analogy are Buckingham and, less frequently, Laud, both of whom had died before 1649, the date of the play's action.

Havard promotes the "majesty misled" theme clearly enough in lines, deleted from performance, against the long-dead Buckingham by Bradshaw (28) and Cromwell (32). Undoubtedly, as Loftis and Liesenfeld point out, the convenient parallel of the kings Charles I and George II and the inherited ministers Buckingham and Walpole is foremost in Havard's mind at these moments.[14] Hume notes that "in performance a good deal of detail reinforcing the parallels to George II and Walpole was cut," and argues that "the suggestion that George II was doing things that might lead him to the block, however tactfully put, must have seemed seditious to many people."[15] But we have no evidence that the play *did* strike its audience this way, nor do we have any reason to regard Bradshaw and Cromwell as reliable narrators.[16] It is at least possible that the deletions indicate that Havard suspected that viewers—but not readers away from the noise of the crowd, with text in hand—would be unable or unwilling to discriminate between the expression of ideology (or statements of opposition commonplace) and the belief in ideology (or the acceptance of commonplace). The notations signaling the deletions have the effect of highlighting particularly egregious instances of cant and hypocrisy.[17]

Bradshaw's and Cromwell's Bolingbrokean swipes at Charles's past are designedly repulsive in the context of a trial presented, as Charles's trial typically was in the period, as trumpery, a violation of law and a backdrop to martyrdom. Justifying his plan for regicide shortly before he prohibits Charles from testifying in his own defense, Bradshaw declares, "'Tis in the Cause that Liberty approves / And every honest *Englishman* must own it" (29). We have no reason to think that apologies for regicide—however framed—were attractive in the 1730s; on the contrary, fear of civil discord is one of the most fundamental and most evident anxieties of the period. Any claim about "parallels" here would need to take into account the speakers as well as what is being spoken: the very types of anarchy use the language of the Bolingbrokean opposition.

Readers of this study will recognize that Havard's line of attack is not unique. As we have seen, the suspicion that Bolingbroke peddled a false and antimonarchic brand of "liberty" was expressed in a host of pamphlets and periodicals written against Bolingbroke and the *Craftsman*. And an ample body of literature demonstrates that mistrust of Bolingbroke and the *Craftsman* was not the prerogative of Walpole's journalists. More specifically, the analogy of Cromwellian and Bolingbrokean "oppositions" that Havard develops is abundant in the period. Havard had plenty of contemporary sources for his subject and his method.

Havard's analogic smear campaign against roundheads and Bolingbrokeans is deliberate and unrelenting. When Cromwell claims that "the lopping off [of Charles's] head" is the "one Blow [that] remains to fix our State" (3), he seems impossibly crude. But Carolinists like Russel and Earbery would have found Cromwell's claim an accurate extrapolation from the tendency among apologists for the Revolution of 1688 to present Charles's reign as an accretion of abuses demanding the remedy of rebellion. And Cromwell's position on the goals of the Civil War recalls the *Craftsman's* stance on the Revolution. Havard's character praises regicide as the rout of the Stuarts: "No more the Royal Tree / Shall, from Legitimacy's Root, presume / To sprout forth Tyrant Branches" (3). A few years earlier in the *Craftsman*, Bolingbroke had declared the Revolution Settlement a means to the same end: "At the Time of the *Revolution*, our *Constitution* received a considerable Strength by *that Act*, which is call'd the *Declaration of Rights*; by which, we hope, an End is put to the dangerous Claims and Practices of some *former Reigns*" (No. 375; 8 Sept. 1733). When Cromwell continues his soliloquy with the exhortation "Down with Nobility—The Commons rule," he lacks the tact of the *Craftsman*. But he gives voice accurately enough to the parliamentary populism of that journal and of Bolingbrokean political theory more generally.

Havard enters the fray over the royal prerogative, which, along with the royal succession, was the dominant issue in English politics from the outbreak of the Civil War in 1642 to the Jacobite's swan song in 1745. For Havard's Cromwell as for the *Craftsman*, "liberty" was coeval with the reduction of monarchic power legislated by the Revolution Settlement and by Williamite parliaments. Cromwell plays "law" and "liberty" against "tyranny" and "prerogative" when he chides Fairfax for counseling leniency toward Charles:

> ... would you obstruct the Law
> In its due Office? Nor permit the Ax
> To fall upon Offenders, such as *Charles*?
> Wou'd you see Tyranny again arise,

> And spread in its Foundation: Let us then
> Seize on our General, Liberty, who still
> Has in the Front of Battle fought our Cause,
> And led us on to Conquest; let us bind him
> In the strong Chains of rough Prerogative,
> And throw him helpless at the Feet of *Charles*:
> He will absolve us then, and praise our Folly.
>
> (49)

Cromwell's "liberty," like the "liberty" that its detractors thought the *Craftsman* was promoting, is a mask for "conquest," an ersatz legalism that sanctions assaults on the monarchy. One should not overlook the cautionary irony of this passage: the false libertarian Cromwell would soon "bind" liberty "in the strong Chains of rough Prerogative" and would thereby usher in a period that the eighteenth century would uniformly pronounce anarchic. As we have seen, a great deal of alarmist literature written against Bolingbroke and the *Craftsman* testifies to the presence of a similar anxiety about the implications of the Bolingbrokean program. When Lady Mary Wortley Montagu wrote of Bolingbroke, "Oh, was your Pow'r like your Intention good! / Your native Land would stream with civil blood," she was expressing a concern that Havard, like many of his contemporaries, seems to have shared, or at least to have been willing to capitalize on.[18]

After Charles is taken away to be executed, Juxon speaks the play's final judgment on him. His eulogy presents Charles's populism as a corollary from his position as monarch rather than a condition for it, or as an acknowledgment by a grateful citizenry rather than the carefully monitored bequest of a powerful parliament.

> [Charles's] Example
> May prove this Maxim's Truth to all Mankind;
> The Subject's Reverence, and the Prince's Love,
> Grasping, and grasp'd, walk Hand in Hand together,
> Strengthened by Union; then, the King's Command
> Is lost in the Obedience of the Subject;
> The King, unask'd, confirm'd the Peoples Rights,
> And by the willing Gift prevents the Claim:
> These are the Virtues that endear a King,
> Adorn a People, and true Greatness bring.
>
> (61)

The curtain speech is the occasion for the play's normative voice, the more certainly as Havard, however clumsily, modeled his play after Shakespeare.[19] The best that one can say of parliamentary libertarianism in the play is that it is unnecessary; the worst, that it is a foil for anarchy. Both positions, of course, are antithetical to Bolingbrokean theory.

The anonymous and suppressed tragedy *Majesty Misled* is similar to *King Charles the First* in some important ways. Although they argue from different political premises, both plays represent generically the collapse of facile libertarianism. *Majesty Misled*'s stridently antigovernment stance is clear enough and has often been commented upon. But no one has observed the play's almost farcical lack of commitment to Bolingbrokean rhetoric. Dedicated to the Jacobitical Lord Mayor of London John Barber, the toast of the City opposition for his role in stymieing Walpole's Excise Bill (1733), *Majesty Misled* seems to be the City's commentary on the Bolingbrokean opposition much as *King Charles the First* is the Carolinist response. H. T. Dickinson notes that Barber and Bolingbroke were on friendly terms; but he and other scholars suggest that the City opposition was not the same thing as the Bolingbrokean opposition, the *Craftsman's* overtures to the City in 1732 and 1733 notwithstanding. And the City and commercial element, generally less squeamish than Bolingbroke about Jacobitism and understandably interested in the parliamentary representation that Bolingbroke could not provide, was under no obligation to the patrician and theoretically-minded Bolingbroke.[20] My own suspicion is that the play's suppression was the result not simply of its anti-Walpole stance—common if unusually strong—but rather of its choice to focus on the unregenerate monarch Edward II and thus to cross the line that separated, as Bolingbroke and his apologists would have it, Bolingbroke himself from his one-time cronies among the Jacobite camp.[21] An incautious play in several ways, *Majesty Misled* is as critical of Bolingbrokean rhetoric as it is of George II and Walpole.

Majesty Misled, which at times recalls Christopher Marlowe's *Edward II* (ca. 1592), presents a cast of grotesques using plainly Bolingbrokean language and everywhere demonstrating their self-interestedness and their contempt for the cits whom they pretend to represent. Edward II's estranged wife Isabella and the earls of Lancaster, Nottingham, Warwick, Leicester, and Warren seem at first to be correctives to the malign statesmen Edward II and the two Hugh Spencers, evil ministers more than usually forthcoming about their intention to usurp the royal prerogative. Isabella speaks to Leicester of their cause as that of "true Patriots" (80) and calls her allies "patriot-barons, at once to free / The people from the tyranny and bondage / Of those two ministers" (56). The queen berates the corrupt government in the stock language of the Bolingbrokean opposition:

> Such ill-court fav'rites, mounted into power,
> Assume the princely reins of government;
> They spur the people with unbridled fury,
> Who, if they cannot cast their riders, must
> Bear tamely their severe chastisement:
> And if such fav'rites' actions they arraign,
> Or bravely censure what they do amiss,
> Fines and imprisonment must be their portion.
>
> (56)

All this is very familiar, down to the lament about censorship reiterated in the *Craftsman* and *Fog's Weekly Journal*, most notably after Richard Francklin's 1731 arrest for printing the "Hague letter." Isabella and her allies, however, are frauds. The conventions of blame (for corruption and venality) and praise (for disinterested patriotism) on which the Bolingbrokean comedies depend are muddied by the refusal of the play to present a normative figure who is as good as his or her rhetoric.

Isabella and her cohorts never confuse speech with sentiment, and the playwright increasingly degrades the characters as the play progresses. The queen finds the grand cadences of opposition rhetoric a convenient cover for her interests in absolutist government and unrestrained sex with her illicit lover, Mortimer. Isabella states her goals with disarming frankness. Once the Spencers have been overthrown, she says,

> Then will I rule with arbitrary sway;
> Stroke off their heads, who have oppos'd my way,
> Recall my *Mortimer*, and ev'ry night,
> With am'rous flames, will revel in delight.
>
> (68)

Lancaster is hardly more attractive. Here he responds to Warwick's claim that the populace supports the rebel cause:

> Be not deceived, my good lord *Warwick*,
> With outward shew; 'tis but a mere appearance.
> In life one observation I have made,
> Nor have I found it false; the vulgar *English*,

> A fickle people, with the current swim,
> And as the tide does ebb or flow, so they
> Will with your int'rest join, and then retreat:
> They've sense enough to choose the strongest side.
>
> (21)

The linguistic analogue to Isabella and (at times) Lancaster is the cruel and totalitarian Spencer, Jr., who, squashing in Edward a sudden and uncharacteristic concern for the "people," says, "'Tis weakness to regard their sighs and groans; / Are they ought else but animated dirt? / A herd of pratling beasts, design'd your slaves" (28).

History supplies the corrective to tragedy in the form of the popular Edward III, but the new king never appears in the play and is mentioned only in passing. The curtain falls on a world in collapse: Lancaster dead, Isabella hopelessly corrupt, Edward II penitent but despairing and discredited, and the remaining earls absent or blindly following Isabella. The cits, Barber's constituency, have rallied meaninglessly behind Isabella after their own resistance to the fleeing king—the one disinterested action in the play. The Bolingbrokean strain has been parodic, and tragedy here is the maintenance of the status quo by titled pseudolibertarians unconcerned with and separate from the populace.

In the plays that I have positioned generically and ideologically "between" the Bolingbrokean comedies and the anti-Bolingbrokean tragedies, the conventions of genre inhibit the diffusion of ideology. Unable to institutionalize the lofty ideologies to which they give voice and uninterested in declaring these ideologies false, the plays convey considerable uncertainty about the Bolingbrokean program. Several tendencies separate them from the more doctrinaire drama of the period. In them, questions of succession are posed but are left unanswered or are answered without conviction. The possibility of achieving libertarian government is offered, but it is either not realized or is realized at the cost of personal stability. Closure, that is, preserves a disjunction between public and private spheres reconciled variously in comedy (through the elevation of both) and tragedy (through the dissolution of both). And closure is rendered unstable by a conflict between, on the one hand, the values of optimism and futurity implicit in the Bolingbrokean ideology that the plays engage and, on the other, the impulse toward tragedy to which they respond. Several of the plays press their points, as *King Charles the First* and *Majesty Misled* do, by assigning the platitudes of the opposition to charlatans. I have arranged my discussion of these plays in order to suggest what I see as degrees of uncertainty about the Bolingbrokean opposition and thus to emphasize the diversity of political drama in the period.

Brooke's *Gustavus Vasa* is a good example of this intermediary sort of play in part because it so earnestly endorses Bolingbrokean ideology. In it, Brooke demonstrates an affinity with "Patriot poets" such as James Thomson and George Lyttleton, who, as Bertrand Goldgar points out, were in the middle and later years of the 1730s producing a literature of "enthusiastic nationalism" that was "hortatory rather than satiric" and was therefore unlike the earlier efforts of the Scriblerian satirists.[22] The new idea was rather to inspire greatness in Frederick, Prince of Wales, than to criticize folly (or worse) in Walpole and in Frederick's father George II.

Goldgar notes that "Bolingbroke's program," as laid out in *The Idea of a Patriot King*, "was to have a profound appeal to the imagination of the later Patriot poets."[23] (By "later," Goldgar means the late 1730s.) Certainly the Bolingbrokean inheritance is evident in *Gustavus Vasa*. Brooke's "Prefatory Dedication to the Subscribers" uses the language of liberty, patriotism, and the ancient constitution even as Brooke proclaims himself innocent of antigovernment intention.[24] The posture of wounded innocence, the appeal to "truth" rather than to "party" (iv), the disclaimer of responsibility for the historical analogy (Sweden/England) hammered upon throughout the dedication—all this recalls not only *The Idea of a Patriot King*, but also the *Remarks on the History of England*, *A Dissertation upon Parties*, many miscellaneous numbers in the *Craftsman*, and, incidentally, quite a few poems by Pope. Brooke's portrait of the ideal monarch might as well have been written by Bolingbroke:

> The Monarch or Head of such a Constitution, is as the Father of a large and well regulated Family, his Subjects are not Servants, but Sons; their Care, their Affections, their Attachments are reciprocal, and their Interest is one, is not to be divided. . . . His Office partakes of the DIVINE INCLINATION, by being exerted to no other End, but the Happiness of a People. (vii)

In Bolingbroke's nearly contemporaneous exploration of government, the "Patriot King" is "the common father of his people."

"The true image of a free people, governed by a Patriot King," Bolingbroke wrote in 1738, "is that of a patriarchal family, where the head and all the members are united by one common interest, and animated by one common spirit."[25] The family-metaphor common to Bolingbroke and Brooke, conventional in any case, is also congruent with the generational fantasies of the patriot-opposition.[26] But Brooke's use of the metaphor is curious: Vasa treats it as a recipe for statescraft without any sustaining correlative in the home. Vasa's kingship removes him from family life and so undermines the metaphor. Rhetorically speaking, the tenor of Brooke's metaphor is rendered unstable by the disappearance of its vehicle.

Initially, Vasa seems everything the patriot-opposition could have wished the dull Prince of Wales (or perhaps the inept Pretender) to be: "unletter'd," but superior to "courts," faction, and bribery (n.p.), and, most importantly, ready to assume the mantle of leadership held out by the Swedish Dalecarlians, oppressed by the Danish and Norwegian King Cristiern and his "vicegerent" Trollio, the stock evil minister.[27] As in *The Fall of Mortimer* and James Ralph's *The Fall of the Earl of Essex* (1731), the hero is the mouthpiece of the mob, which Vasa, disguised as a peasant, leads in the chant "Liberty! Liberty!" (47). Backed by the force of the right-thinking populace, Vasa is swept onto the throne of Sweden, to which he has a hereditary claim. Cristiern conveniently disappears after stabbing Trollio and proclaiming him responsible for the failings of his reign. Monarchy is exonerated and bloated ministry is left to ponder the impossibility of its position: "O," laments the dying Trollio,

> let none aspire
> To be a King's Convenience! Has he Virtues,
> Those are his own; his Vices are his Minister's.
> Who dares to step 'twixt Envy and the Throne,
> Alike to feel the Caprice of his Prince,
> As publick Detestation.
>
> (75)

The audience, accustomed to gullible kings and vicious ministers on stage as in pamphlets and periodicals, would have recognized the conventional tactics of blaming bad ministers for bad monarchies and imaginatively punishing ministers who seemed invincible in real life.

But what makes Brooke's play appear less committed to the opposition than (say) *The Fall of Mortimer* is the element of uncertainty with which it closes. As in the Bolingbrokean comedies, the final act presents an opportunity for a marriage that would validate and fortify the new political order: Cristiern's daughter Cristina loves and is loved by Vasa and has been sought by him in marriage. The union would fuse rival claimants to the throne and neutralize the factionalism habitually lamented by polemicists in the 1730s and targeted by Bolingbroke in his appeals to a unified "country" party. This hypothetical closure would locate tragedy in the fall of the duped Cristiern and would posit the corrective to tragedy in the elevation of Vasa and the promise of a new lineage. Teleology would work much as it does in Lillo's predictable *The Christian Hero.*

Cristina, however, declines to marry. She will devote herself to assisting the physical and ideological regeneration of her father, "abandon'd now by ev'ry supple Wretch / That fed his Years with Flattery" (80), and suddenly sensitized, in his own words, to the dangers of a minister who has placed himself "between the Prince and People; cutting off / Communion from the Ear of Royalty" (74). But Cristiern has abdicated power and has no sons, and his transformation is without teleological or even dramatic significance. Cristina's decision leaves Vasa with no means—and apparently no intention—of producing heirs. In the absence of the conventional equation of heroic action and domestic validation, closure becomes the abandonment of the private sphere and the compensatory elevation of the public sphere. Vasa's final lines call attention to the recent death of his mother and sister and his rupture with Cristina. Public life will be for Vasa a substitute for private life rather than a complement to it:

> Come, come, my Brothers all! Yes I will strive
> To be the Sum of ev'ry Title to ye,
> And you shall be my Sire, my Friend reviv'd,
> My Sister, Mother, all that's kind and dear,
> For so *Gustavus* holds ye—O I will
> Of private Passions all my Soul divest,
> And take my dearer Country to my Breast.
> To publick Good transfer each fond Desire,
> And clasp my *Sweden* with a Lover's Fire.
> Well pleas'd, the Weight of all her Burdens bear;
> Dispense all Pleasure, but engross all Care.
> Still quick to find, to feel my People's Woes,
> And wake that Millions may enjoy Repose.
>
> (81)

Fiery or not, the union that Vasa proposes is sterile, in a sense doomed by its status as metaphor. The diction of desire, consummation, and kinship sidesteps the crucial question of succession that it would seem equipped to address. Surrounded by shouting Dalecarlians ("King!"; "Brother!"; "Father!"; "Friend!" [81]), Vasa selflessly professes his devotion to his "people." But closure does not accommodate an uncluttered vision of futurity as it does in the polemical Bolingbrokean comedies. A play that uses conventional opposition language presents a future founded on nothing stronger than a pathological transference of private needs to public life—a weird corruption of the old notion of the two-bodied king.

In William Duncombe's *Junius Brutus* (1735, performed 1734), the Bolingbrokean program is questioned more consciously. Loftis and Hume have both noted Duncombe's admiration in his play for William III. If one finds the play concerned primarily with the libertarian consul, Brutus, and the tyrant, Tarquin, then one will probably conclude with Loftis that Duncombe "makes a detailed defence of the constitutional principles inherent in the Revolution of 1688." One may even agree with Hume, who believes that the play "hits hard at Walpole via Tarquin's subversion of Roman law."[28] Charges like Hume's were evidently leveled against Duncombe in his own day. Duncombe, sounding like Francis Hare had a few years earlier, expressed "great surprise" at having learned "that an invidious construction has been put on several passages in [the play], as if intended to reflect on the Government, which was the furthest thing from my thoughts."[29]

Duncombe seems to have read his own play quite clearly. *Junius Brutus* is indeed a Williamite play, and Bolingbroke was indeed a Williamite; but for all that, Duncombe's is not a Bolingbrokean play, or even an "opposition" one in any meaningful sense. One might note, for instance, that only an extraordinarily foolish author would have appended to an anti-Walpole play anything like Duncombe's florid dedication to the Walpolite attorney general Philip Yorke, first earl of Hardwicke, who had been involved in two successful cases against Earbery (1717, 1722) (1731) for seditious libel.[30] A closer look at *Junius Brutus* reveals skepticism about the ways in which the patriot-opposition represented the Revolution. The play swells with Bolingbrokean paeans to "liberty," but is unable to translate them into a prescription for government.

Problematically, the character Messala is both the wicked minister and the conduit for the rhetoric of the Bolingbrokean opposition. His mission is to compromise Rome by pitting the military hero, Titus, against his father, Brutus, but he pretends to rally patriotic Romans under Titus's banner in order to vanquish Tarquin. Messala has assembled

> a Band select of faithful Friends,
> Who cannot brook the Yoke of these new Masters;
> Souls Resolute and Bold, whose Hands and Hearts
> Were form'd to shake, or change the Fate of Empires!
>
> (29)

Titus, says Messala, "is *Rome's* chief Support, / The very Life and Soul of all the Party" (30). Messala's refashioning of Titus is the fantasy of the patriot-opposition even as Messala himself is its scourge. The Iago-like plotter Messala easily controls Titus and furthers the action of the play by manipulating Titus's passion for Lucia, daughter of Tarquin.

Messala's disjunctive role as mouthpiece of and actor against Bolingbrokean ideology prevents the play from being the easy endorsement of Revolution principles that some critics would have it be. In his attempt to inspire Titus to claim the power of a king, Messala promotes the synthesis of monarchy and libertarianism that Duncombe, like "Caleb D'Anvers" (and various pro-government polemicists), praised in William III.[31] In Messala's rhetoric, however, the nostalgic Bolingbrokean strain jostles against the diction of conquest and tyranny:

> You may adorn the Name of Conqueror,
> With the more lovely Style of Mediator:
> The Virtues of a *Roman* Citizen
> Are seen in you, illustriously display'd;
> Now practise such as will become a Sovereign.
> Heaven puts into your Power, this happy Moment,
> The Object of your Vows, Revenge and Empire.—
> Bring back those Days, in which our Ancestors
> Weigh'd with impartial Hand, in equal Balance,
> Th'Authority of Kings, and Rights of Subjects.
>
> (63)

Messala's speech quickly becomes a plea for insurrection and parricide. Titus, although mindful of the Roman liberties that he has fought to ensure, allows himself to be tempted into rebellion when Messala claims that Tarquin has promised Lucia to him who restores Tarquin to the throne. Titus's conflict is between his apparently inherent commitment to libertarian government and his desire for Lucia:

> ... to see the *Romans* made a Prey
> To wild Ambition, and to lawless Power,
> I see, and I approve the Paths of Virtue,
> Yet, led by Love, pursue what I condemn!
>
> (70–71)

In conformity to the dictates of tragedy, passion wins and probity loses. Opposition rhetoric becomes hypocrisy in the mouth of Messala and pathos in that of Titus.

As in *Gustavus Vasa*, the rise of libertarian government is the demise of private or domestic life. Brutus's and Titus's recognition that the rebellious Titus must die creates in Brutus a crisis of identity much like that which closes *Vasa*. Brutus, forced to relinquish his claim to family, transfers to the public sphere the language of domesticity and aspires to governance based on the surrogate and sterile sort of "family" posited in Brooke's play. He gently rebukes the senators who would console him for the loss of his son and heir:

> I stand indebted to their Love—But now
> The threat'ning Dangers that surround the *Romans*,
> Claim all our Thoughts, and chase domestic Woes.
> Our Enemies prepare a fresh Attack[;]
> Then let us boldly meet them in the Field,
> Resigning to the Gods our righteous Case.
> I look on all *Rome*'s Citizens as Sons.
>
> (95)

"Domestic" here puns gently and accommodates a shift in emphasis from a literal to a figurative *domus*. As in *Gustavus Vasa*, the home is a useful metaphor but ultimately a hollow one. Titus's death is the purgation needed to rectify the state: "The Fatal Debt is paid to Justice, / And *Rome* is free," says Brutus (95). But the future of the state is not addressed, and again the power of a populist ruler is uninsured. Again like *Vasa* but unlike *The Fall of Mortimer*, *Edward and Eleonora*, or for that matter *Hamlet*, there is no new monarch approaching as the play closes.

Skepticism about opposition rhetoric is thematic in John Tracy's *Periander* (1731), in which the hero rejects the public sphere after failing to institutionalize the patriot-ideology articulated throughout the play. Hume agrees with Loftis that *Peri-*

ander is "a blatant 'propaganda' play denouncing Whig 'luxury' and tyranny, and proposing the restoration of the 'ancient' form of government in the best Bolingbrokean fashion."[32] Certainly this is the direction toward which Tracy's rhetoric tends—indeed, the dedication to Prince Frederick tells us as much. If *Periander* "proposes" anything, however, it does so in the absence of hope. The play is concerned less with promoting libertarian ideology than it is with demonstrating the difficulty of converting this ideology into a workable model of statescraft. As Duncombe does in *Junius Brutus*, Tracy conducts his inquiry (or encourages ours) by presenting closure as disjunctive and by distributing the commonplaces of the opposition among more-or-less attractive characters. But *Periander* denies even the possibility of transitory libertarian government that *Gustavus Vasa* and *Junius Brutus* allow.

The tyrant Procles lends his support to the besieged Periander, King of Corinth, in an effort to extend his own power. Procles and his evil minister Hypsenor appropriate the language of libertarianism in order to appease the Corinthian civic leaders Zeno and Alcander, who, as Loftis suggests, seem to be modeled on Bolingbroke and Pulteney.[33] Procles presents himself to the patriots in their own language:

> To free your Country from its various Ills,
> To fix its former Liberty, I come.
> I come to shew you what a King shou'd be,
> The Guardian, not th'Invader of your Laws.
>
> (15)

Swayed by this rote invocation of a glorious past, Alcander agrees to help Procles gain access to the city, asking only that Procles make more explicit still his promise to "restore" the city's "ancient Liberty" (15). Zeno, more suspicious but equally helpless, simply laments the choice between two bad monarchs.

Zeno and Alcander make a damaging choice in supporting the vicious Procles over the duped but salvageable Periander, and in so doing they hasten the dissolution of the body politic. Procles' incursions against Periander push Corinth to a civil war in which Periander's wife, Melissa, and their righteous son, Lycophron, are killed. (Lycophron's fate reminds us of the danger of seeking "parallels" too eagerly, or else sounds discordantly in a play dedicated to the Prince of Wales.) The death of his son occasions Periander's recollection of his once-forgotten commitment to an "ancient State" (43), which he now describes as an idyllic government of "Rights," "Liberties," and "Laws revive[d]" (60). But ideological regeneration is rendered politically meaningless by the suicide of Periander, grieving for the loss of his son and heir and willing to leave Corinth without a ruler or a line of succession.

Periander abandons all pretense of optimism for goals in themselves attractive. The force of genre compromises the play's ideological interest by making Bolingbrokean ideology the agent of tragedy. Zeno and Alcander fairly explode with opposition jargon, but nothing they say affects positively the political structures represented in the play. Zeno "burn[s] to set [his] suff'ring country, free, / And give the ancient Liberty to *Corinth*" (3). Like Brooke's Vasa and like Lancaster in *Majesty Misled*, he exhorts the populace in the cause of "Liberty" and the "former Fame and Splendor" of the state (11). But Tracy has embedded an irony in the play that makes ideology subservient to genre and that ensures that Zeno and Alcander express sentiments that cannot be realized. Unknown to Zeno and Alcander, populism and monarchy are irreconcilable in Corinth: Periander has promised his dying father to rule the "ancient State" of Corinth as a democratic governor rather than as a king. Periander is convinced that the problems besetting the state are the result of his failure to honor this promise, and the fable shows the tragic ruler purging the state and atoning for his own misuse of power. Zeno and Alcander's noisy and frantic Bolingbrokeanism operates, as it were, outside the generic structure of the play, vainly struggling to create a regenerative comedy from materials that Periander knows are the stuff of tragedy.

Zeno and Alcander eventually identify the insincerity and the menace of Procles and Hypsenor, but they are not empowered by the fall of the evil characters. The language of hopelessness and retreat enters their speech, as when Alcander says,

> . . . far from *Corinth* will I take my Flight,
> No Scene of Horror more shall blast my Eyes,
> But safe from Tyrants in some Desart live,
> Nor with the Thought of Man profane my Breast.
> (57–58)

The movement is toward a radically private sphere, or toward Zeno and Alcander's rejection of the communal implications of the ideology that they have espoused throughout the play. Zeno's curtain speech about Periander employs a generalized moral vocabulary and ends the play with a pat "solution" in which the action of the play has left no room to believe:

> These are thy Spoils, Ambition! these thy Triumphs!
> Infernal Lust of Pow'r! what-e'er it reigns,
> Like furious Storms broke loose, it knows no Bound,
> Rages and roars, and spreads a Waste around,
> Distracts the beauteous Order of the Soul,
> While Reason only can its Rage controul:
> When she breaks forth, like Night it fleets away,
> And leaves behind, a calm unshaded Day.
>
> (64)

For Alcander at least, this "calm unshaded Day" is to be found away from the hubbub of day-to-day politics and the frustrations of implementing a populist government in a self-interested (and predetermined) world. "Reason" here is hopelessly abstract—a vague attempt to redefine philosophically values that have failed politically. It is difficult to imagine a less convincing, or a less convinced, piece of "propaganda."

A more extensive inventory of the history-plays would further suggest that the superabundant "political commonplace" that Hume finds in Restoration and eighteenth-century drama often means in the Walpole era equally the commonplaces of the opposition and those about it. Ralph's *The Fall of the Earl of Essex* closes with a regenerate Elizabeth mindful of the evil of powerful ministers and able to transform her love for the martyred Essex into a useful lesson about governance. The extratextual "closure" of history, however, reminds the viewer or reader that Elizabeth's ideological resuscitation is circumscribed by her failure to marry and to stave off the Stuarts, emblematic in Bolingbrokean historiography, as we have seen, of tyranny and antipopulism. Havard's *Scanderbeg* (1733) presents a libertarian hero who abandons the fruits of his political efforts in a strangely renunciative marriage. As in Aphra Behn's prose "history" *Oroonoko* (ca. 1688), genre subverts ideology when the hero uses pulse-quickening rhetoric to propagate a military conflict that is at bottom a means to reunite him with his lover.[34] We may suspect that Havard's distaste for the Bolingbrokean opposition dates back at least this far when we observe his passionate Hali-Vizen planning the rape of the heroine Deamira and rattling off gross blandishments about

"Liberty," "the great Call of Freedom," and "the gripping Hand of Tyranny" (10–11).

Like much of the other nonce literature of the period, the history-plays discourage us from making generalizations about "coherent" ideology. We would do better to consider them as participants in a noisy debate about liberty, populism, kingship, and the succession. These works are generically equipped to act out the relationship between fine words and fallible or vicious actions. They present anxieties about ideology in ways more complex—and often less conclusive—than those available to polemicists skeptical about or disturbed by the terms of Bolingbroke's bid for the headship of the opposition.

Conclusion

At the beginning of his monograph on Bolingbroke, Isaac Kramnick recited Edmund Burke's question "Who now reads Bolingbroke, who ever read him through?" Kramnick responded, "many have, and many still do."[1] As the reappraisal of Bolingbroke's influence at the end of Kramnick's book demonstrates, Kramnick was right to answer in a way that Burke would not have liked, a question that Burke had not wanted answered in the first place. But *how* has Bolingbroke been read? Before commenting on Bolingbroke's contributions to nineteenth- and twentieth-century thought, Kramnick observes that the Walpolite press "damned" Bolingbroke, as did Walpole's son, Horace.[2] This is not surprising. What Kramnick does not say is that when Burke dismissed Bolingbroke in 1791, he was participating in a reaction against Bolingbroke that had been substantial even at the zenith of Bolingbroke's career, when anti-Bolingbrokeanism cut across party lines that we have tended to regard as rather more rigid.

Samuel Johnson's and Henry Fielding's cynical comments on Bolingbroke's piety and politics, recorded in the introduction of this study, demonstrate that Burke was not the only person to impugn Bolingbroke in the second half of the eighteenth century.[3] H. T. Dickinson has charted the mid-century's reaction against Bolingbroke's *Letters on the Study and Use of History* and his posthumously published writings on religion.[4] Two biographies from this period provide further evidence of the rancor that Bolingbroke inspired after his death.[5] And the present study has shown that, even in the 1730s, Bolingbroke's homogenizing program was regarded with skepticism or hostility by a liberal cross section of the populace that Bolingbroke courted in his polemical works. While there is no point in begrudging Bolingbroke what influence he did have, we should know as well that the rebuttal of Bolingbrokean polemics made common cause for writers as diverse as James Pitt, William Arnall, Lord Hervey, Richard Russel, Matthias Earbery, Joseph Trapp, Francis Hare, William Havard, and John Tracy.

Alongside of Burke's showy snub is a more substantial point

that Kramnick does not address. Comparing Bolingbroke to the deists Anthony Collins, John Toland, Matthew Tindall, Thomas Chubb, and Thomas Morgan, Burke asserts that, like the freethinkers, Bolingbroke (and presumably his "country" party) "never acted in corps, nor were known as a faction in the state, nor presumed to influence, in that name or character, or for the purposes of such a faction, on any of our public concerns."[6] Burke here evinces the practical politician's dislike of the mere theorist, and in this his comment is of a piece with Walpolite apologetics of the 1730s. More condemningly, by stressing the distance of Bolingbroke's activities from the real business of statescraft, Burke disqualifies Bolingbroke even from the (Bolingbrokean) category of "faction." The comment recalls the attempts of Pitt and Arnall to remind Bolingbroke of his "place" in the 1730s.

I have agreed with Burke that Bolingbroke's lack of effectiveness was to some extent a corollary from his position outside the formal structures of politics. *The Remarks on the History of England* attempt to engage the pro-government press in a battle about England's past that the Walpolites could not win and, more to the point, that they quickly realized that they did not need to fight. The Carolinists who opposed Bolingbroke did so in part by reminding him that his vision of politics—founded, like the pro-government position, on "Revolution principles"—was no more legitimate than pro-government orthodoxy. To these writers, Bolingbroke the outsider looked like Walpole the insider and only advertised his own absurdity by proposing to emend the workings of a government from which he was plainly excluded. Finally, a number of historical dramatists of the 1730s played Bolingbrokean ideology off of generic convention and found the former menacing, inert, or simply meaningless. Joel Weinsheimer acutely describes Bolingbroke's career as a study in "sublimated despair." This condition is part of Bolingbroke's anxiety about being excluded from the workings of "history," or, to recast Weinsheimer's point slightly, simply from the sites of political power.[7] And in the 1730s, Bolingbroke had more reminders of his distance from power than even Walpole's busy press corps could have taunted him with. Burke was not the first to charge Bolingbroke with being hopelessly distant from the political sphere that he sought to influence or, even, from the opposition that he claimed to represent.

A dozen years before Burke remarked on Bolingbroke, James Ralph, coeditor with Fielding of the antiministerial *Champion*

(1739–44), commented on the *Craftsman*'s lack of legitimate political power. In *The Case of Authors by Profession or Trade* (1758), Ralph listed as one of three "provinces" of authorship "to write for a Faction in the Name of the Community" (19).⁸ His example is Bolingbroke's partner Nicholas Amhurst; but his comments apply equally to Bolingbroke himself, whose political beliefs guided Amhurst and the *Craftsman* throughout the late '20s and the first half of the '30s. "This Province," wrote Ralph,

> can be but a very narrow one: And I call it the most flattering of all, because the Writer who fills it, is expected to do that without Doors, which his Confederates in a superior Station, find impracticable to do within; because he finds himself consulted and caressed by them on this Account; and because of the Assurances given him, That in the Division of the promised Land, a Lot shall be reserv'd for him.
>
> While, therefore, these occasional Connections hold, while he is useful in collecting the Materials of Opposition, and in working up the whole Mass to a Head, Hope sweetens all his Labours, all his Difficulties, all his Discouragements, and he at least enjoys the Dream, of growing serviceable to himself and his Country together.
>
> (30–31)

When Ralph comments on the status of the party-writer as outsider, he anticipates Burke, allowing for the relative generosity of Ralph's tone. When he turns to the fate of the polemicist, "*left to rot*" like "*an unregarded Bulrush*" after the rise of those whom he had supported (31), Ralph sounds more like Oliver Goldsmith, who in 1770 would remark on Bolingbroke's "almost forgotten" entries in the *Craftsman*.⁹

Burke, Ralph, and Goldsmith variously identify two problems with polemical literature, both of which have concerned me in this study: first, that the opposition polemicist cannot overcome the difficulty of being excluded from political power, and, secondly, that polemicists more generally cannot transcend the limitations imposed by the genre in which they work. So it was with Bolingbroke. His appeals for unity, couched in a language that would have been easily accessible to his contemporary readers, were time-bound attempts to bring the political debate to people who either could not participate in it, or who could participate in it quite well without Bolingbroke's assistance. The progovernment press was justified in reminding its readers that, his gentility notwithstanding, Bolingbroke wrote ephemeral bits of propaganda for an astringent weekly newspaper animated by its hostility toward the king's ministers and perhaps the king himself.

Ralph observes that Amhurst died in poverty in 1742, his tenure with the *Craftsman* well behind him. Bolingbroke, again expatriate when Amhurst died, had the comfort of an estate and an income. But his "Dream," battered by the mid-'30s, also expired in 1742, when Walpole finally stepped down and the "Lots" in Ralph's "promised Land" were meted out quite differently than they might have been five or ten years earlier. There was no room in the new order for Bolingbroke. Dickinson notes that by the middle of 1742, "Bolingbroke was bitterly aware that his major political aims, both for himself and for the Tory-Patriot opposition, had suffered a crippling blow." Pulteney seemed to be priming himself for higher achievement when he "abandoned the idea of a coalition of parties being in the national interest and . . . sold out to his former opponents."[10] But the about-face meant little. When Pulteney refused to cooperate in the formation of the new government, the spoils of the print wars went to the likes of Samuel Sandys; Spencer Compton; and John, Lord Carteret. The hydra-headed "Caleb D'Anvers" remained on the outside.

Burke's, Ralph's, and Goldsmith's variations on the old theme of fleeting mundane glory remind us that the only way to preserve Bolingbroke as a disinterested political theorist is to remove him from the topical milieu of polemical literature and to lodge him in a more Parnassian locale. I have argued against this selective sort of rehabilitation, while acknowledging that Bolingbroke—smart, arrogant, and affiliated with many of the best-known public figures of his day—is a tempting subject for precisely such treatment. But to do this to Bolingbroke is to distort our understanding of the political debate in the Walpole era. We have refashioned Bolingbroke in two ways, both of which fall under the broad rubric of textual history: first, by reprinting his works in ways that obscure their connections to Grub-street journalism, and, second, by giving short shrift to the works that record the eighteenth century's vigorous interrogation of his polemics. If we regard Bolingbroke's political philosophy as distinct from the contexts in which Bolingbroke produced it, we lose sight of what Bolingbroke was to his contemporaries and of how the reaction against his appeals to consensus inflamed, rather than informed, the print wars of the 1730s.

Notes

Introduction

1. See Goldgar, *Walpole and the Wits: The Relation of Politics to Literature, 1722–1742* (Lincoln: University of Nebraska Press, 1976), 6, 3; see Kramnick, *Bolingbroke and His Circle: The Politics of Nostalgia in the Age of Walpole* (Cambridge, Mass.: Harvard University Press, 1968), passim; and Cruickshanks, Introduction to *Ideology and Conspiracy: Aspects of Jacobitism, 1689–1759*, ed. Cruickshanks (Edinburgh: John Donald, 1982), 7. Goldgar elsewhere notes that "the Scriblerian wits were never involved in an organized opposition in the sense of a planned and coordinated literary-political campaign" (42). Howard Erskine-Hill believes that Goldgar's neglect of manuscript materials compromises his analysis of "the great issue of the relation between rulers and writers in the Walpole Era": review of *Walpole and the Wits*, *Review of English Studies* n.s. 30 (February 1979): 92. For the homogenizing effect of the Pretender, James Edward Stuart, on the parliamentary opposition in 1730, see Cruickshanks, *Political Untouchables: The Tories and the '45* (London: Duckworth, 1979), 12–13. Norma Landau notes that Cruickshanks "has not ... addressed the question of the implications of Jacobitism for interpretation of the society in which it appeared": "Country Matters: *The Growth of Political Stability* a Quarter-Century On," *Albion* 25 (Summer 1993): 263.

2. For Bolingbroke's relationship with Pope, see Brean Hammond, *Pope and Bolingbroke: A Study of Friendship and Influence* (Columbia: University of Missouri Press, 1984). The standard biography is H. T. Dickinson, *Bolingbroke* (London: Constable, 1970). My biographical summary is adapted from Dickinson and from Simon Varey, *Henry St. John, Viscount Bolingbroke* (Boston: Twayne, 1984); the quotation is from Dickinson, 177.

3. Fielding, "A Fragment of a Commentary on L. Bolingbroke's Essays," in *Journal of a Voyage to Lisbon* (1755), 249–76 (mispaginated 201–28), 257 (mispaginated 209).

4. Plumb, *The Growth of Political Stability in England, 1675-1725* (London: Macmillan, 1967), 189, xvi; Landau, 264–65. See Colley, *In Defiance of Oligarchy: The Tory Party, 1714–60* (Cambridge: Cambridge University Press, 1982); Monod, *Jacobitism and the English People, 1688–1788* (Cambridge: Cambridge University Press, 1989); and Rogers, *Whigs and Cities: Popular Politics in the Age of Walpole and Pitt* (Oxford: Clarendon, 1989), 3–4. Landau's essay is one of four essays published in *Albion* 25 (Summer 1993) that reevaluate Plumb's thesis; see also Clayton Roberts, "The Growth of Political Stability Reconsidered," 237–55; Stephen Baxter, "A Comment on Clayton Roberts' Perspective," 257–60; and Roberts, "A Reply to Professors Baxter and Landau," 275–77. Jeremy Black discusses "the vexed question of stability" in *Robert Walpole*

and the Nature of Politics in Early Eighteenth-Century England (New York: St. Martin's, 1990), particularly 23–26 (the quotation is from 23).

5. See Colley, 5–7; Monod, 10; and Rogers, 4.

6. McKeon, The Origins of the English Novel, 1600–1740 (Baltimore: Johns Hopkins University Press, 1987), 20.

7. Bender, "A New History of the Enlightenment?," in The Profession of Eighteenth-Century Literature: Reflections on an Institution, ed. Leo Damrosch (Madison: University of Wisconsin Press, 1992), 64–65. Cf. Robert Hume, who argues that "'New Historicism' is a text-based form of close reading that relies upon essentially arbitrary comparisons with other texts": "Texts within Contexts: Notes toward a Historical Method," Philological Quarterly 71 (Winter 1992): 71. For Bender's readings of Defoe and Fielding, see Imagining the Penitentiary: Fiction and the Architecture of Mind in Eighteenth-Century England (Chicago: University of Chicago Press, 1987). Mack's The Garden and the City: Retirement and Politics in the Later Poetry of Pope, 1731–1743 (Toronto: University of Toronto Press, 1969) would seem to fit Bender's "broad definitional traits" perfectly.

8. Lewis, "Addison," in Eighteenth Century English Literature: Modern Essays in Criticism, ed. James Clifford (New York: Oxford University Press, 1959), 152.

9. Pope, Epilogue to the Satires, Dialogue 2, in Imitations of Horace, vol. 4 of The Twickenham Edition of the Poems of Alexander Pope, ed. John Butt (London: Methuen; New Haven: Yale University Press, 1961), l. 248.

10. Lewis, 152.

11. Arnall earns a passing mention in Kramnick, 117, and Varey, 65, but is otherwise absent from discussions of Bolingbroke. Cf. Thomas Horne, "Politics in a Corrupt Society: William Arnall's Defense of Robert Walpole," Journal of the History of Ideas 41 (October–December 1980): 601–14; and see Shelley Burtt's appraisal of Arnall and his fellow Walpolite James Pitt in Virtue Transformed: Political Argument in England, 1688–1740 (Cambridge: Cambridge University Press, 1992), 110–28. More generally, J. G. A. Pocock observes that Bolingbroke's "journalistic adversaries" were "obscure men whose ability has been much underrated": The Machiavellian Moment: Florentine Political Thought and the Atlantic Republican Tradition (Princeton: Princeton University Press, 1975), 480. Earbery's hostility to Bolingbroke has not been noticed since the eighteenth century.

12. McGann, A Critique of Modern Textual Criticism (Chicago: University of Chicago Press, 1983), 43–44. The idea recurs in McGann, The Textual Condition (Princeton: Princeton University Press, 1991), and "Literary Pragmatics and the Editorial Horizon," in Devils and Angels: Textual Editing and Literary Theory, ed. Philip Cohen (Charlottesville: University Press of Virginia, 1991), 1–21.

13. Pat Rogers observes that "the great stroke of the Augustan satirists was to make the world of low literature serve as subject and setting of their works": Grub Street: Studies in a Subculture (London: Methuen, 1971), 3. Rogers overlooks tonal similarities and affective feints (the rage, the sense of threat, the grandstanding) that ally Pope and the "dunces." And Pope's relation to the "low" is of a different order in The Dunciad, Rogers's main concern, than in Peri Bathos (1727) or his anonymous Master Key to Popery (written 1732), both of which are equally immersions in "low literature" and satirical appropriations of it.

14. Pope, *An Epistle from Mr. Pope, to Dr. Arbuthnot*, in *Imitations of Horace*, ll. 219–20.

15. Weinsheimer, *Eighteenth-Century Hermeneutics: Philosophy of Interpretation in England from Locke to Burke* (New Haven: Yale University Press, 1993), 73.

16. Arnall, *Observations on a Pamphlet Intitled, An Answer to One Part of a Late Infamous Libel* (1731), 19, 29. Pulteney's pamphlet is *An Answer to One Part of a Late Infamous Libel, Intitled, Remarks on the Craftsman's Vindication of His Two Honourable Patrons* (1731).

17. Bolingbroke, *A Dissertation upon Parties*, in vol. 2 of *The Works of Lord Bolingbroke* (1844; reprint, New York: Augustus M. Kelley, 1967), 24. Pocock has argued that the new nomenclature actually reasserted early eighteenth-century divisions between "Whigs, who upheld the principles of 1688, and Tories, who could not be trusted to do so" (483).

18. For authorship of essays in the *Craftsman*, see Varey, Introduction to *Lord Bolingbroke: Contributions to the* Craftsman, ed. Varey (Oxford: Clarendon, 1982), xxiii–xxiv. I use Varey's attributions throughout this study.

19. Gunn, *Beyond Liberty and Property: The Process of Self-Recognition in Eighteenth-Century Political Thought* (Kingston, Ontario: McGill-Queen's University Press, 1983), 59.

20. Kenyon, *Revolution Principles: The Politics of Party 1689–1720* (Cambridge: Cambridge University Press, 1977), 75.

21. See Loftis, *The Politics of Drama in Augustan England* (Oxford: Clarendon, 1963), 94–127; and Hume, *Henry Fielding and the London Theatre, 1728–1737* (Oxford: Clarendon, 1988), 77–86. For Hume on "commonplace" and "ideology," see *The Rakish Stage: Studies in English Drama, 1660–1800* (Carbondale: Southern Illinois University Press, 1983), 14–27.

22. For the opposition press's decline in vigor, ca. 1735–37, see Michael Harris, *London Newspapers in the Age of Walpole: A Study of the Origins of the Modern English Press* (Rutherford, N.J.: Fairleigh Dickinson University Press; London: Associated University Presses, 1987), 122–25. For *Fog's* particularly, see Harris, 123.

23. Goldgar, 28.

24. Goldgar, 162; see also 42.

25. Goldgar, 135.

CHAPTER 1. BOLINGBROKE'S *REMARKS ON THE HISTORY OF ENGLAND*

1. *The Craftsman*, 7 vols. (1731; expanded to 14 vols. in 1737); Kramnick, ed., *Lord Bolingbroke: Historical Writings* (Chicago: University of Chicago Press, 1972).

2. McGann, *A Critique of Modern Textual Criticism* (Chicago: University of Chicago Press, 1983), 8.

3. The estimate of the *Craftsman's* sales in 1731 is from *The Danverian History of the Affairs of Europe* (1732); for cautious support, see Michael Harris, *London Newspapers in the Age of Walpole: A Study of the Origins of the Modern English Press* (Rutherford, N.J.: Fairleigh Dickinson University Press; London: Associated University Presses, 1987), 58; and Simon Varey, Introduction, *Lord Bolingbroke: Contributions to the* Craftsman (Oxford: Clarendon, 1982), xiv. In December 1730, the pro-government pamphlet *Liberty and the*

Craftsman estimated the *Craftsman*'s weekly sales at 10,000 to 12,000, and the pro-government *London Journal*'s weekly sales at 2,000 to 3,000 (4). For the *Craftsman*'s circulation more broadly, see Harris, *London Newspapers*, 115–17; and "Figures Relating to the Printing and Distribution of the *Craftsman* 1726 to 1730," *Bulletin of the Institute of Historical Research* 43 (November 1970): 233–42.

4. For figures on the *Grub-street Journal*, see "The Minute Book of the Partners in the *Grub Street Journal*," *Publishing History* 4 (1978): 49–94, 76, 78, 82, 84; the "minute book" does not provide information on No. 25 (25 June 1730)–No. 30 (30 July 1730), or on print runs after March 1731. James Hillhouse notes that the *Journal* "seems to have caught on at once, and to have flourished most prosperously for some five years": *The Grub-Street Journal* (Durham: Duke University Press, 1928), 10. See also contemporary evidence reproduced by Bertrand Goldgar in "Pope and the *Grub-street Journal*," *Modern Philology* 74 (May 1977): 366.

5. Bolingbroke published 27 pieces, including the *Remarks*, in the *Craftsman* from June 1730 to May 1731; this is far more than he contributed during any other period of equal length.

6. Kramnick, Introduction, *Lord Bolingbroke: Historical Writings*, xli.

7. Bolingbroke's narrator concludes his discussion of Machiavelli in the second letter of the *Remarks* by saying, "The Examples, which *Machiavel* cites to shew that the Virtue of particular Men among the *Romans*, did frequently draw that government back to its *original Principles* [i.e., *ricorso*], are so many Proofs that the Duration of *Liberty* depends on keeping the *Spirit* of it alive and warm" (No. 208; 27 June 1730). For Bolingbroke's Machiavellian strain, see Kramnick, *Bolingbroke and His Circle: The Politics of Nostalgia in the Age of Walpole* (Cambridge, Mass.: Harvard University Press, 1968), 25, 33, 75, 104, 130, 163–68; Kramnick, Introduction, *Lord Bolingbroke: Historical Writings*, xix, xx, xxii, xlv, li; and J. G. A. Pocock, *The Machiavellian Moment: Florentine Political Thought and the Atlantic Republican Tradition* (Princeton: Princeton University Press, 1975), 483–86. For Bolingbroke and exemplary historiography generally, see George Nadel, "Philosophy of History before Empiricism," *History and Theory* 3 (1964): 306, 311–12; and Joel Weinsheimer, *Eighteenth-Century Hermeneutics: Philosophy of Interpretation from Locke to Burke* (New Haven: Yale University Press, 1993), 75.

8. See *A Register of Books, 1728–1732, Extracted from the Monthly Chronicle* (London: Gregg-Archive, 1964).

9. See 71–72, below.

10. Amhurst wrote Nos. 239 and 243; the authors of 241 and 244 are unknown. Arnall's series appeared intermittently in the *Free Briton* from 25 Mar. 1731 (No. 69) to 24 June 1731 (No. 82). Amhurst and Pulteney respond to the series in *Craftsman* 251 (24 Apr. 1731). For the sparring over *Craftsman* 255, see Alexander Pettit, "Propaganda, Public Relations, and the *Remarks* on the *Craftsman's Vindication of His Two Hon[oura]ble Patrons*, in His Paper of May 22, 1731," *Huntington Library Quarterly* 57 (Winter 1994): 45–59.

11. See the *Spectator* (1711–12) and the *Tea-Table* (1724).

12. See also *The Case of Opposition Stated, between the Craftsman and the People* (1731; reprinted in *The Craftsman: Four Tracts* [New York: Garland, 1974]) on England before the founding of the *Craftsman*: "Was not all the World at Peace, and the People of *England* happy? Neither Foreign Broils threatned

them, nor Domestick Feuds distracted them; they were satisfied with the Powers above them, which gave all just Protection to them" (5).

13. Varey, who conflates the "narrator" of letter 3 and the speaker of the series, evidently believes that Oldcastle and the Gentleman are one and the same; see *Henry St. John, Viscount Bolingbroke* (Boston: Twayne, 1984), 51, 54. Kramnick says nothing of Bolingbroke's personae in *Bolingbroke and His Circle* or in his introduction to *Lord Bolingbroke: Historical Writings*.

14. Pulteney, *An Answer to a Late Pamphlet, Intituled, Observations on the Writings of the Craftsman* (1730), 16; Pulteney is responding to John, Lord Hervey's *Observations on the Writings of the Craftsman* (1730).

15. See Goldgar, *Walpole and the Wits: The Relation of Politics to Literature, 1722–1742* (Lincoln: University of Nebraska Press, 1976), 87; and Varey, *Henry St. John*, 51.

16. See, for example, Kramnick's introduction to *Lord Bolingbroke: Historical Writings*, particularly xv.

17. Goldsmith, *The Life of Henry St. John, Lord Viscount Bolingbroke* (1770), in vol. 3 of *The Collected Works of Oliver Goldsmith*, ed. Arthur Friedman (Oxford: Clarendon, 1966), 466. Cf. Goldsmith's subsequent claim that "as a political writer, few can equal, and none can exceed [Bolingbroke]. As he was a practical politician, his writings are less filled with those speculative illusions, which are the result of solitude and seclusion. He wrote them with a certainty of their being opposed, sifted, examined, and reviled; he therefore took care to build them up of such materials, as could not be easily overthrown: they prevailed at the times in which they were written, they still continue to the admiration of the present age, and will probably last for ever" (473). Goldsmith wrote the *Life* for an edition of *A Dissertation upon Parties* (see Friedman, Introduction to *The Life of Henry St. John*, 431), which suggests that he had this work in mind here; he may have been unaware that the *Dissertation* first appeared in the *Craftsman*. Goldsmith praises both the *Dissertation* (467) and *The Idea of a Patriot King* (470) in the *Life of Henry St. John*.

18. See Bolingbroke in *Craftsman* 208 (27 June 1730), 210 (11 July 1730), and 219 (12 Sept. 1730); see Amhurst in Nos. 212 (25 July 1730), 220 (19 Sept. 1730), 221 (26 Sept. 1730), 239 (31 Jan. 1730); see Amhurst and Pulteney in No. 236 (9 Jan. 1731); and see also essays by unidentified authors in Nos. 241 (13 Feb. 1731) and 244 (6 Mar. 1731).

19. See Bolingbroke's *Works*: 1754 (2 vols.); 1841 (4 vols., Philadelphia); and 1844 (4 vols.; reprint, New York: Augustus M. Kelley, 1976). All these editions include the *Remarks*. Varey, who uses the folios for his own work, describes the 1844 edition as "not very well edited" and "incomplete," but nonetheless "the standard collection" (*Henry St. John*, 129).

20. For the bibliographical code, see McGann, *The Textual Condition* (Princeton: Princeton University Press, 1991), passim. The quotations are from 56, 51.

21. McGann, *The Textual Condition*, 51.

22. Bornstein, "What Is the Text of a Poem by Yeats?," in *Palimpsest: Editorial Theory in the Humanities*, ed. Bornstein and Ralph Williams (Ann Arbor: University of Michigan Press, 1993), 179.

23. For Bolingbroke as "O," see Varey, Introduction, *Lord Bolingbroke: Contributions to the* Craftsman, xxiii–xxv.

24. Varey holds Francklin responsible for the resequencing; see Introduction, *Lord Bolingbroke: Contributions to the* Craftsman, xxix, note 14. For a compari-

son of numbers and dates in the folios and the 1731 edition, see Herbert Davis, "Reprinting The Craftsman," Book Collector 2 (Winter 1953): 280–81. Davis assigns responsibility, evasively, to "the editor of this edition" (280).

25. Bornstein, 183, 186.

26. Kramnick seems to have used the 1841 (Philadelphia) edition of Bolingbroke's Works as his copy-text, although he notes, misleadingly, that in the "bound editions of 1730 and . . . 1736 [sic]" one may find "the original essays for the Remarks on the History of England" (Introduction, Lord Bolingbroke: Historical Writings, liii). Elsewhere, Kramnick, relying on the resequenced 1731 edition, says that "the essays appeared in The Craftsman on and off from no. 218 (5 Sept. 1730) to no. 255 (22 May 1731)" (Bolingbroke and His Circle, 275, note 58); cf. 145, where Kramnick refers to the folio-date of Bolingbroke's second letter but references the information to the 1841 edition (294, note 27).

27. Significantly, the Letters were printed only privately (by Pope) during Bolingbroke's lifetime and only published after his death (see Varey, Henry St. John, 78). The work's assumptions about audience are therefore different from those of the Remarks.

28. See, for instance, David Nokes, Raillery and Rage: A Study in Eighteenth Century Satire (New York: St. Martin's, 1987).

29. Kramnick, Introduction, Lord Bolingbroke: Historical Writings, xxxix.

30. Kramnick, ed., Lord Bolingbroke: Historical Writings, 320.

31. Varey, Henry St. John, 35.

32. Craftsman 1 (5 Dec. 1731) establishes that "D'Anvers" had left the profession of law but remained a "bencher," or senior member of the Inns of Court.

33. Two items from the Grub-street Journal's "London News" section hint at the social distance between Pulteney and Francklin. The last entry under 6 July 1731 notes that "Mr. Richard Francklin, the reputed Printer of the Craftsman, hath had notice given him by the Sollicitor for the Crown, to prepare for his tryal, upon an information, in the sittings after Term"; the first entry under 7 July notes that "last night about 8 Will. Pulteney, Esq.; and Sir Tho. Lumley Sanderson, Brother to the E. of Scarborough, arrived together at their respective houses in Arlington street, from Sir Rob. Furness's seat near Dover" (No. 79; 8 July 1731).

34. McGann, Critique, 8, 81.

35. McGann, "Literary Pragmatics and the Editorial Horizon," in Devils and Angels: Textual Editing and Literary Theory, ed. Philip Cohen (Charlottesville: University Press of Virginia, 1991), 9–10.

36. The Clarissa Project, gen. ed. Florian Stuber (New York: AMS, 1990–). The quotation is from the title of vol. 11 of the series.

CHAPTER 2. BOLINGBROKE'S ANALOGIC HISTORIOGRAPHY

1. Hervey, Ancient and Modern Liberty Stated and Compar'd (1734; reprint, Los Angeles: Augustan Reprint Society, 1989), 3–4.

2. Hervey's first anti-Bolingbroke pamphlet was An Answer to the Occasional Writer No. II (1727).

3. Hervey's own tendency to define the opposition by its adherence to a common rhetoric is evident throughout Ancient and Modern Liberty Stated and Compar'd.

4. Hervey, The Conduct of the Opposition (1734), 54, 53. For other common homogenizing strategies, see, for instance, The Case of Opposition Stated, be-

tween the *Craftsman and the People* (1731; reprinted in *The Craftsman: Four Tracts* [New York: Garland, 1974]), the author of which makes no effort to distinguish between the *Craftsman* and the "opposition." And see John "Orator" Henley's *Hyp-Doctor*, notable for conflating the *Craftsman* and other opposition journals, as in No. 92 (5 Sept. 1732) and No. 94 (26 Sept. 1732), which merges the *Craftsman* and *Fog's Weekly Journal* in an attack on "the Logick of the CALEBites [and] the *Fog-pates*."

5. Shelley Burtt comments on the difficulty faced by Pitt in his endeavor to answer Bolingbroke's *Remarks* and *A Dissertation upon Parties*, in both of which Bolingbroke had criticized a system of placemanship that plainly existed; see *Virtue Transformed: Political Argument in England, 1688–1740* (Cambridge: Cambridge University Press, 1992), 119.

6. See Laurence Hanson, *Government and the Press 1695–1763* (Oxford: Oxford University Press, 1936), 67, note 1.

7. I am indebted to Simon Varey for the information on the Public Record Office.

8. *Liberty and the Craftsman* seems to be the only source that reports a reprimand; the pamphlet does not mention a date. The author supposes that Francklin's punishment "may cost him three Guineas" but stands to earn him "twenty or thirty Pounds" in sales of papers that discuss the arrest (4); see also *The Danverian History of the Affairs of Europe, for the Memorable Year 1731* (1732), 78–79.

9. Harris says only that "whether this particular prosecution was followed up is doubtful and it was completely overshadowed by the subsequent case against No. 235 of 2 January," that is, by the arrest for printing the "Hague letter" ("Figures Relating to the Printing and Distribution of the *Craftsman* 1726 to 1730," *Bulletin of the Institute of Historical Research* 42 [November 1970]: 234).

10. Varey, *Henry St. John, Viscount Bolingbroke* (Boston: Twayne, 1984), 58.

11. For Francklin's acquittal in 1729 and the opposition's response, see Hanson, 19, 67. See Hanson, 23, for the quotation; for more on the Juries Act and the trial, see Hanson, 67–68, and Varey, *Henry St. John*, 58.

12. For the delay in the trial, see *Craftsman* 263 (17 July 1731); for Francklin's arrest for publishing Pulteney's pamphlet, and for the maneuvering of his counsel on that occasion, see No. 265 (31 July 1731).

13. For the trial and conviction, see vol. 17 of T. B. Howell, ed., *A Complete Collection of State Trials* (1813), 626–75. The date of the sentencing is noted in *Craftsman* 294 (19 Feb. 1732); Francklin had been jailed the week before (see *Craftsman* 293; 12 Feb. 1732). The quotation is from *State Trials*, 675.

14. Varey, "The Craftsman 1726–1752: An Historical and Critical Account" (Ph.D. thesis, Cambridge University, 1976), 284.

15. See Hanson, 16–18, for libel, and 18 for Tutchin.

16. Harris, *London Newspapers in the Age of Walpole: A Study of the Origins of the Modern English Press* (Rutherford, N.J.: Fairleigh Dickinson University Press; London: Associated University Presses, 1987), 147. For Hardwicke's reluctance to prosecute for libel after 1729, see Hanson, 67; and see Harris, *London Newspapers*, 151.

17. Boyer, vol. 42 of *The Political State of Great-Britain* (1732), 88.

18. Varey, *Henry St. John*, 58; Harris, *London Newspapers*, 150.

19. For the opposition in 1729 and 1730, see J. H. Plumb, *Sir Robert Walpole: The King's Minister* (London: Cresset, 1960), 200–1.

20. For the quick collapse in 1727 of the opposition's hopes that George II would not rely upon Walpole as his father had, see Bertrand Goldgar, *Walpole and the Wits: The Relation of Literature to Politics, 1722–1742* (Lincoln: University of Nebraska Press, 1976), 48; for premature speculation about the fall of Walpole early in 1730, see Goldgar, 87.

21. Commenting on the presentation of the *Craftsman*'s position in Pulteney's *Answer to a Late Pamphlet, Intituled, Observations on the Writings of the Craftsman* (1730), Hervey asked, "Would not any one conclude ... that these Writers had carefully avoided not to censure any of those Measures, in which His present Majesty can be suppos'd to have any Hand? And yet, in the very same Page, they forget themselves, and the *Hessians* are brought in by way of Ridicule" (*Farther Observations on the Writings of the Craftsman* [1730], 30; cf. Pulteney, *Answer,* 13–14).

22. Bolingbroke's third letter in the *Remarks* (*Craftsman* 210; 11 July 1730) calls attention to earlier attacks on the series in the *Daily Courant* and the *London Journal*. *London Journal* 577 is titled "*A Continuation of the Observations on Mr. Oldcastle's Remarks upon the English History.*" The pro-government papers sold poorly and are now extremely rare; I have been unable to locate Pitt's earlier essay, presumably a response to the fourth letter of the *Remarks* (*Craftsman* 213; 1 Aug. 1730), the first to discuss English history specifically.

23. Cf. Bolingbroke in *Craftsman* 206 (13 June 1731), 41, above.

24. *The Anti-Craftsman* (1729), 6. See also Hervey, *Observations on the Writings of the Craftsman* (1730): "How they proposed His Majesty should reconcile these general Professions [of loyalty to George II] with such particular Reflexions [against 'every Step of his Measures'] I know not; but I should think that Alternative, they gave him, of being unjust enough to abett the flagrant Iniquities they complain'd of, or blind enough not to perceive them, was one, which neither he, nor any one who has the Honour to know him, would look upon, as any very great Compliment, either to his Head, or his Heart" (14–15).

25. See Harris, *London Newspapers,* 136–40, for Paxton's role in the political press. See Harris, *London Newspapers,* 141, and "Figures," 234–35, for government actions against Amhurst.

26. The authors are identified in the fourteen-volume reprint edition of the *Craftsman* (1731–37) as "A" and "N" respectively; Varey has not identified these contributors.

27. The *Register of Books, 1728–1732, Extracted from the Monthly Chronicle* (London: Gregg-Archive, 1974) notes that the pamphlet was published in October; but the *Grub-street Journal* noted on 10 December 1730 (No. 49) that the pamphlet was published in November. That the pamphlet responds to *Craftsman* 222 (3 Oct. 1730), that the pamphlet continues the legalistic and rhetorical attack on (among others) *London Journal* 577, and that the *Grub-street Journal* had fallen behind in its book-lists in the fall of 1730 make it likely that the pamphlet was published in October.

28. Although such an argument would have had more authority in 1732, when Bolingbroke was negotiating with the French ambassador, Anne-Theodore Chavigny, there is no evidence that in 1730 Bolingbroke (or anyone affiliated with the *Craftsman,* for that matter) was active in the Stuart interest; see H. T. Dickinson, *Bolingbroke* (London: Constable, 1970), 230–32, 240–42.

29. The author of *Liberty and the Craftsman* claims that the *Craftsman* "is aiming at making it absolutely necessary to put a Restraint on Printing; and

then oh the Letchery it would be to him! to have it in his Power to throw such an Infringement of Liberty on his Majesty, the Ministry and present Parliament" (17; see also 30–31). The author of *The Danverian History* argues that regulating the *Craftsman* would be preferable to "a Total Suppression of any News-Paper but what the Court shall think proper" (77). For "guarded Treasons," see Hervey, *Observations*, 7.

30. For Hervey and Walpole in 1730, see Robert Halsband, *Lord Hervey: Eighteenth-Century Courtier* (New York: Oxford University Press, 1974), 93–98; for Walpole and Hervey's anti-opposition writing, see Halsband, 93, 167–68, 209–10. For Walpole and the pro-government press more generally in the early '30s, see Harris, *London Newspapers*, particularly 119–24.

31. See Pulteney, *An Answer to a Late Pamphlet, Intituled, Observations on the Writings of the Craftsman*, 7.

32. *Craftsman* 230 is credited to "D," identified by Varey as Amhurst (Introduction, *Lord Bolingbroke: Contributions to the Craftsman*, xxiv). No. 231 is credited to "D. R."; Varey suggests that "R" may have been Pope's signatory letter in the *Craftsman* (xxvi), but does not comment on this composite signature. It is safest to regard the essay as a collaboration written in part by Amhurst. Bolingbroke's twelfth letter was defended in *Three Pamphlets; Entituled Observations on the Writings of the Craftsman, The Sequel and Farther Observations Examin'd* (Dec. 1730), and *The Doctrine of Innuendo's Discuss'd* (Jan. 1731), examined on 83, below.

33. For Walpole's financial involvement with the pro-government press, see Harris, *London Newspapers*, 102–3, 108–10.

34. The same day, James Pitt ("Francis Osborne") denounced the publication of the "Hague letter" in *London Journal* 597 (9 Jan. 1731); see also *London Journal* 598 (16 Jan. 1731).

35. According to Amhurst in *Craftsman* 237, *Sedition and Defamation Display'd* was published "not above a Day or two before Mr. Francklin was taken up" (16 Jan. 1731). For the pamphlet and Pulteney's erroneous attribution of it to Hervey, see Halsband, 107–10.

36. In the twelfth letter of the *Remarks*, Bolingbroke accuses Walpole, "over whose Head the long gathering Cloud of national Vengeance is ready to burst," of attempting to "destroy" the constitution. Cf. *Liberty and the Craftsman*: "The most daring Presumption of this Writer [i.e., 'D'Anvers'], is his having the Assurance, of late more especially, to write in the Name of the *Generality* of the People; and to affirm and repeat, that the *Majority* are stir'd up by him to a Hatred and Contempt of the Proceedings of the King, Ministry, and both Houses of Parliament" (5).

37. Harris corroborates, or reiterates, the *Craftsman's* claim that the arrest was for *Craftsman* 236 as well as for No. 235 (*London Newspapers*, 223, note 99); but numerous contemporary accounts of the trial leave no doubt that Francklin was ultimately sentenced for printing the "Hague letter." No. 236 is an attack on ministerial writers by Pulteney and Amhurst. For Farley and White, see *Craftsman* Nos. 238 (23 Jan. 1731) and 240 (6 Feb. 1731); for Dodd, Nutt, and the *Craftsman*, see Harris, *London Newspapers*, 39.

38. For graphic evidence of the sharp rise in political pamphleteering from both "sides" in the first six months of 1731, as compared to the same period a year earlier, see *A Register of Books, 1728–1732*.

39. Amhurst's next comment on the subject is more temperate. He argues that the "Hague letter," like many news items, had been presented as a "general

Report," probably but not demonstrably true, rather than as "*Fact*." He concludes, "If We should be call'd upon to defend ourselves in a *Court of Justice*, We must submit to the *Law* and abide the Judgment of our *Country*, after a full Hearing of the Merits on both Sides" (*Craftsman* 239; 31 Jan. 1731).

40. See Halsband, 120; and Goldgar, 88.
41. For the gravity of the charge, see Halsband, 111.
42. See Halsband, 113–16.
43. The author of *An Essay upon Something* subscribes himself "Timothy Scrub"; the *Eighteenth-Century Short-Title Catalogue* notes that the essay is "sometimes attributed to John Kelley." D. F. Foxon notes that Budgell used the pseudonym on occasion; *English Verse, 1701–1750* (Cambridge: Cambridge University Press, 1975), 96, No. B556. In a memo to me, Thomas Lockwood observes that "the mock-abuse of Caleb D'Anvers is just Budgell's line in the early 1730s, when he and the *Craftsman* were linked." Other late entries in the controversy include *A Full and True Account of a Sharp and Bloody Duel* (Jan.[?] 1731); *The Duel; A Poem* (Jan.[?] 1731); *A Letter to Caleb D'Anvers, Esq.; on His Proper Reply to a Late Scurrilous Libel, Entitled, Sedition and Defamation Display'd, &c* (2 Feb. 1731); *Pulteney: Or the Patriot* (15 Feb. 1731); and the *Memoirs of the Life and Conduct of William Pulteney, Esq.* (8 May 1731).
44. Internal evidence indicates that the pamphlet was written in December 1730, between Hervey's *Sequel* and his *Farther Observations*; it was published after the arrest and with a subtitle ("*Being Some Thoughts upon the Present Treatment of the Printer and Publishers of the Craftsman*") that implies a relationship to the arrest that it does not actually have.

Chapter 3. Squaring Off—or Not—over the Revolution of 1688

1. Bolingbroke, *A Final Answer to the Remarks on the Craftsman's Vindication* (1731), in vol. 1 of *The Works of Lord Bolingbroke* (1844; reprint, New York: Augustus M. Kelley, 1967), 465.
2. Gunn, *Beyond Liberty and Property: The Process of Self-Recognition in Eighteenth-Century Political Thought* (Kingston, Ontario: McGill-Queen's University Press, 1983), 59. For Kramnick, see particularly *Bolingbroke and His Circle: The Politics of Nostalgia in the Age of Walpole* (Cambridge, Mass.: Harvard University Press, 1968).
3. Burtt, *Virtue Transformed: Political Argument in England, 1688–1740* (Cambridge: Cambridge University Press, 1992), 91. Burtt's interest in the origins of eighteenth-century political rhetoric, rather than the intersections of history and rhetoric, enables her to stress differences between the Bolingbrokean and Walpolite positions.
4. Wilson, "Inventing Revolution: 1688 and Eighteenth-Century Popular Politics," *Journal of British Studies* 28 (October 1989): 364.
5. Wilson, 368.
6. Wilson, 372.
7. Dickinson paraphrases the position that Bolingbroke took in *A Dissertation upon Parties*: "Even at the height of the Whig-Tory disputes, in the last years of Charles II's reign, the divisions between the two parties had been exaggerated by excessive zeal. The Whigs had not all been republicans and Dissenters and the Tories had not all supported the introduction of absolutism

and religious intolerance. These differences had all been settled by the Revolution" (Bolingbroke, 195); cf. Bolingbroke, *Dissertation*, in vol. 2 of *The Works of Lord Bolingbroke*, 67.

8. See also *Hyp-Doctor* 65 (7 Mar. 1732). The fifteen numbers of the *Free-Mason* interrupted the run of the *Hyp-Doctor* from 13 Nov. 1733 to 19 Feb. 1734; see Graham Midgley, *The Life of Orator Henley* (Oxford: Clarendon, 1973), 263.

9. Simon Varey notes that during the Excise Crisis, the *Craftsman* "ensured success for the Opposition by employing all its argumentative rhetoric on a single major issue"; he adds that the paper was unable to repeat this success in its campaign against the Gin Act (1736): "The *Craftsman* 1726–1752: An Historical and Critical Account" (Ph.D. thesis, Cambridge University, 1976), 266.

10. Plumb, *Sir Robert Walpole: The King's Minister* (London: Cresset, 1960), 325. Plumb adds that "the slope . . . was so gentle that few of his contemporaries perceived it" (325). See also Jeremy Black, *Robert Walpole and the Nature of Politics in Early Eighteenth-Century England* (New York: St. Martin's, 1990), 40–44; B. W. Hill, *Sir Robert Walpole: "Sole and Prime Minister"* (London: Hamish Hamilton, 1989), 181–82; and Paul Langford, *The Excise Crisis: Society and Politics in the Age of Walpole* (Oxford: Clarendon, 1975), 124–50. Bertrand Goldgar, who approvingly reproduces Plumb's comment, notes that "the excise affair marked a significant defeat for [Walpole]," but adds that "the disunited, diverse elements of the opposition were unable to use [this defeat] to their advantage": *Walpole and the Wits: The Relation of Politics to Literature, 1722–1742* (Lincoln: University of Nebraska Press, 1976), 132.

11. Kramnick, "Augustan Politics and English Historiography: The Debate on the English Past, 1730–35," *History and Theory* 6 (1967): 34–38.

12. See also Amhurst: "I think nothing more demonstrable, than that the Court-Whigs of this Age are exactly the same Kind of Creatures with the Court-Tories before the *Revolution*; that, vice versa, the Body of the present Tories have adopted the Spirit of the *old Whigs*" (*Craftsman* 379; 6 Oct. 1733).

13. Hervey, *The Conduct of the Opposition* (1734), 37. See also *Free Briton* 154 (9 Nov. 1732), a reprint of the pamphlet *A Defense of the Measures of the Present Administration* (1731[?]), in which the "Genuine Whiggs" are "the men who had acted sincerely in the *Revolution* . . . attached altogether to the public, [who] knew no Distinction between a Court and Country-Party." Joseph Trapp notes that the change in the meaning of "Whig" was discussed in polemical works published around the time of the trial of the Tory clergyman Henry Sacheverell (1710); see *The Character and Principles of the Present Set of Whigs* (1711), 4.

14. Varey notes that in the *Letters on the Study and Use of History* (1752), "Bolingbroke attributes to the British under William a spirit of liberty, like that spirit his *Remarks* had repeatedly emphasized and tried to revive": *Henry St. John, Viscount Bolingbroke* (Boston: Twayne, 1984), 89.

15. W. A. Speck analyzes the legal wrangling in 1689 over James's departure in *Reluctant Revolutionaries: Englishmen and the Revolution of 1688* (Oxford: Oxford University Press, 1989), 92–114.

16. Varey, *Henry St. John*, 42; and see Bolingbroke, *Occasional Writer* 1 (1727), in vol. 1 of *The Works of Lord Bolingbroke*, 206.

17. Bolingbroke, *Letters on the Study and Use of History*, in vol. 2 of *The Works of Lord Bolingbroke*, 187.

18. Bolingbroke, *A Dissertation upon Parties*, 5.
19. Bolingbroke, *A Dissertation upon Parties*, 5–6.
20. J. P. Kenyon stresses the imprecision of the term "liberty" in *Revolution Principles: The Politics of Party 1689–1720* (Cambridge: Cambridge University Press, 1977), 201. Kenyon notes that the Whig sense of "liberty" hinged on the appropriateness of resisting tyranny, even if it were embodied in a hereditary monarch (6). Obviously, this signification applies equally to all apologists for William III.
21. Bolingbroke, *A Dissertation upon Parties*, 16.
22. Bolingbroke, *A Dissertation upon Parties*, 24.
23. For the politics of the *Whitehall Evening-Post*, see Michael Harris, *London Newspapers in the Age of Walpole: A Study of the Origins of the Modern English Press* (Rutherford, N.J.: Fairleigh Dickinson University Press; London: Associated University Presses, 1987), 122.
24. Dickinson, "The Eighteenth-Century Debate on the 'Glorious Revolution'," *History* 61 (1976): 39.
25. For the struggles of dissent in the period 1732–42, see N. C. Hunt, *Two Early Political Associations: The Quakers and the Dissenting Deputies in the Age of Sir Robert Walpole* (Oxford: Clarendon, 1961), 130–62. In Appendix F, "Note on *The Craftsman's* Appeal to Dissenters" (208), Hunt discusses the tardiness of the *Craftsman's* overtures to dissent. *Grub-street Journal* 195 (20 Sept. 1733) mocks Pitt's argument for dissent but against the repeal of the Test Acts; cf. Amhurst, who sounds like Pitt in his dedication to the 1731 edition of the *Craftsman*: "As Members of the *establish'd Church*, in particular, We shall always endeavour to support it in its just Rights. As Members of the *reform'd Church*, in general, We shall never wish to see any Hardships laid on our *Protestant Brethren*, who cannot comply with the Terms of our Communion" (ix).
26. Hervey, *The Conduct of the Opposition*, 40.
27. Kramnick, *Bolingbroke and His Circle*, 5; Kramnick is commenting on the work of John Brooke, Lucy Sutherland, and Archibald Foord.
28. Kramnick, *Bolingbroke and His Circle*, 17.
29. Earbery sometimes expresses this "contempt" without reference to the Revolution. Writing of *"Whig"* and *"Tory,"* Earbery finds "in both those Parties Men so notoriously Vile, as no Country was ever curs'd with the like": *An Historical Account of the Advantages that Have Accru'd to England, by the Succession in the Illustrious House of Hanover* (1722), 30. See also Russel's characteristic dismissal of both parties as equally "corrupt," in *Grub-street Journal* 230 (23 May 1734). Gunn notes the "impartial distaste for both Whigs and Tories" evident in Earbery's work (144); but his comment that "Earbery made no secret of his preference for republicans over Whigs if only because they too were against a foreign king" (144) ignores the fact that Earbery, in a passage that Gunn alludes to, distinguishes between "the vulgar Whigs" who had sincerely supported Hanover after Anne's accession, and "the Republican Whigs" who had only pretended to (*An Historical Account*, 15). Earbery intends to stress what is loathsome about both sorts of Whiggery.
30. Dickinson, "The Eighteenth-Century Debate," 29.
31. For the Jacobites' reliance on *Fog's Weekly Journal* and for the Pretender's curiously uncommitted "encouragement" to the founding of *Common Sense* in 1737, see Harris, *London Newspapers*, 125. For James's dilatory realization in 1736 "that a paper not directly authorized to speak for him might be a

great convenience," see George Hilton Jones, *The Main Stream of Jacobitism* (Cambridge, Mass.: Harvard University Press, 1954), 197–98.

32. Rogers, "Riot and Popular Jacobitism in Early Hanoverian England," in Eveline Cruickshanks, ed., *Ideology and Conspiracy: Aspects of Jacobitism, 1689–1759* (Edinburgh: John Donald, 1982), 76.

33. *Advocates for Murther and Rebellion, the Pest of Government* (1714), 10–11.

34. Lenman, *The Jacobite Risings in Britain 1689–1746* (London: Eyre Methuen, 1980), 231. For the sorry condition of English Jacobitism between the '15 and the '45, see also Lenman, 231–38; Paul Fritz, *The English Ministers and Jacobitism between the Rebellions of 1715 and 1745* (Toronto: University of Toronto Press, 1975), 126–36; and Frank McLynn, *The Jacobites* (London: Routledge, 1985), 104. That "the four main capital statutes" for "offences against the protestant succession" were passed in 1700, 1701, 1707, and 1744, may reflect Parliament's skepticism regarding Walpole's fear of Jacobitism in the '20s and '30s; for the statutes, see Leon Radzinowicz, vol. 1 of *A History of English Criminal Law and its Administration from 1750* (London: Stevens and Sons, 1948), 614.

35. Earbery, *The Old English Constitution Vindicated, and Set in a True Light* (1717). 35. Howard Erskine-Hill notes the prevalence of rape imagery in Jacobite literature; see "Literature and the Jacobite Cause: Was There a Rhetoric of Jacobitism?," in Cruickshanks, ed., 53–55.

36. Cf. Wilson: "The . . . political climate [under Walpole] forced opposition writers to be selective in their use of real whig arguments and, particularly, to downplay the right of resistance, largely because of its treasonable associations" (373).

37. See also *Daily Courant* 9357 (4 Nov. 1731) and 9390 (13 Dec. 1731), and *Read's Weekly Journal* 350 (4 Dec. 1731). The controversy coincided with the anniversary of William's landing at Torbay on 5 Nov. 1688.

38. Amhurst's essay in observance of the anniversary of William's landing (No. 279; 6 Nov. 1731), published less than two weeks after the Council's decision, says nothing of the proposed statue. Wilson notices some periodical essays from the 1730s that celebrate the landing, as Bolingbroke does in *Craftsman* 375, by contrasting "Revolution principles" and later developments like the Septennial Act of 1716 (367).

39. See *Grub-street Journal* Nos. 97 (11 Nov. 1731), 98 (18 Nov. 1731), 99 (25 Nov. 1731), 100 (2 Dec. 1731), and 102 (16 Dec. 1731). Henley later ridiculed the *Grub-street Journal* for its opposition to the proposed statue (*Hyp-Doctor* 100; 7 Nov. 1732). For the skepticism of *Fog's Weekly Journal* about the statue and about William generally, see No. 164 (25 Dec. 1731); and see a caustically annotated news item on "the Memory of King William" in No. 173 (26 Feb. 1732). No. 177 (25 Mar. 1732), for which the paper's "Printer and publishers" were arrested (see *Grub-street Journal* 117; 30 Mar. 1732), uses the flap over the statue to introduce a pro-City, anti-William leader. *Fog's* continues the anti-Williamite strain in Nos. 183 (6 May 1732) and 184 (13 May 1732).

40. In its quotations, the *Grub-street Journal* alters the *Daily Courant*'s text insignificantly on several occasions, for instance by italicizing differently. In the *Memoirs of the Society of Grub-street* (2 vols., 1737), Russel calls the *Courant*'s article "an Allegorical Account, falsely representing the rejection of the Petition about King William's Statue, and the Controversy betwixt the *Grub-street Journal* and *Free Briton* Occasioned thereby" (2:194). James Hillhouse

says only that No. 102 contains "various accounts in the newspapers of an East India ship attacked by pirates": *The Grub-Street Journal* (Durham: Duke University Press, 1928), 310.

41. A reference in *Occasional Historian* 1 (1731) suggests that Earbery's dislike of Bolingbroke originated in Bolingbroke's lack of support for Francis Atterbury during Atterbury's 1723 conspiracy trial: "If he is afraid of being call'd, or thought a Jacobite, I will give him a Certificate under my Hand, that he is no more one now, than when he advis'd the cutting the Bishop of Rochester's Head off" (68). Earbery refers to the renunciation of Jacobitism in general and Atterbury in specific exacted from Bolingbroke as a condition of his return to England in 1723, for which see G. V. Bennett, *The Tory Crisis in Church and State 1688-1730: The Career of Francis Atterbury Bishop of Rochester* (Oxford: Clarendon, 1975), 276.

42. *Occasional Historian* 2 (1731), 27. Cf. peripheral opposition figure Eustace Budgell, who distinguishes between "the *Liberty of the Press*" and the removal of "*Restraint upon the Press*," and regretfully suggests that the latter only was guaranteed by the Revolution: *A Letter to Cleomenes King of Sparta* (1731), 189.

43. In *The Case of Opposition Stated, between the Craftsman and the People* (1731; reprinted in *The Craftsman: Four Tracts* [New York: Garland, 1974]), Arnall catalogues Bolingbroke's attempts to restrict the press during the period 1710–14 (43–58). See also the derivative pamphlet *The Craftsman's Doctrine and Practice of the Liberty of the Press* (1732), 8–32; and Earbery, *Occasional Historian* 3 (1731), 32. For Bolingbroke's actions in 1711 against "booksellers and publishers for disseminating hostile Whig pamphlets," see Dickinson, *Bolingbroke*, 89; and Varey, "The Craftsman," 274–76.

44. The move to suppress opposition would be codified in Walpole's Licensing Act of 1737, which authorized preperformance censorship of plays. See also Maynard Mack on the "silenc[ing]" of Pope after the publication of the *Epilogue to the Satires* (1738): *Alexander Pope: A Life* (New York: Norton, 1985), 735.

45. Henley, *Hyp-Doctor* 127 (24 Apr. 1733); for more of the same, see *Liberty and the Craftsman* (1730), 17–18.

46. *Mist's* became *Fog's* when its Jacobite printer Nathaniel Mist fled to France in 1728 under pressure from the government; see Harris, *London Newspapers*, 114–15, 148.

47. Although George had sought the executions of Lords Derwentwater, Kenmure, Nithsdale, Wintoun, Carnwath, Nairne, and Widdrington, only the first two were hanged, as were twenty-six commoners; see Speck, *Stability and Strife: England 1714–1760* (London: Edward Arnold, 1977), 183.

48. See 133, below.

49. Speck, *Stability and Strife*, 183.

50. Earbery often omits dates and names; I have compensated for this deficiency as necessary. David Bates suggests that William I's peace with Robert was the result of political necessity rather than native generosity: *William the Conqueror* (London: George Philip, 1989), 160–63. Henry II's political problems with his wife and sons are commonplaces of Norman history.

51. Speck discusses James II, his chief justice George Jeffreys, and "the Bloody Assizes" at Dorchester; see *Reluctant Revolutionaries*, 53–55. James's brutal "clemency" makes small beer of most of Earbery's examples.

52. Although he does not specify, Earbery is presumably thinking of Leo-

pold, who died during the aftermath of the Rebellion but who negotiated more actively with the rebels than his successor had. Linda Frey and Marsha Frey note the prevalence of sympathy for the Protestant Rákóczi among both Whigs and Tories in England: see *A Question of Empire: Leopold I and the War of Spanish Succession, 1701–1705* (Boulder, Colo.: Eastern European Monographs 146; New York: Columbia University Press, 1983), 72. Earbery neglects to mention both Leopold's preference for the annihilation of Hungarian nationalism and its proponents (see Frey and Frey, 81) and the fact that Rákóczi's rebels, unlike their counterparts at Preston, were in a fairly strong position from which to negotiate (see Frey and Frey, 81–85).

53. Add. MS 36,196, f. 167; British Library. The date of the Hicks Hall sentencing was 8 Sept. 1718. Hardwicke was reporting the actions of attorney general Robert, Lord Raymond.

54. Add. MS 36,196, f. 167. The manuscript, Hardwicke's notes on Rex v. Earbery, reveals that one of the charges against Earbery was dropped when he reported to the King's Bench, with the understanding that "if this court . . . shall think fitt to bayl him he must likewise enter into a new Recognizance for that other Misdemeanor." The manuscript is dated 3 July 1732, and contains comments on the case from 1717 to 1722.

55. See *Occasional Historian* 3, 36, 42–43, for Earbery's library. For references to Earbery and torture, see *Occasional Historian* 3, 14, 17–18. In *The Whole System of English Liberty* (1738), Earbery implies that he has been "Witness" to torture, but may or may not be referring to his 1722 imprisonment (35). For the trial at King's Bench, Easter Term, 1723, and the writ of error, see *English Reports* 92 (Edinburgh: William Green and Sons; London: Stevens and Sons, 1909), 751–52. The court's decision was based on the fact that Earbery's offense was a misdemeanor. Add. MS 36,196, f. 167, records Hardwicke's initial objection, possibly in the form of an instruction from Raymond, to Earbery's plea for a writ of error.

56. Earbery, preface to *Occasional Historian* 1 (n.p.).

57. For Earbery's imprisonment, see *The Whole System*, 16. Throughout the *The Whole System*, Earbery fumes about the November decision, which, he claims, had "declared *Magna Charta* to be an *old perished Law*, and the Observation of it inconsistent with modern Practice and modern Law" (7). For more moderate accounts of the motion and the denial, see *English Reports* 94 (Edinburgh: William Green and Sons; London: Stevens and Sons, 1909), 509, 544–45; and Add. MS 36,038, ff. 12b, 31a–b, 45b, 68b; British Library.

58. For what seems to have been the final delay in the trial, see *Common Sense* 55 (18 Feb. 1738). The evidence for acquittal is circumstantial but strong. *Common Sense* 70 (3 June 1738) reprinted a "remarkable paragraph" from a "Vindication" by Earbery—not the *The Whole System* but a source that has evidently not survived—in which Earbery says, "If I had been committed, on the 13th Day of May last, by the Court of King's Bench, and had been permitted to walk thro' the City, which was denied, I design'd to have my Procession with Magna Charta in one Hand, and the Bible in the other, to shew my Esteem for the two Charters of Salvation and Liberty; with a Chain over my Shoulders, to declare my Detestation of Slavery." The obvious implication is that Earbery was not "committed." It is inconceivable that Earbery would have allowed the *The Whole System*, written under his own name and probably printed under his direction, to be released during the trial.

59. For the Usages Controversy, see J. H. Overton, *The Nonjurors: Their Lives,*

Principles, and Writings (London: Smith, Elder, 1902), 290–308; and Henry Broxap, *The Later Non-Jurors* (Cambridge: Cambridge University Press, 1924), 37–65. Earbery favored ending the controversy; see Broxap, 40; and Earbery to Brett 19 Sept. 1727(?) (MS Eng. Th. C 30, ff. 87–88; Bodleian Library). For Russel's opposition to the reconciliation, see Broxap, 153, 315; and Goldgar, "Pope and the *Grub-street Journal*," *Modern Philology* 74 (May 1977): 370. Their different stances would account for the otherwise confusing fact that Earbery and Russel do not acknowledge one another in print. Possible support for the hypothesis appears in Brett's postscript to a letter to Russel dated 3 Feb. 1733, in which Brett says, "Though you think fit to join with those who seem to have entered into a combination not to communicate with me upon any Terms, yet that shall not hinder me from doing you or any of them any Brotherly of Friendly office within my power" (MS Eng. Th. C 42, f. 176; Bodleian Library). If Russel had written off the august Brett, from whom he had once respectfully sought advice on the controversy (Russel to Brett, 19 Mar. 1718; MS Eng. Th. C 26, ff. 223–34; Bodleian Library), it presumably would have been easy for him to shun Earbery. Earbery's distance from the antiaccommodationist branch is clear in Earbery to Brett, 11 Sept. 1733 (MS Eng. Th. C 32, ff. 229–30; Bodleian Library); Russel's intractability is suggested by Overton's comment that the efforts of the "Usager" Brett and the "non-Usager" George Smith produced "a partial reunion of the two sections [i.e., factions] of Nonjurors in 1731" (321).

60. Earbery to the bishop of Norwich; Rawlinson MS C 735, f. 181; Bodleian Library. The Bodleian's cataloguers have not deciphered the letter's scribbled date, but the letter was certainly written after Earbery's arrest for writing *Universal Spy* 12, and probably written late in the decade. The bishop of Norwich from February 1733 to June 1738 was the ultra-Walpolite William Baker; his successor was the milder Thomas Gooch. This suggests that Gooch was Earbery's correspondent. It is possible (but beyond demonstration) that Earbery was finally convinced to swear allegiance by the government's response to *The Whole of English Liberty*. On the recto of the (unpaginated) first leaf of the Bodleian Library's copy of the *The Whole System*, Richard Rawlinson notes that "this book was seized by the Secretary of State, [and] very few escaped the Fire ordeal." Earbery's defeated tone in the letter to Norwich contrasts notably to the ebullience of the passage reproduced in *Common Sense* 70 (3 June 1738); see note 58, above. Gunn's summation of Earbery's career is curious: "Though Earbery's extra-parliamentary pinpricks were not granted the same immunity as those of [the Jacobite] William Shippen inside Parliament, it still speaks volumes for the relative liberality of Walpole's administration that such a doughty opponent enjoyed [!] a long career" (145).

61. Earbery's *Some Impartial Reflexions upon Dr Burnet's Posthumous History* responds to the first volume of Burnet's *History of His Own Time* (1724–34). Earbery flirts briefly with sedition when he criticizes Burnet for having "transferr'd all his Allegiance" to William III from "his natural Prince" James II (102).

62. *Occasional Historian* Nos. 1–3 were written against, respectively, *Craftsman* Nos. 225 (24 Oct. 1730); 242 (20 Feb. 1731); and 241 (13 Feb. 1731). *Occasional Historian* 4, "an HISTORICAL ESSAY Upon, and in Defense of English *Hereditary Right*" (t.p.) is a broader criticism of Bolingbroke's hostility toward the doctrine that Earbery held sacred.

63. Gunn perhaps strains to find in *Occasional Historian* 2 evidence of Earb-

ery's "able spokesman[ship] for the interests of the nonjurors and others who failed to flourish under the Whig oligarchy" (239–40).

64. James II is a mediocrity in *Occasional Historian* 1 (see 61). *Universal Spy* 12 (22 Sept. 1732), for which Earbery was arrested, attacks the low-church leanings of the ministry and the monarchy by ridiculing Queen Caroline's famous Hermitage. No. 8 (26 Aug. 1732) is an allegory meant to reflect poorly on George II's court. No copies of Nos. 4 and 9 seem to have survived, so any discussion of the journal is necessarily tentative. Gunn's reliance on the Bodleian Library's incomplete collection prompts him to say that the *Universal Spy* "appears to have had no more than three issues" (144).

65. *Occasional Historian* 2, 44.

66. Shakespeare, *Troilus and Cressida*, 1.1.90 in the Riverside edition.

CHAPTER 4. THE CAROLINIST CHALLENGE

1. See 87, above.

2. For the scantness of material that William III offered propagandists, see Earl Miner, Introduction, *Poems on the Reign of William III* (Los Angeles: Augustan Reprint Society, 1974), v.

3. Potter, *Secret Rites and Secret Writing: Royalist Literature 1641–1660* (Cambridge: Cambridge University Press, 1989), passim.

4. Charles in fact adjourned Parliament for eleven years, from March 1629 until April 1640. Cf. Pitt's earlier charge that Bolingbroke in the *Remarks* was overly generous to James I and Charles I (*London Journal* Nos. 604 [27 Feb. 1731] and 612 [17 Apr. 1731]; the ludicrous claim suggests Pitt's uneasiness about the proximity of his own position to Bolingbroke's.

5. Kennett, *A Sermon Preached before the Lords [. . .] the xxxth of January, M.DCC.XIX* (1720), 26. Kennett seems to conflate Charles I and Charles II. Thomas Hearne calls the sermon "sad stuff" in his diary for 13 Mar. 1720; see Hearne, *Remarks and Collections*, ed. C. E. Doble, D. W. Rannie, and H. E. Salter (Oxford: Oxford University Press, 1885–1921), 7:104.

6. Hervey, *Ancient and Modern Liberty Stated and Compar'd* (1734; reprint, Los Angeles: Augustan Reprint Society, 1989), 30.

7. Earbery, *The Whole System of English Liberty* (1738), 14, 15.

8. Harris, *London Crowds in the Reign of Charles II: Propaganda and Politics from the Restoration until the Exclusion Crisis* (Cambridge: Cambridge University Press, 1987), 134. See also Phillip Harth, *Pen for a Party: Dryden's Tory Propaganda in Its Contexts* (Princeton: Princeton University Press, 1993), e.g., 71. Discussing Jacobitism in the 1710s, Nicholas Rogers mentions, but does not discuss, the conflation of "roundheads" and eighteenth-century Whigs; see "Riot and Popular Jacobitism in Early Hanoverian England," in Eveline Cruickshanks, ed., *Ideology and Conspiracy: Aspects of Jacobitism, 1689–1759* (Edinburgh: John Donald, 1982), 74, 83.

9. For "the cult of Charles I" after 1688, see J. P. Kenyon, *Revolution Principles: The Politics of Party 1689–1720* (Cambridge: Cambridge University Press, 1977), 61–82. Like Harris, Kenyon does not extend his research into the 1730s.

10. Sharpe, *The Personal Rule of Charles I* (New Haven: Yale University Press, 1992), e.g., xv.

11. Anselment, *Loyalist Resolve: Patient Fortitude in the English Civil War* (Newark: University of Delaware Press, 1988), 18.

12. In presenting a "discussion of the decade before the political crisis [that] emphasizes the interaction between myth and history" (18), Anselment notes his debt to various "revisionist historians," including Sharpe and Conrad Russel (187–88, note 41).

13. Cf. L. J. Reeve's generally critical *Charles I and the Road to Personal Rule* (Cambridge: Cambridge University Press, 1989).

14. Randall, "The Rise and Fall of a Martyrology: Sermons on Charles I," *Huntington Library Quarterly* 10 (February 1947): 138.

15. Trapp, *A Sermon Preach'd before the Right Honourable the Lord Mayor and Aldermen of the City of London [. . .] on Friday, January 30. 1729* (1730), 1. Many seventeenth- and eighteenth-century clerics made what Kenyon calls "the obvious comparison [of Charles] with Jesus Christ" (70); see also Randall, 142–44, 148. Randall notes that the regicides "overlooked the fact that the second lesson for the 30th of January, appointed in the Book of Common Prayer, was the 27th chapter of St. Matthew, on the trial and crucifixion of Christ" (137). Randall observes that this was Trapp's text for his sermon and that in the sermon Trapp "was reviving the parallel with Christ" (158).

16. Potter, 157. Referring to Charles's stutter, Potter argues that "perhaps [Charles's] speech impediment contributed to his preference for self-presentation through visual rather than aural means, but he made it a matter of choice as well as necessity" (157). Cf. Sharpe: "There is no doubt that Charles could and did upon occasions speak lucidly and forcefully. . . . For all the famous stutter, contemporaries testify to his clarity in expounding a position" (179).

17. Potter, 165. Sharpe's brief analysis of portraits of Charles and the royal family suggests a less ethereal aspect of Caroline portraiture (see 184–87).

18. Potter, 158.

19. Potter, 169.

20. Potter, 210.

21. Potter, 210.

22. In an essay probably cowritten by Nicholas Amhurst, the *Craftsman* took another tack when it condemned the "pernicious Measures" of Charles's advisor Thomas Wentworth, earl of Strafford, whom the journal accused of "endeavouring too long and obstinately, though at last in vain, to screen [Charles] from the Justice of the Nation" (No. 372; 18 Aug. 1733). The use of the *Craftsman's* beloved "screen" charge links Strafford and Walpole; the journal's attitude toward George II is clear when the author or authors add that Strafford's scheming "brought not only his *own head* to the Block, but likewise That of his *unhappy Master.*" For the charge that Charles had erred by supporting Strafford and his predecessor, Buckingham, see Amhurst in *Craftsman* 309 (3 June 1732) and 501 (7 Feb. 1736).

23. Because Walpole had served under George I before serving under George II, Buckingham's position under James I and Charles I was a convenience for Charles's detractors in the opposition. See, for example, Amhurst in *Craftsman* 298 (1 Apr. 1732); and see the anonymous *The Fate of Favourites; Exemplified in the Fall of Villiers, Duke of Buckingham* (1734), e.g., 27.

24. For Dodsley and the *Grub-street Journal*, see Bertrand Goldgar, "The Grub-Street Journal," *British Literary Magazines: The Augustan Age and the Age of Johnson, 1698–1788*, ed. Alvin Sullivan (Westport, Conn.: Greenwood, 1983), 145. Dodsley's comments on Charles are an amalgam of commonplace rather than an endorsement of the Carolinist position; see, for instance, his

Craftsman-like remark that "[Charles I] was a pious and religious Prince, and wrote many godly Books. . . . Howbeit he did that which was Evil in the Sight of the Lord, in following the Steps of his Father, and aspiring to absolute Power" (45).

25. See Croxall, *A Sermon Preach'd before the Honourable House of Commons [. . .] on Friday, January xxx, 1729* (1730). Goldgar discusses the pro-government response to the sermon in *Walpole and The Wits: The Relation of Politics to Literature, 1722–1742* (Lincoln: University of Nebraska Press, 1976), 88–89. Elsewhere, he comments on the *Grub-street Journal*'s interest in the sermon: "Pope and the *Grub-street Journal*," *Modern Philology* 74 (May 1977): 375. Hearne remarked on the rhetorical slipperiness of Croxall's sermon in his diary for 12 Feb. 1730 (10:250).

26. Charles Carlton evidently believes the anecdote about the cane; see *Charles I: The Personal Monarch* (London: Ark-Routledge, 1983), 350.

27. Potter, 209.

28. The series begins with a satire on church manners in No. 207 (13 Dec. 1733), continues through Nos. 210 (3 Jan. 1734) and 212 (17 Jan. 1734), and concludes in No. 224 (11 Apr. 1734), in which Charles I is "the exactest pattern of public devotion which his subjects could propose to themselves for their imitation."

29. See, for example, Pope, *The Dunciad* (1728) in *The Dunciad*, vol. 5 of *The Twickenham Edition of the Poems of Alexander Pope*, ed. James Sutherland (London: Methuen; New Haven: Yale University Press, 1951), ll. 3.181–86. The passage is misquoted on the frontispiece of *Impartial Memorials of the Life and Writings of Thomas Hearne, M.A. By Several Hands* (1736), published by the notorious Edmund Curll.

30. For George I, see, e.g., Hearne's diary for 9 July 1716 (5:262); for "James III," see, e.g., diary for 10 Nov. 1717 (6:106); for Charles I, see diary for 10 Aug. 1718 (6:212).

31. For Hearne on Charles and Ireland, see diary for 24 Feb. 1714 (4:314); for Scotland, see diary for 30 Apr. 1732 (11:53). For a succinct account of the Irish affair, see G. E. Aylmer, *Rebellion or Revolution?: England from Civil War to Restoration* (Oxford: Oxford University Press, 1986), 26–27; Carlton is more useful on Charles in Scotland (308–14).

32. Hearne diary 11 Aug. 1715 (5:87). But recall what Samuel Johnson said of "the spirit of any person appearing after death": "All argument is against it; but all belief is for it": James Boswell, *Boswell's Life of Johnson*, ed. George Birbeck Hill, revised by Lawrence Powell (Oxford: Clarendon, 1934–50), 3:230.

33. For the supposed disinterment, see Hearne's diary for 9 Jan. 1724 (8:155–56); for the handkerchief, see the diary for 17 May 1725 (8:369). C. V. Wedgwood notes that some observers of the execution "managed to dip handkerchiefs in the King's blood, or even to scrape up fragments of earth from below the scaffold or tear off pieces of the blood-soaked pall": *A Coffin for King Charles: The Trial and Execution of Charles I* (New York: Macmillan, 1964), 225; she adds that "on all sides stories were circulated, in print and by word of mouth, telling of the miracles wrought by scraps of linen stained with [Charles's] precious blood" (242).

34. Anselment, 21.

35. Writing of polemics in the period 1689–1720, Kenyon notes that "if [Charles's execution] was wrong, it was difficult to resist the conclusion that the nation's treatment of James II was wrong, too; conversely, if the Revolution

could be justified, so could Charles's death, and along much the same lines" (66). Bolingbrokean polemics consistently opposes this logic.

36. Earbery, *Occasional Historian* 1 (1731), n.p.; the "Advertisement" first appeared in *London Evening-Post* 438 (26 Sept. 1730). On both occasions Earbery appended an anonymous quotation: "When it was a babe it was Liberty, when it could walk alone it was Rebellion, and when it came to its Fulness of Stature it was compleat absolute Tyranny."

37. For the passing reference to Earbery, see William Pulteney, *An Answer to a Late Pamphlet, Intituled, Observations on the Writings of the Craftsman* (1730), 8.

38. Sharpe, 758; Sharpe argues that "traditional accounts that make the trial sound like a travesty of justice are themselves a travesty of truth" (760). Sharpe's account of the trial, like his lengthy examination of Caroline history, contradicts Bolingbrokean historiography in ways that would have pleased Earbery. The Star Chamber, a court of law descended from the old King's Council, had considerable scope and power under the Tudors and, however much Earbery argued otherwise, under Charles I as well; see Sharpe, 665–83. Sharpe notes the seventeenth-century origins of the "myth" of a sinister Caroline Star Chamber (665-66); the *Craftsman* plays on this myth in No. 241.

39. See Hearne's diary for 7 June 1717 (6:61), and 7 Jan. 1721 (7:205).

40. "Oxoniensis" published a sketchy list of Trapp's contributions to the *Grub-street Journal* in *Gentleman's Magazine* 56 (1786): 661–62. Goldgar accepts its authenticity; see "Pope," 374, note 18. Trapp's 1738 political pamphlet is *The Ministerial Virtue: Or, Long-Suffering Extolled in a Great Man*.

41. See note 15, above.

42. It is difficult to determine the extent of Jacobitism in City government. George Hilton Jones discusses "the Jacobite group in the governing bodies of the City of London, led by Alderman Barber" around 1730; the Namierite Lucy Sutherland, discussing the period around the fall of Walpole (1742), says of "City Jacobitism": "the more [it] is examined, the more it appears to be nothing other than a vague and unorganized dislike of authorities." Paul Langford is skeptical about Jacobitism, City or otherwise, in the 1730s; but he acknowledges the power in City government of "individual Jacobites," notably Barber. See Jones, *The Main Stream of Jacobitism* (Cambridge, Mass.: Harvard University Press, 1954), 178; Sutherland, "The City of London in Eighteenth-Century Politics," in *Essays Presented to Sir Lewis Namier*, ed. Richard Pares and A. J. P. Taylor (London: MacMillan; New York: St. Martin's, 1956), 64; Langford, *The Excise Crisis: Society and Politics in the Age of Walpole* (Oxford: Clarendon, 1975), 55.

43. In Trapp's sermon, Charles II has "many amiable and endearing Qualities," but is accused of "ungratefully flinging those wonderful Blessings behind his Back, and indulging himself in Ease, Luxury, and unlawful Pleasures"; James II is "a *bigotted Papist*" (16). Hearne called the sermon "an invective on the Rebellion and a Panegyrick on the King [i.e., Charles I], but withall a Satyr on the succeeding Royal Family" (diary, 4 Mar. 1730; 10:250).

44. The *Craftsman* spoke out against standing armies as early as 6 Jan. 1728 (No. 79); the flap over the Hessian mercenaries reached its peak in 1730.

45. Trapp's sermon is the subject of an "advertisement" appended to the anonymous *Anti-Papismus: Or, a Letter to the Reverend Dr. Trapp* (1731). The author claims that in his sermon, Trapp "mistakingly . . . confounds the Notions of *Civil War,* and *Rebellion,* as synonimous; and does not distinguish

between a *deplorable Murder, and self-preserving Defence of Civil Rights and Liberties;*—nor yet the Act of *a few Miscreants* . . . from the Act of the Nation" (5).

46. In framing the point, Swift pairs the regicides and those who would observe the day without due rigor; see *A Sermon upon the Martyrdom of K. Charles I [. . .] Jan. 30, 1725–26* (1726), reprinted in *Irish Tracts 1720–1723 and Sermons,* vol. 9 of *The Prose Works of Jonathan Swift,* ed. Herbert Davis and Louis Landa (Oxford: Basil Blackwell, 1963), e.g., 219.

47. The complexity of this transaction is thematic to Howard Weinbrot, *Augustus Caesar in "Augustan" England: The Decline of a Classical Norm* (Princeton: Princeton University Press, 1978); see also Howard Erskine-Hill, *The Augustan Idea in English Literature* (London: Edward Arnold, 1983).

48. Russel's verses in *Grub-street Journal* 116 (23 Mar. 1732) accuse James Pitt of subverting the maxim as Cromwell did.

49. "Marchmont Nedham's History of the Rebellion," in Morgan, ed., *Phoenix Britannicus* (1732), 175. See Marchamont Nedham, *A Short History of the English Rebellion* (1661), 3–4.

CHAPTER 5. CAROLINISM AND THE CHURCH

1. H. T. Dickinson, *Bolingbroke* (London: Constable, 1970), 186.

2. See chapter 1, note 4, above. By August 1730, the *Journal* was routinely printed in runs of over one thousand; from November 1730 to March 1731 (the last month recorded in the *Journal's* "Minute Book"), the runs are all over fifteen hundred.

3. Hillhouse, *The Grub-Street Journal* (Durham: Duke University Press, 1928), 6–7, note 2; Goldgar, *Walpole and the Wits: The Relation of Politics to Literature, 1722–1742* (Lincoln: University of Nebraska Press, 1976), 94; Hammond, *Pope and Bolingbroke: A Study of Friendship and Influence* (Columbia: University of Missouri Press, 1984), 54–56.

4. In addition to Hillhouse, see Goldgar, who comments on the "anti-Walpole and occasionally Jacobite bias of the paper, a bias well recognized by its contemporaries despite its claims of political neutrality": "Pope and the Grub-street Journal," *Modern Philology* 74 (May 1977): 371. Citing letters from Russel to his son James written from 1747 to 1753, Goldgar observes that "what appears to have been at least a passive Jacobitism on Russel's part was softened by neither advancing age nor the experience of the '45" ("Pope," 370). The letters (Add. MS 41,169; British Library) contain one reference to Charles Edward Stuart but express no interest in seeing him on the throne; see Russel to James Russel, 4 Nov. 1748 (f. 16b). The *Journal* offers an oblique consideration of the affairs of the Pretender in Nos. 127, 128, 129 (8, 15, 22 June 1732); a dense Jacobitical allegory entitled *The State of the Nation,* by "John Gabriel," appears in Nos. 144 (5 Oct. 1732), 152 (23 Nov. 1732), 161 (25 Jan. 1733), and 170 (29 Mar. 1733).

5. Sutherland, "The City of London in Eighteenth-Century Politics," in *Essays Presented to Sir Lewis Namier,* ed. Richard Pares and A. J. P. Taylor (London: Macmillan; New York: St. Martin's, 1956), 62.

6. The details of Russel's life have been assembled by Thomas Lounsbury, Hillhouse, and Goldgar: see Lounsbury, *The Text of Shakespeare* (New York: Scribner's, 1908), 394–97; Hillhouse, 40-45; and Goldgar, "Pope," 369–72. "The Minute Book of the Partners in the *Grub Street Journal*" sheds light on the

paper's management; see *Publishing History* 4 (1978): 49–94; and see Michael Harris's companion piece, "The Management of the London Newspaper Press During the Eighteenth Century," *Publishing History* 4 (1978): 95–112. Goldgar and Harris stress Russel's editorial power, but Harris suggests that it was reduced in the *Journal*'s later years: see Goldgar, "Pope," 369; and Goldgar, "The Grub-street Journal," in *British Literary Magazines: The Augustan Age and the Age of Johnson, 1698–1788,* ed. Alvin Sullivan (Westport, Conn.: Greenwood, 1983), 145; cf. Harris, "Management," 104; and Harris, *London Newspapers in the Age of Walpole* (Rutherford, N.J.: Fairleigh Dickinson University Press; London: Associated University Presses, 1987), 77. In attributing authorship of articles from the *Journal,* I have relied whenever possible upon the *Memoirs of the Society of Grub-street* (2 vols., 1737), in which the initials "B" for "Bavius" and "M" for Maevius are appended to the reprinted pieces; Hillhouse reprints this information in an appendix to *The Grub-Street Journal* (298–345). It is now generally accepted, and is suggested by Russel's preface to the *Memoirs* (1:xxix–xxx), that Russel and John Martyn, a partner in the early 1730s, used "Bavius," and that Russel alone used "Maevius."

7. For the *Journal*'s response to Pitt, see No. 22 (4 June 1730). Russel lost the livings of Alfriston and Selmeston in January 1716 (see Hillhouse, 43; and Goldgar, "Pope," 369). Citing Hillhouse and George Sherburn's review of Hillhouse (*Modern Philology* 26 [February 1929]: 361–67), Goldgar summarizes Russel's itinerant way of life in "Pope," 369.

8. Roberts, "Grub Street and its Journal," *The Bookworm* 1 (1888): 96.

9. Goldgar, *Walpole and the Wits,* 96. The author of No. 84 is "Elkanah Conundrum." Hillhouse thinks Conundrum is Russel; see 298. The *Memoirs* credit the piece to Maevius (2:113).

10. Russel supports the politics of *Fog's* while mocking its claim that Locke poses an acceptable alternative to "the distemper" of "DEISM *and* INFIDELITY" (No. 46; 19 Nov. 1730). The *Journal* rebukes *Fog's* for making light of the clergy in No. 340 (1 July 1736).

11. The preface to the *Memoirs* was originally printed in *Grub-street Journal* Nos. 381 (14 Apr. 1737), 417 (22 Dec. 1737), and 418 (29 Dec. 1737); parts of it appeared in different form in No. 58 (11 Feb. 1731). Hillhouse and Raymond Williamson attribute the preface to Russel; see Hillhouse, 45; and Williamson, "John Martyn and the *Grub-street Journal,*" *Medical History* 5 (October 1961): 362. Pat Rogers says that the preface is "almost certainly" Russel's work: *Grub Street: Studies in a Subculture* (London: Methuen, 1972), 353.

12. See *Occasional Historian* 3 (1731), 32–33; and see 132–33, above.

13. Rogers, 354.

14. See C. J. Abbey, "Church Fabrics and Services," in *The English Church in the Eighteenth Century,* by Abbey and J. H. Overton, 2d ed. (1887), 474.

15. Oldmixon, *Memoirs of the Press* (1742), 35. Frank McLynn observes that "even within the sphere of doctrine it is doubtful if Jacobite ideology can be described as 'anachronistic' in, say, 1745, unless we restrict the said ideology narrowly to a belief in divine, hereditary and indefeasible right": *The Jacobites* (London: Routledge and Kegan Paul, 1985), 88. Russel's position in the 1730s admits this restriction.

16. For the 1701–2 and 1714 oaths, see J. H. Overton, *The Nonjurors: Their Lives, Principles, and Writings* (London: Smith, Elder, 1902), 2–3; for the 1722 oath, see Overton, 310; and Paul Fritz, *The English Ministers and Jacobitism between the Rebellions of 1715 and 1745* (Toronto: University of Toronto Press,

1975), 84 and 105, note 23. W. A. Speck notes that the increase in taxation followed the Atterbury Plot: *Stability and Strife: England 1714–1760* (London: Edward Arnold, 1977), 220.

17. See Arthur Scouten, ed., part 3, vol. 1 of *The London Stage 1660–1800* (Carbondale: Southern Illinois University Press, 1961), 404–5. The *Journal* attacked the play in No. 109 (3 Feb. 1732). As late as 1775, when asked by Boswell if, as Cibber had alleged, the nonjurors slept with their patrons' wives, Dr. Johnson replied, "I am afraid many of them did": *Boswell's Life of Johnson*, ed. George Birbeck Hill, revised by Lawrence F. Powell (Oxford: Clarendon, 1934–50), 2:322.

18. See also John Henley in *Hyp-Doctor* Nos. 97 (17 Oct. 1732), 100 (7 Nov. 1732), and 110 (16 Jan. 1733). In No. 97, "Nebulo," a caricature of the Jacobite journalist Nathaniel Mist, says to "*Runt Russel* the *Chaplain* of the ['*GRUB STREET*'] Company": "I thought you were all High-Church, honest old *Cavaliers*, tho' out at Heels, as well as out of Fashion?"

19. Wakeman, *An Introduction to the History of the Church of England*, 11th ed. (London: Rivingtons, 1927), 416.

20. This seems to be Trapp's piece "Upon Impudence," noted in an entry on Trapp and the *Journal* by "Oxoniensis" in *Gentleman's Magazine* 56 (1786): 662.

21. Goldgar, *Walpole and the Wits*, 97.

22. See *Grub-street Journal* 160 (18 Jan. 1733) and 267 (6 Feb. 1735) for more on "Noll Protector" and his alleged progeny.

23. See also two 1716 pamphlets by Russel: *A Discourse Concerning the Nature and Obligation of Oaths* and *The Obligation of Acting According to Conscience*. The former is translated by Russel from Robert Sanderson (1646) and has a preface by Russel; the latter is Russel's "Farewel Sermon" (t.p.).

24. The author is "D. D.," a frequent contributor. This may be Trapp's piece on "Bribery and Perjury"; see "Oxoniensis," 662. D. D.'s interest in classical literature—he translated many of Anacreon's odes for the *Journal*—may suggest Trapp, translator of Virgil in 1718–20. The initials replicate the short form of Trapp's (not unusual) title, "Doctor of Divinity."

25. Paul Langford notes the strength of dissent "among precisely those elements most discontented with the excise scheme, the small traders and businessmen in the towns": *The Excise Crisis: Society and Politics in the Age of Walpole* (Oxford: Clarendon, 1975), 117. Russel's hatred of dissent is reiterated throughout the *Journal*. The role of the City in the downfall of Charles I occasionally figures in Carolinist apologetics, as in Earbery, *Occasional Historian* 3, 79, and as in lines reprinted in 1732: "The new-form'd Priests first led the way, / And said it was no sin / By force to drive the King away, / And draw the City in"; see "Marchmont Nedham's History of the Rebellion," in Joseph Morgan, ed., *Phoenix Britannicus* (1732), 174; and see Marchamont Nedham, *A Short History of the English Rebellion* (1661), 2.

26. Goldgar, "The Grub-street Journal," 146; see also Goldgar, *Walpole and the Wits*, 94. Goldgar notes the high circulation of numbers on City politics ("The Grub-street Journal," 147); Harris, however, attributes the unusually large run of No. 48 (3 Dec. 1730) to the fact that the portrait of the Lord Mayor on the first page was a novelty; see *London Newspapers*, 164.

27. Rudé, *Hanoverian London 1714–1808* (Berkeley: University of California Press, 1971), 143–44.

28. Goldgar, *Walpole and the Wits*, 97.

29. See also a letter from the female "Fiddle-Faddle Club" in *Grub-street Journal* 176 (10 May 1733); and see *The Commodity Excised: Or, the Women in an Uproar* (1733), an unstaged play by "Timothy Smoke."

30. The essay is continued in Nos. 174 (26 Apr. 1733), and 176 (10 May 1733). Less apparent than the debt to the *The Dunciad* is that to the *Universal Spectator, and Weekly Journal:* "What I wou'd humbly offer is, that the Excise might rather be laid on a *Staple* Nusance of this Kingdom, call'd *Dulness*, which might prevent a great many present Inconveniencies both in Church and State" (*Universal Spectator* 231; 10 Mar. 1733); the essay concludes in No. 233 (24 Mar. 1733).

31. Foord, *His Majesty's Opposition 1714–1830* (Oxford: Clarendon, 1964), 177, note 1.

32. See N. C. Hunt, "Note on *The Craftsman's* Appeal to Dissenters," Appendix F, *Two Early Political Associations: The Quakers and the Dissenting Deputies in the Age of Sir Robert Walpole* (Oxford: Clarendon, 1961), 208–10.

33. For *Fog's* against relief for dissent and against the *London Journal's* support of dissent, see No. 121 (16 Jan. 1731).

34. The *Journal's* prolonged campaign against the Quakers' Tythes Bill in 1736 caused a rift between its staff and its publisher, the Quaker John Huggonson; see Hillhouse, 243–46.

35. See W. A. Speck, *Reluctant Revolutionaries* (Oxford: Oxford University Press, 1988), 95–96, 173–74.

36. Hillhouse, 248.

37. For King Charles Day sermons in the seventeenth and eighteenth centuries, see Helen Randall, "The Rise and Fall of a Martyrology: Sermons on Charles I," *Huntington Library Quarterly* 10 (February 1947): 135–67; Louis Landa, Introduction to *Sermons*, by Jonathan Swift, in *Irish Tracts 1720–1723 and Sermons*, vol. 9 of *The Prose Works of Jonathan Swift*, ed. Herbert Davis and Landa (Oxford: Basil Blackwell, 1963), 120–24; E. W. Rosenheim, Jr., "Swift and the Martyred Monarch," *Philological Quarterly* 54 (Winter 1975): 178–94; Landa, review of Randall, *Philological Quarterly* 27 (April 1948): 128; and J. P. Kenyon, *Revolution Principles: The Politics of Party 1689–1720* (Cambridge: Cambridge University Press, 1977), 69–82.

38. Randall surveys a handful of King Charles Day sermons and traces changes in them during the approximate periods 1649–70, 1670–1700, and the eighteenth century. Her division of dates, strange in any case, causes Randall to homogenize the eighteenth century: "'Respectably staid' describes fairly well not only the [eighteenth-century] discussion of the Anniversary but the character of most of the sermons themselves" (159). Randall says nothing about Hare or the controversy that he caused.

39. For Hare and Marlborough, see Robert Horn, "Marlborough's First Biographer: Dr. Francis Hare," *Huntington Library Quarterly* 20 (February 1957): 145–62; for Hare's tutorship, see Horn, 147, 162; and *DNB* on Hare. The letters of 8 Aug. and 16 Nov. 1700 are printed in vol. 2 of William Coxe, *Memoirs of the Life and Administration of Sir Robert Walpole* (1798), 1–2. Hare published 12 pro-Marlborough pamphlets in 1711, the responses to which included Manley and Swift, *A Learned Comment upon Dr. Hare's Sermon* (1711), and Swift, *The Conduct of the Allies* (1711). For Pelham's letter to Hare of 22 Sept. 1722, informing Hare that Walpole had nominated him for the ushership, see *The Manuscripts of the Earl of Buckinghamshire, The Earl of Lindsey, The Earl of Onslow, Lord Emly, Theodore J. Hare, Esq., and James Round, Esq., M.P.* (1895),

234–35. Norman Sykes says that Hare accepted the post: *Church and State in England in the Eighteenth Century* (Hamden, Conn.: Archon, 1962), 44. Reed Browning, on good evidence, calls Hare a "friend" of Newcastle: *The Duke of Newcastle* (New Haven: Yale University Press, 1975), 100; cf. Basil Williams, who, discussing their correspondence of the 1730s, calls him a "political friend" of the duke: "The Duke of Newcastle and the Election of 1734," *English Historical Review* 12 (July 1897): 467. For Gibson's correspondence with Hare in 1736, see Hunt, 97; three letters from Hare to Gibson (1737–39) are in an uncatalogued volume of Gibson's correspondence at the Huntington Library. Speck calls Hare's case "a spectacular example" of rising in the church through political connections: *Stability and Strife*, 98.

40. See Bradshaw, *A Sermon Preach'd before the Lords [. . .] on Friday January 30. 1729/30* (1730); and Clavering, *A Sermon Preach'd before the Lords [. . .] on Saturday, January XXX, 1730* (1731).

41. Hare, *A Sermon Preached before the House of Lords [. . .] January 31, 1731* (8 Feb. 1732).

42. The following sources, published in 1732, concern the sermon: *The B[isho]p and the D[octo]r Reconcil'd* (22 Feb.); "P. C.," *A Letter to [. . .] the Lord Bishop of Chichester* (9 Mar.); "C. P.," *A Defence of the Bishop of Chichester's Sermon* (20 Mar.); "P. C.," *A Letter to the Author of the Defence of the Bishop of Chichester's Sermon* (27 Mar.); *Craftsman* 298 (1 Apr.); Thomas Gordon, *An Examination of the Facts and Reasonings in the Lord Bishop of Chichester's Sermon* (1 Apr.); Earbery, *Universal Spy* 2 (6 May); *A Letter to the Author of the Examination of the Facts and Reasonings in [. . .] Chichester's Sermon* (9 May); *The Examiner Examined* (16 May); *The Principles and Facts of the Lord Bishop of Chichester's Sermon* (31 May); *Fog's Weekly Journal* 186, 187 (27 May, 3 June); "Titus Britannicus," *The Present Government of England in Church and State Asserted against the Oppugners of the Lord Bishop of Chichester's Sermon* (17 June).

43. Hare's *Sermon Preached at St. Mary's Church in Cambridge* (1709) analogically links Jews at the time of Christ and various alleged enemies of Hanover; his anti-Jacobite *Sermon Preached at the Cathedral Church of Worcester* (1716) praises the monarchy for placating dissent and neutralizing its threat to the church. In *Scripture Vindicated from the Misinterpretations of the Lord Bishop of Bangor* (1721; in vol. 2 of *The Works of the Late Right Reverend and Learned Dr. Francis Hare* [1746], 45–284), Hare is less sanguine, arguing for "severe Laws to curb and check the first Beginnings of Disorders from them" (75–76). Hare's attacks on Hoadly are *Church-Authority Vindicated* (1719), *A New Defense of the Lord Bishop of Bangor's Sermon* (1720), and *Scripture Vindicated*; the responses are the ironic *A Letter of Thanks from a Young Clergyman to the Reverend Dr. Hare* (1719); Hoadly, *An Answer to [. . .] Church-Authority Vindicated* (1720); Daniel Neal, *A Letter to the Reverend Dr. Francis Hare [. . .] Occasion'd by His Reflections on the Dissenters* (1720); and Richard Steele, *The D[ea]n of W[orceste]r Still the Same* (1720). Hare's position on dissent is criticized in all four pamphlets. The *DNB* erroneously states that Hare's role in the Bangorian Controversy prompted the loss of his chaplaincy "about 1718"; this is the result of a misreading of a report in John Nichols, vol. 5 of *Literary Anecdotes of the Eighteenth Century* (1812), 97–98, note. There is no contemporary support for the claim.

44. See Hunt, 128–29. For Gibson and dissent, see Browning, 78–79; and see Gibson, *The Dispute Adjusted, about the Proper Time of Applying for*

a *Repeal of the Corporation and Test Acts: by Shewing, That No Time Is Proper* (1732).

45. Walpole may even have orchestrated the "decision" of the Dissenting Deputies—an ad hoc pressure group formed in 1732 to promote repeal—to table their agitation; see Hunt, 133–34, 163–78.

46. *London Journal* 661 (26 Feb. 1732); see also Nos. 704 (23 Dec. 1732) and 741 (8 Sept. 1733). Henley's pro-government *Hyp-Doctor* also opposed repeal; see No. 107 (26 Dec. 1732).

47. Swift, *Upon the Martyrdom of King Charles I* (1726), in *Irish Tracts 1720–1723 and Sermons*, 219–31. For criticism of Hare's analogy of the 1640s and the 1730s, see "P. C.," *Letter [. . .] to Chichester*, 22–24; *Letter to the Author*, 20; Gordon, 40–41; and *Principles and Facts*, 33.

48. Sharp, *A Sermon Preached before the Lords [. . .] on the Thirtieth of January, 1699–1700* (1700); cf. Swift, *Upon the Martyrdom of King Charles I*, 231.

49. Kennett, *A Sermon Preached before the Lords [. . .] the xxxth of January, M.DCC.XIX* (1720); for Bradshaw and Clavering, see note 40, above.

50. See also, for example, Earbery, *Universal Spy* 10 (9 Sept. 1732); and "Philomeides I" in *Grub-street Journal* 57 (4 Feb. 1731).

51. See also Gordon, 43; and *Principles and Facts*, 5.

52. Hervey, vol. 1 of *Some Materials towards Memoirs of the Reign of King George II*, ed. and rev. by Romney Sedgwick (London: King's Printers, 1931), 88. Sedgwick notes that "Hervey seems to have begun the Memoirs early in 1733" (lvii). Gordon also considered Hare a turn-coat (3). Horn accepts Hervey's inaccurate charge of Hare's about-face (161).

53. *Titus Britannicus* (21) also takes offense at "P. C."'s statement about "High-church Spirit."

54. The *Craftsman* preferred to observe 5 November, the anniversary of the failure of the Gunpowder Plot of 1605 and of William III's landing at Torbay in 1688: see Nos. 70 (4 Nov. 1727), 174 (1 Nov. 1729), and 279 (6 Nov. 1731).

55. Clarke, *A Sermon Preached before the Honourable House of Commons [. . .] on Monday January XXXI, 1731* (1732); Warren, *The Glorious Reward of Christian Fortitude: A Sermon Preach'd before the Right Honourable the Lord Mayor, Aldermen, and Citizens of London [. . .] on Monday the 31st of January 1731* (1732). The *Grub-street Journal* did not reprint all the passages that I cite; my citations are to the original sermons. Clarke's text is Ps. 78.8 ("And might not be as their fathers, a stubborn and rebellious generation; a generation that set not their heart aright, and whose spirit was not stedfast with God"); Warren's is Rev. 3.21 ("To him that overcometh will I grant to sit with me in my throne, even as I also overcame, and am set down with my Father in his throne"). For *Fog's Weekly Journal* against Clarke's sermon, see No. 174 (4 Mar. 1732).

56. Warren despises "modern Advocates for the *Perfection* of the *Law of Nature exclusive of revelation*" (1), and analogically links Christ and Charles (14); his praise for Charles's "*Devotions*" (14) anticipates *Grub-street Journal* 224 (11 Apr. 1734).

57. The italicized portion is paraphrased from Clarke's sermon; see Clarke, 20.

58. Hare's 1746 *Works* includes "C. P."'s *A Defence of the Bishop of Chichester's Sermon*; the *Eighteenth-Century Short-Title Catalogue* does not endorse the attribution.

59. Hare's letters to his son are printed in *The Manuscripts of [. . .] Theodore J. Hare*, 235–57; Hare to Gibson, 29 Nov. 1739 and 29 Dec. 1739, are in the uncatalogued volume at the Huntington. According to Hervey, Hare's devotion to Walpole nearly paid off in 1737, when only Hervey's intervention kept Walpole from appointing Hare archbishop of Canterbury: see vol. 2 of Hervey, *Memoirs of the Reign of George the Second*, ed. John Wilson Croker (1884), 285; the account is accepted by the *DNB* and Horn (162).

60. Hare to Newcastle, Add. MS 32,688, f. 135; British Library. Hare's letters to Newcastle in 1734 have a similar tone; see Add. MS 32,689, ff. 220, 355; British Library.

61. For Hare and the 1734 election, see Williams, 567–68; for Newcastle and dissent, see Browning, 79, 307.

62. The ellipses appear in the manuscript.

CHAPTER 6. ACTING OUT THE UNSTABLE OPPOSITION

1. Loftis, *The Politics of Drama in Augustan England* (Oxford: Clarendon, 1963), 118–19. More recently, Loftis has argued that dramatists of the period 1728–37 "made use of their characters and fables to provide expositions of systems embodying principles resembling the systematic formulations of political theorists": "Political and Social Thought in the Drama," in *The London Theatre World, 1660–1800*, ed. Robert Hume (Carbondale: Southern Illinois University Press, 1980), 255. Loftis finds the drama of the period overwhelmingly hostile to Walpole: see *The Politics of Drama*, 94–127; and see "Thomson's *Tancred and Sigismunda* and the Demise of the Drama of Political Opposition," in *The Stage and the Page: London's 'Whole Show' in the Eighteenth-Century Theatre*, ed. George Winchester Stone, Jr. (Berkeley: University of California Press, 1981), e.g., 35. Bertrand Goldgar qualifies Loftis's political reading of Fielding's *Pasquin* (1736), although he is generally in accord with Loftis's appraisal of the politics of the drama: *Walpole and the Wits: The Relationship of Politics to Literature, 1722–1742* (Lincoln: University of Nebraska Press, 1976), 6; 151–52; 239, note 44. Jean Kern leaves political readings of political satire to Loftis; see *Dramatic Satire in the Age of Walpole, 1720–1750* (Ames: Iowa State University Press, 1976), 16–17. Robert Hume, although more mindful than other critics of the difficulty of defining political intention in the drama, considers as political (i.e., opposition) "the plays treated as political by Loftis, Goldgar, and Kern": *Henry Fielding and the London Theatre* (Oxford: Clarendon, 1988), 77–78. Vincent Liesenfeld notes "the hostility to the government that dominated the London stage during the 1730s": Introduction to *The Stage and the Licensing Act, 1729–1739*, ed. Liesenfeld (New York: Garland, 1981), x; cf. the more balanced tone of his introduction to Liesenfeld, *The Licensing Act of 1737* (Madison: University of Wisconsin Press, 1984), 3–5.

2. Writing about "content and meaning" in Restoration and eighteenth-century drama, Hume distinguishes "commonplace"—"belief ingrained at the level of unexamined assumption"—from "ideology"—"a matter of conscious and examined belief, something not believed by everyone": *The Rakish Stage: Studies in English Drama, 1660–1800* (Carbondale: Southern Illinois University Press, 1983), 16–17.

3. Bolingbroke, *Occasional Writer* 1 (1727), in vol. 1 of *The Works of Lord Bolingbroke* (1844; reprint, New York: Augustus M. Kelley, 1967), 209.

4. Hume, *Henry Fielding*, 78. The following plays, discussed in this chapter, are reprinted in Liesenfeld, ed., *The Stage and the Licensing Act: The Fall of Mortimer, King Charles the First*, and *Gustavus Vasa*. For *The Christian Hero*, see *The Plays of George Lillo*, ed. Trudy Drucker, 2 vols. (New York: Garland, 1979), vol. 1; for *Edward and Eleonora*, see *The Plays of James Thomson*, ed. Percy Adams (New York: Garland, 1979). Drucker selects *The Works of Mr. George Lillo* (1775) as the base-text for *The Christian Hero*; I have used the second edition of 1735, reprinted in *The Works of the Late Mr. George Lillo* (1740). Adams chooses the "corrected" 1768 edition of Thomson's Works as his source for *Edward and Eleonora*; I have preferred the first edition. In all other cases, I have used first editions.

5. For the evolution of *The Fall of Mortimer* as political drama, see Lance Bertelsen, "The Significance of the 1731 Revisions to *The Fall of Mortimer*," *Restoration and 18th Century Theatre Research*, 2d series, 2 (Winter 1987): 8–25.

6. The line is deleted in the 1768 edition.

7. See Loftis, *The Politics of Drama*, 120, 124; Liesenfeld, *The Licensing Act*, 82–83; Liesenfeld, Introduction to *The Stage and the Licensing Act*, xx–xxii; Hume, *Henry Fielding*, 85, 239–40. Chesterfield in 1737 found *King Charles the First* "a most tragical Story" with "a Catastrophe too recent, too melancholy, and of too solemn a Nature, to be heard of any where but from the Pulpit"; *The E[arl] of C[hester]f[iel]d's Speech in the H[ou]se of L[or]ds, against the Bill for Licensing All Dramatic Performances* (Dublin, 1749), 5–6.

8. See the following for biographical information on Havard: Robert Bruce, Introduction to William Boyce, *Three Birthday Odes for Prince George: 1749 or 1750, 1751, 1752* (London: Stainer and Bell, 1989), ix–x; William Chetwood, *The British Theatre* (Dublin, 1750), 185; John Doran, vol. 2 of *Annals of the English Stage from Thomas Betterton to Edmund Kean*, ed. Robert Lowe (1888), 61–62, 290; Philip Highfill, Jr., et al., vol. 7 of *A Biographical Dictionary of Actors, Actresses, Musicians, Dancers, Managers, and Other Stage Personnel in London, 1660–1800* (Carbondale: Southern Illinois University Press, 1973–), 184–91; Arthur Scouten, ed., part 3, vol. 1 of *The London Stage, 1660–1800* (Carbondale: Southern Illinois University Press, 1961), xlv, lxxxi–ii, clxxi; vol. 1 of *The Thespian Dictionary* (1805). None of these sources suggests that Havard had any sympathy for the opposition. The Cibberish lyrics that Havard wrote for Boyce's odes demonstrate that in his later life Havard was anything but subversive; and Havard's "New Epilogue upon His Leaving the Stage" (1768) recounts a life dedicated only to the theater (in Highfill, et al., 188). Paul Whitehead's epitaph for his friend Havard is probably accurate enough: "Fair peace he cherish'd, as he hated strife, / And lov'd and liv'd an inoffensive life" (in Highfill, et al., 189).

9. Liesenfeld, *The Licensing Act*, 83; see also Hawkins, *The Life of Samuel Johnson, LL.D.*, 2d ed. (1787), 73–74.

10. Hawkins, no friend to the theater, may be responsible for the first graft of opposition sentiment onto Havard's play. Disregarding the play's success, Hawkins comments on "the indignation of the public" against a play that "perpetuate[d] . . . enmity between the friends to and the opponents of our ecclesiastical and civil establishment" (73–74). Liesenfeld reproduces much of the section (*The Licensing Act*, 83; also Introduction to *The Stage and the Licensing Act*, xxi–ii), but omits the comment on the public's response and so removes the sole (dubious) prop for Hawkins's reading. I find no evidence from

the 1730s to support Hawkins's claim, but Liesenfeld seems to extrapolate from it when he comments on "the political significance audiences found in the play" (83)—a claim not supported in his text or his apparatus.

11. Hume, *Henry Fielding*, 239.

12. Hume, *Henry Fielding*, 239.

13. John Genest, refreshingly, notes that "Havard is a little partial to the King, but not grossly so": vol. 3 of *Some Account of the English Stage, from the Restoration in 1660 to 1830* (Bath, 1832), 513.

14. See Loftis, *The Politics of Drama*, 120; Liesenfeld quotes and endorses Loftis in *The Licensing Act*, 83; see also Liesenfeld, Introduction to *The Stage and the Licensing Act*, xx–xxi. The "majesty misled" theme crops up in the prologue to Havard's play, written "By a Friend," for which see 125, above. It would be foolish to lean too heavily on a recitation of commonplace in a part of the play typically reserved for such.

15. Hume, *Henry Fielding*, 239.

16. As far as I know, no one but Hawkins imagined a partisan reaction to the play until 1794. In April of that year, riots were set off in Edinburgh when some theatergoers refused to remove their hats for the singing of "God Save the King" before a production of what the (London) *Morning Chronicle* called "Havard's insipid tragedy of Charles I" (18 Apr. 1794). See Marilyn Morris, "The Monarchy as an Issue in English Political Argument in the Decade of the French Revolution" (Ph.D. thesis, University of London, 1988), 267–68. The *Morning Chronicle*'s critical instincts were intact, but its claim that the play inflamed political passions is suspect.

17. Loftis's contention that the deletions constitute "censorship" is puzzling; see "Political and Social Thought," 274.

18. Montagu, "P[ope] to Bolingbroke" (1734–35), in *Essays and Poems and Simplicity, A Comedy*, ed. Robert Halsband and Isobel Grundy (Oxford: Clarendon, 1977), ll. 40–43.

19. Of Havard's self-proclaimed Shakespearean "imitation" (see Havard's title page), Genest quipped, "Havard was quite right to inform the public that King Charles the 1st was written in imitation of Shakespeare, as no one could otherwise have discovered the circumstance" (611).

20. For Barber and Bolingbroke, see H. T. Dickinson, *Bolingbroke* (London: Constable, 1970), 189, 217, 220, 233; and see 220 for Bolingbroke's lack of "influence" with the mercantile interest in the City opposition. For the addresses of "Bolingbroke and his circle" to the "lesser gentry" as distinguished from "the big urban centres" that formed "the vanguard of a more broadly based opposition to the ruling order," see Nicholas Rogers, "The Urban Opposition to Whig Oligarchy, 1720–60," in *The Origins of Anglo-American Radicalism*, ed. Margaret Jacob and James Jacob (Atlantic Highlands, N.J.: Humanities, 1991), 153.

21. Loftis, however, may be correct in speculating that the play was "perhaps not written to be performed, so palpable and gross are the political parallels included" ("Political and Social Thought," 273).

22. Goldgar, *Walpole and the Wits*, 137.

23. Goldgar, *Walpole and the Wits*, 139.

24. Goldgar notes that the duchess of Marlborough also found the play politically inoffensive; he explains, however, that "in the highly charged atmosphere of 1739 . . . speaking on the side of liberty had indeed become a great offense, especially in plays coming from the circle around the prince and boasting the

usual trappings of Patriot drama (corrupt ministers, heroic saviors, and the like)" (*Walpole and the Wits*, 181).

25. Bolingbroke, *The Idea of a Patriot King*, in vol. 2 of *The Works of Lord Bolingbroke*, 401. Mabel Hessler Cable argues that *Vasa* "is really a dramatization of Bolingbroke's ideas": "The Idea of a Patriot King in the Propaganda of the Opposition to Walpole," *Philological Quarterly* 18 (April 1939): 124. Although the *Idea* was not published in an authorized edition until 1749, the manuscript and possibly some of Pope's printed copies were in circulation in 1738: see Dickinson, 260; and Simon Varey, *Henry St. John, Viscount Bolingbroke* (Boston: Twayne, 1984), 98.

26. See, for instance, James Thomson's *Britannia* (1729), in which the personified England repeatedly refers to the English as her "sons."

27. Varey discusses the common tendency to regard Frederick as the "patriot king" but considers the possibility that Bolingbroke might have had the young pretender, Charles Edward Stuart, in mind; see *Henry St. John*, 98–101.

28. Loftis, *The Politics of Drama*, 122; Hume, *Henry Fielding*, 84. Calhoun Winton observes that *Junius Brutus* is "a line-by-line prose translation of [Voltaire's] *Le Brutus* [1731]": "The Roman Play in the Eighteenth Century," *Studies in the Literary Imagination* 10 (Spring 1977): 80. As Winton points out, Voltaire addressed his preface to Bolingbroke (80); but Winton's findings seem to argue against ascribing too much English topicality to Duncombe.

29. Duncombe to Charlotte Clayton, Viscountess Sundon, vol. 1 of *Memoirs of Viscountess Sundon*, ed. Katherine Thomson (1847), 394. Sundon was Queen Caroline's mistress of the robes.

30. For Earbery, see 107–8, above. In his letter to Sundon, Duncombe claims that "Lady Hardwicke, and other of her friends . . . all approved [the play]" (395).

31. In Duncombe's dedication to Hardwicke, William III is "that Heroic Prince, whom Providence raised up in the Day of Distress, to rescue these Nations from Civil and Ecclesiastical Tyranny, and fix our Liberties on a firm and Lasting foundation" (n.p.).

32. Hume, *Henry Fielding*, 85; see Loftis, *The Politics of Drama*, 109.

33. Loftis, *The Politics of Drama*, 109.

34. See also Thomas Whincop's *Scanderbeg*, published in 1747 but written before Havard's *Scanderbeg* and Lillo's *The Christian Hero*.

Conclusion

1. Kramnick, *Bolingbroke and His Circle: The Politics of Nostalgia in the Age of Walpole* (Cambridge, Mass.: Harvard University Press, 1968), 1; see Burke, *Reflections on the Revolution in France* (1791), in *The French Revolution, 1790–1794*, vol. 8 of *The Writings and Speeches of Edmund Burke*, ed. L. G. Mitchell (Oxford: Clarendon, 1988), 140.

2. Kramnick, 261. For more on Bolingbroke's influence, see H. T. Dickinson, *Bolingbroke* (London: Constable, 1970), 302–10; and J. G. A. Pocock, *The Machiavellian Moment: Florentine Political Thought and the Atlantic Republican Tradition* (Princeton: Princeton University Press, 1975), 507.

3. Burke, 175. For Fielding and Johnson, see 17, above.

4. Dickinson, 297–300.

5. See *The Life and History of the Right Honourable Henry St. John, Lord*

Visc. Bolingbroke (1754); and Thomas Hunter, *A Sketch of the Philosophical Character of the Late Lord Viscount Bolingbroke* (1770).

6. Burke, 140.

7. Weinsheimer, *Eighteenth-Century Hermeneutics: Philosophy of Interpretation in England from Locke to Burke* (New Haven: Yale University Press, 1993), 73.

8. Reprinted in The Case of Authors by Profession or Trade *(1758) Together with* The Champion *(1739–1740)*, ed. Philip Stevick (Gainesville, Fla.: Scholars' Facsimiles and Reprints, 1966), 1–76.

9. Goldsmith, *The Life of Henry St. John, Lord Viscount Bolingbroke* (1770), in vol. 3 of *The Collected Works of Oliver Goldsmith*, ed. Arthur Friedman (Oxford: Clarendon, 1966), 466; see also 48, above.

10. Dickinson, 273, 276.

Bibliography

Manuscript Sources

Brett, Thomas. Letter to Richard Russel, 3 February 1733. MS Eng. Th. C 42, f. 176. Bodleian Library.

Earbery, Matthias. Letter to Thomas Brett, 19 September 1727(?). MS Eng. Th. C 30, ff. 87–88. Bodleian Library.

———. Letter to Thomas Brett, 11 September 1733. MS Eng. Th. C 32, ff. 229–30. Bodleian Library.

———. Letter to Thomas Gooch(?), bishop of Norwich, ca. 1738. Rawlinson MS C 735, f. 181. Bodleian Library.

Hare, Francis, bishop of Chichester. Letter to Edmund Gibson, bishop of London, 29 November 1739. Uncatalogued volume of Gibson's correspondence. Huntington Library.

———. Letter to Edmund Gibson, bishop of London, 29 December 1739. Uncatalogued volume of Gibson's correspondence. Huntington Library.

———. Letter to Thomas Pelham-Holles, duke of Newcastle, 18 August 1733. Add. MS 32,688, f. 135. British Library.

———. Letters to Thomas Pelham-Holles, duke of Newcastle, 1734. Add. MS 32,689, ff. 220, 355. British Library.

Russel, Richard. Letters to James Russel, 1748–53. Add. MS 41,169. British Library.

———. Letter to Thomas Brett, 19 March 1718. MS Eng. Th. C 26, ff. 223–34. Bodleian Library.

Yorke, Philip, 1st earl of Hardwicke. Notes on King's Bench cases, 1733–34. Add. MS 36,038. British Library.

———. Notes on Exchequer and King's Bench cases, 1717–33. Add. MS 36,196. British Library.

Original Sources in Print

(Unless otherwise indicated, the place of publication is London. Reprinted works that I mention but from which I do not quote are identified by year of original publication, as, of course, are works that have not been reprinted. I have identified periodicals by author when authorship is well known or is evidently stable during the years on which I focus in this study.)

Addison, Joseph. *Cato.* 1713.

———, and Richard Steele. *The Spectator.* 1711–12.

Advocates for Murther and Rebellion, the Pest of Government. 1714.

The Anti-Craftsman. 1729.

Anti-Papismus: Or, a Letter to the Reverend Dr. Trapp. 1731.

An Appeal to the Nation: Or, the Case of the Present Minister of Great Britain Truly Stated. 1731.

Applebee's Original Weekly Journal. 1720(?)–36(?).

Arnall, William [Francis Walsingham, pseud.]. *The Free Briton.* 1729–35.

Arnall, William. *Observations on a Pamphlet Intitled, An Answer to One Part of a Late Infamous Libel.* 1731.

―――. *Remarks on the Craftsman's Vindication of His Two Hon[oura]ble Patrons, in His Paper of May 22, 1731.* 1731.

Behn, Aphra. *Oroonoko.* Ca. 1688.

The B[isho]p and the D[octo]r Reconcil'd. 1732.

Bolingbroke, Henry St. John, 1st Viscount. *A Dissertation upon Parties.* 1733–34. In vol. 2 of *The Works of Lord Bolingbroke* (1967), 5–172.

―――. *A Final Answer to the Remarks on the Craftsman's Vindication.* 1731. In vol. 1 of *The Works of Lord Bolingbroke* (1967), 456–73.

―――. *The Idea of a Patriot King.* 1749. In vol. 2 of *The Works of Lord Bolingbroke* (1967), 372–429.

―――. *Letters on the Study and Use of History.* 1752. In vol. 2 of *The Works of Lord Bolingbroke* (1967), 173–334.

―――. *Lord Bolingbroke: Contributions to the* Craftsman. Edited by Simon Varey. Oxford: Clarendon, 1982.

―――. *Lord Bolingbroke: Historical Writings.* Edited by Isaac Kramnick. Chicago: University of Chicago Press, 1972.

―――. *The Occasional Writer.* 1727. In vol. 1 of *The Works of Lord Bolingbroke* (1967), 201–35.

―――. *The Philosophical Works of the Late Right Honourable Henry St. John, Lord Viscount Bolingbroke.* 5 vols. 1754–77.

―――. *Remarks on the History of England.* 1730–31.

―――. *The Works of Lord Bolingbroke.* 4 vols. Philadelphia, 1841.

―――. *The Works of Lord Bolingbroke.* 4 vols. 1844. Reprint. New York: Augustus M. Kelley, 1967.

―――. *The Works of the Right Honourable Henry St. John, Lord Viscount Bolingbroke.* 5 vols. 1754.

Bond, William. *The Tuscan Treaty.* 1733.

Boswell, James. *Boswell's Life of Johnson.* Edited by George Birbeck Hill, revised by Lawrence Powell. 6 vols. Oxford: Clarendon, 1934–50.

Boyer, Abel. Vol. 42 of *The Political State of Great-Britain.* 1732.

Bradshaw, William, bishop of Bristol. *A Sermon Preach'd before the Lords Spiritual and Temporal, in Parliament Assembled, in the Abbey-Church of Westminster, on Friday January 30. 1729/30.* 1730.

Britannicus, Titus [pseud.]. *The Present Government of England in Church and State Asserted against the Oppugners of the Lord Bishop of Chichester's Sermon.* 1732.

Brooke, Henry. *Gustavus Vasa.* 1739. Reprinted in *The Stage and the Licensing Act,* edited by Vincent Liesenfeld. New York: Garland, 1979.

Budgell, Eustace(?) [Timothy Scrub, pseud.]. *An Essay upon Something, or Something of an Essay.* 1731.

———. *A Letter to Cleomenes King of Sparta.* 1731.

Burke, Edmund. *Reflections on the Revolution in France.* 1791. In *The French Revolution, 1790–1794*, edited by L. G. Mitchell. Vol. 8 of *The Writings and Speeches of Edmund Burke*, edited by Paul Langford, et al. Oxford: Clarendon, 1988. 52–293.

C., P. [pseud.]. *A Letter to the Author of the Defence of the Bishop of Chichester's Sermon.* 1732.

———. *A Letter to the Right Reverend the Lord Bishop of Chichester.* 1732.

The Case of Opposition Stated, between the Craftsman and the People. 1731. Reprinted in *The Craftsman: Four Tracts.* New York: Garland, 1974.

Chesterfield, Philip Dormer Stanhope, 4th Earl of. *The E[arl] of C[hester]f[iel]d's Speech in the H[ou]se of L[or]ds, against the Bill for Licensing All Dramatic Performances.* 1737. Dublin, 1749.

Chetwood, William. *The British Theatre.* Dublin, 1750.

Cibber, Colley. *The Nonjuror.* 1717.

Clarke, Alured. *A Sermon Preached before the Honourable House of Commons, at St. Margaret's Westminster, on Monday January XXXI, 1731.* 1732.

Clavering, Robert, bishop of Peterborough. *A Sermon Preach'd before the Lords Spiritual and Temporal in Parliament Assembled, in the Abby-Church Westminster, on Saturday, January XXX, 1730.* 1731.

A Coalition of Patriots Delineated. 1735.

Common Sense. 1737–43.

The Compromise: Or, a Dialogue between W[alpole] and P[ulteney]. 1731.

The Country Journal; Or, the Craftsman. 1726–52.

Coxe, William. *Memoirs of the Life and Administration of Sir Robert Walpole.* 3 vols. 1798.

The Craftsman. 14 vols. 1731–37.

The Craftsman's Doctrine and Practice of the Liberty of the Press. 1732.

Croxall, Samuel. *A Sermon Preach'd before the Honourable House of Commons, at St. Margaret's, Westminster, on Friday, January xxx, 1729.* 1730.

The Daily Courant. 1702–35.

The Daily Journal. 1720–42.

The Daily Post. 1719–46(?).

The Danverian History of the Affairs of Europe, for the Memorable Year 1731. 1732.

A Defense of the Measures of the Present Administration. 1731(?). Reprinted in *Free Briton* 154 (9 Nov. 1732).

Defoe, Daniel. *Moll Flanders.* 1722.

The Doctrine of Innuendo's Discuss'd. 1731.

Dodsley, Robert [Nathan Ben Saddi, pseud.]. *Chronicle of the Kings of England from the Norman Conquest unto the Present Time.* 1742.

Dodsley, Robert. *The King and the Miller of Mansfield.* 1737.

———. *Sir John Cockle at Court.* 1738.

The Duel; A Poem. 1731.

Duncombe, William. *Junius Brutus*. 1735.

———. Letter to Charlotte Clayton, Viscountess Sundon. In vol. 1 of *Memoirs of Viscountess Sundon*, edited by Katherine Thomson, 394–96. 1847.

Earbery, Matthias. *An Historical Account of the Advantages That Have Accru'd to England, by the Succession in the Illustrious House of Hanover*. 1722.

———. *The History of the Clemency of Our English Monarchs*. 1717.

———. *The Occasional Historian*. 1731–32.

———. *The Old English Constitution Vindicated, and Set in a True Light*. 1717.

———. *Some Impartial Reflexions upon Dr Burnet's Posthumous History*. 1724.

———, trans. *De Statu Mortuorum*, by Thomas Burnet. 2 vols. 1727.

———. *The Universal Spy; Or, the Royal Oak Journal Reviv'd*. 1732.

———. *Vindication of the History of the Clemency, with Reflections upon the Late Proceedings against the Author*. 1718.

———. *The Whole System of English Liberty*. 1738.

Eikon Basilike. 1649.

The Examiner Examined. 1732.

The Fate of Favourites; Exemplified in the Fall of Villiers, Duke of Buckingham. 1734.

Fielding, Henry. "A Fragment of a Commentary on L. Bolingbroke's Essays." In *Journal of a Voyage to Lisbon*, 201–28 (for 249–76). 1755.

———. *Shamela*. 1741.

———. *Tom Jones*. 1749.

Fog's Weekly Journal. 1728–37.

Freeman, R. [pseud.]. *The Merits of the Crafts-Men Consider'd*. 1734.

A Full and True Account of a Sharp and Bloody Duel. 1731.

A Full and True Account of the Sad and Deplorable Death of Caleb D'Anvers Esq. 1731.

Gay, John. *The Beggar's Opera*. 1727.

Gibson, Edmund, bishop of London. *The Dispute Adjusted, about the Proper Time of Applying for a Repeal of the Corporation and Test Acts: by Shewing, That No Time Is Proper*. 1732.

Goldsmith, Oliver. *The Life of Henry St. John, Lord Viscount Bolingbroke*. 1770. In vol. 3 of *The Collected Works of Oliver Goldsmith*, edited by Arthur Friedman, 437–73. Oxford: Clarendon, 1966.

Gordon, Thomas. *An Examination of the Facts and Reasonings in the Lord Bishop of Chichester's Sermon*. 1732.

The Grub-street Journal. 1730–37.

Hare, Francis, bishop of Chichester. *Church-Authority Vindicated*. 1719.

———. Correspondence. 1737–40. In *The Manuscripts of the Earl of Buckinghamshire, The Earl of Lindsey, The Earl of Onslow, Lord Emly, Theodore J. Hare, Esq., and James Round, Esq., M.P.*, 235–57. 1895.

———. *A New Defense of the Lord Bishop of Bangor's Sermon*. 1720.

———. *Scripture Vindicated from the Misinterpretations of the Lord Bishop of Bangor*. 1721. In vol. 2 of *The Works of the Late Right Reverend and Learned Dr. Francis Hare*, 45–284. 1746.

———. *Sermon Preached at St. Mary's Church in Cambridge.* 1709.

———. *Sermon Preached at the Cathedral Church of Worcester.* 1716.

———. *A Sermon Preached before the House of Lords, in the Abbey-Church at Westminster, upon Monday, January 31, 1731.* 1732.

———. *Two Sermons on Rom. 13.1,2.* 1722.

Hatchett, William(?). *The Fall of Mortimer.* 1731. Reprinted in *The Stage and the Licensing Act,* edited by Vincent Liesenfeld. New York: Garland, 1979.

Havard, William. *King Charles the First.* 1737. Reprinted in *The Stage and the Licensing Act,* edited by Vincent Liesenfeld. New York: Garland, 1979.

———. *Scanderbeg.* 1733.

———. Text. *Three Birthday Odes for Prince George: 1749 or 1750, 1751, 1752,* by William Boyce. London: Stainer and Bell, 1989.

Hawkins, Sir John. *The Life of Samuel Johnson, LL.D.* 2d ed. 1787.

Haywood, Eliza. *The Tea-Table.* 1724.

Hearne, Thomas. *Remarks and Collections.* Edited by C. E. Doble, D. W. Rannie, and H. E. Salter. 11 vols. Oxford: Oxford University Press, 1885–1921.

Henley, John. *The Free-Mason.* 1733–34.

———. *The Hyp-Doctor.* 1730–42.

Hervey, John Hervey, Baron. *Ancient and Modern Liberty Stated and Compar'd.* 1734. Reprint. Los Angeles: Augustan Reprint Society, 1989.

———. *An Answer to the Occasional Writer No. II.* 1727.

———. *The Conduct of the Opposition.* 1734.

———. *Farther Observations on the Writings of the Craftsman.* 1730.

———. Vol. 2 of *Memoirs of the Reign of George the Second,* edited by John Wilson Croker. 1884.

———. *Observations on the Writings of the Craftsman.* 1730.

———. *Sequel of a Pamphlet Intitled Observations on the Writings of the Craftsman.* 1730.

———. Vol. 1 of *Some Materials towards Memoirs of the Reign of King George II,* edited by Romney Sedgwick. London: King's Printers, 1931.

Hoadly, Benjamin, bishop of Bangor. *An Answer to Dr. Hare's Sermon, Intitul'd Church-Authority Vindicated.* 1720.

Howell, T. B., ed. Vol. 17 of *A Complete Collection of State Trials.* 1813.

Hunter, Thomas. *A Sketch of the Philosophical Character of the Late Lord Viscount Bolingbroke.* 1770.

Impartial Memorials of the Life and Writings of Thomas Hearne, M.A. By Several Hands. 1736.

Johnson, Samuel. *A Dictionary of the English Language.* 1755.

Kennett, White, bishop of Peterborough. *A Sermon Preached before the Lords Spiritual and Temporal, in the Abbey-Church at Westminster, the xxxth of January, M.DCC.XIX.* 1720.

A Letter of Thanks from a Young Clergyman to the Reverend Dr. Hare. 1719.

A Letter to Caleb D'Anvers, Esq.; on His Proper Reply to a Late Scurrilous Libel, Entitled, Sedition and Defamation Display'd, &c. 1731.

A Letter to the Author of the Examination of the Facts and Reasonings in the Lord Bishop of Chichester's Sermon. 1732.

Liberty and the Craftsman: A Project for Improving the Country Journal. 1730.

The Life and History of the Right Honourable Henry St. John, Lord Visc. Bolingbroke. 1754.

Lillo, George. *The Christian Hero.* 2d ed. 1735. In *The Works of the Late Mr. George Lillo.* 1740.

———. *The Christian Hero.* 1735. Reprinted in vol. 1 of *The Plays of George Lillo,* edited by Trudy Drucker. New York: Garland, 1979.

London Evening-Post. 1727–(?).

Majesty Misled. 1734.

Memoirs of the Life and Conduct of William Pulteney, Esq. 1731.

"The Minute Book of the Partners in the Grub Street Journal." *Publishing History* 4 (1978): 49–94.

Mist's Weekly Journal. 1725–28.

Montagu, Lady Mary Wortley. "P[ope] to Bolingbroke." 1734–35. In *Essays and Poems and Simplicity, A Comedy,* edited by Robert Halsband and Isobel Grundy, 279–84. Oxford: Clarendon, 1977.

Morgan, Joseph, ed. *Phoenix Britannicus.* 1732.

Morning Chronicle. 18 April 1794.

Neal, Daniel. *A Letter to the Reverend Dr. Francis Hare, Dean of Worcester, Occasion'd by His Reflections on the Dissenters.* 1720.

Nedham, Marchamont. "Marchmont Nedham's History of the Rebellion." 1661. In *Phoenix Britannicus,* edited by Joseph Morgan, 174–86. 1732.

———. *A Short History of the English Rebellion.* 1661.

Nichols, John. Vol. 5 of *Literary Anecdotes of the Eighteenth Century.* 1812.

Observations on the Occasional Writer, the Craftsman, and Other Papers. 1729.

Oldmixon, John. *Memoirs of the Press.* 1742.

Oxoniensis [pseud.]. Letter to the editor. *Gentleman's Magazine* 56 (1786): 661–62.

P., C. [pseud.]. *A Defence of the Bishop of Chichester's Sermon.* 1732.

Pelham, Henry. Letter to Francis Hare, 22 September 1722. In *The Manuscripts of the Earl of Buckinghamshire, The Earl of Lindsey, The Earl of Onslow, Lord Emly, Theodore J. Hare, Esq., and James Round, Esq., M.P.,* 234–35. 1895.

Pitt, James [Francis Osborne, pseud.]. *The London Journal.* 1719–44.

Pope, Alexander. *The Dunciad.* 1728. In *The Dunciad,* edited by James Sutherland. Vol. 5 of *The Twickenham Edition of the Poems of Alexander Pope,* edited by John Butt, et al. London: Methuen; New Haven: Yale University Press, 1951. 59–200.

———. *Epilogue to the Satires, Dialogue 2.* 1738. In *Imitation of Horace,* edited by John Butt. Vol. 4 of *The Twickenham Edition of the Poems of Alexander Pope,* edited by John Butt, et al. London: Methuen; New Haven: Yale University Press, 1941. 313–27.

———. *An Epistle from Mr. Pope, to Dr. Arbuthnot.* 1735. In *Imitations of Horace,* 95–127.

———. *A Master Key to Popery.* 1949 (written 1732).

———. *Peri Bathos.* 1727.

The Principles and Facts of the Lord Bishop of Chichester's Sermon. 1732.

Pulteney: Or the Patriot. 1731.

Pulteney, William. *An Answer to a Late Pamphlet, Intituled, Observations on the Writings of the Craftsman.* 1730.

———. *An Answer to One Part of a Late Infamous Libel, Intitled, Remarks on the Craftsman's Vindication of His Two Honourable Patrons.* 1731.

———. *A Proper Reply to a Late Scurrilous Libel; Intitled, Sedition and Defamation Display'd.* 1731.

Ralph, James. *The Case of Authors by Profession or Trade.* 1758. Reprinted in *The Case of Authors by Profession or Trade (1758) Together with The Champion (1739–1740),* edited by Philip Stevick, 1–76. Gainesville, Fla.: Scholars' Facsimiles and Reprints, 1966.

———. *The Fall of the Earl of Essex.* 1731.

Rapin de Thoyras, Paul. *History of England.* Translated by Nicholas Tindal. 15 vols. 1725–31.

Read's Weekly Journal. 1730–61.

A Register of Books, 1728–1732, Extracted from the Monthly Chronicle. London: Gregg-Archive, 1964.

Richardson, Samuel. *Clarissa.* 1747–49.

———. *Pamela.* 1740–41.

Russel, Richard, trans. *A Discourse Concerning the Nature and Obligation of Oaths,* by Robert Sandersen. 1716.

———. *The Impeachment: Or, the Church Triumphant.* 1711.

———, ed. *Memoirs of the Society of Grub-street.* 2 vols. 1737.

———. *The Obligation of Acting According to Conscience.* 1716.

Sharp, John, archbishop of York. *A Sermon Preached before the Lords Spiritual and Temporal in Parliament Assembled, in the Abbey-Church at Westminster, on the Thirtieth of January, 1699–1700.* 1700.

Smoke, Timothy [pseud.]. *The Commodity Excised: Or, the Women in an Uproar.* 1733.

Steele, Richard. *The D[ea]n of W[orceste]r Still the Same.* 1720.

Swift, Jonathan. *The Conduct of the Allies.* 1711.

———. *A Learned Comment upon Dr. Hare's Sermon.* 1711.

———. *A Sermon upon the Martyrdom of K. Charles I. Preached at St. Patrick's, Dublin, Jan. 30, 1725–6.* 1726. In *Irish Tracts 1720–1723 and Sermons,* edited by Herbert Davis and Louis Landa. Vol. 9 of *The Prose Works of Jonathan Swift,* edited by Davis, et al. Oxford: Basil Blackwell, 1963. 219–31.

———. *A Tale of a Tub.* 1704.

The Thespian Dictionary. 1805.

Thomson, James. *Britannia.* 1729.

———. *Edward and Eleonora.* 1739.

———. *Edward and Eleonora.* Corrected ed. 1768. Reprinted in *The Plays of James Thomson,* edited by Percy Adams. New York: Garland, 1979.

Three Pamphlets; Entituled Observations on the Writings of the Craftsman, The Sequel and Farther Observations Examin'd. 1730.

Tracy, John. *Periander.* 1731.

Trapp, Joseph. *The Character and Principles of the Present Set of Whigs.* 1711.

———. *The Ministerial Virtue: Or, Long-Suffering Extolled in a Great Man.* 1738.

———. *A Sermon Preach'd before the Right Honourable the Lord Mayor and Aldermen of the City of London, at the Cathedral Church of St. Paul, on Friday, January 30. 1729.* 1730.

Universal Spectator. 1728–46.

Warren, Robert. *The Glorious Reward of Christian Fortitude: A Sermon Preach'd before the Right Honourable the Lord Mayor, Aldermen, and Citizens of London, at the Cathedral of St. Paul, on Monday the 31st of January 1731.* 1732.

Weekly Miscellany. 1732–41.

Whig and Tory: Or, Wit on Both Sides. 1713.

Whincop, Thomas. *Scanderbeg.* 1747.

Whitehall Evening-Post. 1718–1800(?).

Yonge, William. *Sedition and Defamation Display'd.* 1731.

Secondary Sources

Abbey, C. J. "Church Fabrics and Services." In *The English Church in the Eighteenth Century*, by Abbey and J. H. Overton, 403–75. 2d ed. 1887.

Anselment, Raymond. *Loyalist Resolve: Patient Fortitude in the English Civil War.* Newark: University of Delaware Press, 1988.

Aylmer, G. E. *Rebellion or Revolution?: England from Civil War to Restoration.* Oxford: Oxford University Press, 1986.

Bates, David. *William the Conqueror.* London: George Philip, 1989.

Baxter, Stephen. "A Comment on Clayton Roberts' Perspective." *Albion* 25 (Summer 1993): 257–60.

Bender, John. *Imagining the Penitentiary: Fiction and the Architecture of Mind in Eighteenth-Century England.* Chicago: University of Chicago Press, 1987.

———. "A New History of the Enlightenment?" In *The Profession of Eighteenth-Century Literature: Reflections on an Institution*, edited by Leo Damrosch, 62–83. Madison: University of Wisconsin Press, 1992.

Bennett, G. V. *The Tory Crisis in Church and State 1688–1730: The Career of Francis Atterbury Bishop of Rochester.* Oxford: Clarendon, 1975.

Bertelsen, Lance. "The Significance of the 1731 Revisions to *The Fall of Mortimer*." *Restoration and 18th Century Theatre Research*, 2d series, 2 (Winter 1987): 8–25.

Black, Jeremy. *Robert Walpole and the Nature of Politics in Early Eighteenth-Century England.* New York: St. Martin's, 1990.

Bornstein, George. "What Is the Text of a Poem by Yeats?" In *Palimpsest: Editorial Theory in the Humanities*, edited by Bornstein and Ralph Williams, 167–93. Ann Arbor: University of Michigan Press, 1993.

Browning, Reed. *The Duke of Newcastle.* New Haven: Yale University Press, 1975.

Broxap, Henry. *The Later Non-Jurors.* Cambridge: Cambridge University Press, 1924.

Bruce, Robert. Introduction to *Three Birthday Odes for Prince George: 1749 or 1750, 1751, 1752*, by William Boyce. London: Stainer and Bell, 1989.

Burtt, Shelley. *Virtue Transformed: Political Argument in England, 1688–1740.* Cambridge: Cambridge University Press, 1992.

Cable, Mabel Hessler. "The Idea of a Patriot King in the Propaganda of the Opposition to Walpole." *Philological Quarterly* 18 (April 1939): 119–30.

Carlton, Charles. *Charles I: The Personal Monarch.* London: Ark-Routledge, 1983.

Colley, Linda. *In Defiance of Oligarchy: The Tory Party, 1714–60.* Cambridge: Cambridge University Press, 1982.

Cruickshanks, Eveline. Introduction to *Ideology and Conspiracy: Aspects of Jacobitism, 1689–1759*, edited by Cruickshanks. Edinburgh: John Donald, 1982.

———. *Political Untouchables: The Tories and the '45.* London: Duckworth, 1979.

Davis, Herbert. "Reprinting *The Craftsman*." *Book Collector* 2 (Winter 1953): 279–82.

Dickinson, H. T. *Bolingbroke.* London: Constable, 1970.

———. "The Eighteenth-Century Debate on the 'Glorious Revolution'." *History* 61 (February 1976): 28–45.

Doran, John. Vol. 2 of *Annals of the English Stage from Thomas Betterton to Edmund Kean*, edited by Robert Lowe. London: Nimmo, 1888.

English Reports, vols. 92, 94. Edinburgh: William Green and Sons; London: Stevens and Sons, 1909.

Erskine-Hill, Howard. *The Augustan Idea in English Literature.* London: Edward Arnold, 1983.

———. "Literature and the Jacobite Cause: Was There a Rhetoric of Jacobitism?" In *Ideology and Conspiracy: Aspects of Jacobitism, 1689–1759*, edited by Eveline Cruickshanks, 49–69. Edinburgh: John Donald, 1982.

———. Review of *Walpole and the Wits: The Relation of Politics to Literature, 1722–1742*, by Bertrand Goldgar. *Review of English Studies* n.s. 30 (February 1979): 90–94.

Foord, Archibald. *His Majesty's Opposition 1714–1830.* Oxford: Clarendon, 1964.

Frey, Linda, and Marsha Frey. *A Question of Empire: Leopold I and the War of Spanish Succession, 1701–1705.* Boulder, Colo.: Eastern European Monographs 146; New York: Columbia University Press, 1983.

Friedman, Arthur. Introduction to *The Life of Henry St. John, Lord Viscount Bolingbroke*. In vol. 3 of *The Collected Works of Oliver Goldsmith*, edited by Friedman, 431–33. Oxford: Clarendon, 1966.

Fritz, Paul. *The English Ministers and Jacobitism between the Rebellions of 1715 and 1745.* Toronto: University of Toronto Press, 1975.

Genest, John. Vol. 3 of *Some Account of the English Stage, from the Restoration in 1660 to 1830.* Bath, 1832.

Goldgar, Bertrand. "The Grub-street Journal." In *British Literary Magazines: The Augustan Age and the Age of Johnson, 1698–1788*, edited by Alvin Sullivan, 144–49. Westport, Conn.: Greenwood, 1983.

———. "Pope and the Grub-street Journal." *Modern Philology* 74 (May 1977): 366–80.

———. *Walpole and the Wits: The Relation of Politics to Literature, 1722–1742.* Lincoln: University of Nebraska Press, 1976.

Gunn, J. A. W. *Beyond Liberty and Property: The Process of Self-Recognition in Eighteenth-Century Political Thought.* Kingston, Ontario: McGill-Queen's University Press, 1983.

Halsband, Robert. *Lord Hervey: Eighteenth-Century Courtier.* New York: Oxford University Press, 1974.

Hammond, Brean. *Pope and Bolingbroke: A Study of Friendship and Influence.* Columbia: University of Missouri Press, 1984.

Hanson, Laurence. *Government and the Press 1695–1763.* Oxford: Oxford University Press, 1936.

Harris, Michael. "Figures Relating to the Printing and Distribution of the *Craftsman* 1726 to 1730." *Bulletin of the Institute of Historical Research* 43 (November 1970): 233–42.

———. *London Newspapers in the Age of Walpole: A Study of the Origins of the Modern English Press.* Rutherford, N.J.: Fairleigh Dickinson University Press; London: Associated University Presses, 1987.

———. "The Management of the London Newspaper Press During the Eighteenth Century." *Publishing History* 4 (1978): 95–112.

Harris, Tim. *London Crowds in the Reign of Charles II: Propaganda and Politics from the Restoration until the Exclusion Crisis.* Cambridge: Cambridge University Press, 1987.

Harth, Phillip. *Pen for a Party: Dryden's Tory Propaganda in Its Contexts.* Princeton: Princeton University Press, 1993.

Highfill, Philip, Jr., et al. "William Havard." Vol. 7 of *A Biographical Dictionary of Actors, Actresses, Musicians, Dancers, Managers, and Other Stage Personnel in London, 1660–1800.* Carbondale: Southern Illinois University Press, 1982.

Hill, B. W. *Sir Robert Walpole: "Sole and Prime Minister".* London: Hamish Hamilton, 1989.

Hillhouse, James. *The Grub-Street Journal.* Durham: Duke University Press, 1928.

Horn, Robert. "Marlborough's First Biographer: Dr. Francis Hare." *Huntington Library Quarterly* 20 (February 1957): 145–62.

Horne, Thomas. "Politics in a Corrupt Society: William Arnall's Defense of Robert Walpole." *Journal of the History of Ideas* 41 (October–December 1980): 601–14.

Hume, Robert. *Henry Fielding and the London Theatre, 1728–1737.* Oxford: Clarendon, 1988.

———. *The Rakish Stage: Studies in English Drama, 1660–1800.* Carbondale: Southern Illinois University Press, 1983.

———. "Texts within Contexts: Notes toward a Historical Method." *Philological Quarterly* 71 (Winter 1992): 69–100.

Hunt, N. C. *Two Early Political Associations: The Quakers and the Dissenting Deputies in the Age of Sir Robert Walpole.* Oxford: Clarendon, 1961.

Jones, George Hilton. *The Main Stream of Jacobitism.* Cambridge, Mass.: Harvard University Press, 1954.

Kenyon, J. P. *Revolution Principles: The Politics of Party 1689–1720.* Cambridge: Cambridge University Press, 1977.

Kern, Jean. *Dramatic Satire in the Age of Walpole, 1720–1750.* Ames: Iowa State University Press, 1976.

Kramnick, Isaac. "Augustan Politics and English Historiography: The Debate on the English Past, 1730–35." *History and Theory* 6 (1967): 33–56.

———. *Bolingbroke and His Circle: The Politics of Nostalgia in the Age of Walpole.* Cambridge, Mass.: Harvard University Press, 1968.

———. Introduction to *Lord Bolingbroke: Historical Writings,* edited by Kramnick. Chicago: University of Chicago Press, 1972.

Landa, Louis. Introduction to *Sermons.* In *Irish Tracts 1720–1723 and Sermons,* edited by Herbert Davis and Landa. Vol. 9 of *The Prose Works of Jonathan Swift,* edited by Davis, et al. Oxford: Basil Blackwell, 1963. 97–137.

———. Review of "The Rise and Fall of a Martyrology: Sermons on Charles I," by Helen Randall, in *Huntington Library Quarterly* 10 (February 1947): 135–67. *Philological Quarterly* 27 (April 1948): 128.

Landau, Norma. "Country Matters: *The Growth of Political Stability* a Quarter-Century On." *Albion* 25 (Summer 1993): 261–74.

Langford, Paul. *The Excise Crisis: Society and Politics in the Age of Walpole.* Oxford: Clarendon, 1975.

Liesenfeld, Vincent. Introduction to *The Stage and the Licensing Act, 1729–1739,* edited by Liesenfeld. New York: Garland, 1981.

———. *The Licensing Act of 1737.* Madison: University of Wisconsin Press, 1984.

Lenman, Bruce. *The Jacobite Risings in Britain 1689–1746.* London: Eyre Methuen, 1980.

Lewis, C. S. "Addison." In *Eighteenth Century English Literature: Modern Essays in Criticism,* edited by James Clifford, 144–56. New York: Oxford University Press, 1959.

Lockwood, Thomas. Electronic memorandum to author, 3 March 1994.

Loftis, John. "Political and Social Thought in the Drama." In *The London Theatre World, 1660–1800,* edited by Robert Hume, 253–85. Carbondale: Southern Illinois University Press, 1980.

———. *The Politics of Drama in Augustan England.* Oxford: Clarendon, 1963.

———. "Thomson's *Tancred and Sigismunda* and the Demise of the Drama of Political Opposition." In *The Stage and the Page: London's 'Whole Show' in the Eighteenth-Century Theatre,* edited by George Winchester Stone, Jr., 34–54. Berkeley: University of California Press, 1981.

Lounsbury, Thomas. *The Text of Shakespeare.* New York: Scribner's, 1908.

Mack, Maynard. *Alexander Pope: A Life.* New York: Norton, 1985.

———. *The Garden and the City: Retirement and Politics in the Later Poetry of Pope, 1731–1743.* Toronto: University of Toronto Press, 1969.

McGann, Jerome. *A Critique of Modern Textual Criticism.* Chicago: University of Chicago Press, 1983.

———. "Literary Pragmatics and the Editorial Horizon." In *Devils and Angels: Textual Editing and Literary Theory,* edited by Philip Cohen, 1–21. Charlottesville: University Press of Virginia, 1991.

———. *The Textual Condition*. Princeton: Princeton University Press, 1991.

McKeon, Michael. *The Origins of the English Novel, 1600–1740*. Baltimore: Johns Hopkins University Press, 1987.

McLynn, Frank. *The Jacobites*. London: Routledge, 1985.

Midgley, Graham. *The Life of Orator Henley*. Oxford: Clarendon, 1973.

Miner, Earl. Introduction to *Poems on the Reign of William III*, edited by Miner. Los Angeles: Augustan Reprint Society, 1974.

Monod, Paul Kléber. *Jacobitism and the English People, 1688–1788*. Cambridge: Cambridge University Press, 1989.

Morris, Marilyn. "The Monarchy as an Issue in English Political Argument in the Decade of the French Revolution." Ph.D. thesis, University of London, 1988.

Nadel, George. "Philosophy of History before Empiricism." *History and Theory* 3 (1964): 291–313.

Nokes, David. *Raillery and Rage: A Study in Eighteenth Century Satire*. New York: St. Martin's, 1987.

Overton, J. H. *The Nonjurors: Their Lives, Principles, and Writings*. London: Smith, Elder, 1902.

Pettit, Alexander. "Propaganda, Public Relations, and the *Remarks on the Craftsman's Vindication of His Two Hon[oura]ble Patrons, in His Paper of May 22, 1731*." *Huntington Library Quarterly* 57 (Winter 1994): 45–59.

Plumb, J. H. *The Growth of Political Stability in England, 1675–1725*. London: Macmillan, 1967.

———. *Sir Robert Walpole: The King's Minister*. London: Cresset, 1960.

Pocock, J. G. A. *The Machiavellian Moment: Florentine Political Thought and the Atlantic Republican Tradition*. Princeton: Princeton University Press, 1975.

Potter, Lois. *Secret Rites and Secret Writing: Royalist Literature 1641–1660*. Cambridge: Cambridge University Press, 1989.

Radzinowicz, Leon. Vol. 1 of *A History of English Criminal Law and its Administration from 1750*. London: Stevens and Sons, 1948.

Randall, Helen. "The Rise and Fall of a Martyrology: Sermons on Charles I." *Huntington Library Quarterly* 10 (February 1947): 135–67.

Reeve, L. J. *Charles I and the Road to Personal Rule*. Cambridge: Cambridge University Press, 1989.

Roberts, Clayton. "The Growth of Political Stability Reconsidered." *Albion* 25 (Summer 1993): 237–55.

———. "A Reply to Professors Baxter and Landau." *Albion* 25 (Summer 1993): 275–77.

Roberts, W. "Grub Street and its Journal." *The Bookworm* 1 (1888): 94–99.

Rogers, Nicholas. "Riot and Popular Jacobitism in Early Hanoverian England." In *Ideology and Conspiracy: Aspects of Jacobitism, 1689–1759*, edited by Eveline Cruickshanks, 70–88. Edinburgh: John Donald, 1982.

———. "The Urban Opposition to Whig Oligarchy, 1720–60." In *The Origins of Anglo-American Radicalism*, edited by Margaret Jacob and James Jacob, 152–68. Atlantic Highlands, N.J.: Humanities, 1991.

———. *Whigs and Cities: Popular Politics in the Age of Walpole and Pitt.* Oxford: Clarendon, 1989.

Rogers, Pat. *Grub Street: Studies in a Subculture.* London: Methuen, 1971.

Rosenheim, E. W., Jr. "Swift and the Martyred Monarch." *Philological Quarterly* 54 (Winter 1975): 178–94.

Rudé, George. *Hanoverian London 1714–1808.* Berkeley: University of California Press, 1971.

Scouten, Arthur, ed. Part 3, vol. 1 of *The London Stage, 1660–1800.* Carbondale: Southern Illinois University Press, 1961.

Sedgwick, Romney. Introduction to *Some Materials towards Memoirs of the Reign of King George II*, by John, Lord Hervey. London: King's Printers, 1931.

Sharpe, Kevin. *The Personal Rule of Charles I.* New Haven: Yale University Press, 1992.

Sherburn, George. Review of *The Grub-Street Journal*, by James Hillhouse. *Modern Philology* 26 (February 1929): 361–67.

Speck, W. A. *Reluctant Revolutionaries: Englishmen and the Revolution of 1688.* Oxford: Oxford University Press, 1989.

———. *Stability and Strife: England 1714–1760.* London: Edward Arnold, 1977.

Stuber, Florian, gen. ed. The *Clarissa* Project. 8 vols. to date. New York: AMS, 1990– .

Sutherland, Lucy. "The City of London in Eighteenth-Century Politics." In *Essays Presented to Sir Lewis Namier*, edited by Richard Pares and A. J. P. Taylor, 49–74. London: MacMillan; New York: St. Martin's, 1956.

Sykes, Norman. *Church and State in England in the Eighteenth Century.* Hamden, Conn.: Archon, 1962.

Varey, Simon. "The *Craftsman* 1726–1752: An Historical and Critical Account." Ph.D. thesis, Cambridge University, 1976.

———. *Henry St. John, Viscount Bolingbroke.* Boston: Twayne, 1984.

———. Introduction to *Lord Bolingbroke: Contributions to the* Craftsman, edited by Varey. Oxford: Clarendon, 1982.

Wakeman, Henry Offley. *An Introduction to the History of the Church of England.* 11th ed. London: Rivingtons, 1927.

Wedgwood, C. V. *A Coffin for King Charles: The Trial and Execution of Charles I.* New York: Macmillan, 1964.

Weinbrot, Howard. *Augustus Caesar in "Augustan" England: The Decline of a Classical Norm.* Princeton: Princeton University Press, 1978.

Weinsheimer, Joel. *Eighteenth-Century Hermeneutics: Philosophy of Interpretation in England from Locke to Burke.* New Haven: Yale University Press, 1993.

Williams, Basil. "The Duke of Newcastle and the Election of 1734." *English Historical Review* 12 (July 1897): 448–88.

Williamson, Raymond. "John Martyn and the Grub-street Journal." *Medical History* 5 (October 1961): 361–74.

Wilson, Kathleen. "Inventing Revolution: 1688 and Eighteenth-Century Popular Politics." *Journal of British Studies* 28 (October 1989): 349–86.

Winton, Calhoun. "The Roman Play in the Eighteenth Century." *Studies in the Literary Imagination* 10 (Spring 1977): 77–90.

Index

"Bolingbrokean polemics" identifies the work of Lord Bolingbroke and other writers affiliated with or sympathetic to the *Craftsman*, particularly Nicholas Amhurst and William Pulteney. "Carolinist polemics" identifies the work of Matthias Earbery, Richard Russel, and others discussed in sections of this book indexed here under Carolinism. "Pro-government polemics" identifies the writings of William Arnall, Lord Hervey, James Pitt, and others affiliated with or sympathetic to the administration of Sir Robert Walpole. References in subentries to Russel are to Richard Russel; those to Walpole are to Sir Robert Walpole.

Abbey, C. J., 214 n. 14
Abjuration Oaths (1701–2, 1714). See loyalty oaths
Act of Settlement (1701), 94, 95, 100
Adams, Percy, 220 n. 4
Addison, Joseph, 40, 55; *Cato*, 170
Advocates for Murther and Rebellion, 101, 122, 205 n. 33
Amhurst, Nicholas: on Carolinist opposition to Walpole, 119; and *Craftsman*, 15, 35, 36, 39, 42–43, 48–54, 59, 66–71, 79, 92–93, 119, 201 nn. 32, 35, and 37, 201–2 n. 39, 203 n. 12, 204 n. 25, 205 n. 38, 210 nn. 22 and 23; on dissent, 204 n. 25; on pro-government polemics, 42, 48, 197 n. 18, 201 n. 37; Ralph on, 191–92; on Revolution of 1688–89, 203 n. 12; on Whigs and Tories, 92–93, 203 n. 12; on William III, 205 n. 38
analogies, historical: in Bolingbrokean polemics, 26, 36–38, 39, 58–60, 62–77, 80, 82–84, 111, 135, 167–68, 179, 198 n. 3, 210 nn. 22 and 23; in Carolinist polemics, 106–8, 121, 122, 124, 129–30, 137–38, 149, 150, 159, 161–62, 172–74, 209 n. 8; in history plays, 172–74, 179, 185, 221 n. 21; in King Charles Day sermons, 29, 135, 152, 156–57, 159–62, 210 n. 15, 218 nn. 47 and

56; in pro-government polemics, 58, 84, 217 n. 43
Ancient and Modern Liberty Stated and Compar'd (Hervey), 58, 84, 94, 120, 198 n. 3
Anselment, Raymond, 123, 127–28, 210 n. 12
Answer to a Late Pamphlet, An (Pulteney), 46, 72, 74–75, 200 n. 21, 201 n. 31
Answer to Dr. Hare's Sermon, An (Hoadley), 217 n. 43
Answer to One Part of a Late Infamous Libel, An (Pulteney), 61, 79, 195 n. 16
Answer to the Occasional Writer No. II, An (Hervey), 198 n. 2
Anti-Craftsman, The, 65, 200 n. 24
Anti-Papismus, 136, 212–13 n. 45
"Apotheosis of That Ever Blessed Martyr King Charles I," 127
Appeal to the Nation, An, 56
Applebee's Original Weekly Journal, 59
Arnall, William (pseud. Francis Walsingham): on Bolingbrokean opposition, 24, 40, 41, 48, 98–99, 112, 189–90, 206 n. 43; *History of Patriotism*, 40, 196 n. 10; *Observations on a Pamphlet*, 24, 195 n. 16; *Remarks on the Craftsman's Vindication of His Two Hon[oura]ble Pa-*

237

trons, 61, 79; responses to, 61, 119, 147–48; scholarship on, 22, 194 n. 11; on William III, 102–3. See also Free Briton
Atterbury, Francis, bishop of Rochester, 139, 144, 206 n. 41, 215 n. 16
Aylmer, G. E., 211 n. 31

Bævius. See Martyn, John; Russel, Richard
Baker, William, bishop of Norwich, 208 n. 60
Bangorian Controversy (1717), 121, 154, 217 n. 43. See also Hoadley, Benjamin
Barber, John, 134–35, 176, 212 n. 42
Bastwick, John, 131–33
Bates, David, 206 n. 50
Baxter, Stephen, 193 n. 4
Beggar's Opera, The (Gay), 165
Behn, Aphra: *Oroonoko*, 43, 187
Bender, John, 19–20, 194 n. 7
Bennett, G. V., 206 n. 41
Bertelsen, Lance, 220 n. 5
Bill of Rights (1689), 91, 93–94, 96, 112, 119
B[ishop] and the D[octo]r Reconcil'd, The, 217 n. 42
Black, Jeremy, 193–94 n. 4, 203 n. 10
Bolingbroke, Henry St. John, 1st viscount, 15–17, 22–26, 35–57, 62–70; and Barber, 176; on Bill of Rights, 112; on 1st duke of Buckingham, 36; Burke on, 189–92; Caroline (queen of England) allegedly attacked by, 69, 74; in Carolinist polemics, 27–28, 90, 102, 110–14, 115–16, 117, 129–33, 134–36, 141, 149, 151, 173–75, 189, 194 n. 11, 206 nn. 41 and 43; on Charles I, 39, 54, 112, 120, 132, 209 n. 4; and Church of England, 139; and City of London, 176, 221 n. 20; consensus promoted by, 15–16, 17, 22, 24–26, 35, 38, 40–43, 58–59, 87–90, 111, 139, 144, 164, 165, 181, 188, 191–92; on constitutional monarchy, 37, 39, 44–45, 93; and *Craftsman*, 15–16, 17, 35–46, 89, 196 n. 5; on divine-right monarchy, 208 n. 62; on Edward III, 39, 63; on Edward IV, 39, 69, 73, 84; on Elizabeth I, 37, 112, 132; and exemplary historiography, 115, 196 n. 7; H. Fielding on, 17, 189; on *Fog's Weekly Journal*, 41, 44; on George I, 48, 94; on George II, 36, 37, 39, 44, 64, 69, 71, 74, 76; and earl of Godolphin, 48; Goldsmith on, 48–49, 191–92, 197 n. 17; Hanoverian monarchy attacked by, 64–69; Hanoverian monarchy supported by, 17, 53, 67–68, 117, 170; on Henry IV, 66; on Henry VI, 66; on Henry VIII, 36; historical analogies used by, 26, 36–38, 39, 58–60, 62–77, 80, 82–84, 96, 108, 111; history plays as responses to, 165–88, 222 nn. 25 and 28; history theorized by, 26, 37–38, 41, 93–94, 166, 170; and Jacobitism, 17, 76, 89–90, 97, 102, 105, 200 n. 28, 206 n. 41; on James I, 112, 209 n. 4; on James II, 95; Johnson on, 17, 189; on liberty and English history, 26, 37–38, 41–42, 43, 45, 53, 92–93, 96–97, 102, 104, 112, 128, 137, 166, 169, 173–76, 179–80, 182, 196 n. 7, 203 n. 14, 221–22 n. 24; on liberty of the press, 104–5, 206 n. 43; life of, 16–17, 30, 35–36, 150, 192, 196 n. 5, 206 n. 41; and literary opposition to Walpole, 30; influence of Machiavelli on, 37, 196 n. 7; and duke of Marlborough, 48; on parliament, 170; personae used by, 36–37, 40–45, 52–53, 64, 66, 69, 197 n. 13; and Pope, 15, 20–24, 45, 198 n. 27; in pro-government polemics, 24, 36, 40, 42, 46, 48, 58–61, 64–67, 71–78, 81–84, 92, 94, 175, 189, 194 n. 11, 200 n. 22, 206 n. 43, 209 n. 4; on pro-government polemics, 36, 39, 42, 44, 48, 67, 75, 87; on Pulteney, 36, 48, 53, 87; on *Remarks on the History of England*, 23, 37, 48; on Revolution of 1688–89, 17, 37, 88–89, 92–97, 102, 115, 170–71, 174; on Richard II, 37, 63, 66; textual status of works by, 26, 35, 40, 47–57, 192, 197 n. 19, 198 n. 26; on Walpole, 17, 26, 27, 37, 39, 69, 76, 95–97, 115, 167, 201 n. 36; on earl of Warwick, 69; on William III, 94–95,

102–3, 203 n. 14; on Elizabeth Woodville, 69. See also *Craftsman*; Dickinson, H. T.; Goldgar, Bertrand; Gunn, J. A. W.; Kramnick, Isaac; Varey, Simon

Bolingbroke, Henry St. John, 1st viscount (works): *A Dissertation upon Parties*, 17, 24, 59, 87, 91, 95–97, 166, 179, 197 n. 17, 199 n. 5, 202–3 n. 7; *The Famous Dedication to the Pamphlet, Entitled, A Dissertation upon Parties*, 96–97, 98; *A Final Answer to the Remarks on the Craftsman's Vindication*, 23, 57, 87; *The Idea of a Patriot King*, 46, 166, 169, 179–80, 197 n. 17; *Letters on the Study and Use of History*, 46, 51–52, 95, 189, 198 n. 27, 203 n. 14; *Occasional Writer*, 17, 38, 73, 95, 96, 167; *Philosophical Works*, 17; *Remarks on the History of England*, 17, 22–24, 25–26, 30, 35–57, 58–84, 87, 89, 91, 92, 95, 96, 108, 110–14, 119, 120, 129, 130, 166, 168, 172, 179, 190, 197 n. 13, 199 n. 5, 200 n. 22, 209 n. 4; *Works*, 49, 52, 57, 197 n. 19, 198 n. 26

Bond, William: *The Tuscan Treaty*, 168–69, 170–71

Bornstein, George, 49, 51, 57

Boswell, James, 211 n. 32, 215 n. 17

Boyce, William, 220 n. 8

Boyer, Abel, 62

Bradshaw, William, bishop of Bristol, 153, 156

Brett, Thomas, 109, 136, 144, 208 n. 59

Britannia (Thomson), 222 n. 26

Britannicus, Titus (pseud.): *The Present Government of England in Church and State Asserted*, 160–61, 217 n. 42, 218 n. 53

British Theatre, The (Chetwood), 220 n. 8

Brocas, Richard, 134–35

Brooke, Henry: *Gustavus Vasa*, 166, 169, 179–82, 184, 185, 186, 220 n. 4, 222 n. 25; "Prefatory Dedication to the Subscribers," 179

Brooke, John, 204 n. 27

Browning, Reed, 217 nn. 39 and 44, 219 n. 61

Broxap, Henry, 208 n. 59

Bruce, Robert, 220 n. 8

Brutus, Le (Voltaire), 222 n. 28

Buckingham, George Villiers, 1st duke of, 36, 65, 126, 173, 210 nn. 22 and 23

Buckingham, Henry Stafford, duke of, 73

Budgell, Eustace: *A Letter to Cleomenes King of Sparta*, 206 n. 42; *An Essay upon Something* (Budgell[?]), 81, 202 n. 43

Burke, Edmund, 189–92

Burnet, Gilbert: *History of His Own Time*, 110, 208 n. 61

Burnet, Thomas: *De Statu Mortuorum*, 110

Burton, Henry, 132–33

Burtt, Shelley, 88, 194 n. 11, 199 n. 5

C., P. (pseud.): *A Letter to the Author of the Defence of the Bishop of Chichester's Sermon*, 217 n. 42; *A Letter to the Right Reverend the Lord Bishop of Chichester*, 153, 159–60, 217 n. 42, 218 nn. 47 and 53

Cable, Mabel Hessler, 222 n. 25

Carlton, Charles, 211 n. 26

Caroline (queen of England), 109, 153, 209 n. 64, 222 n. 29

Carolinism, 27–29, 100–105, 115–38, 139–63; Bolingbrokean and progovernment ideologies conflated in polemics of, 27–28, 90, 110–14, 115–16, 128–34, 173–74, 190; Church of England and, 28–29, 121, 139, 141, 143–45, 155, 157, 160, 161–63, 210 n. 15, 218 n. 53; City of London and, 102–3, 134–35, 141, 147–49, 215 nn. 25 and 26; Civil War in polemics of, 126, 129, 139, 143, 149; Cromwell in polemics of, 28, 137, 146, 172–75, 213 n. 48, 215 n. 22; dissent in polemics of, 150–51, 152, 157, 204 n. 25, 215 n. 25, 218 n. 50; divine-right monarchy in polemics of, 116–17, 121, 135, 143, 145–47, 208 n. 62, 214 n. 15; Dodsley and, 126, 210–11 n. 24; Earbery and, 27–28, 90, 100–102, 110–14, 116, 119, 121, 127, 129–34,

143, 151, 152, 157, 174; Excise Crisis in polemics of, 134, 147–49, 216 n. 29; *Fog's Weekly Journal* in polemics of, 142, 214 n. 10; George II in polemics of, 27, 111, 122, 135, 172–73, 209 n. 64; Hare and, 28–29, 140, 152, 155–63, 218 nn. 47 and 53; Havard and, 125–26, 169, 171–76, 220 n. 7, 221 nn. 13 and 14; Hearne and, 28, 105, 116, 127–28, 132, 152; and historical analogies, 27–28, 115–16, 121–23, 125–26, 129–30, 131, 132, 142–43, 156–57, 159–60, 172–73, 218 nn. 47 and 56; history plays and, 125–26, 169, 171–76, 220 n. 7, 221 nn. 13 and 14; Jacobitism contrasted to, 27–28, 90, 100–101, 105, 109–10, 128–29, 151; James II in polemics of, 103–4, 208 n. 61, 209 n. 64, 212 n. 43; James Edward Stuart in polemics of, 28, 100–101, 127, 135, 213 n. 4; and King Charles Day sermons, 28–29, 126, 134–36, 140, 151–52, 155–59, 161–63, 210 n. 15, 218 nn. 47, 55, and 56; and liberty and English history, 102, 104–5, 112, 128, 130, 135–36, 157, 172–76; mythopoeia of, 28, 90, 115, 117–18, 127–28, 132–34, 211 n. 35; responses to, 119–20, 136, 159–63, 210 nn. 22 and 23, 220 n. 7; Revolution of 1688–89 in polemics of, 27–28, 100–114, 116, 121, 128–29, 134, 139, 146, 152, 174; Russel and *Grub-street Journal* and, 27, 28, 90, 100–101, 116, 126, 127, 129–30, 137, 139–49, 151–52, 157, 161–63, 174, 211 n. 28, 213 n. 48, 215 n. 22; Trapp and, 28, 116, 134–36, 146–47, 151, 212–13 n. 45; Walpole in polemics of, 27–28, 90, 102, 111, 122, 135, 139, 141, 163, 166; William III in polemics of, 100, 102–4, 145–46, 205 n. 39, 208 n. 61. See also Charles I; Earbery, Matthias; *Grub-street Journal*; Russel, Richard

Carteret, John Carteret, baron (later earl Granville), 192

Case of Authors by Profession or Trade, The (Ralph), 190–92

Case of Opposition Stated, The, 196–97 n. 12, 198–99 n. 4, 206 n. 43

Catholicism, 29, 100, 144, 158

Cato (Addison), 17

Champion, 190

Character and Principles of the Present Set of Whigs, The (Trapp), 134, 203 n. 13

Charles I: in Bolingbrokean polemics, 119–21, 132, 172–73, 209 n. 4, 210 nn. 22 and 23, 210–11 n. 24, 211–12 n. 35; in Carolinist polemics, 27–28, 90, 101, 107, 112, 116–21, 122, 124–28, 129, 132–33, 139, 143, 149, 151–52, 155–59, 161–62, 169, 172–76, 209 n. 9, 210 n. 15, 210–11 n. 24, 211 n. 28, 215 n. 25, 218 n. 56, 220 n. 7, 221 nn. 13, 14; in King Charles Day sermons, 126, 135, 151–52, 155–57, 159, 161–62, 210 n. 15, 218 n. 56; mythopoetic appeal of, 117, 124–25, 127–28, 210 n. 16, 211 n. 33; in pro-government polemics, 119–21, 209 n. 4; scholarship on, 123–25, 210 nn. 16 and 17, 211 nn. 26, 31, and 33, 212 n. 38. See also Carolinism

Charles II, 107–8, 116, 212 n. 43

Charles Edward Stuart ("Bonnie Prince Charlie," "the young pretender"), 101, 180, 213 n. 4, 222 n. 27. See also Jacobitism

Charleton, Walter, 128

Chavigny, Anne-Theodore, 200 n. 28

Chesterfield, Philip Dormer Stanhope, 4th earl of, 17, 171–72, 220 n. 7

Chetwood, William: *The British Theatre*, 220 n. 8

Christian Hero, The (Lillo), 170–71, 181, 220 n. 4, 222 n. 34

Chronicale of the Kings of England (Dodsley), 126

Chubb, Thomas, 190

Church-Authority Vindicated (Hare), 154, 217 n. 43

Church of England, 134, 143–44, 155, 204 n. 25, 215 n. 18; Bolingbroke and, 139; Carolinism and, 28–29, 121, 139, 141, 143–45, 155, 157, 160, 161–63, 210 n. 15, 218 n. 53;

Hare and, 152, 155, 159, 217 n. 39. See also King Charles Day sermons; nonjurors
Cibber, Colley, 94; *The Nonjuror*, 144, 215 n. 17
Civil War (1642–49), 117, 124–25; in Carolinist polemics, 126, 129, 139, 143, 149; in King Charles Day sermons, 120, 135, 161, 212–13 n. 45. See also Cromwell, Oliver
Clarendon, Edward Hyde, 1st earl of: *True Historical Narrative of the Rebellion*, 120
Clarissa (Richardson), 43
Clarissa Project, 57
Clarke, Alured, 160, 161–63, 218 n. 55
Clarke, Samuel, 109
Clavering, Robert, bishop of Peterborough, 153, 156
Coalition of Patriots Deliniated, A, 99
Coe, Margaret, 118, 124, 127
Colley, Linda, 18–19
Collins, Anthony, 190
comedy, 168–69, 178, 186. See also history plays: comedies
Commodity Excised, The ("Smoke"), 216 n. 29
Common Council, London, 102–3, 147–48
Common Sense, 204 n. 31, 207 n. 58, 208 n. 60
Compromise, The, 56
Compton, Spencer. See Wilmington
Conduct of the Allies, The (Swift), 216 n. 39
Conduct of the Opposition, The (Hervey), 59, 84, 93, 98–99, 204 n. 26
consensus. See Bolingbroke: consensus promoted by; opposition (to Sir Robert Walpole): consensus alleged among
"Constitution Clap'd, The," 148
Conundrum, Elkanah. See Russel, Richard
Convention Parliament (1689), 94
Country Journal: Or, the Craftsman. See *Craftsman*
country party, 149, 181, 190, 203 n. 13. See also Bolingbroke: consensus promoted by
Coxe, William, 216 n. 39

Craftsman, 25–27, 35–51, 59–84, 87; Amhurst and, 15, 35, 36, 39, 42–43, 48–54, 59, 66–71, 79, 92–93, 119, 201 nn. 32, 35, and 37, 201–2 n. 39, 203 n. 12, 204 n. 25, 205 n. 38, 210 nn. 22 and 23; authorship of essays in, 195 n. 18, 197 n. 23, 200 n. 26, 201 n. 32; Bolingbroke and, 15–16, 17, 35–46, 89, 196 n. 5; in Carolinist polemics, 102, 104, 110–14, 119, 130–34, 136, 142, 148–49, 173–75; on Charles I, 119–20, 172–73; and City of London, 141, 176; "Caleb D'Anvers" as editor of, 36, 42–43, 55, 81–82, 87, 90, 198 n. 32; on dissent, 150, 204 n. 25; and Excise Crisis, 147–48, 203 n. 9; and *Fog's Weekly Journal*, 30, 41, 44, 89, 140; Francklin and, 50–51, 197 n. 24; on George II, 210 n. 22; on Gin Act, 203 n. 9; Goldsmith on, 48–49, 191–92; *Grub-street Journal* and, 140, 142; "Hague letter" in, 39–40, 51, 61, 76, 78–80, 84, 104–5, 131–32, 177, 201 nn. 34 and 37, 201–2 n. 39; Hanoverian monarchy supported by, 30, 67, 77; harassment of, 26, 40, 52–53, 60–62, 65–71, 74–81, 92, 199 n. 16, 201 nn. 32 and 35, 201–2 n. 39; on Hessian troops, 135, 212 n. 44; historical analogies in, 26, 36, 37, 179, 210 n. 22; history of, 15, 30, 35–36, 195–96 n. 3; on James I, 120; on liberty of the press, 177; and *Mist's Weekly Journal*, 30; in pro-government polemics, 41, 59–60, 64–65, 71–78, 83–84, 90–92, 94, 98, 105, 131, 141–42, 196–97 n. 12, 198–99 n. 4, 200 nn. 21, 24, and 27; on pro-government polemics, 48, 131; Pulteney and, 15, 25; Ralph on, 191–92; *Remarks on the History of England* in, 25–26, 36–46, 48–49, 53–54; on Revolution of 1688–89, 27, 89, 92–95, 129, 174, 203 n. 12; 1731 edition of, 35, 49–53, 197 n. 24, 198 n. 26, 204 n. 25; on standing armies, 135, 212 n. 44; on Star Chamber, 131–32, 212 n. 38; on Walpole, 68–69, 79; on William III, 102, 183, 205 n. 38, 218 n. 54. See also Bolingbroke: *A Dissertation upon Parties*; Bolingbroke: *Remarks on the History of England*; Francklin, Richard: legal history of *Craftsman's Doctrine and Practice of the Liberty of the Press, The*, 206 n. 43

Cromwell, Oliver, 117, 121; in Carolinist polemics, 28, 137, 146, 172–75, 213 n. 48, 215 n. 22. See also Civil War

Croxall, Samuel, 126

Cruickshanks, Eveline, 16, 27, 193 n. 1

Curll, Edmund, 110, 211 n. 29

D., D. See Trapp, Joseph

Daily Courant, 42, 44, 103, 200 n. 22, 205 nn. 37 and 40

Daily Journal, 142

Daily Post, 118

Danverian History of the Affairs of Europe, The, 82, 105, 195 n. 3, 199 n. 8, 201 n. 29

D'Anvers, Caleb (pseud.). See *Craftsman*

Davis, Herbert, 198 n. 24

D[ea]n of W[orceste]r Still the Same, The (Steele), 217 n. 43

Defence of the Bishop of Chichester's Sermon, A ("C. P."), 160, 217 n. 42

Defense of the Measures of the Present Administration, A, 203 n. 13

Defoe, Daniel, 22, 43, 117

deism, 17, 109, 160, 161, 214 n. 10

Dickinson, H. T.: on Bolingbroke, 97–98, 176, 189, 192, 193 n. 2, 200 n. 28, 202–3 n. 7, 206 n. 43, 213 n. 1, 221 n. 20, 222 nn. 25 and 2; on Revolution of 1688–89 in eighteenth-century polemics, 97–98, 100, 104

Discourse Concerning the Nature and Obligation of Oaths, A (Sanderson), 215 n. 23

Dispute Adjusted, The (Gibson), 217–18 n. 44

dissent, Protestant: in Bolingbrokean polemics, 150, 204 n. 25; in Carolinist polemics, 150–51, 152, 157, 204 n. 25, 215 n. 25, 218 n. 50; *Fog's Weekly Journal* on, 150, 216 n. 33; George I and, 154; Hare on, 29, 152, 154–58, 160, 217 n. 43; James II and, 150–51, 216 n. 35; in King Charles Day sermons, 29, 152, 154–58, 160, 161; duke of Newcastle on, 164, 219 n. 61; in pro-government polemics, 98, 154–55, 160, 204 n. 25, 216 n. 33, 218 n. 46; and Test and Corporation Acts, 29, 98, 150, 152, 154, 158; Walpole and, 29, 154–55, 218 n. 45

Dissertation upon Parties, A (Bolingbroke), 17, 24, 59, 87, 91, 95–97, 166, 179, 197 n. 17, 199 n. 5, 202–3 n. 7

Doctrine of Innuendo's Discuss'd, The, 83, 87, 91–92, 201 n. 32

Dodd, Ann (Anne), 78

Dodsley, Robert: *Chronicle of the Kings of England*, 126–27, 210–11 n. 24; in *Grub-street Journal*, 126, 210 n. 24; *King and the Miller of Mansfield, The*, 170–71; *Sir John Cockle at Court*, 171

Doran, John, 220 n. 8

Doubtful, Consciencious (pseud.), 162

drama, historical. See history plays

Drucker, Trudy, 220 n. 4

Duel, The, 202 n. 43

Dunciad, The (Pope), 21, 90, 138, 194 n. 13, 211 n. 29, 216 n. 30

Duncombe, William: *Junius Brutus*, 182–84, 185, 222 n. 31

Earbery, Matthias (general information), 15, 27–28, 104–14, 129–34; on Bolingbroke and Bolingbrokean polemics, 22, 27, 90, 104, 110–14, 116, 117, 119, 120–21, 129–34, 141, 189, 194 n. 11, 206 nn. 41 and 43, 212 n. 36; and Brett, 109, 208 n. 59; on Caroline (queen of England), 209 n. 64; and Carolinism, 27–28, 90, 100–102, 110–14, 116, 119, 121, 127, 129–34, 143, 151, 152, 157, 174; on Charles II, 107, 108; on S. Clarke, 109; and Curll, 110; on dissent, 157, 218 n. 50; on divine-right monarchy, 145, 208 n. 62; on Edward II, 107; on Elizabeth I, 112, 132; on George I, 106, 108, 111; on George II, 111, 209 n. 64; and Francis Hare controversy, 140, 153, 163, 164, 217 n. 42; on Henry II, 106–7;

INDEX 243

on Henry IV, 107; on Henry VI, 107; historical analogies used by, 106–8; and Jacobitism, 100–101, 105–7, 109; on James I, 112; on James II, 107, 208n. 61, 209n. 64; on Joseph I, 107; on Leopold I, 107, 207n. 52; on liberty of the press, 104–5, 132–33, 143; life and legal history of, 105–11, 182, 207nn. 54, 55, 57, and 58, 208n. 60, 209n. 64; on Locke, 109; and nonjurors, 100, 105, 109, 208n. 59, 208–9n. 63; on pro-government polemics, 27, 111, 113–14, 116, 117, 119, 120–21, 131, 153–54, 163; Pulteney and, 109, 133, 212n. 37; on Rákóczi, 107, 207n. 52; on Revolution of 1688–89, 100, 101–2, 110, 112, 174; on Richard III, 107; and Russel, 109, 131, 141, 208n. 59; on Star Chamber, 106, 132–33; and Usages Controversy, 109, 208n. 59; on Walpole, 111, 163, 166; on Whigs and Tories, 204n. 29; on William I, 106; on William III, 100, 145, 208n. 61; on Wills, 106–8; on Woolston, 109
Earbery, Matthias (works): *An Historical Account of the Advantages That Have Accru'd to England*, 204n. 29; *The History of the Clemency of Our English Monarchs*, 106–9, 206n. 50; *Occasional Historian*, 104, 109, 110–14, 119, 130–34, 143, 157, 206nn. 41 and 43, 207n. 55, 208n. 62, 208–9n. 63, 209n. 64; *The Old English Constitution Vindicated*, 101–2; *Some Impartial Reflexions upon Dr Burnet's Posthumous History*, 110, 208n. 61; *De Statu Mortuorum* (trans. Earbery), 110; *Universal Spy*, 109, 110–11, 119, 153, 163, 208n. 60, 209n. 64, 217n. 42, 218n. 50; *Vindication of the History of the Clemency*, 107–9; *The Whole System of English Liberty*, 109, 121, 207nn. 55, 57, and 58, 208n. 60
eastward adoration, 143
Edward I, 170–71
Edward II, 107, 176, 178
Edward III, 39, 63, 171, 178
Edward IV, 39, 69, 73, 84

Edward V, 73
Edward and Eleonora (Thomson), 166, 170–71, 184, 220n. 4
Eikon Basilike, 123
Elizabeth I, 37, 112, 132, 187
Epilogue to the Satires (Pope), 21, 42, 137
Epistle to Dr. Arbuthnot, An (Pope), 21, 23, 24
Erastianism, 144, 146, 152, 154, 161
Erskine-Hill, Howard, 193n. 1, 205n. 35, 213n. 47
Essay upon Something, An (Budgell[?]), 81, 202n. 43
Examination of the Facts and Reasonings in the Lord Bishop of Chichester's Sermon, An (Gordon), 140, 153–54, 156–57, 160, 217n. 42, 218nn. 47, 51, and 52
Examiner Examined, The, 159, 160, 217n. 42
Excise Crisis (1732–33), 164, 176, 203n. 10, 215n. 25; in Bolingbrokean polemics, 59, 92, 105, 147, 203n. 9; in Carolinist polemics, 134, 147–49, 216n. 29; Walpole and, 59, 92, 148, 164
"excremental poems" (Swift), 138

Fall of Mortimer, The (Hatchett[?]), 170–71, 180, 184, 220nn. 4 and 5
Fall of the Earl of Essex (Ralph), 180, 187
Famous Dedication to the Pamphlet, Entitled, A Dissertation upon Parties, The (Bolingbroke), 96–97, 98
Farley, Felix, 78
Farther Observations on the Writings of the Craftsman (Hervey), 74–75, 76, 77, 200n. 21, 202n. 44
Fate of Favourites, The, 210n. 23
Fielding, Henry, 17, 55, 73, 125, 189, 190; "A Fragment of a Commentary on L. Bolingbroke's Essays," 193n. 3; *Jonathan Wild*, 21; *Pasquin*, 219n. 1; *Shamela*, 21; *Tom Jones*, 101
Fielding, Sarah, 125
Final Answer to the Remarks on the Craftsman's Vindication, A (Bolingbroke), 23, 57, 87
Fog's Weekly Journal: in Bolingbro-

kean polemics, 41, 44; in Carolinist polemics, 142, 214n. 10; and City of London, 205n. 39; on A. Clarke, 218n. 55; and *Craftsman*, 30, 41, 44, 89, 140; on dissent, 150, 216n. 33; harassment of, 30, 195n. 22; on Francis Hare controversy, 153, 160, 217n. 42; on Hessian troops, 135; and Jacobitism, 30, 100, 105, 204n. 31, 206n. 46; and James Edward Stuart, 100; and liberty of the press, 30, 105, 177, 195n. 22; and Mist, 206n. 46; and *Mist's Weekly Journal*, 30, 105, 206n. 46; in pro-government polemics, 77, 98, 105, 199n. 4; on Walpole, 167; on William III, 205n. 39

Foord, Archibald, 150, 204n. 27

Foxon, D. F., 202n. 43

"Fragment of a Commentary on L. Bolingbroke's Essays" (H. Fielding), 193n. 3

Francklin, Richard, 198n. 33; legal history of, 37, 39, 40, 51, 52–53, 60–62, 65–71, 74, 76, 78–79, 95, 104, 105, 131, 177, 199nn. 8, 9, 11, 12, 13, and 16, 201nn. 35 and 37; and 1731 edition of *Craftsman*, 50–51, 197n. 24. See also *Craftsman*: harassment of

Frederick (Prince of Wales), 30, 179–80, 185, 221–22n. 24, 222n. 27

Free Briton (Arnall), 40, 147, 196n. 10, 203n. 13, 205–6n. 40. See also Arnall, William

Freeman, R. (pseud.): *The Merits of the Crafts-Men Consider'd*, 60

Free-Mason (Henley), 203n. 8

Frey, Linda, 207n. 52

Frey, Marsha, 207n. 52

Fritz, Paul, 205n. 34, 214–15n. 16

Full and True Account of a Sharp and Bloody Duel, A, 202n. 43

Full and True Account of the Sad and Deplorable Death of Caleb D'Anvers, A, 81–82

Gabriel, John (pseud.): *The State of the Nation*, 213n. 4

Gay, John, 17; *The Beggar's Opera*, 165

Genest, John, 221nn. 13 and 19

George I: accession of, 94, 101, 129; and Bangorian Controversy, 154; Bolingbroke on, 48, 94; and dissent, 154; Earbery on, 106, 108, 111; and Jacobitism, 101, 106, 108, 206n. 47; and Walpole, 200n. 20, 210n. 23

George II: in Bolingbrokean polemics, 36, 37, 39, 44–45, 60, 64, 67, 69, 71, 74, 76, 170, 210nn. 22 and 23; in Carolinist polemics, 27, 111, 122, 135, 172–73, 209n. 64; Hare on, 159; history plays allude to, 172–73, 176; in pro-government polemics, 60, 74, 119; and Walpole, 63–65, 95, 111, 117, 200nn. 20 and 24, 210nn. 22 and 23

Gibson, Edmund, bishop of London, 153, 154–55, 163–64, 217n. 39; *The Dispute Adjusted*, 217–18n. 44

Gin Act (1736), 203n. 9

Glorious Revolution. See Revolution of 1688–89

Godolphin, Sidney Godolphin, earl of, 48

Goldgar, Bertrand: on Bolingbroke, 30, 46–47, 179; on Croxall, 211n. 25; on Excise Crisis, 203n. 10; on literary opposition to Walpole, 16, 21, 30–31, 179, 193n. 1, 200n. 20, 219n. 1, 221–22n. 24; on Pulteney, 30, 202n. 40; on Russel and *Grub-street Journal*, 140–42, 147, 196n. 4, 208n. 59, 210n. 24, 211n. 25, 212n. 40, 213n. 4, 213–14n. 6, 214n. 7, 215n. 26

Goldsmith, Oliver: *The Life of Henry St. John*, 48–49, 191–92, 197n. 17

Gooch, Thomas, bishop of Norwich, 208n. 60

Gordon, Thomas, 155, 163, 164; *An Examination of the Facts and Reasonings in the Lord Bishop of Chichester's Sermon*, 140, 153–54, 156–57, 160, 217n. 42, 218nn. 47, 51, and 52

Grub, Oliver (pseud.), 148

Grub-street Journal, 28, 139–51, 161–63; authorship of essays in, 212n. 40, 214nn. 6, 9, and 11, 215nn. 20 and 24; on Bolingbroke and Bolingbrokean polemics, 28, 102, 113, 139–42, 147–51; book-lists in,

200 n. 27; and Carolinism, 28, 127, 129–30, 137, 139–45, 148, 151, 157, 161–63, 211 n. 28, 218 n. 56; and Church of England, 139, 155; and City of London, 147–49, 215 n. 26; on Cromwell, 146, 215 n. 22; on Croxall, 211 n. 25; on dissent, 150–51, 204 n. 25, 218 n. 50; Dodsley in, 126, 210 n. 24; and Excise Crisis, 147–49, 216 n. 29; and *Fog's Weekly Journal*, 142; on Francis Hare controversy, 161–63; history and management of, 36, 140, 141, 196 n. 4, 213 n. 2, 213–14 n. 6, 216 n. 34; and Jacobitism, 141, 144, 151, 213 n. 4; on James II, 103–4; on loyalty oaths, 146–47, 150–51; and *Mist's Weekly Journal*, 142; and nonjurors, 141, 144–45; and Pope, 148; in pro-government polemics, 141–42, 144, 205 nn. 39 and 40; on pro-government polemics, 102–3, 113, 144–45, 147, 149, 205–6 n. 40, 214 n. 7; on Quakers' Tythes Bill, 216 n. 34; on Revolution of 1688–89, 129; Russel and, 28, 90, 139–51, 213 n. 48, 213–14 n. 6; 214 nn. 9, 10, and 11; Trapp in, 134, 145–47, 212 n. 40, 215 nn. 20 and 24; on Walpole, 28, 102, 139, 141; on Whigs and Tories, 102, 130; on William III, 102–3, 145–46, 205 n. 39. See also Russel, Richard

Gunn, J. A. W.: on Bolingbroke and opposition to Walpole, 27, 87–88, 100; on Earbery, 204 n. 29, 208 n. 60, 208–9 n. 63, 209 n. 64

Gunpowder Plot (1605), 218 n. 54

Gustavus Vasa (Brooke), 166, 169, 179–82, 184, 185, 186, 220 n. 4, 222 n. 25

"Hague letter," 39–40, 51, 61, 76, 78–80, 84, 104–5, 131–32, 177, 201 nn. 34 and 37, 201–2 n. 39

Halifax, George Savile, marquis of, 150–51

Halsband, Robert, 201 nn. 30 and 35, 202 nn. 40, 41, and 42

Hammond, Brean, 141, 193 n. 2

Hanson, Laurence, 61, 199 nn. 6, 11, 15, and 16

Hardwicke, Margaret Yorke, Lady, 222 n. 30

Hardwicke, Philip Yorke, 1st earl of, 61, 107–8, 182, 199 n. 16, 207 n. 55

Hare, Francis, bishop of Chichester, 29, 152–64; and Bangorian Controversy, 154, 163, 217 n. 43; in Carolinist polemics, 140, 153–54, 161–63, 164; Carolinist rhetoric used by, 29, 152, 157, 162–63; on Charles I, 155–59; and Church of England, 152, 155, 159, 217 n. 39; controversy regarding 1732 King Charles Day sermon by, 29, 140, 152–64, 182, 217 nn. 42 and 43; on dissent, 29, 152, 154–58, 160, 217 n. 43; *Fog's Weekly Journal* on, 153, 160; on George II, 159; and Gibson, 153, 217 n. 39; Gordon on, 140, 153, 160; Hervey on, 160, 164, 219 n. 59; historical analogies used by, 29, 156–57, 159–61, 162; and Jacobitism, 29, 158, 217 n. 43; life of, 153–54, 163–64, 216–17 n. 39, 217 n. 43; and duke of Newcastle, 153, 164, 217 n. 39, 219 n. 60; and Walpole, 153, 164, 216–17 n. 39, 219 n. 59. Works: *Church-Authority Vindicated*, 154, 217 n. 43; *A New Defense of the Lord Bishop of Bangor's Sermon*, 217 n. 43; *Scripture Vindicated from the Misinterpretations of the Lord Bishop of Bangor*, 217 n. 43; *Sermon Preached at St. Mary's Church in Cambridge*, 217 n. 43; *Sermon Preached at the Cathedral Church of Worcester*, 217 n. 43; *Two Sermons on Rom. 13.1,2*, 158

Harris, Michael: on *Common Sense*, 204 n. 31; on *Craftsman*, 195–96 n. 3; on *Fog's Weekly Journal*, 204 n. 31, 206 n. 46; on *Grub-street Journal*, 214 n. 6, 215 n. 26; on harassment of opposition press, 62, 199 nn. 9 and 16, 200 n. 25, 201 n. 37; on *Mist's Weekly Journal*, 206 n. 46; on opposition press's decline, 195 n. 22; on pro-government press, 201 nn. 30 and 33, 204 n. 23

Harris, Tim, 123

Harth, Phillip, 209 n. 8

246 INDEX

Hatchett, William: *The Fall of Mortimer* (Hatchett[?]), 170–71, 180, 184, 220 nn. 4 and 5

Havard, William, 172, 189, 220 n. 8; *King Charles the First*, 125–26, 127, 169, 171–76, 179, 220 nn. 4 and 7, 220–21 n. 10, 221 nn. 13, 14, 16, 17, and 19; "New Epilogue upon His Leaving the Stage," 220 n. 8; *Scanderbeg*, 187–88, 222 n. 34

Hawkins, Sir John, 172, 220–21 n. 10

Haywood, Eliza, 22, 40

Hearne, Thomas: and Carolinism, 28, 105, 116, 127–28, 132, 152; on Samuel Croxall, 211 n. 25; *Impartial Memorials of the Life and Writings of Thomas Hearne*, 211 n. 29; and Jacobitism, 127, 132; on Kennett, 209 n. 5; and nonjurors, 144; on Trapp, 134, 212 n. 43

Henley, John ("Orator"): on Charles I, 119; on *Craftsman*, 90–91, 105, 199 n. 4; on dissent, 218 n. 46; on *Fog's Weekly Journal*, 199 n. 4; *FreeMason*, 203 n. 8; *Hyp-Doctor*, 199 n. 4, 203 n. 8; on Revolution of 1688–89, 129; on Russel and *Grub-street Journal*, 205 n. 39, 215 n. 18; on William III, 90–91

Henry II, 106–7, 171

Henry IV, 107

Henry VI, 107

Henry VIII, 36

Hervey, John Hervey, baron of Ickworth: bisexuality of, 79–80, 202 n. 41; on Bolingbrokean opposition, 48, 58, 92, 112, 166, 189 (see also under individual works); on Charles I, 120; on Hare, 160, 164, 219 n. 59; on James II, 94; and Pulteney, 79–80, 81–82, 197 n. 14, 202 n. 43; and Walpole, 74, 79; on William III, 94–95. Works: *Ancient and Modern Liberty Stated and Compar'd*, 58, 84, 94, 120, 198 n. 3; *An Answer to the Occasional Writer No. II*, 198 n. 2; *The Conduct of the Opposition*, 59, 84, 93, 98–99, 204 n. 26; *Farther Observations on the Writings of the Craftsman*, 74–75, 76, 77, 200 n. 21, 202 n. 44; *Memoirs of the Reign of George the Second*, 219 n. 59; *Observations on the Writings of the Craftsman*, 71–72, 74, 75, 77, 84, 197 n. 14, 200 nn. 24 and 27; introduction to *Sedition and Defamation Display'd* (Yonge), 76–77; *Sequel of a Pamphlet Intitled Observations on the Writings of the Craftsman*, 72–73, 77, 202 n. 44; *Some Materials towards Memoirs of the Reign of King George II*, 160, 218 n. 52

Highfill, Philip, Jr., 220 n. 8

Hill, B. W., 203 n. 10

Hillhouse, James, 140, 151, 196 n. 4, 205–6 n. 40, 213 n. 6, 214 nn. 7, 9, and 11, 216 n. 34

Historical Account of the Advantages That Have Accru'd to England (Earbery), 204 n. 29

historiography, analogic. See analogies, historical

historiography, exemplary, 37, 115. See also analogies, historical

History of England (Rapin-Thoyras), 56, 70–71

History of His Own Time (G. Burnet), 110, 208 n. 61

History of Patriotism (Arnall), 40, 196 n. 10

History of the Clemency of Our English Monarchs, The (Earbery), 106–9, 206 n. 50

history plays, 29, 165–88, 190; Bolingbrokean rhetoric in, 165–69, 170–88, 190; closure in, 168–69, 170–71, 178, 181–82, 184, 185, 187; comedies, 168–69, 170–71, 177, 182; generic hybrids, 168–69, 178–87; genre and ideology in, 29, 168–69, 178, 186, 188, 190; George II in, 172–73, 176; tragedies, 168–69, 171–78; Walpole in, 165–66, 173, 176, 182, 219 n. 1; William III in, 222 n. 31

Hoadley, Benjamin, bishop of Bangor, 154, 163, 217 n. 43; *An Answer to Dr. Hare's Sermon*, 217 n. 43. See also Bangorian Controversy.

Horn, Robert, 216 n. 39, 218 n. 52, 219 n. 59

INDEX

Horne, Thomas, 194 n. 11
Huggonson, John, 216 n. 34
Hume, Robert, 29, 166, 168, 171–73, 182, 187, 194 n. 7, 219 nn. 1 and 2
Hunt, N. C., 154, 204 n. 25, 216 n. 32, 217 n. 44, 218 n. 45
Hunter, Thomas: *A Sketch of the Philosophical Character of the Late Lord Viscount Bolingbroke*, 223 n. 5
Hyp-Doctor (Henley), 199 n. 4, 203 n. 8

Idea of a Patriot King, The (Bolingbroke), 46, 166, 169, 179–80, 197 n. 17
Impartial Memorials of the Life and Writings of Thomas Hearne, 211 n. 29
Indemnity Acts, 154–55
Irish Rebellion (1641), 127
Isabella (queen of England), 171, 176–78

Jacobitism: Bolingbroke and, 17, 76, 89–90, 97, 102, 105, 200 n. 28, 206 n. 41; Carolinism contrasted to, 27–28, 90, 100–1, 105, 109–10, 128–29, 151; in Carolinist polemics, 141, 144–45, 214 n. 4; City of London and, 101, 135, 141, 147, 176, 212 n. 42; Earbery and, 100–1, 105–7, 109; *Fog's Weekly Journal* and, 30, 100, 105, 204 n. 31, 206 n. 46; George I and, 101, 106, 108, 206 n. 47; Hare and, 29, 158, 217 n. 43; life of, 153–54, 163–64, 216–17 n. 39, 217 n. 43; Hearne and, 127, 132; in pro-government polemics, 100, 144, 153, 158, 217 n. 43; and rebellions of 1715 and 1745, 16, 94, 100, 106, 121, 129, 174, 206 n. 47; between rebellions of 1715 and 1745, 16, 18, 27, 100–102, 109–10, 128, 135, 141, 143, 147, 154, 176, 193 n. 1, 205 n. 34, 212 n. 42, 214 n. 15; Russel and *Grub-street Journal* and, 100–101, 105, 141, 143–44, 151, 213 n. 4, 214 n. 15; Walpole and, 101, 141. See also Charles Edward Stuart; James Edward Stuart
James I, 59–60, 112, 120, 209 n. 4
James II: in Bolingbrokean polemics, 95, 121, 210 n. 23; in Carolinist polemics, 103–4, 208 n. 61, 209 n. 64, 212 n. 43; departure from throne of, 94, 117, 203 n. 15, 211–12 n. 35; and dissent, 150–51; and Monmouth's Rebellion, 107, 206 n. 51; in pro-government polemics, 94, 121
James Edward Stuart ("James III," "the old pretender"), 107; and Bolingbroke, 17; in Carolinist polemics, 28, 100–101, 127, 135, 213 n. 4; and opposition press, 100–101, 204–5 n. 31; and parliamentary opposition to Walpole, 193 n. 1. See also Jacobitism
Jeffreys, George, 206 n. 51
Johnson, Samuel, 17, 133, 189, 211 n. 32, 215 n. 17
Jonathan Wild (H. Fielding), 21
Jones, George Hilton, 204–5 n. 31, 212 n. 42
Joseph I (Hapsburg emperor), 107
Junius Brutus (Duncombe), 182–84, 185
Juries Act (1730), 61
Juxon, William, bishop of London, 125–26, 172, 175

Kelley, John, 202 n. 43
Kennett, White, bishop of Peterborough, 70, 139; 1720 King Charles Day sermon by, 119–20, 126, 151–52, 153, 156, 209 n. 5
Kenyon, J. P., 28, 204 n. 20, 209 n. 9, 210 n. 15, 211–12 n. 35, 216 n. 37
Kern, Jean, 219 n. 1
King and the Miller of Mansfield, The (Dodsley), 170–71
King Charles Day sermons, 151–52, 216 nn. 37 and 38; Carolinism and, 28–29, 126, 134–36, 140, 151–52, 155–59, 161–63, 210 n. 15, 218 nn. 47, 55, and 56; Civil War in, 120, 135, 161, 212–13 n. 45; dissent in, 29, 152, 154–58, 160–61; historical analogies in, 135, 152, 156–57, 159, 160, 161–62, 210 n. 15, 218 n. 56; Russel and *Grub-street Journal* on, 161–63. See also Bradshaw, William; Clarke, Alured; Clavering, Robert; Croxall, Samuel; Hare, Francis; Kennett, White; Sharp, John;

Swift, Jonathan; Trapp, Joseph; Warren, Robert

King Charles the First (Havard), 125–26, 127, 169, 171–76, 179, 220 nn. 4 and 7, 220–21 n. 10, 221 nn. 13, 14, 16, 17, and 19

Knapton, George, 71

Kramnick, Isaac: on Bolingbrokean opposition to Walpole, 16, 25, 27, 48, 52, 88, 99–100, 104, 189–90, 196 n. 7, 197 nn. 13 and 16; *Lord Bolingbroke: Historical Writings* (ed. Kramnick), 35, 40, 47, 51–57, 197 n. 13, 198 n. 26; on Whigs and Tories, 93

Landa, Louis, 216 n. 37
Landau, Norma, 18, 193 n. 1
Langford, Paul, 203 n. 10, 212 n. 42, 215 n. 25
Laud, William, archbishop of Canterbury, 27, 122, 126, 137–38, 139, 173
Learned Comment upon Dr. Hare's Sermon, A (Swift and Manley), 216 n. 39
Leisenfeld, Vincent, 171–73, 219 n. 1, 220–21 n. 10, 221 n. 14
Lenman, Bruce, 101, 205 n. 34
Leopold I (Hapsburg emperor), 107, 206–7 n. 52
Letter of Thanks from a Young Clergyman to the Reverend Dr. Hare, A, 217 n. 43
Letter to Caleb D'Anvers, Esq., A, 202 n. 43
Letter to Cleomenes King of Sparta, A (Budgell), 206 n. 42
Letter to the Author of the Defence of the Bishop of Chichester's Sermon, A ("P. C."), 217 n. 42
Letter to the Author of the Examination of the Facts and Reasonings in the Lord Bishop of Chichester's Sermon, A, 217 n. 42, 218 n. 47
Letter to the Reverend Dr. Francis Hare, A (Neal), 217 n. 43
Letter to the Right Reverend the Lord Bishop of Chichester, A ("P. C."), 153, 159–60, 217 n. 42, 218 nn. 47 and 53
Letters on the Study and Use of History (Bolingbroke), 46, 51–52, 95, 189, 198 n. 27, 203 n. 14

Lewis, C. S., 21

liberty: in Bolingbrokean polemics, 26, 37–38, 41–42, 43, 45, 53, 92–93, 96-97, 102, 104, 112, 128, 137, 166, 169, 171, 173–76, 179–80, 182, 186, 196 n. 7, 203 n. 14, 204 n. 20, 221–22 n. 24; in Carolinist polemics, 102, 104–5, 112, 128, 130, 135–36, 157, 172–76, 207 n. 58, 212 n. 36; in pro-government polemics, 94–95, 98, 112, 120, 128, 204 n. 20. *See also* press, liberty of

Liberty and the Craftsman, 61, 72, 74, 76, 195–96 n. 3, 200–201 n. 29, 201 n. 36, 206 n. 45

Licensing Act. *See* Stage Licensing Act

Life and History of the Right Honourable Henry St. John, The, 222–23 n. 5

Life of Henry St. John, The (Goldsmith), 48, 197 n. 17

Lillo, George: *The Christian Hero,* 170–71, 181, 220 n. 4, 222 n. 34

Locke, John, 109, 214 n. 10

Lockwood, Thomas, 202 n. 43

Loftis, John, 29, 166, 171–73, 182, 185, 219 n. 1, 221 nn. 17 and 21

London, City of: Bolingbroke and Bolingbrokean polemics and, 102–3, 141, 147, 149, 176, 221 n. 20; Carolinism and, 102–3, 134–35, 141, 147–49, 215 nn. 25 and 26; *Fog's Weekly Journal* and, 205 n. 39; Jacobitism and, 101, 135, 141, 147, 176, 212 n. 42; *Majesty Misled* alludes to, 176–78; pro-government polemics and, 102

London Evening-Post, 212 n. 36

London Journal: on Bolingbrokean opposition to Walpole, 42, 78, 80, 200 nn. 22 and 27, 201 n. 34; in Bolingbrokean polemics, 39, 42, 131; in Carolinist polemics, 102, 111, 113, 131, 136; and dissent, 155, 216 n. 33; sales of, 196 n. 3. *See also* Pitt, James

Lounsbury, Thomas, 213 n. 6

loyalty oaths, 144, 146–47, 150–51

Lyttleton, George (later 1st baron Lyttleton), 30, 79
Machiavelli, Niccolò, 37, 196 n. 7
Mack, Maynard, 20, 194 n. 7, 206 n. 44
Mævius. *See* Russel, Richard
Majesty Misled, 169, 176–78, 179, 186
Manley, Mary de la Riviere (Delarivier Manley), 153; *A Learned Comment upon Dr. Hare's Sermon* (Manley and Swift), 216 n. 39
Mansion House Fund, 154
"Marchmont Nedham's History of the Rebellion" (Nedham), 213 n. 49, 215 n. 25
Marlborough, John Churchill, 1st duke of, 48, 153, 154, 216 n. 39
Marlborough, Sarah Churchill, duchess of, 221 n. 24
Martyn, John, 214 n. 6
Mary II, 127
Master Key to Popery, A (Pope), 194 n. 13
McGann, Jerome, 22, 26, 35, 47, 49, 52, 56–57, 194 n. 12
McKeon, Michael, 19–20
McLynn, Frank, 205 n. 34, 214 n. 15
Memoirs of the Life and Conduct of William Pulteney, Esq, 202 n. 43
Memoirs of the Press (Oldmixon), 143, 214 n. 15
Memoirs of the Reign of George the Second (Hervey), 219 n. 59
Memoirs of the Society of Grub-street (ed. Russel), 104, 142–43, 205 n. 40, 214 nn. 6 and 11
Merits of the Crafts-Men Consider'd, The ("Freeman"), 60
Midgley, Graham, 203 n. 8
Miner, Earl, 209 n. 2
Ministerial Virtue, The (Trapp), 212 n. 40
Mist, Nathaniel, 206 n. 46, 215 n. 18
Mist's Weekly Journal, 30, 105, 142, 206 n. 46. *See also Fog's Weekly Journal*
Moll Flanders (Defoe), 43
monarchy, constitutional, 116; in Bolingbrokean polemics, 27, 37, 39, 44–45, 75, 95, 119, 166; in pro-government polemics, 27, 75, 89, 93, 98, 119, 156, 159

monarchy, divine-right: in Bolingbrokean polemics, 89, 208 n. 62; in Carolinist polemics, 116–17, 121, 135, 143, 145–47, 208 n. 62, 214 n. 15
monarchy, limited. *See* monarchy, constitutional
Monmouth's Rebellion (1685), 107, 206 n. 51
Monod, Paul Kléber, 18–19
Montagu, Lady Mary Wortley, 175
Monthly Chronicle, 39, 200 n. 27, 201 n. 38
Morgan, Joseph: *Phoenix Britannicus* (ed. Morgan), 137–38
Morgan, Thomas, 190
Morning Chronicle, 221 n. 16
Morris, Marilyn, 221 n. 16

Nadel, George, 196 n. 7
Namier, Sir Lewis, 99
Neal, Daniel: *A Letter to the Reverend Dr. Francis Hare*, 217 n. 43
Nedham, Marchamont: "Marchmont Nedham's History of the Rebellion," 213 n. 49, 215 n. 25; *A Short History of the Rebellion*, 213 n. 49, 215 n. 25
Newcastle, Thomas Pelham-Holles, 1st duke of: and dissent, 164; and harassment of Francklin and *Craftsman*, 60–61, 76, 80, 84; and Hare, 153, 164, 217 n. 39, 219 n. 60
New Defense of the Lord Bishop of Bangor's Sermon, A (Hare), 217 n. 43
"New Epilogue upon His Leaving the Stage" (Havard), 220 n. 8
new historicism, 19–20, 194 n. 7
Nichols, John, 217 n. 43
Nokes, David, 198 n. 28
Nonjuror, The (Cibber), 144, 215 n. 17
nonjurors, 121, 152, 214–15 n. 16; Brett, 109, 136, 144, 208 n. 59; Cibber on, 215 n. 17; Earbery and, 100, 105, 109, 208 n. 59, 208–9 n. 63; Hearne and, 144; Johnson on, 215 n. 17; Rawlinson, 144, 208 n. 60; Russel and *Grub-street Journal* and, 100, 109, 141, 143–45, 150–51; Smith, 208 n. 59; Usages Controversy among, 109, 143, 207–8 n. 59; William III and, 144, 152. *See also*

Earbery, Matthias; Hearne, Thomas; Russel, Richard
Normandy, Robert Curthose, duke of, 106, 206 n. 50
Nottingham, Daniel Finch, 2nd earl of, 106
Nutt, Elizabeth, 78

obedience, passive. See monarchy, divine-right; nonjurors
Obligation of Acting According to Conscience, The (Russel), 215 n. 23
Observations on a Pamphlet (Arnall), 24, 195 n. 16
Observations on the Occasional Writer, the Craftsman, and Other Papers, 64–65
Observations on the Writings of the Craftsman (Hervey), 71–72, 74, 75, 77, 84, 197 n. 14, 200 nn. 24 and 27
Occasional Conformity Act (1711), 154
Occasional Historian (Earbery), 104, 109, 110–14, 119, 130–34, 143, 157, 206 nn. 41 and 43, 207 n. 55, 208 n. 62, 208–9 n. 63, 209 n. 64
Occasional Writer (Bolingbroke), 17, 38, 73, 95, 96, 167
Oldcastle, Humphrey. See Bolingbroke: personae used by
Old English Constitution Vindicated, The (Earbery), 101–2
Oldmixon, John: *Memoirs of the Press*, 143, 214 n. 15
opposition (to Sir Robert Walpole): City of London and, 176, 212 n. 42, 215 n. 25, 221 n. 20; consensus alleged among, 15–16, 18–19, 22, 26–30, 35, 58–59, 84, 87–90, 91, 96–100, 111, 114, 198 n. 3, 198–99 n. 4; the literary, 16, 21, 30–31, 179, 184–85, 193 n. 1, 200 n. 20, 219 n. 1, 221–22 n. 24; the parliamentary, 27, 63, 141, 150; and "patriots," 30, 179–82, 184–85, 192, 221–22 n. 24. See also under individual newspapers and polemicists; Carolinism; Jacobitism
Oroonoko (Behn), 43, 187
Osborne, Francis. See Pitt, James
Overton, J. H., 207–8 n. 59, 214 n. 16

Oxoniensis (pseud.), 212 n. 40, 215 nn. 20 and 24
P., C. (pseud.), *A Defence of the Bishop of Chichester's Sermon*, 160, 217 n. 42
Pamela (Richardson), 43, 73
parallels. See analogies, historical
Pasquin (H. Fielding), 219 n. 1
Patriot literature, 30, 179, 184–85, 221–22 n. 24. See also Thomson, James
Paxton, Nicholas, 68, 84
Pearce, Mrs., 78
Pelham, Henry, 153, 216 n. 39
Periander (Tracy), 184–87
Peri Bathos (Pope), 21, 194 n. 13
Perspective, Sir John. See Earbery, Matthias
Pettit, Alexander, 196 n. 10
Philomeides I (pseud.), 218 n. 50
Philosophical Works (Bolingbroke), 17
Phoenix Britannicus (ed. Morgan), 137–38
Pitt, James (pseud. Francis Osborne): on Bolingbrokean opposition, 59–60, 64, 65, 67, 74–75, 80, 98, 112, 131, 141–42, 199 n. 5, 201 n. 34, 209 n. 4; in Bolingbrokean polemics, 131; in Carolinist polemics, 113, 131, 214 n. 7; on Carolinist polemics, 141–42, 144; on Charles I, 119–20; on dissent, 204 n. 25; on *Fog's Weekly Journal*, 98; on Revolution of 1688–89, 129; scholarship on, 194 n. 11. See also *London Journal*
Plumb, J. H., 18–19, 93, 193–94 n. 4, 199 n. 19, 203 n. 10
Pocock, J. G. A., 194 n. 11, 195 n. 17, 196 n. 7, 222 n. 2
Pope, Alexander: and Bolingbroke, 15, 20–24, 45, 198 n. 27; and *Craftsman*, 201 n. 32; and *Grub-street Journal*, 148; possible harassment of, 206 n. 44; satirical method of, 15, 24, 58, 125, 194 n. 13. Works: *The Dunciad*, 21, 24, 90, 138, 194 n. 13, 211 n. 29, 216 n. 30; *Epilogue to the Satires*, 21, 42, 137; *Epistle to Bathurst*, 24; *An Epistle to Dr. Arbuth-*

not, 21, 23, 24; Horatian imitations, 24; *A Master Key to Popery*, 194 n. 13; *Peri Bathos*, 21, 194 n. 13. See also satire, Scriblerian
Potter, Lois, 117, 124–26, 127–28, 210 n. 16
"Prefatory Dedication to the Subscribers" (Brooke), 179
Present Government of England in Church and State Asserted, The ("Britannicus"), 160–61, 217 n. 42, 218 n. 53
press, liberty of: in Bolingbrokean polemics, 104–5, 131–32, 143, 177; Bolingbroke's actions against, 206 n. 43; in Carolinist polemics, 104–5, 131–33, 143; *Fog's Weekly Journal* and, 30, 105, 177, 195 n. 22; in pro-government polemics, 105, 200–201 n. 29, 206 nn. 42 and 43. See also *Craftsman*: harassment of; Earbery, Matthias: life and legal history of; Francklin, Richard: legal history of
Principles and Facts of the Lord Bishop of Chichester's Sermon, The, 157, 217 n. 42, 218 nn. 47 and 51
Proper Reply to a Late Scurrilous Libel, A (Pulteney), 79–80
Protestant dissent. See dissent, Protestant
Prynne, William, 131–33
Pulteney: Or the Patriot, 202 n. 43
Pulteney, William (later 1st earl of Bath): *An Answer to a Late Pamphlet*, 46, 72, 74, 75, 200 n. 21, 201 n. 31; *An Answer to One Part of a Late Infamous Libel*, 61, 79, 195 n. 16; Bolingbroke on, 36, 48, 53, 87; and *Craftsman*, 15, 25; and Earbery, 109, 133, 212 n. 37; and Francklin, 198 n. 33; Hanoverian monarchy supported by, 72; and Hervey, 79–80, 81–82, 197 n. 14, 202 n. 43; and opposition to Walpole, 30, 192; *Periander* alludes to, 185; in pro-government polemics, 24, 40, 74–77, 81–82, 94; on pro-government polemics, 46, 79, 197 n. 18, 201 nn. 35 and 37; *A Proper Reply to a Late Scurrilous Libel*, 79–80; and Walpole, 79

Quakers' Tythes Bill (1736), 150, 216 n. 34

Radzinowicz, Leon, 205 n. 34
Rákóczi, Ferenc, 107, 207 n. 52
Ralph, James: *The Case of Authors by Profession or Trade*, 190–91; *The Fall of the Earl of Essex*, 180, 187
Randall, Helen, 124, 210 n. 15, 216 nn. 37 and 38
Rapin-Thoyras, Paul de, 56, 70–71
Rawlinson, Richard, 144, 208 n. 60
Raymond, Robert, Lord, 108, 207 nn. 53 and 55
Read's Weekly Journal, 205 n. 37
Reeve, L. J., 210 n. 13
Register of Books, 1728–1738, Extracted from the Monthly Chronicle, A, 39, 200 n. 27, 201 n. 38
Remarks on the Craftsman's Vindication of His Two Hon[oura]ble Patrons (Arnall), 61, 79
Remarks on the History of England (Bolingbroke), 17, 22–24, 25–26, 30, 35–57, 58–84, 87, 89, 91, 92, 95, 96, 108, 110–14, 119, 120, 129, 130, 166, 168, 172, 179, 190, 197 n. 13, 199 n. 5, 200 n. 22, 209 n. 4
Revolution of 1688–89, 87–114; in Bolingbrokean polemics, 17, 26–27, 37, 75, 88–90, 92–97, 99–100, 102, 115–16, 121, 128–29, 170–71, 174, 183, 190, 202–3 n. 7, 203 n. 12, 211–12 n. 35; Budgell on, 206 n. 42; in Carolinist polemics, 27–28, 100–14, 116, 121, 128–29, 134, 139, 146, 152, 174; Hare on, 156, 158; in history plays, 170–71, 174, 182; in pro-government polemics, 27, 88–95, 97–100, 116, 121, 128–29, 190, 203 n. 13. See also William III
Revolution Settlement (1689). See Revolution of 1688–89
Richard II, 37, 63, 66
Richard III, 73, 107
Richardson, Samuel, 125; *Clarissa*, 43; *Pamela*, 43, 73
Robert (son of William I). See Normandy
Roberts, Clayton, 193 n. 4
Roberts, W., 142

Rogers, Nicholas, 18–19, 101, 209 n. 8, 221 n. 20
Rogers, Pat, 143, 194 n. 13, 214 n. 11
Rosenheim, E. W., Jr., 216 n. 37
Rudé, George, 147, 149
Russel, Conrad, 210 n. 12
Russel, James, 213 n. 4
Russel, Richard, 27–28, 100–105, 129–30, 139–51: on Bolingbrokean polemics, 27–28, 90, 116, 149, 189; and Brett, 208 n. 59; and Carolinism, 27–28, 90, 100–101, 116, 126, 127, 129–30, 139–49, 152, 157, 163, 174, 213 n. 48, 215 n. 22; on dissent, 150–51, 215 n. 25; and Earbery, 109, 131, 141, 208 n. 59; on Fog's Weekly Journal, 214 n. 10; and Grub-street Journal, 28, 90, 139–51, 213 n. 48, 213–14 n. 6; 214 nn. 9, 10, and 11; on Francis Hare controversy, 163, 164; and Jacobitism, 100–101, 105, 141, 143–44, 213 n. 4, 214 n. 15; on liberty of the press, 104; life of, 144, 213 n. 4, 213–14 n. 6, 214 n. 7; on Locke, 214 n. 10; on loyalty oaths, 144, 146–47, 150–51; and nonjurors, 100, 109, 143–45, 150–51; in pro-government polemics, 141–42, 215 n. 18; on pro-government polemics, 27–28, 90, 116, 148, 213 n. 48; on Revolution of 1688–89, 27–28, 100, 129, 174; and Usages Controversy, 109, 208 n. 59; on Whigs and Tories, 104–5, 204 n. 29; on William III, 100, 145. Works: *A Discourse Concerning the Nature and Obligation of Oaths* (trans. Russel), 215 n. 23; *The Impeachment*, 122; *Memoirs of the Society of Grub-street* (ed. Russel), 104, 142–43, 205 n. 40, 214 nn. 6 and 11; *The Obligation of Acting According to Conscience*, 215 n. 23. See also *Grub-street Journal*

Sacheverell, Henry, 121, 129, 153, 203 n. 13
Saddi, Nathan Ben. See Dodsley, Robert
"Said to Be Found upon a Great Lady's Toylet," 121–22
Sanderson, Robert: *Discourse Concerning the Nature and Obligation of Oaths, A*, 215 n. 23
Sandys, Samuel, 192
satire, Scriblerian, 15, 20–25, 125, 137, 179
Scanderbeg (Havard), 187–88, 222 n. 34
Scanderbeg (Whincop), 222 n. 34
Schism Act (1714), 154
Scouten, Arthur, 215 n. 17, 220 n. 8
Scripture Vindicated from the Misinterpretations of the Lord Bishop of Bangor (Hare), 217 n. 43
Scrub, Timothy. See Budgell, Eustace
Sedgwick, Romney, 218 n. 52
Sedition and Defamation Display'd (Yonge), 76–78, 79, 91–92, 105
Septennial Act (1716), 205 n. 38
Sequel of a Pamphlet Intitled Observations on the Writings of the Craftsman (Hervey), 72–73, 77, 202 n. 44
Sermon Preached at St. Mary's Church in Cambridge (Hare), 217 n. 43
Sermon Preached at the Cathedral Church of Worcester (Hare), 217 n. 43
Shamela (H. Fielding), 21, 73
Sharpe, John, archbishop of York, 155–56
Sharpe, Kevin, 123, 157, 210 nn. 12, 16, and 17, 212 n. 38
Sherburn, George, 214 n. 7
Short History of the Rebellion, A (Nedham), 213 n. 49, 215 n. 25
Sir John Cockle at Court (Dodsley), 171
Sketch of the Philosophical Character of the Late Lord Viscount Bolingbroke, A (Hunter), 223 n. 5
Smith, George, 208 n. 59
Smoke, Timothy (pseud.): *The Commodity Excised*, 216 n. 29
Some Impartial Reflexions upon Dr Burnet's Posthumous History (Earbery), 110, 208 n. 61
Some Materials towards Memoirs of the Reign of King George II (Hervey), 160, 218 n. 52
Speck, W. A.: on Hare, 217 n. 39; on

Jacobitism, 106, 206 n. 47; on James II and dissent, 216 n. 35; on Monmouth's Rebellion, 206 n. 51; on nonjurors and taxation, 215 n. 16; on Revolution of 1688–89, 203 n. 15
St. John, Henry. See Bolingbroke
Stage Licensing Act (1737), 29, 30, 84, 134, 166, 206 n. 44
standing armies, 135, 212 n. 44. See also troops, Hessian
Star Chamber, 106, 120, 131–33, 212 n. 38
State of the Nation, The ("Gabriel"), 213 n. 4
Statu Mortuorum, De (T. Burnet), 110
Steele, Richard, 40; *The D[ea]n of W[orceste]r Still the Same*, 217 n. 43
Strafford, Thomas Wentworth, earl of, 210 n. 22
Stuart, Charles Edward. See Charles Edward Stuart
Stuart, James Edward. See James Edward Stuart
Sundon, Charlotte Clayton, viscountess, 222 nn. 29 and 30
Sutherland, Lucy, 141, 204 n. 27, 212 n. 42
Swift, Jonathan, 17, 21, 73, 153; *The Conduct of the Allies*, 216 n. 39; "excremental poems," 138; *A Learned Comment upon Dr. Hare's Sermon* (Swift and Manley), 216 n. 39; 1726 King Charles Day sermon by, 136, 155–56, 213 n. 46; *A Tale of a Tub*, 43
Sykes, Norman, 217 n. 39

Tale of a Tub, A (Swift), 43
Test and Corporation Acts (1661, 1673), 29, 98, 150, 152, 154, 158. See also dissent, Protestant
textual editing, 26, 35, 47–57
Thomson, James, 30, 179; *Britannia*, 222 n. 26; *Edward and Eleonora*, 166, 170–71, 184, 220 n. 4
Three Pamphlets, 201 n. 32
Tindall, Matthew, 190
Toland, John, 190
Toryism, contested definition of, 15–16, 24, 92–93, 98, 102, 104–5, 144, 195 n. 17, 202–3 n. 7, 203 n. 12, 204 n. 29

Tracy, John, 189; *Periander*, 184–87
Traffick, Will (pseud.), 148
tragedy, 168–69, 178, 184, 186. See also history plays: tragedies
Trapp, Joseph: on Bolingbrokean polemics, 116, 135–36, 189; and Carolinism, 28, 116, 134–36, 146–47, 151, 212–13 n. 45; *The Character and Principles of the Present Set of Whigs*, 134, 203 n. 13; on Charles II, 212 n. 43; on George II, 135; in *Grub-street Journal*, 134, 145–47, 212 n. 40, 215 nn. 20 and 24; Hearne on, 134, 212 n. 43; on James II, 212 n. 43; *The Ministerial Virtue*, 212 n. 40; and opposition to Walpole, 116, 134–36; 1730 King Charles Day sermon by, 124, 134–36, 151, 152, 210 n. 15, 212 n. 43
troops, Hessian, 63, 78, 135, 200 n. 21, 212 n. 44
True Historical Narrative of the Rebellion, The (Clarendon), 120
Tuscan Treaty, The (Bond), 168–69, 170–71
Tutchin, John, 62
Two Sermons on Rom. 13.1,2 (Hare), 158
Tyrell, Mr., 128

Universal Spectator, 216 n. 30
Universal Spy (Earbery), 109, 110–11, 119, 153, 163, 208 n. 60, 209 n. 64, 217 n. 42, 218 n. 50
Usages Controversy, 109, 143, 207–8 n. 59
Utrecht, Treaty of (1713), 45

Varey, Simon: on Bolingbroke, 95, 193 n. 2, 197 n. 23, 198 n. 27, 203 n. 14, 206 n. 43, 222 nn. 25 and 27; on *Craftsman*, 55, 61, 62, 195 nn. 18 and 3, 197 nn. 23 and 24, 199 nn. 7 and 11, 200 n. 26, 201 n. 32, 203 n. 9; on *Remarks on the History of England*, 47, 61, 197 nn. 13, 19, and 23
Vienna, 2nd Treaty of (1731), 40, 78, 80, 82
Vindication of the History of the Clemency (Earbery), 107–9
Voltaire, François-Marie Arouet de, 17; *Le Brutus*, 222 n. 28

Wakeman, Henry Offley, 144
Walpole, Horace, 189
Walpole, Sir Robert (later 1st earl of Orford): in Bolingbrokean polemics, 17, 26, 27, 37, 39, 63, 68–69, 79, 95–97, 134, 167, 201 n. 36; career of, 30, 93, 142, 192; in Carolinist polemics, 27–28, 90, 102, 111, 122, 135, 139, 141, 163, 166; and Civil List, 63; and dissent, 29, 154–55, 218 n. 45; and Excise Crisis, 59, 92, 148, 164; in *Fog's Weekly Journal*, 167; and George I, 200 n. 20, 210 n. 23; and George II, 63–65, 95, 111, 117, 200 nn. 20 and 24, 210 nn. 22 and 23; and harassment of *Craftsman*, 68, 80; and Hare, 153, 164, 216–17 n. 39, 219 n. 59; and Hervey, 74, 79; history plays allude to, 165–66, 173, 176, 182, 219 n. 1; and Jacobitism, 101, 141; and 2nd Treaty of Vienna, 40, 78, 82. See also opposition (to Sir Robert Walpole)
Walsingham, Francis. *See* Arnall, William
Warren, Robert, 160, 161–63, 218 nn. 55 and 56
Warwick, Richard Neville, earl of, 69
Wedgwood, C. V., 211 n. 33
Weekly Miscellany, 155
Weinbrot, Howard, 213 n. 47
Weinsheimer, Joel, 23, 190, 196 n. 7
Whig and Tory: Or, Wit on Both Sides, 121
Whiggism, contested definition of, 15–16, 24, 92–93, 97–98, 102, 104–5, 130, 134, 195 n. 17, 202–3 n. 7, 203 nn. 12 and 13, 204 n. 29

Whincop, Thomas: *Scanderbeg*, 222 n. 34
White, John, 78
Whitehall Evening-Post, 97
Whitehead, Paul, 220 n. 8
Whole System of English Liberty, The (Earbery), 109, 121, 207 nn. 55 and 57, and 58, 208 n. 60
William I ("William the Conqueror"), 106, 206 n. 50
William III: accession of, 117, 127; in Bolingbrokean polemics, 89, 94–95, 102–3, 121, 182–83, 203 n. 14, 205 n. 38, 218 n. 54, 222 n. 31; in Carolinist polemics, 100, 102–4, 145–46, 205 n. 39, 208 n. 61; *Fog's Weekly Journal* on, 205 n. 39; *Junius Brutus* alludes to, 182–83, 222 n. 31; nonjurors and, 144, 152; in pro-government polemics, 90–92, 94–95, 97, 102–3, 121, 183; proposed statue of, 102–3, 205 nn. 37, 38, 39, and 40. See also Revolution of 1688–89
Williams, Basil, 217 n. 39, 219 n. 61
Williams, John, 134–35
Williamson, Raymond, 214 n. 11
Wills, Charles, 106–8
Wilmington, Spencer Compton, earl of, 192
Wilson, Kathleen, 89, 205 nn. 36 and 38
Winton, Calhoun, 222 n. 28
Woodville, Elizabeth (queen of England), 69
Woolston, Thomas, 109

Yonge, William (later Sir William Yonge), 76–78, 79, 91–92, 105

Zeal, Timothy (pseud.), 141